E SOURCE

The Prentice Hall ENGINEERING SOURCE

Introduction to AutoCAD®

Second Edition

Mark Dix and Paul Riley

CAD Support Associates

PEARSON
Prentice Hall

Upper Saddle River, NJ 07458

Library of Congress Cataloging-in-Publication Data on file

Vice President and Editorial Director, ECS: *Marcia J. Horton*
Executive Editor: *Eric Svendsen*
Associate Editor: *Dee Bernhard*
Vice President and Director of Production and Manufacturing, ESM: *David W. Riccardi*
Executive Managing Editor: *Vince O'Brien*
Managing Editor: *David A. George*
Production Editor: *Scott Disanno*
Art Director: *Jayne Conte*
Cover Designer: *Bruce Kenselaar*
Art Editor: *Greg Dulles*
Manufacturing Manager: *Trudy Pisciotti*
Manufacturing Buyer: *Lisa McDowell*
Senior Marketing Manager: *Holly Stark*

PEARSON
Prentice Hall

Pearson Prentice Hall
Pearson Education, Inc.
Upper Saddle River, NJ 07458

Drawing credits: Hearth Drawing courtesy of Thomas Casey: Double Bearing Assembly compliments of David Sumner; King Philip Technical Drawing: Isometric Drawing Flanged Coupling courtesy of Richard F. Ross; Isometric drawing of Garage courtesy of Thomas Casey

Printed in the United States of America

10 9 8 7 6 5 4

ISBN 0-13-147509-6

Pearson Education Ltd., *London*
Pearson Education Australia Pty. Ltd., *Sydney*
Pearson Education Singapore, Pte. Ltd.
Pearson Education North Asia Ltd., *Hong Kong*
Pearson Education Canada, Inc., *Toronto*
Pearson Educación de Mexico, S.A. de C.V.
Pearson Education—Japan, *Tokyo*
Pearson Education Malaysia, Pte. Ltd.
Pearson Education, Inc., *Upper Saddle River, New Jersey*

About ESource

ESource—The Prentice Hall Engineering Source—www.prenhall.com/esource

ESource—The Prentice Hall Engineering Source gives professors the power to harness the full potential of their text and their first year engineering course. More then just a collection of books, ESource is a unique publishing system revolving around the ESource website—www.prenhall.com/esource. ESource enables you to put your stamp on your book just as you do your course. It lets you:

Control You choose exactly what chapter or sections are in your book and in what order they appear. Of course, you can choose the entire book if you'd like and stay with the authors' original order.

Optimize Get the most from your book and your course. ESource lets you produce the optimal text for your students needs.

Customize You can add your own material anywhere in your text's presentation, and your final product will arrive at your bookstore as a professionally formatted text. Of course, all titles in this series are available as stand-alone texts, or as bundles of two or more books sold at a discount. Contact your PH sales rep for discount information.

ESource ACCESS

Professors who choose to bundle two or more texts from the ESource series for their class, or use an ESource custom book will be providing their students with an on-line library of intro engineering content—ESource Access. We've designed ESource ACCESS to provide students a flexible, searchable, on-line resource. Free access codes come in bundles and custom books are valid for one year after initial log-on. Contact your PH sales rep for more information.

ESource Content

All the content in ESource was written by educators specifically for freshman/first-year students. Authors tried to strike a balanced level of presentation, an approach that was neither formulaic nor trivial, and one that did not focus too heavily on advanced topics that most introductory students do not encounter until later classes. Because many professors do not have extensive time to cover these topics in the classroom, authors prepared each text with the idea that many students would use it for self-instruction and independent study. Students should be able to use this content to learn the software tool or subject on their own.

While authors had the freedom to write texts in a style appropriate to their particular subject, all followed certain guidelines created to promote a consistency that makes students comfortable. Namely, every chapter opens with a clear set of **Objectives**, includes **Practice Boxes** throughout the chapter, and ends with a number of **Problems**, and a list of **Key Terms**. **Applications Boxes** are spread throughout the book with the intent of giving students a real-world perspective of engineering. **Success Boxes** provide the student with advice about college study skills, and help students avoid the common pitfalls of first-year students. In addition, this series contains an entire book titled ***Engineering Success*** by Peter Schiavone of the University of Alberta intended to expose students quickly to what it takes to be an engineering student.

Creating Your Book

Using ESource is simple. You preview the content either on-line or through examination copies of the books you can request on-line, from your PH sales rep, or by calling 1-800-526-0485. Create an on-line outline of the content you want, in the order you want, using ESource's simple interface. Insert your own material into the text flow. If you are not ready to order, ESource will save your work. You can come back at any time and change, re-arrange, or add more material to your creation. Once you're finished you'll automatically receive an ISBN. Give it to your bookstore and your book will arrive on their shelves four to six weeks after they order. Your custom desk copies with their instructor supplements will arrive at your address at the same time.

To learn more about this new system for creating the perfect textbook, go to www.prenhall.com/esource. You can either go through the on-line walkthrough of how to create a book, or experiment yourself.

Supplements

Adopters of ESource receive an instructor's CD that contains professor and student resources and **350 PowerPoint transparencies** created by Jack Leifer of University of Kentucky–Paducah for various books in the series. Professors can either follow these transparencies as pre-prepared lectures or use them as the basis for their own custom presentations.

Titles in the ESource Series

Design Concepts for Engineers, 2/e
0-13-093430-5
Mark Horenstein

Engineering Success, 2/e
0-13-041827-7
Peter Schiavone

Engineering Design and Problem Solving, 2E
0-13-093399-6
Steven K. Howell

Exploring Engineering
0-13-093442-9
Joe King

Engineering Ethics
0-13-784224-4
Charles B. Fleddermann

Introduction to Engineering Analysis, 2/e
0-13-145332-7
Kirk D. Hagen

Introduction to Engineering Communication
0-13-146102-8
Hillary Hart

Introduction to Engineering Experimentation
0-13-032835-9
Ronald W. Larsen, John T. Sears, and Royce Wilkinson

Introduction to Mechanical Engineering
0-13-019640-1
Robert Rizza

Introduction to Electrical and Computer Engineering
0-13-033363-8
Charles B. Fleddermann and Martin Bradshaw

Introduction to MATLAB 7
0-13-147492-8
Delores Etter and David C. Kuncicky, with Holly Moore

MATLAB Programming
0-13-035127-X
David C. Kuncicky

Introduction to Mathcad 2000
0-13-020007-7
Ronald W. Larsen

Introduction to Mathcad 11
0-13-008177-9
Ronald W. Larsen

Introduction to Maple 8
0-13-032844-8
David I. Schwartz

Mathematics Review
0-13-011501-0
Peter Schiavone

Power Programming with VBA/Excel
0-13-047377-4
Steven C. Chapra

Introduction to Excel 2002
0-13-008175-2
David C. Kuncicky

Introduction to Excel, 2/e
0-13-016881-5
David C. Kuncicky

http://www.prenhall.com/esource/

Engineering with Excel, 2/e
0-13-147511-8
Ronald W. Larsen

Introduction to Word 2002
0-13-008170-1
David C. Kuncicky

Introduction to PowerPoint 2002
0-13-008179-5
Jack Leifer

Graphics Concepts
0-13-030687-8
Richard M. Lueptow

Graphics Concepts with SolidWorks, 2/e
0-13-140915-8
Richard M. Lueptow and Michael Minbiole

Graphics Concepts with Pro/ENGINEER
0-13-014154-2
Richard M. Lueptow, Jim Steger, and Michael T. Snyder

Introduction to AutoCAD, 2/e
0-13-147509-6
Mark Dix and Paul Riley

Introduction to UNIX
0-13-095135-8
David I. Schwartz

Introduction to the Internet, 3/e
0-13-031355-6
Scott D. James

Introduction to Visual Basic 6.0
0-13-026813-5
David I. Schneider

Introduction to C
0-13-011854-0
Delores Etter

Introduction to C++
0-13-011855-9
Delores Etter

Introduction to FORTRAN 90
0-13-013146-6
Larry Nyhoff and Sanford Leestma

Introduction to Java
0-13-919416-9
Stephen J. Chapman

http://www.prenhall.com/esource/

About the Authors

No project could ever come to pass without a group of authors who have the vision and the courage to turn a stack of blank paper into a book. The authors in this series, who worked diligently to produce their books, provide the building blocks of the series.

Martin D. Bradshaw was born in Pittsburg, KS in 1936, grew up in Kansas and the surrounding states of Arkansas and Missouri, graduating from Newton High School, Newton, KS in 1954. He received the B.S.E.E. and M.S.E.E. degrees from the University of Wichita in 1958 and 1961, respectively. A Ford Foundation fellowship at Carnegie Institute of Technology followed from 1961 to 1963 and he received the Ph.D. degree in electrical engineering in 1964. He spent his entire academic career with the Department of Electrical and Computer Engineering at the University of New Mexico (1961–1963 and 1991–1996). He served as the Assistant Dean for Special Programs with the UNM College of Engineering from 1974 to 1976 and as the Associate Chairman for the EECE Department from 1993 to 1996. During the period 1987–1991 he was a consultant with his own company, EE Problem Solvers. During 1978 he spent a sabbatical year with the State Electricity Commission of Victoria, Melbourne, Australia. From 1979 to 1981 he served an IPA assignment as a Project Officer at the U.S. Air Force Weapons Laboratory, Kirkland AFB, Albuquerque, NM. He has won numerous local, regional, and national teaching awards, including the George Westinghouse Award from the ASEE in 1973. He was awarded the IEEE Centennial Medal in 2000.

Acknowledgments: Dr. Bradshaw would like to acknowledge his late mother, who gave him a great love of reading and learning, and his father, who taught him to persist until the job is finished. The encouragement of his wife, Jo, and his six children is a never-ending inspiration.

Stephen J. Chapman received a B.S. degree in Electrical Engineering from Louisiana State University (1975), the M.S.E. degree in Electrical Engineering from the University of Central Florida (1979), and pursued further graduate studies at Rice University. Mr. Chapman is currently Manager of Technical Systems for British Aerospace Australia, in Melbourne, Australia. In this position, he provides technical direction and design authority for the work of younger engineers within the company. He also continues to teach at local universities on a part-time basis.

Mr. Chapman is a Senior Member of the Institute of Electrical and Electronics Engineers (and several of its component societies). He is also a member of the Association for Computing Machinery and the Institution of Engineers (Australia).

Steven C. Chapra presently holds the Louis Berger Chair for Computing and Engineering in the Civil and Environmental Engineering Department at Tufts University. Dr. Chapra received engineering degrees from Manhattan College and the University of Michigan. Before joining the faculty at Tufts, he taught at Texas A&M University, the University of Colorado, and Imperial College, London. His research interests focus on surface water-quality modeling and advanced computer applications in environmental engineering. He has published over 50 refereed journal articles, 20 software packages and 6 books. He has received a number of awards including the 1987 ASEE Merriam/Wiley Distinguished Author Award, the 1993 Rudolph Hering Medal, and teaching awards from Texas A&M, the University of Colorado, and the Association of Environmental Engineering and Science Professors.

Acknowledgments: To the Berger Family for their many contributions to engineering education. I would also like to thank David Clough for his friendship and insights, John Walkenbach for his wonderful books, and my colleague Lee Minardi and my students Kenny William, Robert Viesca and Jennifer Edelmann for their suggestions.

Mark Dix began working with AutoCAD in 1985 as a programmer for CAD Support Associates, Inc. He helped design a system for creating estimates and bills of material directly from AutoCAD drawing databases for use in the automated conveyor industry. This system became the basis for systems still widely in use today. In 1986 he began collaborating with Paul Riley to create AutoCAD training materials, combining Riley's background in industrial design and training with Dix's background in writing, curriculum development, and programming. Mr. Dix received the M.S. degree in education from the University of Massachusetts. He is currently the Director of Dearborn Academy High School in Arlington, Massachusetts.

Delores M. Etter is a Professor of Electrical and Computer Engineering at the University of Colorado. Dr. Etter was a faculty member at the University of New Mexico and also a Visiting Professor at Stanford University. Dr. Etter was responsible for the Freshman Engineering Program at the University of New Mexico and is active in the Integrated Teaching Laboratory at the University of Colorado. She was elected a Fellow of the Institute of Electrical and Electronics Engineers for her contributions to education and for her technical leadership in digital signal processing.

Charles B. Fleddermann is a professor in the Department of Electrical and Computer Engineering at the University of New Mexico in Albuquerque, New Mexico. All of his degrees are in electrical engineering: his Bachelor's degree from the University of Notre Dame, and the Master's and Ph.D. from the University of Illinois at Urbana-Champaign. Prof. Fleddermann developed an engineering ethics course for his department in response to the ABET requirement to incorporate ethics topics into the undergraduate engineering curriculum. *Engineering Ethics* was written as a vehicle for presenting ethical theory, analysis, and problem solving to engineering undergraduates in a concise and readily accessible way.

Acknowledgments: I would like to thank Profs. Charles Harris and Michael Rabins of Texas A & M University whose NSF sponsored workshops on engineering ethics got me started thinking in this field. Special thanks to my wife Liz, who proofread the manuscript for this book, provided many useful suggestions, and who helped me learn how to teach "soft" topics to engineers.

Kirk D. Hagen is a professor at Weber State University in Ogden, Utah. He has taught introductory-level engineering courses and upper-division thermal science courses at WSU since 1993. He received his B.S. degree in physics from Weber State College and his M.S. degree in mechanical engineering from Utah State University, after which he worked as a thermal designer/analyst in the aerospace and electronics industries. After several years of engineering practice, he resumed his formal education, earning his Ph.D. in mechanical engineering at the University of Utah. Hagen is the author of an undergraduate heat transfer text.

Mark N. Horenstein is a Professor in the Department of Electrical and Computer Engineering at Boston University. He has degrees in Electrical Engineering from M.I.T. and U.C. Berkeley and has been involved in teaching engineering design for the greater part of his academic career. He devised and developed the senior design project class taken by all electrical and computer engineering students at Boston University. In this class, the students work for a virtual engineering company developing products and systems for real-world engineering and social-service clients.

Acknowledgments: I would like to thank Prof. James Bethune, the architect of the Peak Performance event at Boston University, for his permission to highlight the competition in my text. Several of the ideas relating to brainstorming and teamwork were derived from a workshop on engineering design offered by Prof. Charles Lovas of Southern Methodist University. The principles of estimation were derived in part from a freshman engineering problem posed by Prof. Thomas Kincaid of Boston University.

Steven Howell is the Chairman and a Professor of Mechanical Engineering at Lawrence Technological University. Prior to joining LTU in 2001, Dr. Howell led a knowledge-based engineering project for Visteon Automotive Systems and taught computer-aided design classes for Ford Motor Company engineers. Dr. Howell also has a total of 15 years experience as an engineering faculty member at Northern Arizona University, the University of the Pacific, and the University of Zimbabwe. While at Northern Arizona University, he helped develop and implement an award-winning interdisciplinary series of design courses simulating a corporate engineering-design environment.

Douglas W. Hull is a graduate student in the Department of Mechanical Engineering at Carnegie Mellon University in Pittsburgh, Pennsylvania. He is the author of *Mastering Mechanics I Using Matlab 5*, and contributed to *Mechanics of Materials* by Bedford and Liechti. His research in the Sensor Based Planning lab involves motion planning for hyper-redundant manipulators, also known as serpentine robots.

Scott D. James is a staff lecturer at Kettering University (formerly GMI Engineering & Management Institute) in Flint, Michigan. He is currently pursuing a Ph.D. in Systems Engineering with an emphasis on software engineering and computer-integrated manufacturing. He chose teaching as a profession after several years in the computer industry. "I thought that it was really important to know what it was like outside of academia. I wanted to provide students with classes that were up to date and provide the information that is really used and needed."

Acknowledgments: Scott would like to acknowledge his family for the time to work on the text and his students and peers at Kettering who offered helpful critiques of the materials that eventually became the book.

Joe King received the B.S. and M.S. degrees from the University of California at Davis. He is a Professor of Computer Engineering at the University of the Pacific, Stockton, CA, where he teaches courses in digital design, computer design, artificial intelligence, and computer networking. Since joining the UOP faculty, Professor King has spent yearlong sabbaticals teaching in Zimbabwe, Singapore, and Finland. A licensed engineer in the state of California, King's industrial experience includes major design projects with Lawrence Livermore National Laboratory, as well as independent consulting projects. Prof. King has had a number of books published with titles including M*atlab*, MathCAD, Exploring Engineering, and Engineering and Society.

David C. Kuncicky is a native Floridian. He earned his Baccalaureate in psychology, Master's in computer science, and Ph.D. in computer science from Florida State University. He has served as a faculty member in the Department of Electrical Engineering at the FAMU–FSU College of Engineering and the Department of Computer Science at Florida State University. He has taught computer science and computer engineering courses for over 15 years. He has published research in the areas of intelligent hybrid systems and neural networks. He is currently the Director of Engineering at Bioreason, Inc. in Sante Fe, New Mexico.

Acknowledgments: Thanks to Steffie and Helen for putting up with my late nights and long weekends at the computer. Finally, thanks to Susan Bassett for having faith in my abilities, and for providing continued tutelage and support.

Ron Larsen is a Professor of Chemical Engineering at Montana State University, and received his Ph.D. from the Pennsylvania State University. He was initially attracted to engineering by the challenges the profession offers, but also appreciates that engineering is a serving profession. Some of the greatest challenges he has faced while teaching have involved non-traditional teaching methods, including evening courses for practicing engineers and teaching through an interpreter at the Mongolian National University. These experiences have provided tremendous opportunities to learn new ways to communicate technical material. Dr. Larsen views modern software as one of the new tools that will radically alter the way engineers work, and his book *Introduction to MathCAD* was written to help young engineers prepare to meet the challenges of an ever-changing workplace.

Acknowledgments: To my students at Montana State University who have endured the rough drafts and typos, and who still allow me to experiment with their classes—my sincere thanks.

Sanford Leestma is a Professor of Mathematics and Computer Science at Calvin College, and received his Ph.D. from New Mexico State University. He has been the long-time co-author of successful textbooks on Fortran, Pascal, and data structures in Pascal. His current research interest are in the areas of algorithms and numerical computation.

Jack Leifer is an Assistant Professor in the Department of Mechanical Engineering at the University of Kentucky Extended Campus Program in Paducah, and was previously with the Department of Mathematical Sciences and Engineering at the University of South Carolina–Aiken. He received his Ph.D. in Mechanical Engineering from the University of Texas at Austin in December 1995. His current research interests include the analysis of ultra-light and inflatable (Gossamer) space structures.

Acknowledgments: I'd like to thank my colleagues at USC–Aiken, especially Professors Mike May and Laurene Fausett, for their encouragement and feedback; and my parents, Felice and Morton Leifer, for being there and providing support (as always) as I completed this book.

Richard M. Lueptow is the Charles Deering McCormick Professor of Teaching Excellence and Associate Professor of Mechanical Engineering at Northwestern University. He is a native of Wisconsin and received his doctorate from the Massachusetts Institute of Technology in 1986. He teaches design, fluid mechanics, an spectral analysis techniques. Rich has an active research program on rotating filtration, Taylor Couette flow, granular flow, fire suppression, and acoustics. He has five patents and over 40 refereed journal and proceedings papers along with many other articles, abstracts, and presentations.

Acknowledgments: Thanks to my talented and hardworking co-authors as well as the many colleagues and students who took the tutorial for a "test drive." Special thanks to Mike Minbiole for his major contributions to Graphics Concepts with SolidWorks. Thanks also to Northwestern University for the time to work on a book. Most of all, thanks to my loving wife, Maiya, and my children, Hannah and Kyle, for supporting me in this endeavor. (Photo courtesy of Evanston Photographic Studios, Inc.)

Holly Moore is a professor of engineering at Salt Lake Community College, where she teaches courses in thermal science, materials science engineering, and engineering computing. Dr. Moore received the B.S. degree in chemistry, the M.S. degree in chemical engineering from South Dakota School of Mines and Technology, and the Ph.D. degree in chemical engineering from the University of Utah. She spent 10 years working in the aerospace industry, designing and analyzing solid rocket boosters for both defense and space programs. She has also been active in the development of hands-on elementary science materials for the state of Utah.

Acknowledgments: Holly would like to recognize the tremendous influence of her father, Professor George

Moore, who taught in the Department of Electrical Engineering at the South Dakota School of Mines and Technology for almost 20 years. Professor Moore earned his college education after a successful career in the United States Air Force, and was a living reminder that you are never too old to learn.

Larry Nyhoff is a Professor of Mathematics and Computer Science at Calvin College. After doing bachelor's work at Calvin, and Master's work at Michigan, he received a Ph.D. from Michigan State and also did graduate work in computer science at Western Michigan. Dr. Nyhoff has taught at Calvin for the past 34 years—mathematics at first and computer science for the past several years.

Paul Riley is an author, instructor, and designer specializing in graphics and design for multimedia. He is a founding partner of CAD Support Associates, a contract service and professional training organization for computer-aided design. His 15 years of business experience and 20 years of teaching experience are supported by degrees in education and computer science. Paul has taught AutoCAD at the University of Massachusetts at Lowell and is presently teaching AutoCAD at Mt. Ida College in Newton, Massachusetts. He has developed a program, Computer-aided Design for Professionals that is highly regarded by corporate clients and has been an ongoing success since 1982.

Robert Rizza is an Assistant Professor of Mechanical Engineering at North Dakota State University, where he teaches courses in mechanics and computer-aided design. A native of Chicago, he received the Ph.D. degree from the Illinois Institute of Technology. He is also the author of *Getting Started with Pro/ENGINEER*. Dr. Rizza has worked on a diverse range of engineering projects including projects from the railroad, bioengineering, and aerospace industries. His current research interests include the fracture of composite materials, repair of cracked aircraft components, and loosening of prostheses.

Peter Schiavone is a professor and student advisor in the Department of Mechanical Engineering at the University of Alberta, Canada. He received his Ph.D. from the University of Strathclyde, U.K. in 1988. He has authored several books in the area of student academic success as well as numerous papers in international scientific research journals. Dr. Schiavone has worked in private industry in several different areas of engineering including aerospace and systems engineering. He founded the first Mathematics Resource Center at the University of Alberta, a unit designed specifically to teach new students the necessary *survival skills* in mathematics and the physical sciences required for success in first-year engineering. This led to the Students' Union Gold Key Award for outstanding contributions to the university. Dr. Schiavone lectures regularly to freshman engineering students and to new engineering professors on engineering success, in particular about maximizing students' academic performance.

Acknowledgements: Thanks to Richard Felder for being such an inspiration; to my wife Linda for sharing my dreams and believing in me; and to Francesca and Antonio for putting up with Dad when working on the text.

David I. Schneider holds an A.B. degree from Oberlin College and a Ph.D. degree in Mathematics from MIT. He has taught for 34 years, primarily at the University of Maryland. Dr. Schneider has authored 28 books, with one-half of them computer programming books. He has developed three customized software packages that are supplied as supplements to over 55 mathematics textbooks. His involvement with computers dates back to 1962, when he programmed a special purpose computer at MIT's Lincoln Laboratory to correct errors in a communications system.

David I. Schwartz is an Assistant Professor in the Computer Science Department at Cornell University and earned his B.S., M.S., and Ph.D. degrees in Civil Engineering from State University of New York at Buffalo. Throughout his graduate studies, Schwartz combined principles of computer science to applications of civil engineering. He became interested in helping students learn how to apply software tools for solving a variety of engineering problems. He teaches his students to learn incrementally and practice frequently to gain the maturity to tackle other subjects. In his spare time, Schwartz plays drums in a variety of bands.

Acknowledgments: I dedicate my books to my family, friends, and students who all helped in so many ways.

Many thanks go to the schools of Civil Engineering and Engineering & Applied Science at State University of New York at Buffalo where I originally developed and tested my UNIX and Maple books. I greatly appreciate the opportunity to explore my goals and all the help from everyone at the Computer Science Department at Cornell.

John T. Sears received the Ph.D. degree from Princeton University. Currently, he is a Professor and the head of the Department of Chemical Engineering at Montana State University. After leaving Princeton he worked in research at Brookhaven National Laboratory and Esso Research and Engineering, until he took a position at West Virginia University. He came to MSU in 1982, where he has served as the Director of the College of Engineering Minority Program and Interim Director for BioFilm Engineering. Prof. Sears has written a book on air pollution and economic development, and over 45 articles in engineering and engineering education.

Michael T. Snyder is President of Internet startup company Appointments 123.com. He is a native of Chicago, and he received his Bachelor of Science degree in Mechanical Engineering from the University of Notre Dame. Mike also graduated with honors from Northwestern University's Kellogg Graduate School of Management in 1999 with his Masters of Management degree. Before Appointments123.com, Mike was a mechanical engineer in new product development for Motorola Cellular and Acco Office Products. He has received four patents for his mechanical design work. "Pro/ENGINEER was an invaluable design tool for me, and I am glad to help students learn the basics of Pro/ENGINEER."

Acknowledgments: Thanks to Rich Lueptow and Jim Steger for inviting me to be a part of this great project. Of course, thanks to my wife Gretchen for her support in my various projects.

Jim Steger is currently Chief Technical Officer and cofounder of an Internet applications company. He graduated with a Bachelor of Science degree in Mechanical Engineering from Northwestern University. His prior work included mechanical engineering assignments at Motorola and Acco Brands. At Motorola, Jim worked on part design for two-way radios and was one of the lead mechanical engineers on a cellular phone product line. At Acco Brands, Jim was the sole engineer on numerous office product designs. His Worx stapler has won design awards in the United States and in Europe. Jim has been a Pro/ENGINEER user for over six years.

Acknowledgments: Many thanks to my co-authors, especially Rich Lueptow for his leadership on this project. I would also like to thank my family for their continuous support.

Royce Wilkinson received his undergraduate degree in chemistry from Rose-Hulman Institute of Technology in 1991 and the Ph.D. degree in chemistry from Montana State University in 1998 with research in natural product isolation from fungi. He currently resides in Bozeman, MT and is involved in HIV drug research. His research interests center on biological molecules and their interactions in the search for pharmaceutical advances.

http://www.prenhall.com/esource/

ESource Reviewers

We would like to thank everyone who helped us with or has reviewed texts in this series.

Christopher Rowe, *Vanderbilt University*
Steve Yurgartis, *Clarkson University*
Heidi A. Diefes-Dux, *Purdue University*
Howard Silver, *Fairleigh Dickenson University*
Jean C. Malzahn Kampe, *Virginia Polytechnic Institute* and State University
Malcolm Heimer, *Florida International University*
Stanley Reeves, *Auburn University*
John Demel, *Ohio State University*
Shahnam Navee, *Georgia Southern University*
Heshem Shaalem, *Georgia Southern University*
Terry L. Kohutek, *Texas A & M University*
Liz Rozell, *Bakersfield College*
Mary C. Lynch, *University of Florida*
Ted Pawlicki, *University of Rochester*
James N. Jensen, *SUNY at Buffalo*
Tom Horton, *University of Virginia*
Eileen Young, *Bristol Community College*
James D. Nelson, *Louisiana Tech University*
Jerry Dunn, *Texas Tech University*
Howard M. Fulmer, *Villanova University*
Naeem Abdurrahman, *University of Texas, Austin*
Stephen Allan, *Utah State University*
Anil Bajaj, *Purdue University*
Grant Baker, *University of Alaska–Anchorage*
William Beckwith, *Clemson University*
Haym Benaroya, *Rutgers University*
John Biddle, *California State Polytechnic University*
Tom Bledsaw, *ITT Technical Institute*
Fred Boadu, *Duk University*
Tom Bryson, *University of Missouri, Rolla*
Ramzi Bualuan, *University of Notre Dame*
Dan Budny, *Purdue University*
Betty Burr, *University of Houston*
Dale Calkins, *University of Washington*
Harish Cherukuri, *University of North Carolina –Charlotte*
Arthur Clausing, *University of Illinois*
Barry Crittendon, *Virginia Polytechnic and* State University
James Devine, *University of South Florida*
Ron Eaglin, *University of Central Florida*
Dale Elifrits, *University of Missouri, Rolla*
Patrick Fitzhorn, *Colorado State University*
Susan Freeman, *Northeastern University*
Frank Gerlitz, *Washtenaw College*
Frank Gerlitz, *Washtenaw Community College*
John Glover, *University of Houston*
John Graham, *University of North Carolina–Charlotte*
Ashish Gupta, *SUNY at Buffalo*
Otto Gygax, *Oregon State University*
Malcom Heimer, *Florida International University*
Donald Herling, *Oregon State University*
Thomas Hill, *SUNY at Buffalo*
A.S. Hodel, *Auburn University*
James N. Jensen, *SUNY at Buffalo*
Vern Johnson, *University of Arizona*
Autar Kaw, *University of South Florida*
Kathleen Kitto, *Western Washington University*
Kenneth Klika, *University of Akron*
Terry L. Kohutek, *Texas A&M University*
Melvin J. Maron, *University of Louisville*
Robert Montgomery, *Purdue University*
Mark Nagurka, *Marquette University*
Romarathnam Narasimhan, *University of Miami*
Soronadi Nnaji, *Florida A&M University*
Sheila O'Connor, *Wichita State University*
Michael Peshkin, *Northwestern University*
Dr. John Ray, *University of Memphis*
Larry Richards, *University of Virginia*
Marc H. Richman, *Brown University*
Randy Shih, *Oregon Institute of Technology*
Avi Singhal, *Arizona State University*
Tim Sykes, *Houston Community College*
Neil R. Thompson, *University of Waterloo*
Raman Menon Unnikrishnan, *Rochester Institute of* Technology
Michael S. Wells, *Tennessee Tech University*
Joseph Wujek, *University of California, Berkeley*
Edward Young, *University of South Carolina*
Garry Young, *Oklahoma State University*
Mandochehr Zoghi, *University of Dayton*

Contents

2 Circles and Drawing Aids 32

3 Layers, Colors, and Linetypes 62

1

Lines

Overview

Drawing in AutoCAD can be a fascinating and highly productive activity. AutoCAD 2004 is full of features that will enhance your CAD performance. Here and throughout this book, our goal will be to get you drawing as quickly and efficiently as possible. Discussion and explanation is limited to what will be most useful and relevant at the moment, but also give you an understanding of the program to make you a more powerful user.

This chapter introduces some of the basic tools you will use whenever you draw in AutoCAD. You will begin to find your way around AutoCAD 2004 menus and toolbars, and learn to control basic elements of the Drawing Window. You will produce drawings involving straight lines and learn to undo your last command with the U command. Your drawings will be saved, if you wish, using the SAVE or SAVEAS commands.

Sections

Objectives

After reading this chapter, you should be able to:

- Begin a new drawing.
- Explore the drawing window.
- Explore command entry methods.
- Draw and undo lines.
- Save and open drawings.
- Draw a grate.
- Draw a design.
- Draw a shim.

1.1 BEGINNING A NEW DRAWING

When you load AutoCAD 2004 you will find yourself in the Drawing Window with the Startup dialog box open. The Drawing Window is where you do most of your work with AutoCAD. You can begin a new drawing from scratch or open a previously saved drawing or template file. In this section you will begin a NEW drawing using the "Start from Scratch" option.

- **From the Windows Startup screen, choose Programs, then the AutoCAD 2004 folder, and then the AutoCAD 2004 program.**

  Or, if your system has an AutoCAD 2004 shortcut icon on the Windows desktop, double click on the icon to start AutoCAD.

- **Wait...**

  When you see the AutoCAD 2004 screen with the Startup dialog box in the foreground, as shown in Figure 1.1, you are ready to begin.

NOTE: If you do not see the Start From Scratch dialog box shown in Figure 1.1, the following simple procedure will turn it on.

1. At the command prompt at the bottom left of your screen, type "startup" and press enter.
2. Type "1" and press enter. This changes the setting of the startup system variable from 0 to 1. You should now see the dialog box as shown.

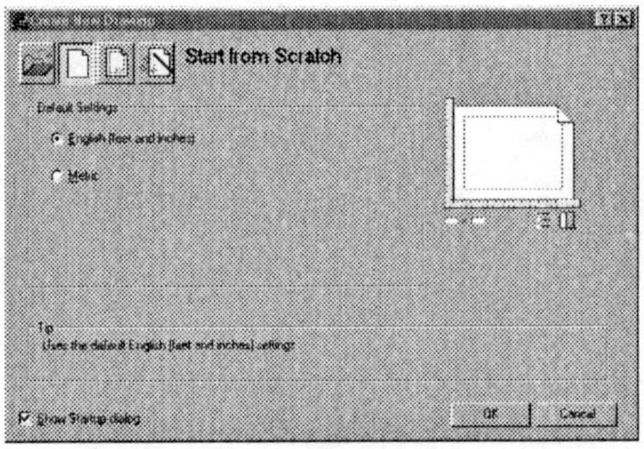

Figure 1.1

The Startup dialog box gives you four options, indicated by the four icons at the top. You can open a previously saved file, start from scratch, use a template, or use a Wizard, which guides you through setup. For our purposes it will be best to start from scratch to ensure that your Drawing Window shows the same AutoCAD 2004 default settings as are used in this chapter. We will explore other possibilities later.

You should see your cursor arrow somewhere on the screen. If you do not see it, move your pointing device to the middle of your drawing area or digitizer. When you see the arrow, you are ready to proceed.

- **Move your pointing device until the arrow is inside the second icon.**

  You should see the words "Start from Scratch" to the right of the icons in the Startup dialog box.

- **Click on the second icon so that "Start from Scratch" shows in the dialog box.**
- **Click on "English" in the Default Setting box.**
- **Click on Okay to exit the dialog box and start your new drawing.**

  Pressing Enter will also work.

The dialog box will disappear and your screen should resemble Figure 1.2. You are now ready to proceed.

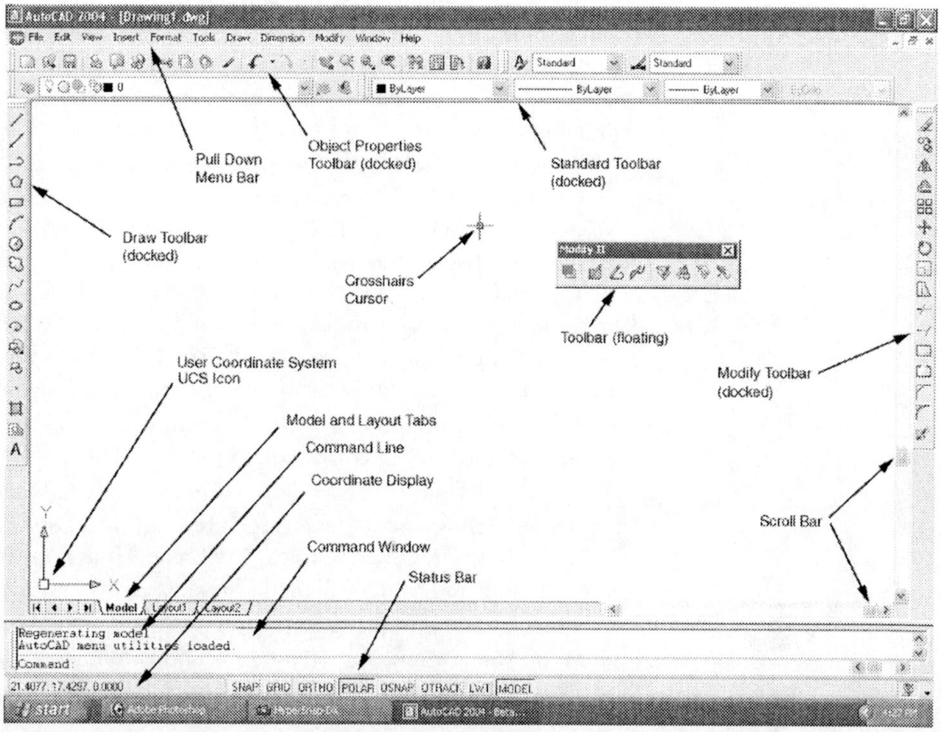

Figure 1.2

1.2 EXPLORING THE DRAWING WINDOW

You are looking at the AutoCAD Drawing Window. There are many ways that you can alter it to suit a particular drawing application. To begin with, there are a number of features that can be turned on and off using your mouse or the F-keys on your keyboard.

1.2.1 The Screen

The AutoCAD 2004 Drawing Window has many features that are common to all Windows programs. At the top of the screen you will see the title bar, with the AutoCAD 2004 icon on the left and the standard Windows minimize, maximize, and close buttons on the right.

Below the title bar you will see AutoCAD 2004's pull-down menu bar, including the titles for the File, Edit, View, Insert, Format, Tools, Draw, Dimension, Modify, Window, and Help pull-down menus. Pull-down menus work in AutoCAD just as in other Windows applications and are discussed later in this section.

The next line down is the standard toolbar. This toolbar is one of many toolbars that can be displayed on the AutoCAD 2004 screen. There are 28 toolbars available in the standard AutoCAD 2004 toolbar dialog box. Toolbars can be created and modified. They can be moved, resized, and reshaped. They are a convenience, but they can also make your drawing area overly cluttered. For our purposes you will not need more than a few of the available toolbars. The use of toolbars will also be discussed later in this chapter.

The next line is the Object Properties toolbar, which displays the current layer and linetype. It also includes tools for changing other object properties.

Below these toolbars you will see the drawing area with the Draw toolbar positioned vertically along the left side and the Modify toolbar and a vertical scroll bar along the right side. You may see a bar at the top of the drawing area with the current drawing name, "Drawing1," on the left side. This indicates that you are in an AutoCAD drawing window. You can have more than one drawing window open in a single AutoCAD session, but this will not be necessary at this point. If the drawing name bar is showing, you can eliminate it and expand your drawing window slightly by clicking on the maximize button at the top right of the drawing name bar.

At the bottom of the drawing area you will see arrows and tabs with the words "Model," "Layout1," and "Layout2." These tabs allow you to switch among the drawing and different layouts that you create for printing or plotting. You will have no immediate need for this feature. At the bottom and along the right side of the drawing area you will see scroll bars. These work like the scroll bars in any Windows application. Clicking on the arrows or clicking and dragging the square sliders will move your drawing to the left or right, up or down within the drawing area. We will demonstrate these in a moment.

Beneath the scroll bar you will see the command prompt area. Typed commands are one of the basic ways of working in AutoCAD.

At the bottom of the Drawing Window is the status bar, with the coordinate display on the left, currently showing three numbers, and eight mode indicators (Snap, Grid, Ortho, Polar, Osnap, Otrack, LWT, and Model) in the center. The coordinate display and mode indicators will be discussed shortly.

Finally, the bottom of your screen will show the Windows taskbar, with the Start button on the left and any open applications following. You should see the AutoCAD icon here, indicating that you have an AutoCAD window open.

TIP: You can gain more room for your drawing area by hiding the Windows taskbar. This can be done by pointing to the top of the taskbar and dragging it down off the bottom of the screen. It will move down, leaving only the top edge showing. To get it back, point to this top edge again and drag it upward.

1.2.2 Switching Screens

⊕ **Press F2.**

This brings up the AutoCAD Text Window. AutoCAD uses this window to display text that will not fit in the command area. As soon as the Text Window opens, Windows adds a button with a text icon on the taskbar at the bottom of the screen. Now you can open and close the Text Window using the taskbar buttons or F2.

⊕ **Press F2 again, or click on the AutoCAD icon button on the taskbar.**

This brings you back to the Drawing Window. Once used, the AutoCAD Text Window operates like an open application. It remains "open" but may be visible or invisible until you close it using the close button in the upper right corner.

⊕ **Press F2 or the AutoCAD Text Window button to view the Text Window again.**

⊕ **Click on the close button (X) in the upper right corner of the Text Window to close the text window.**

NOTE: Sometimes AutoCAD switches to the Text Window automatically when there is not enough room in the command area for prompts or messages. If this happens, use F2 when you are ready to return to the drawing area.

1.3 INTERACTING WITH THE DRAWING WINDOW

There are many ways to communicate with the Drawing Window. In this section we will explore the mouse, cross hairs, arrow, and other simple features. In the next section we will begin to enter drawing commands.

1.3.1 The Mouse

Most of your interaction with the Drawing Window will be communicated through your mouse. Given the toolbar and menu structure of AutoCAD and Windows, a two-button mouse is sufficient for most applications. In this book we will assume two buttons. If you have a digitizer or a more complex pointing device, the two button functions will be present along with other functions that we will not address.

On a common two-button mouse the left button is called the pickbutton and will be used for point selection, object selection, and menu or tool selection. All mouse instructions refer to this left button, unless specifically stated otherwise. The right button sometimes functions as an alternative to the enter key on the keyboard, but more often calls up shortcut menus as in other Windows applications. The menu that is called depends on the context. Learning how and when to use these menus can increase your efficiency. We will point them out as we go along. In this section, most instructions are for the left button. If you hit the right button accidentally and open an unwanted shortcut menu, close it by clicking with the left button at any point not on the shortcut menu.

1.3.2 Cross Hairs and Pickbox

You should see a small cross with a box at its intersection somewhere in the display area of your screen. If you do not see it, move your pointing device until it appears. The two perpendicular lines are the cross hairs, or screen cursor, which tell you where your pointing device is located on your digitizer or mouse pad.

The small box at the intersection of the cross hairs is called the pickbox and is used to select objects for editing. You will learn more about the pickbox later.

- **Move the mouse and see how the cross hairs move in coordination with your hand movements.**
- **Move the mouse so that the cross hairs move to the top of the screen.**

  When you leave the drawing area, your cross hairs will be left behind and you will see an arrow pointing up and to the left. The arrow will be used as in other Windows applications to select tools and to pull down menus from the menu bar.

NOTE: Here and throughout this book we show the AutoCAD 2004 versions of AutoCAD screens in our illustrations. If you are working with another version, your screen may show significant variations.

- **Move the cursor back into the drawing area and the selection arrow will disappear.**

1.3.3 The Coordinate Display

The coordinate display at the bottom left of the status line keeps track of coordinates as you move the pointer. The coordinate display is controlled using the F6 key or by clicking on the display itself.

- **Move the cross hairs around slowly and keep your eye on the three numbers at the bottom of the screen.**

They should be moving very rapidly through four-place decimal numbers. When you stop moving, the numbers will be showing coordinates for the location of the pointer. These coordinates are standard coordinate values in a three-dimensional coordinate system originating from (0,0,0) at the lower left corner. The first value is the *x* value, showing the horizontal position of the cross hairs, measuring left to right across the screen. The second value is *y*, or the vertical position of the cross hairs, measured from bottom to top on the screen. Points also have a *z* value, but it will always be 0 in two-dimensional drawing and can be ignored until you begin to draw in 3D. In this book we will usually not include the *z* value if it is 0, as it will not be relevant until we get into 3D drawings.

Press F6 or click on the coordinate display.

The numbers will freeze and the coordinate display will turn gray.

Move the cross hairs slowly.

Now when you move the cross hairs you will see that the coordinate display does not change. You will also see that it is grayed out. The display is now in static mode, in which the numbers will only change when you select a new point by pressing the left button on your mouse. Try it.

Move the cross hairs to any point on the screen and press the left button on your mouse.

Notice that the first two numbers in the coordinate display change, but the display is still grayed out. Take a moment to ensure that you understand these values. The *x* value measuring horizontally, the *y* value measuring vertically, and the *z* value (0).

Move the cross hairs to another point on the screen.

You will see that AutoCAD opens a box on the screen, as shown in Figure 1.3. *You are not drawing anything with this box.* This is the object selection window, used to select objects for editing. It will have no effect now since there are no objects on your screen. You will give two points to define the window and then it will vanish because there is nothing there to select.

AutoCAD prompts for the other corner of the selection window. You will see this in the command area:

Specify opposite corner:

Pick a second point.

This will complete the object selection window. The window will vanish. Notice the change in the static coordinate display numbers.

Press F6 to return the coordinate display to dynamic mode.

The coordinate display actually has two different dynamic modes, but this will not be apparent until you enter a drawing command such as LINE (Section 1.4), which asks for point selection.

NOTE: The units AutoCAD uses for coordinates, dimensions, and for measuring distances and angles can be changed at any time using the UNITS command. For now we will accept the AutoCAD default values, including the four-place decimals. In the next chapter we will be changing to two-place decimals. The F-keys are switches only; they cannot be used to change settings.

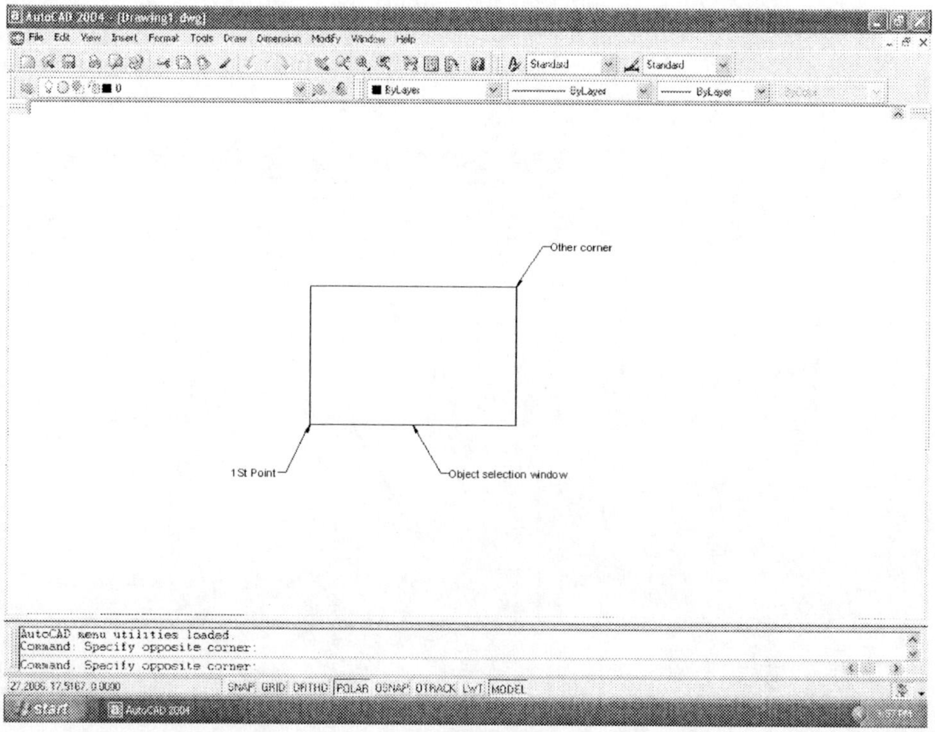

Figure 1.3

1.3.4 The Grid

- **Press F7 or click on the word GRID on the status bar.**

  This will turn on the grid. When the grid is on, the GRID button will appear in the "down" position on the status bar, as illustrated in Figure 1.4. The grid will initially appear at the left side of the drawing area, as illustrated.

  The following procedure will enlarge and center the grid, as shown in Figure 1.5. It makes use of the ZOOM command, which is presented in Chapter 3. For now, all you need is this:

- **At the command prompt, type Z and press enter.**
- **In response to the prompt, type A and press enter.**

The grid is simply a matrix of dots that helps you find your way around on the screen. It will not appear on your drawing when it is plotted, and it may be turned on and off at will. You may also change the spacing between dots using the GRID command.

The grid is presently set up to emulate the shape of an A-size (12 × 9 inch) piece of paper, with grid points at 0.50 inch increments. There are 20 grid points from bottom to top, numbered 0, 0.5, 1.0, 1.5, and so forth, up to 9.0. There are 26 points from left to right, numbered 0 to 12, including all 0.5 unit increments. The AutoCAD command that controls the outer size and shape of the grid is LIMITS. Until then we will continue to use the present format.

You should be aware from the beginning that there is no need to scale AutoCAD drawings while you are working on them. That can be handled when you get ready to plot or print your drawing on paper. You will always draw at full scale, where one unit of length on the screen equals one unit of length in real space. This full-scale drawing space is called "model space." Notice the word "MODEL" on the right end of the status bar, indicating that you are currently working in model space. The actual size of drawings printed out on paper may be handled in "paper space." When you are in paper space you will see the word "PAPER" on the status bar in place of the word "MODEL." For now, all your work will be done in model space, and you do not need to be concerned with paper space.

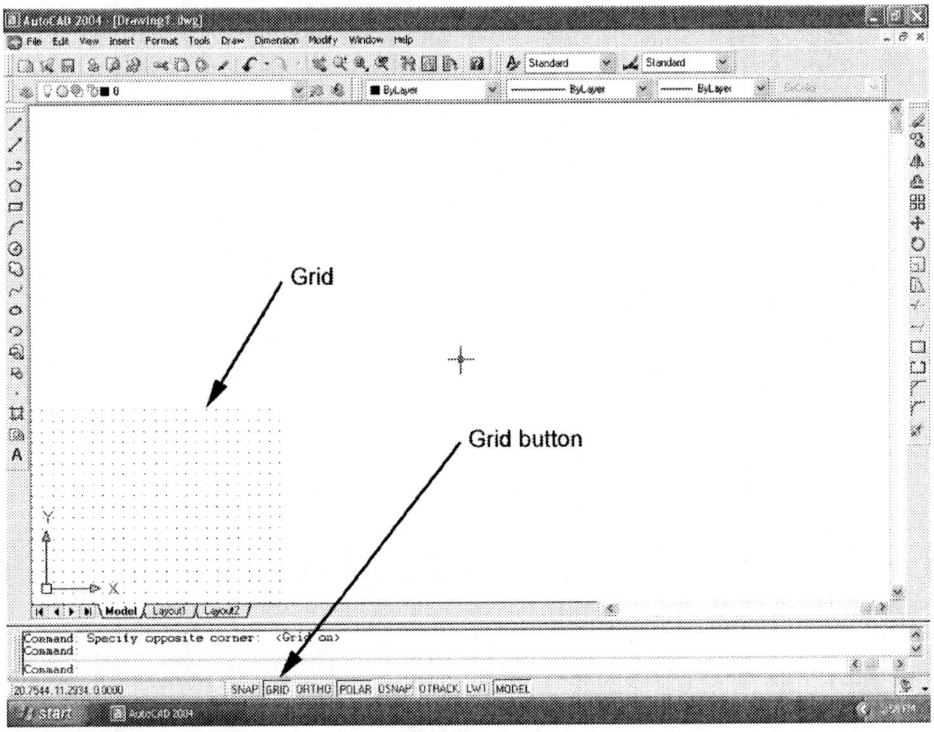

Figure 1.4

1.3.5 Scroll Bars

⌗ **Click on the left arrow on the horizontal scroll bar at the bottom of the screen.**

Your grid will move a little to the right.

⌗ **Click the left arrow again.**

As you see, the movement is slight and the grid moves in the direction opposite to where the arrow is pointing. This may seem backwards. Think about the scroll bars controlling the drawing window rather than the drawing itself. As you move the window to the left, the drawing within the window appears to move to the right.

⌗ **Hold the mouse button down so that the grid moves continuously across the screen.**

⌗ **Work with the left and right buttons until the grid is centered within the drawing area, as shown in Figure 1.5.**

Notice that moving the grid in this way does not change the coordinate value of dots on the grid. The position of grid points has changed relative to the screen but not relative to other points on the grid.

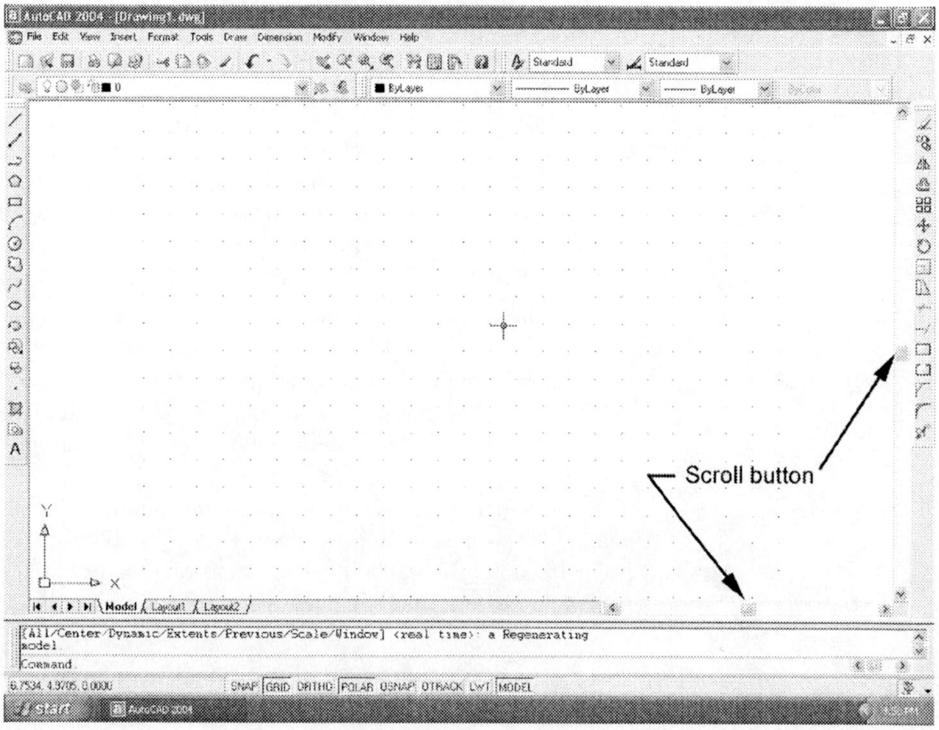

Figure 1.5

1.3.6 Snap

Snap is an important concept in AutoCAD 2004 and CAD in general. There are several AutoCAD features through which an approximate screen cursor location will lock onto a precise numerical point, a point on an object, or the extension of an object. This means that the operator does not have to hunt or visually guess at precise point locations. The simplest form of snap is called incremental snap or grid snap, because it is conceptually related to the screen grid. Try this:

⌗ **Press F9 or click on the word SNAP on the status bar.**

The SNAP button should go into the down position, indicating that the snap mode is now on.

⌗ **Move the cross hairs slowly around the drawing area.**

Look closely and you will see that the cross hairs jump from point to point. If your grid is on, notice that it is impossible to make the cross hairs touch a point that is not on the grid. Try it.

⌗ **If your coordinate display is in the static mode, press F6 to switch to dynamic mode.**

⌗ **Move the cursor and watch the coordinate display.**

You will see that the coordinate display shows only values ending in 0.0000 or 0.5000.

⌗ **Press F9 or click on SNAP again.**

Snap should now be off and the SNAP button will be in the up or off position on the status bar again.

If you move the cursor in a circle now, you will see that the cross hairs move more smoothly, without jumping. You will also observe that the coordinate display moves rapidly through a full range of four-place decimal values again.

F9 turns snap on and off. With snap off you can, theoretically, touch every point on the screen. With snap on you can move only in predetermined increments. With the Start from Scratch default settings snap is set to a value of 0.5000 so that you can move only in half unit increments. In future discussions you will learn how to change this setting using the SNAP command. For now we will leave the snap setting alone. A snap setting of 0.5000 will be adequate for the drawings at the end of this chapter.

Using an appropriate snap increment is a tremendous timesaver. It also allows for a degree of accuracy that is not possible otherwise. If all the dimensions in a drawing fall into 1-inch increments, for example, there is no reason to deal with points that are not on a 1-inch grid. You can find the points you want much more quickly and accurately if all those in between are temporarily eliminated. The snap setting will allow you to do that.

TIP: Incremental snap is more than a convenience. In many cases it is a necessity. With snap off it is virtually impossible to locate any point precisely. If you try to locate the point (6.5000,6.5000,0.0000) with snap off, for example, you may get close, but the probability is very small that you will actually be able to select that exact point. Try it.

1.3.7 Other Buttons on the Status Bar

All of the status bar buttons are important and can be used to turn powerful features on and off. Some of the features are so powerful, however, that they will interfere with your learning and ability to control the cursor at this stage. For this reason we will encourage you to keep some features off until you need them. Generally you will want Snap, Grid, and Model to be on and all other buttons to be off. Ortho and Polar are discussed later in this chapter and you can use them at your discretion. Osnap, which stands for Object Snap, is a very important feature that will force the selection of a geometrically definable point on an object, such as the endpoint or midpoint of a line. Otrack stands for Object Snap Tracking. Otrack is an outgrowth of Object Snap and we will save it for Chapter 6 as well. LWT stands for Lineweight, which we will introduce in Chapter 3.

1.3.8 The User Coordinate System Icon

At the lower left of the screen you will see the User Coordinate System (UCS) icon (see Figure 1.2). These two perpendicular arrows clearly indicate the directions of the *x* and *y* axes, which are currently aligned with the sides of your screen. To do 3D drawings, you can define your own coordinate systems, which can be turned at any angle and originate at any point in space. At that time the icon is a very useful visual aid. However, it is hardly necessary in 2D drawing and may be distracting. For this reason you may want to turn it off now and keep it turned off until you actually need it.

☩ **Type "ucsicon."**

Notice that the typed letters are displayed on the command line to the right of the colon.

☩ **Press the enter key on your keyboard.**

AutoCAD will show the following prompt on the command line:

Enter an option [ON/OFF/All/Noorigin/ORigin] <ON>:

As you explore AutoCAD commands you will become familiar with many prompts like this one. First comes the prompt, then a series of options inside brackets [ ] separated by slashes (/). The current setting is shown between the arrows < >. For now we only need to know about "On" and "Off."

⌖ **Type "off" and press enter.**

The UCS icon will disappear from your screen. Anytime you want to see it again, type "ucsicon" and then type "on." Alternatively, you can click on "View" on the menu bar, then highlight "Display" and "Ucsicon" and click "On." This will turn the icon on if it is off. If the ucsicon is on, the word on the menu will be "Off." In this case selecting Off will turn the icon off.

1.4 EXPLORING COMMAND ENTRY METHODS

You've entered your first command, the UCSICON command, using the keyboard. You can also communicate drawing instructions to AutoCAD by selecting items from a toolbar, a pull-down menu, a shortcut menu, or a tablet menu. Each method has its advantages and disadvantages depending on the situation, and most tasks can be accomplished in several different ways. Often a combination of two or more methods is the most efficient way to carry out a complete command sequence. The instructions in this book are not always specific about which to use. All operators develop their own preferences.

An important concept in AutoCAD is what is termed "Heads-up Design." What this means is that optimal efficiency is achieved when the CAD operator can keep his or her attention focused on the screen, in particular the drawing area and the objects being worked on. The less time and effort spent looking away from the screen the better. Staying heads-up certainly works as a general rule, and we will provide you with many techniques to support it as we go along.

Each of the basic command entry methods is described briefly. You do not have to try them all out at this time. Read them over to get a feel for the possibilities and then proceed to the LINE command.

1.4.1 The Keyboard and the Command Line

The keyboard is the most primitive and fundamental method of interacting with AutoCAD, and is still of great importance despite the goal of staying heads-up. Toolbars and menus all function in part by automating basic command sequences as they would be typed on the keyboard. Being familiar with the keyboard procedures will increase your understanding of AutoCAD even if other methods are sometimes faster. The keyboard is the most basic, the most comprehensive, and changes the least from one release of AutoCAD to the next. It is literally at your fingertips and if you know the command you want, you will not have to go looking for it. For this reason, some excellent CAD operators rely too heavily on the keyboard. Do not limit yourself by typing everything. If you know the keyboard sequence, try out the other methods to see how they vary and how you can use them to save time and to stay screen-focused. Ultimately, you will want to type as little as possible and use the differences between the toolbar and menu systems to your advantage.

As you type commands and responses to prompts, the characters you are typing will appear on the command line after the colon. Remember that you must press enter to complete your commands and responses. The command line can be moved and reshaped, or you can switch to the text screen using F2 when you want to see more lines, including previously typed entries.

Many of the most often used commands, such as LINE, ERASE, and CIRCLE, have "aliases." These one- or two-letter abbreviations are very handy. A few of the most commonly used aliases are shown in Figure 1.6. There are also a large number of two- and three-letter aliases, some of which we will introduce as we go along.

COMMAND ALIAS CHART		
LETTER + ENTER		= COMMAND
A	↵	ARC
C	↵	CIRCLE
E	↵	ERASE
F	↵	FILLET
L	↵	LINE
M	↵	MOVE
O	↵	OFFSET
P	↵	PAN
R	↵	REDRAW
S	↵	STRETCH
Z	↵	ZOOM

Figure 1.6

1.4.2 Pull-Down Menus

Pull-down menus and toolbars have the great advantage that instead of typing a complete command, you can simply "point and shoot" to select an item, without looking away from the screen. The pull-down menus are always available and contain most commands that you will use regularly. Menu selections and toolbar selections often duplicate each other.

Pull-down menus work in AutoCAD as they do in any Windows application. To use a menu, move the cross hairs up into the menu bar so that the selection arrow appears. Then move the arrow to the menu heading you want. Select it with the pickbutton (the left button on your mouse). A menu will appear. Run down the list of items to the one you want. Press the pickbutton again to select the item (see Figure 1.7). Items followed by a triangle have "cascading" submenus. Submenus open automatically when an item is highlighted. Picking an item that is followed by an ellipsis (…) will call up a dialog box.

Dialog boxes are familiar features in all Windows programs. They require a combination of pointing and typing that is fairly intuitive. We will discuss many dialog boxes and dialog box features as we go along.

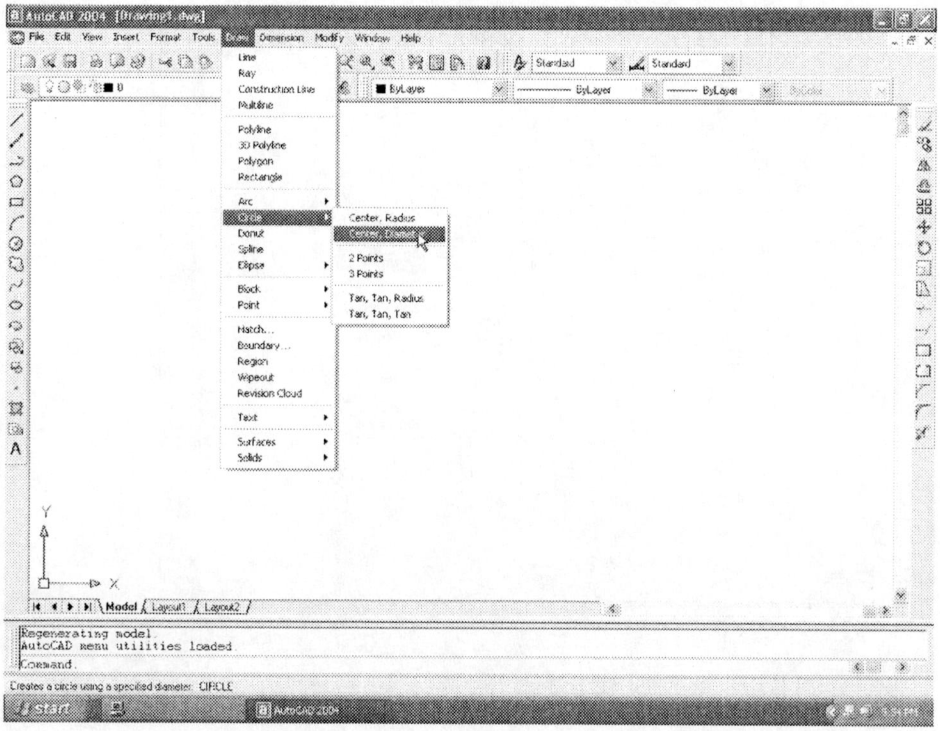

Figure 1.7

1.4.3 Toolbars

Toolbars are also a standard Windows feature. They are comprised of buttons with icons that give one-click access to commands. Twenty-four toolbars can be opened from the Toolbars dialog box accessible from the bottom of the View pull-down menu or from a shortcut menu opened by right clicking on any open toolbar.

Once opened, toolbars can "float" anywhere on the screen, or can be "docked" along the edges of the drawing area. Toolbars can be a nuisance, since they cover portions of your drawing space, but they can be opened and closed quickly. Beyond the Standard, Object Properties, Draw, and Modify toolbars, which are open by default, you will probably only wish to open a toolbar if you are doing a whole set of procedures involving one toolbar. In dimensioning an object, for example, you may wish to have the Dimensioning toolbar open. Do not use too many toolbars at once, and remember that you can move toolbars or use the scroll bars to move your drawing right, left, up, and down behind the toolbars.

The icons used on toolbars are also a mixed blessing. One picture may be worth a thousand words, but with so many pictures, you may find that a few words can be very helpful as well. As in other Windows applications, you can get a label for an icon simply by allowing the selection arrow to rest on the button for a moment without selecting it. These labels are called "Tooltips." Try this:

⌗ **Position the selection arrow on the top button of the Draw toolbar, as shown in Figure 1.8, but do not press the pickbutton.**

Figure 1.8

You will see a yellow label that says "Line," as shown in Figure 1.8. This label identifies this button as the LINE command button.

When a tooltip is displayed, you will also see a phrase in the status bar in place of the coordinate display. This phrase will describe what the tool or menu item does and is called a "Helpstring." The LINE helpstring says "Creates straight line segments: line." The word following the colon identifies the command as you would type it in the command area.

1.5 DRAWING AND UNDOING LINES

Now that you know about the drawing window and command entry methods, it is time to begin drawing some lines.

⌖ **In preparation, make sure that your status line resembles ours, as shown in Figure 1.9.**

Figure 1.9

In particular, note that SNAP, GRID, and MODEL are in the on position (down), while ORTHO, POLAR, OSNAP, OTRACK, and LWT are off (up). This will keep things simple and uncluttered for the present. ***This is very important.*** While features like Osnap and Polar tracking are very powerful, they also can get in your way when used at the wrong time. You will have plenty of use for them later on.

Now it is time to enter the LINE command and start drawing.

- **Type "L" or select the Line icon from the Draw toolbar, or Line under Draw on the pull-down menu (remember to press enter if you are typing).**

Look at the command area. You should see this, regardless of how you enter the command:

Specify first point:

This is how AutoCAD asks for a start point for your line.

Also, notice that the pickbox disappears from the cross hairs when you have entered a drawing command.

Most of the time when you are drawing you will want to point rather than type. To do this you need to pay attention to the grid and the coordinate display.

- **If snap is off switch it on (F9 or click on SNAP).**
- **Move the cursor until the display reads "1.0000, 1.0000, 0.000."**
- **Press the pickbutton.**

AutoCAD registers your first point and asks for a second point. You should see this in the command area:

Specify next point or [Undo]:

This prompts you to pick a second point. The "Undo" option will be discussed shortly.

1.5.1 Rubber Band

There are several other new things to be aware of. One is the "rubber band," which extends from the start point to the cross hairs on the screen. If you move the cursor, you will see that this visual aid stretches, shrinks, or rotates like a tether, keeping you connected to the start point. In this case the rubber band represents the line you are about to draw.

1.5.2 Absolute (xyz) and Polar Coordinates

Another feature to watch is the coordinate display. If it is off (no change in coordinates when the cursor moves), press F6 to turn it on. Once it is on it will show either absolute coordinates or polar coordinates. Absolute coordinates are the familiar coordinate numbers (x, y, z) discussed previously. They are distances measured from the origin (0,0,0) of the coordinate system at the lower left corner of the grid. If your display shows three four-digit numbers, then these are the absolute coordinates.

If your display shows something like "4.2426 < 45,0.0000", it is set on polar coordinates.

- **Press F6 or click on the coordinate display and then move your cursor.**

Which type of coordinates is displayed?

- **Press F6 and move your cursor again.**

Observe the coordinate display. As you continue to press F6, you will see that there are three coordinate display modes: static (no change until you select a point), xyz (x, y, and z values separated by a comma), and polar (length 6 angle, z).

- **Press F6 once or twice more until you see polar coordinates.**

Polar coordinates are in a length, angle, z format and are given relative to the last point you picked. They look something like this: 5.6569 6 45,0.0000. There are three values here: 5.6569, 45, and 0.0000. The first number (5.6569) is the distance from the starting point of the line to the cross hairs. The second (45) is an angle of rotation, measuring counterclockwise, with 0 degrees being straight out to the right. The third value (0.0000) is the z coordinate, which will remain zero in 2D drawing. In LINE, as well as many other draw commands, polar coordinates are very useful because the first number will give you the length of the segment you are currently drawing.

Now switch back to absolute coordinates and complete a line between (1.0000, 1.0000, 0.0000) and (8.0000, 8.0000, 0.0000), as follows:

⌖ **Press F6 to read xyz coordinates.**

⌖ **Pick the point (8.0000, 8.0000, 0.0000).**

Your screen should now resemble Figure 1.10. AutoCAD has drawn a line between (1,1) and (8,8) and is asking for another point.

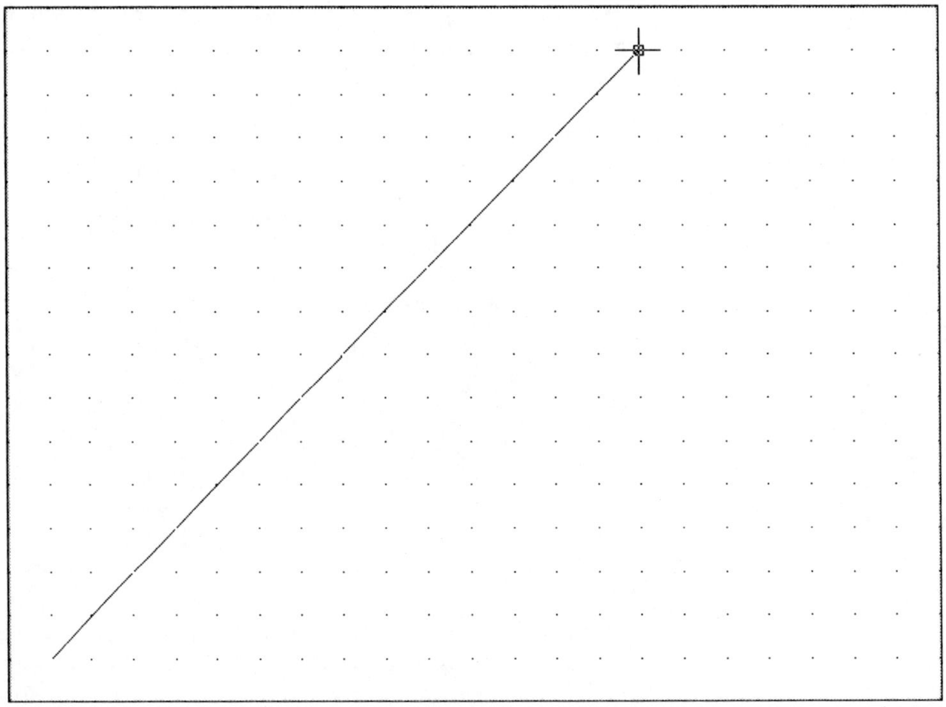

Figure 1.10

Specify next point or [Undo]:

This prompt allows you to stay in the LINE command to draw a whole series of connected lines if you wish. You can draw a single line from point to point, or a series of lines from point to point to point to point. In either case, you must tell AutoCAD when you are finished by pressing enter or the space bar.

NOTE: When you are drawing a continuous series of lines, the polar coordinates on the display are given relative to the most recent point, not the original starting point.

⌖ **Press enter or the space bar to end the LINE command.**

You should be back to the "Command:" prompt again, and the pickbox will have reappeared at the intersection of the cross hairs.

1.5.3 Space Bar and Enter Key

In most cases AutoCAD allows you to use the space bar as a substitute for the enter key. Although this is one of the oldest of AutoCAD features, it is a major contributor to the goal of heads-up drawing. It is a great convenience, since the space bar is easy to locate with one hand (your left hand if the mouse is on the right side) while the other hand is on the pointing device. For example, the LINE command can be entered without removing your right hand from your pointing device by typing the "L" on the keyboard with your left index finger and then hitting the space bar with your left thumb. The major exception to the use of the space bar as an enter key is when you are entering text. Since a space may be part of a text string, the space bar must have its usual significance there.

1.5.4 Right Mouse Button and Shortcut Menus

The right button on your mouse may also be used in place of the enter key sometimes, but in most cases there will be an intervening step involving a shortcut menu with choices. This, too, is a major heads-up feature, which we will explore as we go along. For now, try this:

☩ **Press the right button on your mouse (this action will be called right click from now on).**

This calls up a shortcut menu, as shown in Figure 1.11. The top line is a Repeat Line option that can be used to re-enter the LINE command. You will have no use for the other options until later chapters.

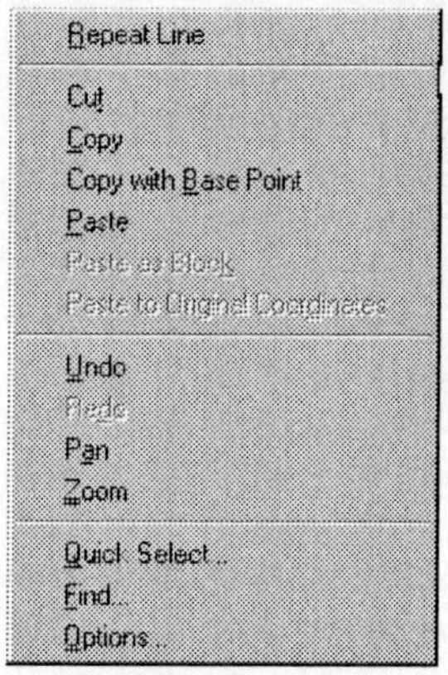

Figure 1.11

Shortcut menus are context sensitive; the menu that is called depends on the situation. Often the last command entered can be repeated by selecting the top option.

TIP: You can also repeat the last command by hitting the space bar or the enter key at the command prompt. We recommend that you use this major convenience often.

☩ **Move the cursor anywhere outside of the cursor menu and press the pick-button (the left mouse button).**

The cursor menu will disappear, but AutoCAD will take the picked point as the first point in an object selection window.

⌗ **Pick any second point to close the object selection window.**

There are many context-sensitive shortcut menus in AutoCAD 2004. We will not attempt to present every one, but encourage you to explore. You will find many possibilities simply by clicking the right mouse button while in a command or dialog box.

1.5.5 Direct Distance Entry

Another convenient drawing method is called Direct Distance Entry. In this method, you pick the first point and then show the direction of the line segment you wish to draw, but instead of picking the other endpoint you type in a value for the length of the line. Try it:

⌗ **Repeat the LINE command by pressing enter or the space bar.**

AutoCAD prompts for a first point.

TIP: If you press enter or the space bar at the "Specify first point:" prompt, AutoCAD will select the last point entered, so that you can begin drawing from where you left off.

⌗ **Press enter or the space bar to select the point (8,8,0), the endpoint of the previously drawn line.**

AutoCAD prompts for a second point.

⌗ **Pull the rubber band diagonally down to the right, as shown in Figure 1.12.**

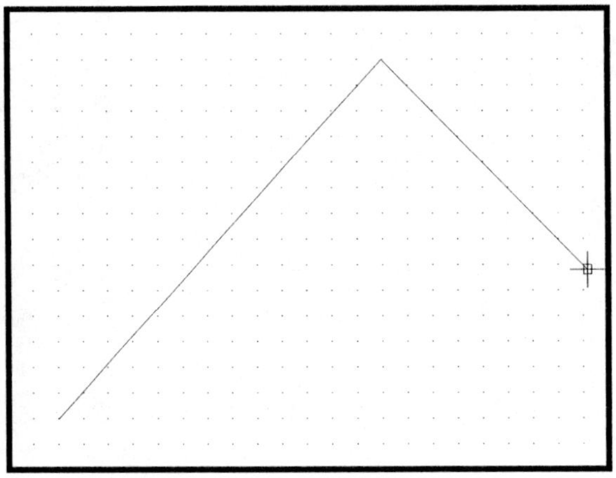

Figure 1.12

Moving along the diagonal set of grid points will put you at a −45 degree angle, as shown. The length of the rubber band does not matter, only the direction.

⌗ **With the rubber band stretched out as shown, type "3."**

⌗ **Press enter or hit the space bar.**

AutoCAD will draw a 3.0000 line segment at the angle you have shown.

⌗ **Press enter or the space bar to exit the LINE command.**

Your screen should resemble Figure 1.13.

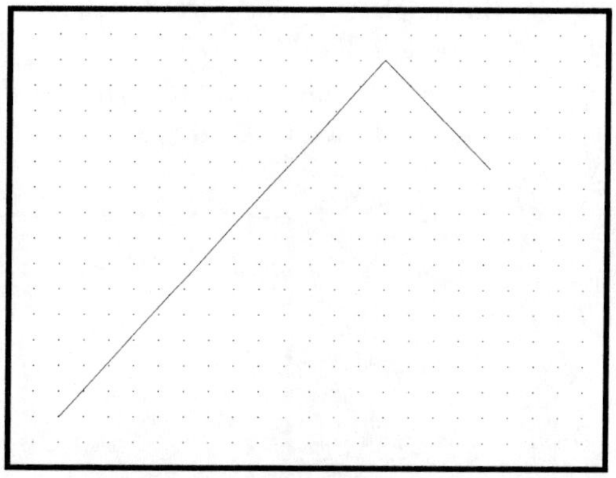

Figure 1.13

1.5.6 Undoing Commands with U

⌗ **To undo the line you just drew, type "U" <enter> or select the Undo tool from the Standard toolbar, as shown in Figure 1.14.**

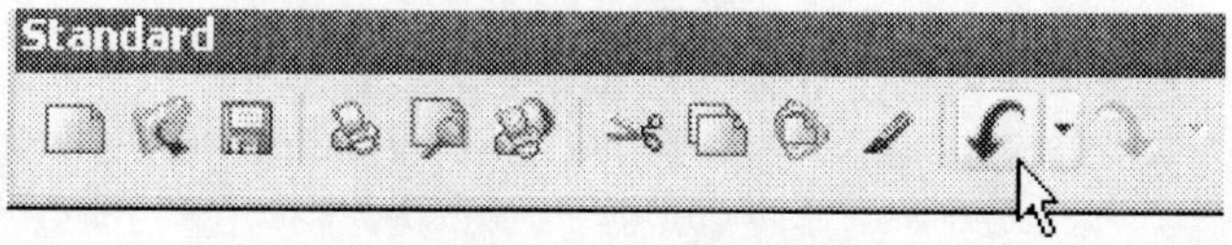

Figure 1.14

U undoes the last command, so if you have done anything else since drawing the line, you will need to type "U" <enter> more than once. In this way you can walk backward through your drawing session, undoing your commands one by one. As mentioned previously, there is also an Undo option within the LINE command so that you can undo the last segment drawn without leaving the command.

⌗ **Select the Redo tool, which is to the right of the Undo tool on the Standard toolbar.**

REDO only works immediately after U, and it only works once. That is, you can only REDO the last U and only if it was the last command executed.

NOTE: The Undo tool executes a command called U. AutoCAD also has an UNDO command that can be entered at the command line by typing "undo." U is not an alias for UNDO, which is more elaborate. REDO can be used to reverse either U or UNDO. Also note that R is **not** an alias for REDO.

⌗ **Use the Redo tool to ensure that there is at least one line in your drawing. Or, draw a new line.**

1.5.7 Erasing Lines

In this section, we will discuss the ERASE command in its simplest form. Using ERASE brings up the techniques of object selection which are common to all editing commands.

The simplest form of object selection requires that you point to an object and then click the pickbutton. Try this:

⌖ **Move the cross hairs so that they are over one of the lines on your screen, as shown in Figure 1.15.**

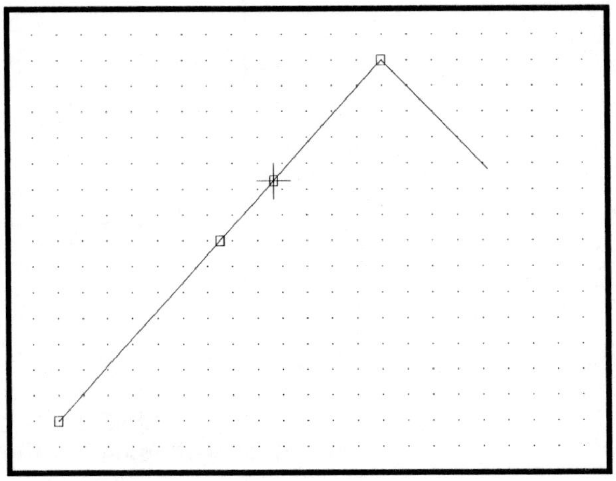

Figure 1.15

⌖ **Press the pickbutton.**

You will see that the line becomes dotted, indicating that it has been selected. You will also see small blue boxes at the middle and at each end of the line. You can ignore these for now.

Now that the line is selected, you can enter the ERASE command to erase it.

⌖ **Type "e" with the middle finger of your left hand and hit the space bar with your left thumb.**

The line will disappear. Notice the left-hand alias and space-bar technique again.

⌖ **Before going on, use U or ERASE to remove all lines from your drawing, leaving a blank drawing area.**

Be aware that undoing ERASE will cause a line to reappear.

1.5.8 Ortho

Before completing this section on line drawing, we suggest that you try the ortho and polar tracking modes.

⌖ **Type "L" <enter> or select the Line tool from the Draw toolbar.**

⌖ **Pick a starting point. Any point near the center of the screen will do.**

⌖ **Press F8 or click on the word ORTHO, so that the button goes down.**

⌖ **Move the cursor in slow circles.**

Notice how the rubber band jumps between horizontal and vertical without sweeping through any of the angles between. Ortho forces the pointing device to pick up points only along the horizontal and vertical quadrant lines from a given starting point. With ortho on you can select points at 0, 90, 180, and 270 degrees of rotation from your starting point only (see Figure 1.16).

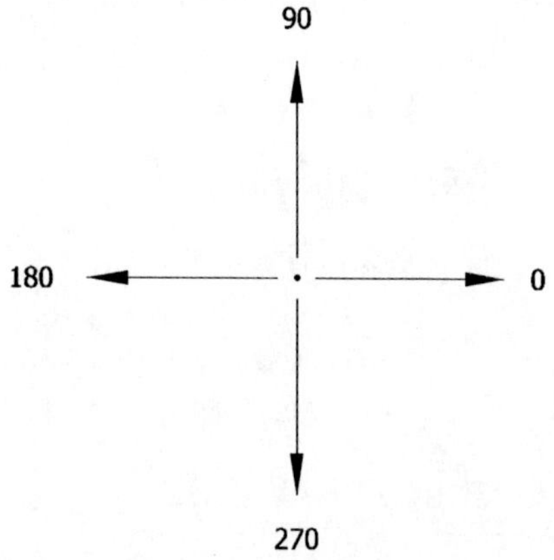

Figure 1.16

The advantages of ortho are similar to the advantages of snap mode, except that it limits angular rather than linear increments. It ensures that you will get precise and true right angles and perpendiculars easily when that is your intent. Ortho will become more important as drawings grow more complex. In this chapter it is hardly necessary, though it will be convenient in drawings 1 and 3.

1.5.9 Polar Tracking

Polar tracking is an AutoCAD feature that can replace ORTHO for many purposes. Try it out:

⌖ **Press F10 or select the POLAR button to turn on polar tracking.**

Notice that POLAR and ORTHO are mutually exclusive. They cannot both be on at the same time. When you turn POLAR on, ORTHO shuts off automatically.

⌖ **Move your cursor in a slow circle around the starting point of your line, just as you did with ORTHO on.**

With POLAR tracking on, you will see that when the rubber band crosses a vertical or horizontal axis (i.e., when the rubber band is at 0, 90, 180, or 270 degrees), a dotted line appears that extends to the edge of the drawing area. You will also see a tooltip label giving a value like "Polar 6.5000<0°" (see Figure 1.17).

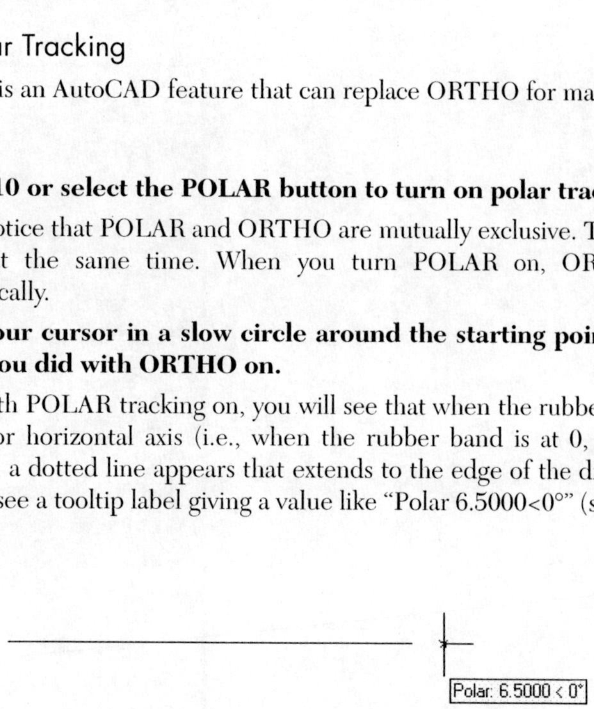

Figure 1.17

The value is a polar coordinate, without the z value. By default, polar tracking is set to respond on the orthogonal axes. In later chapters you will see that it can be set to track at any angle. For now you should leave it off and focus on basic line drawing and point selection.

⌖ **Press F10 or click on the POLAR button to turn polar tracking off.**

⌖ **Move the cross hairs in a circle and observe that polar tracking is no longer in effect.**

1.5.10 The Esc key

⌖ **While still in the LINE command, press the "Esc" (escape) key.**

This will abort the LINE command and bring back the "Command:" prompt. Esc is used to cancel a command that has been entered. Sometimes it will be necessary to press Esc twice to exit a command and return to the command prompt.

1.6 SAVING AND OPENING DRAWINGS

Saving drawings in AutoCAD is just like saving a file in other Windows applications. Use SAVE to save an already named drawing. Use SAVEAS to name a drawing as you save it or save a named drawing under a new name. In all cases, a .dwg extension is added to file names to identify them as AutoCAD drawing files. This is automatic when you name a file.

1.6.1 The SAVE Command

To save a drawing without leaving the drawing window, select "Save" from the File pull-down menu, or select the Save tool from the Standard toolbar, as shown in Figure 1.18.

Figure 1.18

If the current drawing is already named, AutoCAD will save it without intervening dialog. If it is not named, it will open the SAVEAS dialog box and allow you to give it a name before it is saved. SAVEAS is described next.

1.6.2 The SAVEAS Command

To rename a drawing or to give a name to a previously unnamed drawing, type "Saveas," select "Saveas..." from the File pull-down menu, or, in an unnamed drawing, select the Save tool from the Standard Toolbar.

Any of these methods will call the Save Drawing As dialog box (see Figure 1.19). The cursor will be blinking in the area labeled "Files:", waiting for you to enter a file name. Include a drive designation, (i.e., "A:1-1") if you are saving your work on a floppy disk. AutoCAD will add the .dwg extension automatically. SAVEAS will also allow you to save different versions of the same drawing under different names while continuing to edit.

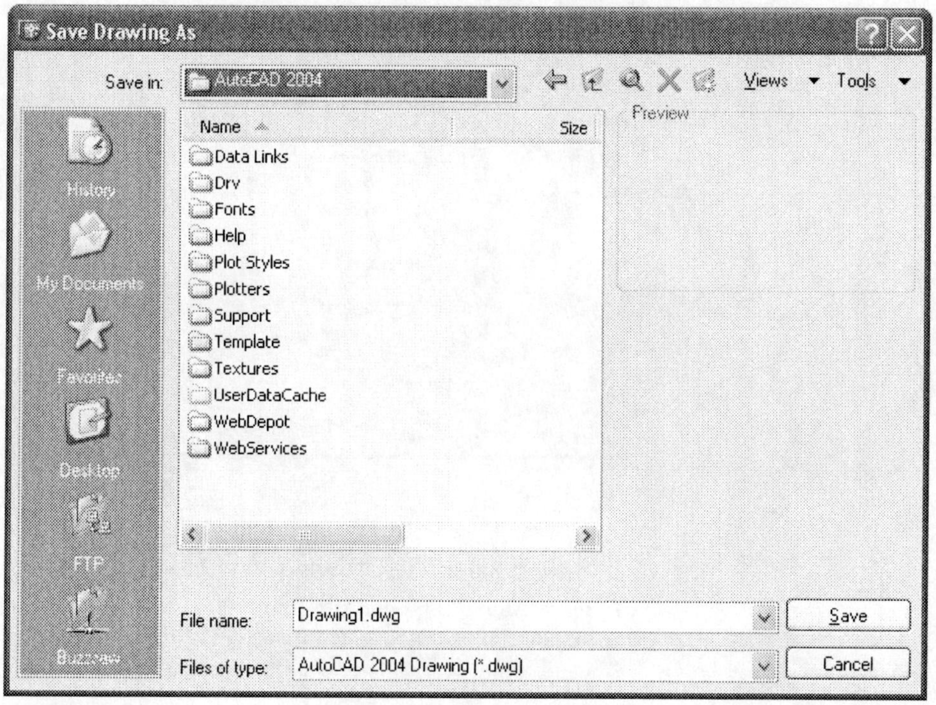

Figure 1.19

1.6.3 OPENing Saved Drawings

To open a previously saved drawing, type "open," select "Open" from the File pull-down menu, or select the Open tool from the Standard toolbar, as shown in Figure 1.20.

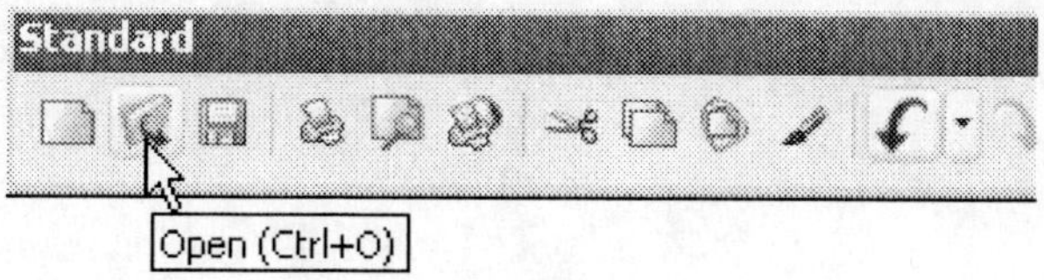

Figure 1.20

Once you have saved a drawing you will need to use the OPEN command to return to it later. Entering the OPEN command by any method will bring up the Select File dialog box shown in Figure 1.21. You can select a file directory in the box at the left and then a file from the box at the right. When you select a file, AutoCAD will show a preview image of the selected drawing in the Preview image box at the right. This way you can be sure that you are opening the drawing you want.

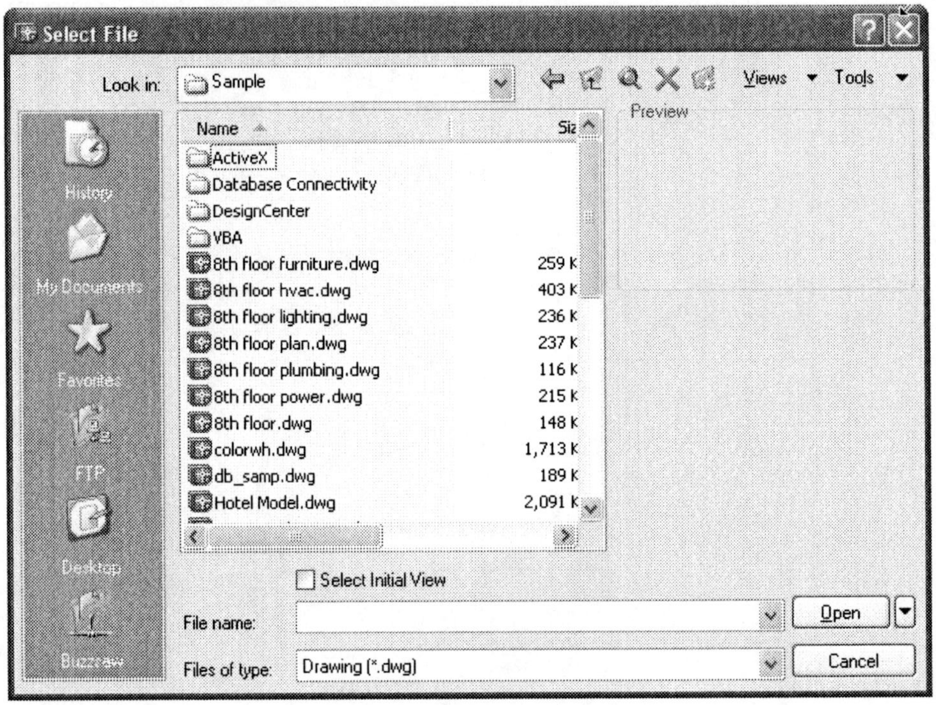

Figure 1.21

1.6.4 Exiting the Drawing Window

To leave AutoCAD, open the File pull-down menu and select "Exit," or click the Windows close button (X) at the upper right of the screen. If you have not saved your current drawing, AutoCAD will ask whether you wish to save your changes before exiting.

1.7 REVIEW MATERIAL

1.7.1 Questions

Before going to the drawings, review the following questions and problems. Then you should be ready for Drawing 1.

1. What function key opens and closes the text window?
2. What are the three different modes of the coordinate display and how does each mode appear? What are two ways to switch between modes?
3. Explain and describe the differences among absolute, relative, and polar coordinates.
4. You have just entered the point (1,1,0) and you now wish to enter the point two units straight up from this point. How would you identify this point using absolute, relative, and polar coordinates?

5. What is the value and limitation of having SNAP on?
6. Name three different ways to enter the LINE command.
7. Name and describe three different methods of point selection in AutoCAD.
8. What does the U command do?
9. What is the main limitation of the REDO command?
10. What key do you use to cancel a command?
11. What command would you use to save a new version of a drawing under a new file name? How would you enter it?

PROFESSIONAL SUCCESS

Will the Computer Replace Pencil and Paper Drawings?

Not too long ago, a student entering an engineering graphics class would likely encounter rows of large drafting tables used in the production of precision drawings by hand. Today, computerized drawing programs like AutoCAD have, for the most part, replaced mechanical drawing.

Though computer-aided drafting software has become almost ubiquitous, technical sketching by hand is still an essential tool for the successful engineer. Just as an electronic calculator is not used in every circumstance (some calculations are more easily done in your head), hand sketching sometimes proves to be the most convenient means of rapidly producing a drawing.

Hand sketches, with practice, should be neither imprecise nor sloppy; any type of engineering drawing that can be produced via computer or mechanical drafting methods can be rapidly realized by sketch.

A major advantage of sketching is that it can be done anywhere. Quick sketches may be produced by an engineer on a plant tour for the purpose of recording a particular design or layout. A group of engineers at a restaurant or party may resort to sketching on napkins as they work as a group to refine an idea into a conceptual design. In such cases, sketches are being used as a means of communication among engineers, as it is often easier to express an idea pictorially than in words. Until computers are as small, light and as easy to use as a pencil and tablet (or a napkin!), hand sketching will remain among the most important skills that an engineer can master.

Commands

ERASE	OPEN	SAVEAS
LINE	REDO	UCSICON
NEW	SAVE	

1.8 DRAWING PROBLEMS

1. Draw a line from (3,2) to (4,8) using the keyboard only.
2. Draw a line from (6,6) to (7,5) using the mouse only.
3. Draw a line from (6,6) to (6,8) using the direct distance method.
4. Undo (U) all lines on your screen.
5. Draw a square with corners at (2,2), (7,2), (7,7), and (2,7). Then erase it using the ERASE command.

TIP: Closing a Set of Lines
For drawing an enclosed figure like the one in step 5, the LINE command provides a convenient Close option. "Close" will connect the last in a continuous series of lines back to the starting point of the series. In drawing a square, for instance, you would simply type "C" <enter> in lieu of drawing the last of the four lines. For this to work, the whole square must be drawn without leaving the LINE command.

DRAWING 1

Grate

Before beginning, look over the drawing page. Notice the status bar mode reminders and other drawing information below. *It is important to keep the modes as shown.*

The first two drawings in this chapter are given without dimensions. Instead, we have drawn them as you will see them on the screen, against the background of a half-unit grid. All of these drawings were done using the default half-unit snap, but all points will be found on one-unit increments.

Drawing Suggestions

- If you are beginning a new drawing, type or select "New..." and then select Start from Scratch in the Startup dialog box. Notice that AutoCAD 2004 remembers your last selection and it becomes the default. Because of this you may be able simply to press enter or select OK to get started.
- Remember to watch the coordinate display when searching for a point.
- Be sure that GRID, SNAP, and the coordinate display are all turned on and that OSNAP, OTRACK, and LWT are turned off. ORTHO or POLAR may be on or off as you wish.
- Draw the outer rectangle first. It is six units wide and seven units high, and its lower left-hand corner is at the point (3.0000,1.0000). The three smaller rectangles inside are 4 × 1.
- The Close option can be used in all four of the rectangles.

If You Make a Mistake—U This is a reminder that you can stay in the LINE command as you undo the last line you drew, or the last two or three if you have drawn a series.

- Type "U" <enter>. The last line you drew will be gone or replaced by the rubber band, awaiting a new endpoint. If you want to go back more than one line, type "U" <enter> again, as many times as you need.
- If you have already left the LINE command, the U command will undo the last continuous series of lines. In Grate this could be the whole outside rectangle, for instance.
- Remember, if you have mistakenly undone something, you can get it back by using the Redo tool. You cannot perform other commands between U and REDO.

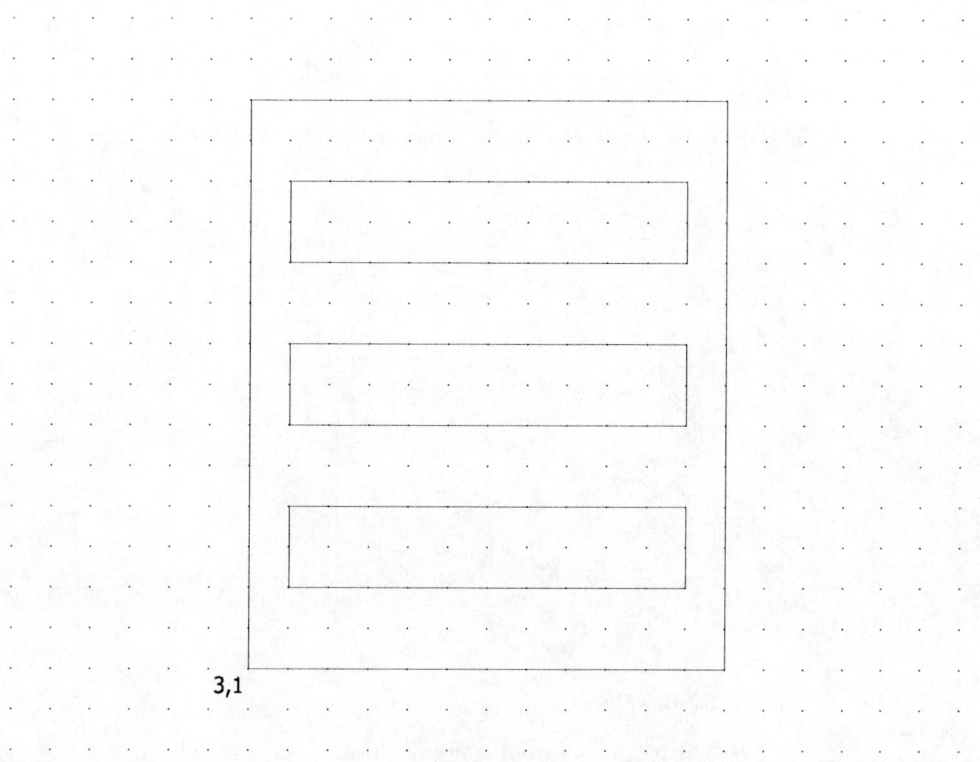

GRATE

DRAWING 2

Design

This design will give you further practice with the LINE command.

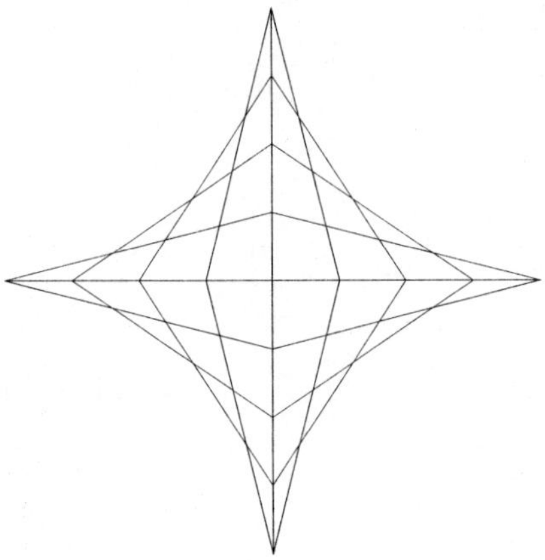

Drawing Suggestions

- If you are beginning a new drawing, type or select "New..." and then check the Startup dialog box to ensure that you Start from Scratch.
- Draw the horizontal and vertical lines first. Each is eight units long.
- Notice how the rest of the lines work—outside point on horizontal to inside point on vertical, then working in, or vice versa.
- You will want ORTHO off to do this drawing.
- Placing the bottom tip of the design at (6,0.5) as shown will keep your drawing well positioned on the grid.

Repeating a Command Remember, you can repeat a command by pressing enter or the space bar at the Command: prompt. This will be useful in this drawing, since you have several sets of lines to draw.

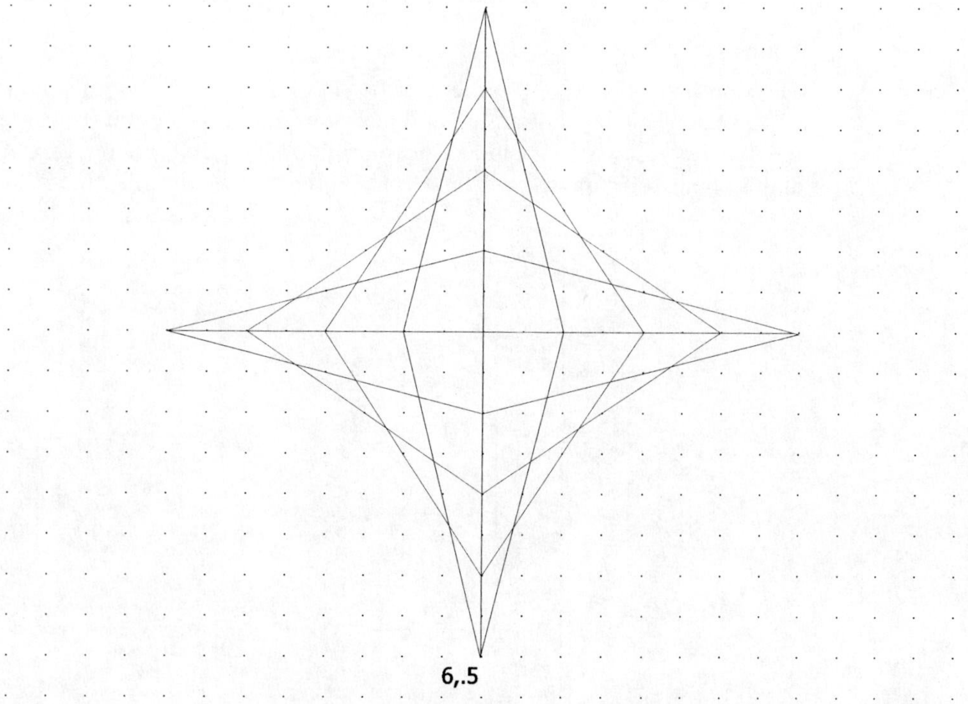

DESIGN #1

DRAWING 3

Shim

This drawing will give you further practice in using the LINE command. In addition, it will give you practice in translating dimensions into distances on the screen. Note that the dimensions are only included for your information; they are not part of the drawing at this point. Your drawing will appear like the reference drawing that follows.

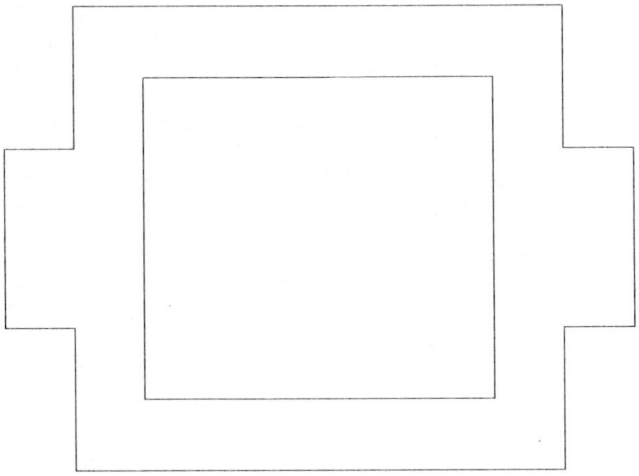

Drawing Suggestions

- If you are beginning a new drawing, type or select "New..." and Start from Scratch.
- It is most important that you choose a starting point that will position the drawing so that it fits on your screen. If you begin with the bottom left-hand corner of the outside figure at the point (3,1), you should have no trouble.
- Read the dimensions carefully to see how the geometry of the drawing works. It is good practice to look over the dimensions before you begin drawing. Often the dimension for a particular line may be located on another side of the figure or may have to be extrapolated from other dimensions. It is not uncommon to misread, misinterpret, or miscalculate a dimension, so take your time.

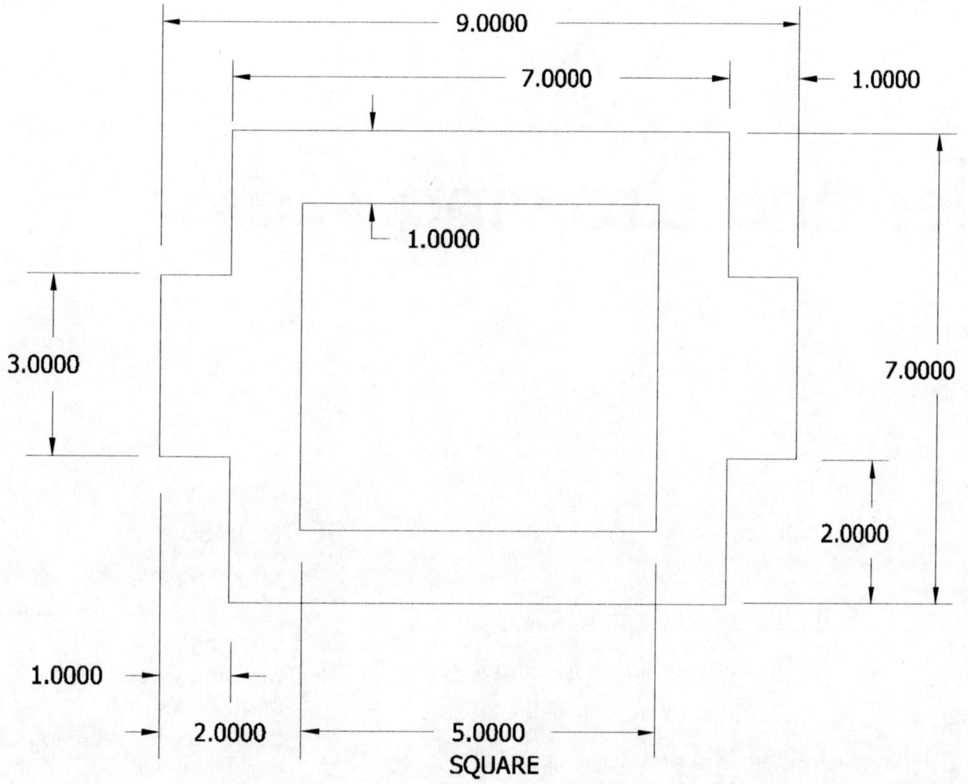
9.0000
7.0000
1.0000
1.0000
3.0000
7.0000
2.0000
1.0000
2.0000
5.0000
SQUARE

SHIM

2

Circles and Drawing Aids

OVERVIEW

This chapter is loaded with new material and techniques. Here you will begin to gain control of your drawing environment by changing the spacing of the grid and the snap and the units in which coordinates are displayed. You will add to your repertoire of objects by drawing circles with the CIRCLE command and rectangles with the RECTANGLE command. You will explore the many methods of object selection as you continue to learn editing procedures with the ERASE command. You will gain access to convenient HELP features and begin to learn AutoCAD's extensive plotting and printing procedures.

SECTIONS

OBJECTIVES

After reading this chapter, you should be able to:

- Change the grid spacing.
- Change the snap spacing.
- Change units.
- Draw three concentric circles using the center point, radius method.
- Draw three more concentric circles using the center point, diameter method.
- Access AutoCAD HELP features.
- ERASE the circles, using four selection methods.
- Draw a rectangle.
- Print or plot a drawing.
- Draw an aperture wheel.
- Draw a roller.
- Draw a switch plate.

2.1 CHANGING THE GRID SETTING

When you begin a new drawing from scratch in AutoCAD 2004, the grid and snap are set with a spacing of 0.5000. Previously, all drawings were done without altering the grid and snap spacings from the default value. Usually you will want to change this to a value that reflects your application. You may want a 10-mile snap for a mapping project, or a 0.010-inch snap for a printed circuit diagram. The grid may match the snap setting or may be set independently.

- **To begin, open a new drawing by selecting the New tool from the Standard toolbar, and then selecting Start from Scratch and English units in the Start Up dialog box.**

  Once again, this ensures that you begin with the settings we have used in preparing this chapter.

- **Using F7 and F9, or clicking on the status bar, be sure that GRID and SNAP are both on.**
- **Type "grid."**

  We will no longer remind you to press enter after typing a command or response to a prompt. Do not use the pull-down menu or toolbar yet. We will get to those procedures momentarily.

  The command area prompt will appear like this, with options separated by slashes (/):

  Specify grid spacing(X) or [ON/OFF/Snap/Aspect] <0.5000>:

  You can ignore the options for now. The number <0.5000> shows the current setting. AutoCAD uses this format (<default>) in many command sequences to show you a current value or default setting. It usually comes at the end of a series of options. Pressing the enter key or space bar at this point will confirm the default setting.

- **In answer to the prompt, type "1" and watch what happens (of course you remembered to press enter).**

  The screen will change to show a one-unit grid.

- **Move the cursor around to observe the effects of the new grid setting.**

  The snap setting has not changed, so you still have access to all half-unit points, but the grid shows only single-unit increments.

- **Try other grid settings. Try 2, 0.25, and 0.125.**

  Remember that you can repeat the last command, GRID, by pressing enter or the space bar.

- **What happens when you try 0.05?**

  When you get too small (smaller than 0.109 on our screen), the grid becomes too dense to display, but the snap can still be set smaller.

- **Before going on to Section 2.2, set the grid back to 0.5000.**

2.2 CHANGING THE SNAP SETTING

The process for changing the snap setting is the same as changing the grid. In fact, the two are similar enough to cause confusion. The grid is only a visual reference. It has no effect on selection of points. Snap is invisible, but it dramatically affects point selection. Grid and snap may or may not have the same setting.

2.2.1 Using the Drafting Settings Dialog Box

Snap may be changed using the SNAP command at the prompt, as we did with the GRID command in the last section. Both can also be changed in the Drafting Settings dialog box, as we will do in this section. The procedure is somewhat different, but the result is the same.

⌗ **Type "ds" or open the Tools pull-down menu and click on "Drafting Settings..." as shown in Figure 2.1.**

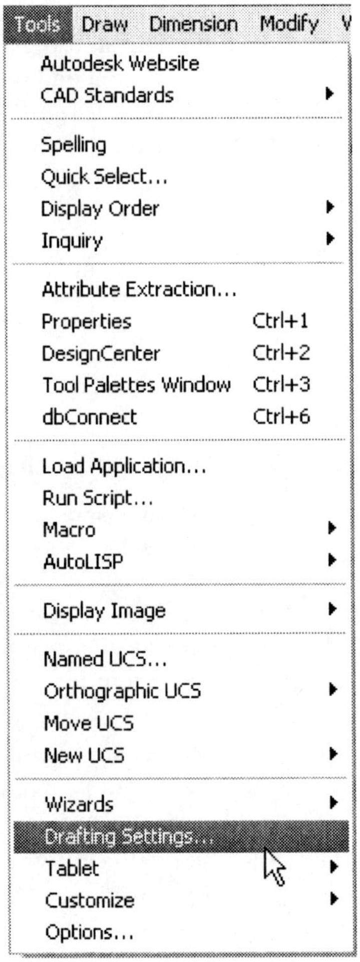

Figure 2.1

This will open The Drafting Settings dialog box shown in Figure 2.2. DSETTINGS is the command that calls up this dialog box, and "ds" is the command alias. Look at the dialog box. It contains some common features, including tabs, check boxes, radio buttons, and edit boxes.

2.2.2 Tabs

At the top of the dialog box you will see an arrangement that resembles a well-ordered set of three tabbed index cards with the words "Snap and Grid," "Polar Tracking," and

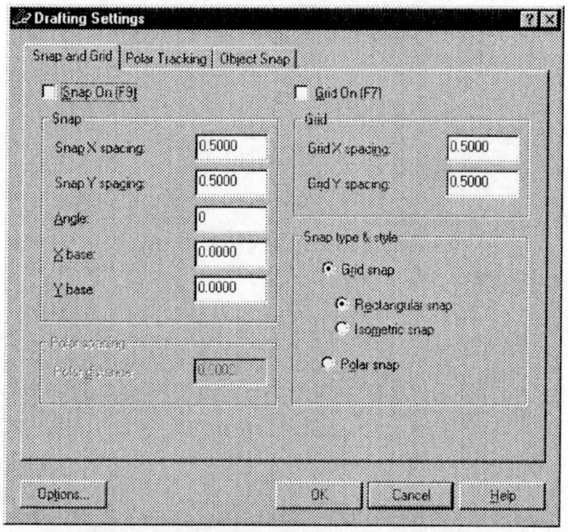

Figure 2.2

"Object Snap" on the tabs. Tabbed dialog boxes are common in Windows programs. With this tabbed arrangement, a single dialog box can provide access to a large variety of related features. By clicking on a tab you can bring the related "index card" to the top of the "stack" so that is visible in front of the others. We will not need to access the Polar Tracking or Object Snap cards at this time.

⌗ **If the Snap and Grid card is not on top, click its tab to bring it up.**

2.2.3 Check Boxes

Below the tabs you will see check boxes labeled "Snap on" and "Grid on." You can turn snap and grid on and off by moving the arrow inside the appropriate check box and pressing the pickbutton. A checked box is on, while an empty box is off. In your dialog box, check boxes should show that both Snap and Grid are on.

2.2.4 Panels

On the Snap and Grid card you will see four bordered and labeled areas. Most dialog boxes are divided into sections in this way. We will refer to these labeled sections as panels. The four panels here are Snap, Grid, Snap type & style, and Polar spacing. In this section we will look at the Snap and Grid panels only.

2.2.5 Edit Boxes

The snap and grid settings are shown in edit boxes, labeled Snap X spacing, Snap Y spacing, Grid X spacing, and Grid Y spacing. Edit boxes contain text or numerical information that can be edited as you would in a text editor. You can highlight the entire box to replace the text, or point anywhere inside to do partial editing.

To change the snap setting, do the following:

⌗ **Move the arrow into the edit box labeled "Snap X spacing."**

NOTE: The dialog box has places to set both x and y spacing. It is unlikely that you will want to have a grid or snap matrix with different horizontal and vertical increments, but the capacity is there if you do. Also notice that you can change the snap angle. Setting the snap angle to 45, for example, would turn your snap and grid at a 45-degree angle. When you alter the grid or snap angle, you may also want to designate x and y base points around which to rotate. This is the function of the x and y base point settings.

- **Double click to highlight the entire number 0.5000 in the Snap X spacing edit box.**
- **Type "1" and press Enter.**

  Pressing enter at this point is like clicking on OK in the dialog box. It will take you out of the dialog box and back to the screen.

  Snap is now set at 1 and grid is still at 0.5. This makes the snap setting larger than the grid setting. Move the cursor around the screen and you will see that you can only access half of the grid points. This type of arrangement is not too useful. Try some other settings.

TIP: Another way to open the Drafting settings dialog box is to right click while pointing at the Grid or Snap button on the status bar. This will open a shortcut menu with On, Off, and Settings... options. Selecting Settings... will open the Drafting settings dialog box.

- **Open the dialog box again by right clicking on the Snap button on the status bar and then choosing Settings... from the shortcut menu.**
- **Change the snap x spacing to 0.25.**

  Move the cursor slowly and observe the coordinate display. This is a more efficient type of arrangement. With grid set "coarser" than snap, you can still pick exact points easily, but the grid is not so dense as to be distracting.
- **Set the snap to 0.05.**

  Remember what happened when you tried to set the grid to 0.05?
- **Move the cursor and watch the coordinate display.**

  Observe how the snap setting is reflected in the available coordinates. How small a snap will AutoCAD accept?
- **Try 0.005.**

  Move the cursor and observe the coordinate display.
- **Try 0.0005.**

  You could even try 0.0001, but this would be like turning snap off, since the coordinate display is registering four decimal places anyway. Unlike the grid, which is limited by the size of your screen, you can set snap to any value you like.
- **Finally, before you leave this section, set the snap back to 0.25 and leave the grid at 0.5.**

TIP: If you wish to keep snap and grid the same, set the grid to "0" in the Drafting Settings dialog box, or enter the GRID command and then type "s," for the Snap option. The grid will then change to match the snap and will continue to change any time you reset the snap. To free the grid, just give it its own value again using the GRID command or the dialog box.

2.3 CHANGING UNITS

In this section we will learn about specifying units in AutoCAD, and also see why drop-down lists are a handy time-saver.

2.3.1 Drop-Down Lists and the Drawing Units Dialog Box

The Drawing Units dialog box makes use of drop-down lists, another common dialog box feature. Lists give you quick access to settings, files, and other items that are organized as a list of options.

⌗ **Type "Units" or select Units... from the Format menu.**

This will call up the Drawing Units dialog box shown in Figure 2.3. This four-panel dialog box has five drop-down lists for specifying various characteristics of linear and angular drawing units, and a Sample Output area at the bottom. Drop-down lists show a current setting next to an arrow that is used to open the list of other possibilities. Your dialog box should show that the current length type in your drawing is Decimal units precise to 0.0000 places, and Angle type is Decimal Degrees with 0 places.

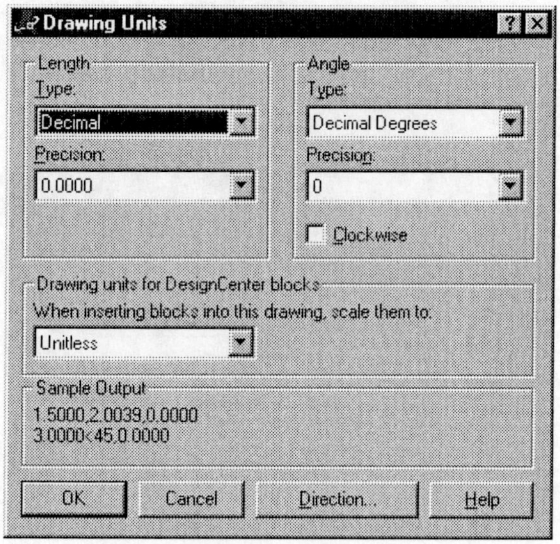

Figure 2.3

⌗ **Click on the arrow to the right of the word "Decimal," under Type in the Length panel of the dialog box.**

A list will drop down with the following options:

Architectural
Decimal
Engineering
Fractional
Scientific

Architectural units display feet and fractional inches (1'–3 $\frac{1}{2}$"). Engineering units display feet and decimal inches (1'–3.50"). Fractional units display units in a mixed number format (15 $\frac{1}{2}$). Scientific units use exponential notation for the display of very large or very small numbers (1.55E+01). With the exception of Engineering and Architectural formats, these formats can be used with any basic unit of measurement. For example, decimal mode works for metric units as well as English units.

Through most of this book we will stick to decimal units. Obviously, if you are designing a house you will want architectural units. If you are building a bridge you may want engineering-style units. You might want scientific units if you are mapping subatomic particles.

Whatever your application, once you know how to change units, you can do so at any time. However, as a drawing practice you will want to choose appropriate units when you first begin work on a new drawing.

⌖ **Click on Decimal, or click anywhere outside the list box to close the list without changing the setting.**

Now we will change the precision setting to 2-place decimals.

⌖ **Click the arrow next to 0.0000 in the Precision list box in the Length panel.**

This will open a list with options ranging from 0 to 0.00000000 as shown in Figure 2.4. Notice the scroll bars on the right of the list. These appear any time the list is too large to be contained entirely within the box.

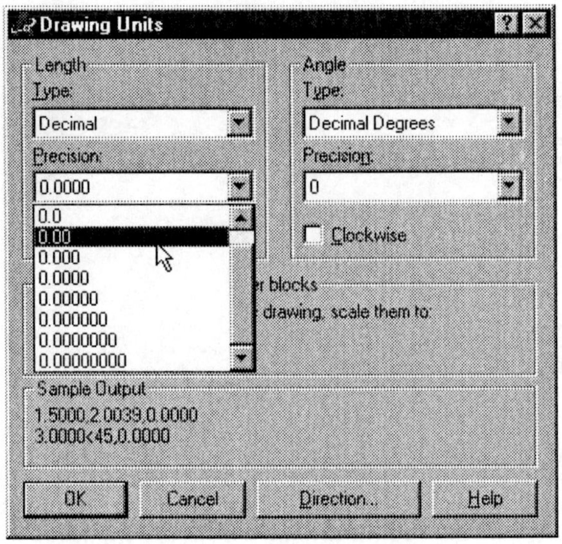

Figure 2.4

We will use 2-place decimals because they are practical and more common than any other choice.

⌖ **Run your cursor arrow down the list until 0.00 is highlighted, as shown in Figure 2.4.**

⌖ **Click on 0.00.**

The list will close and 0.00 will replace 0.0000 as the current precision for units of length. Notice that the Sample Output has also changed to reflect the new setting.

The area to the right allows you to change the units in which angular measures, including polar coordinates, are displayed. If you open the angle-type list you will see the following options:

Decimal Degrees
Deg/Min/Sec
Grads
Radians
Surveyor's Units

The default system is standard decimal degrees with 0 decimal places, measured counterclockwise, with 0 being straight out to the right (3 o'clock), 90, straight up (12 o'clock), 180 to the left (9 o'clock), and 270 straight down (6 o'clock). We will leave these settings alone.

- **Check to see that you have 2-place decimal units for length and 0-place decimal degree units for angles. Then click OK to close the dialog.**

TIP: All dialog boxes can be moved on the screen. This is done by clicking in the gray title area at the top of the dialog box, holding down the pickbutton, and dragging the box across the screen.

2.4 DRAWING CIRCLES GIVING CENTER POINT AND RADIUS

Circles can be drawn by giving AutoCAD a center point and a radius, a center point and a diameter, three points on the circle's circumference, two points that determine a diameter, two tangent points on other objects and a radius, or three tangent points. In this chapter we will use the first two options.

We will begin by drawing a circle with radius 3 and center at the point (6, 5). Then we will draw two smaller circles centered at the same point. Later we will erase them using the ERASE command.

- **Grid should be set to 0.5, snap to 0.25, and units to 2-place decimal.**
- **Type "c," select Circle from the Draw menu, or select the Circle tool from the Draw toolbar, illustrated in Figure 2.5.**

The prompt that follows will look like this:

Specify center point for circle or [3P/2P/Ttr (tan tan radius)]/<Center point>:

- **Type coordinates or point to the center point of the circle you want to draw. In our case it will be the point (6, 5).**

AutoCAD assumes that a radius or diameter will follow and shows the following prompt:

Specify radius of circle or [Diameter]:

If we type or point to a value now, AutoCAD will take it as a radius, since that is the default.

Figure 2.5

- **Move your cursor and observe the rubber band and dragged circle.**
- **If your coordinate display is not showing polar coordinates, click on it once or twice until you see something like "3.00<0, 0.00."**
- **Press the pickbutton to show the radius endpoint at a distance of 3.00 from the center.**

  You should now have your first circle complete.

- **Draw two more circles using the same center point, radius method. They will be centered at (6, 5) and have radii of 2.50 and 2.00.**

  The results are illustrated in Figure 2.6.

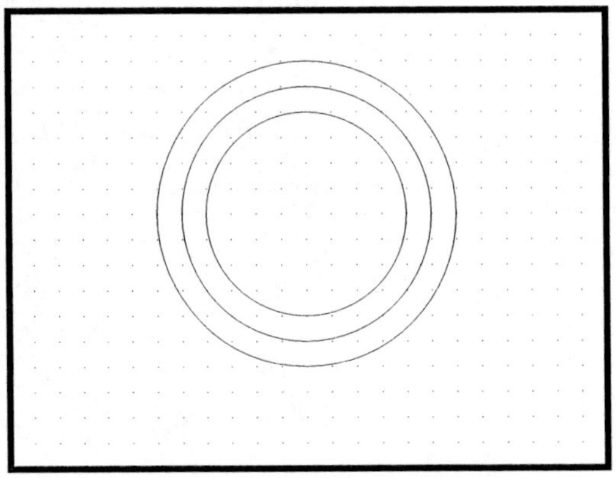

Figure 2.6

2.5 DRAWING CIRCLES GIVING CENTER POINT AND DIAMETER

We will draw three more circles centered on (6, 5) having diameters of 1, 1.5, and 2. Drawing circles this way is almost the same as the radius method, except you will not use the default, and you will see that the rubber band works differently.

- **Press enter or the space bar to repeat the CIRCLE command.**
- **Indicate the center point (6, 5) by typing coordinates or pointing.**
- **Answer the prompt with a "d," for diameter.**

  Notice that the cross hairs are now outside the circle you are dragging on the screen (see Figure 2.7). This is because AutoCAD is looking for a diameter, but the last point you gave was a center point. So the diameter is being measured from the center point out, twice the radius. Move the cursor around, in and out from the center point, to get a feel for this.

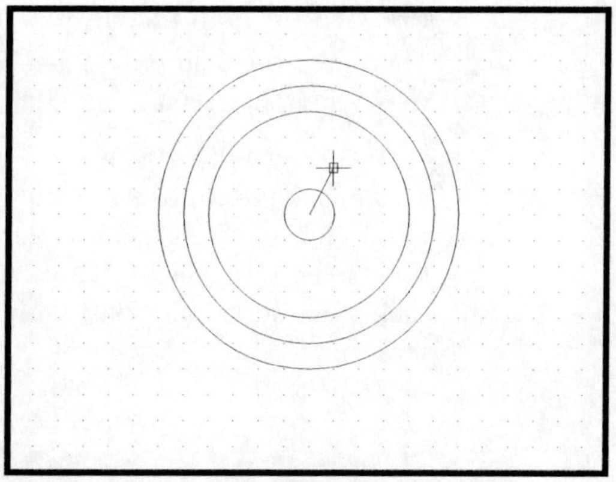

Figure 2.7

- **Point to a diameter of 1.00, or type "1."**

  You should now have four circles.

- **Draw two more circles with diameters of 1.50 and 2.00.**

  When you are done, your screen should look like Figure 2.8.

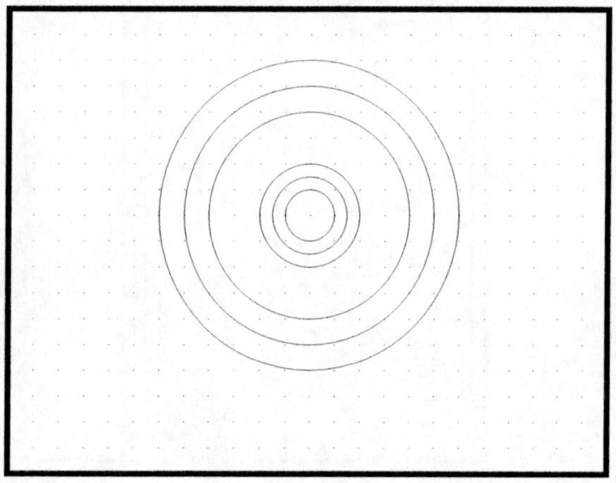

Figure 2.8

2.6 ACCESSING AUTOCAD HELP FEATURES

The AutoCAD HELP command gives access to an extraordinary amount of information in a comprehensive library of AutoCAD references and information. The procedures for using HELP are standard Windows procedures and access the Command Reference, the AutoCAD User's Guide, the AutoCAD Customization Guide, and the AutoCAD Driver and Peripheral Guide. In this section we will focus on the use of the Index feature, which pulls information from all of the references, depending on the topic you select. For demonstration, we will look for further information on the CIRCLE command.

⌖ **To begin, you should be at the command prompt.**

HELP is context sensitive, meaning that it will go directly to the AutoCAD Command Reference if you ask for help while in the middle of a command sequence. You should try this later.

⌖ **Press F1 or open the Help menu and select Help.**

This opens the help system and places an orange AutoCAD 2004 Help button on your Windows taskbar.

⌖ **Click the orange button.**

This opens the AutoCAD Help dialog box shown in Figure 2.9. If the Contents tab is showing, you will see the list of available references. These contain the same information as the actual AutoCAD manuals, and you can browse through their contents as you would with the books. It is usually quicker to use the Index, however.

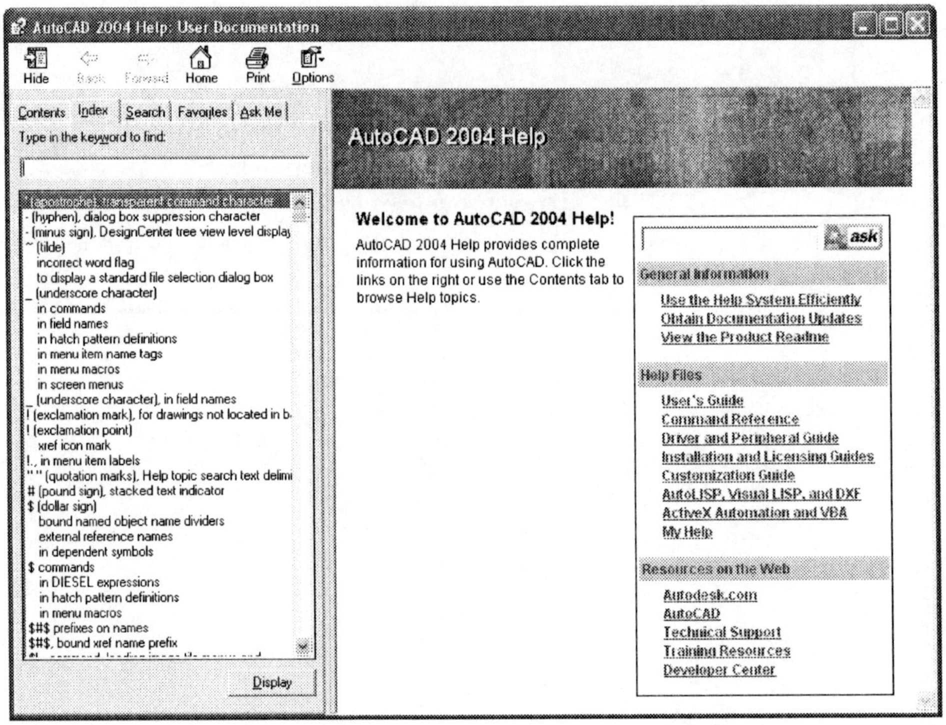

Figure 2.9

⌗ **If necessary, click on the Index tab.**

You should see the Index as shown in Figure 2.9. The list of topics is very long, so it is rare that you will use the scroll bar on the right. Most often you will type in a command or topic. The list will update as you type, so you may not need to type the complete word or command.

⌗ **Type "Cir."**

Do this slowly, one letter at a time, and you will see how the index follows along. When you have typed "cir" you will be at the Circle (Draw menu) options entry. Adding the rest of the letters "cle" will have no further effect.

The entry we want is the CIRCLE command entry, which is just below the Draw menu options.

⌗ **Double click on "CIRCLE command," or highlight it and then press enter or click on display.**

This will call up a second smaller dialog box with three options. We want the first option.

⌗ **Double click on "CIRCLE command," again, or press enter or click on display.**

AutoCAD will display the CIRCLE command page from the AutoCAD Command Reference, as shown in Figure 2.10. Links to additional information on items on this page are available for words underlined and shown in green.

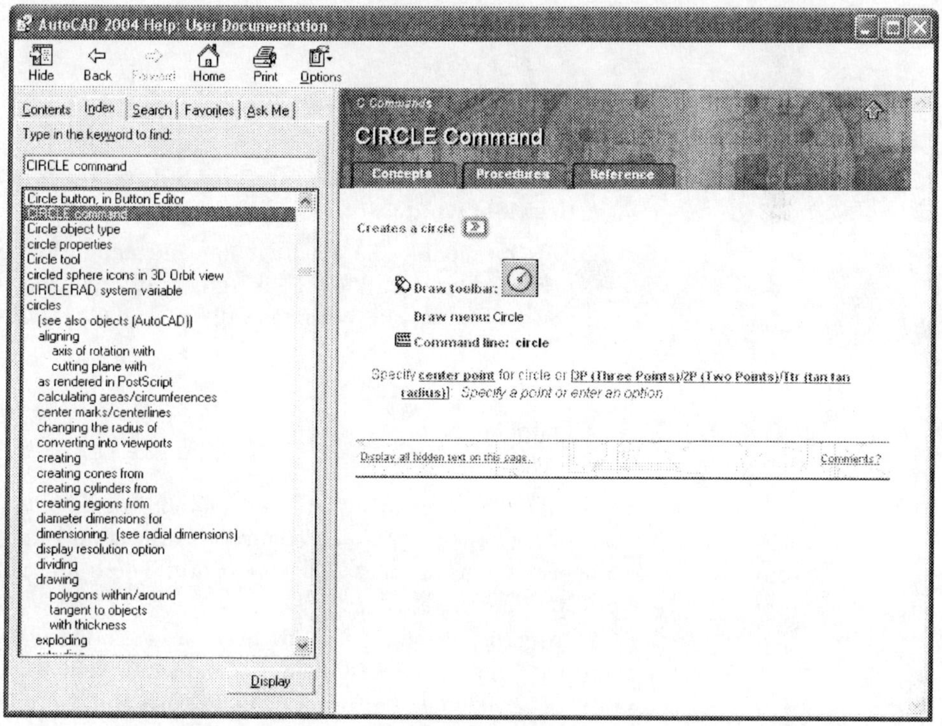

Figure 2.10

⌖ **Click on "TTR — Tangent, Tangent, Radius."**

This will call up the page for the Tangent, Tangent, Radius option of the CIRCLE command, shown in Figure 2.11.

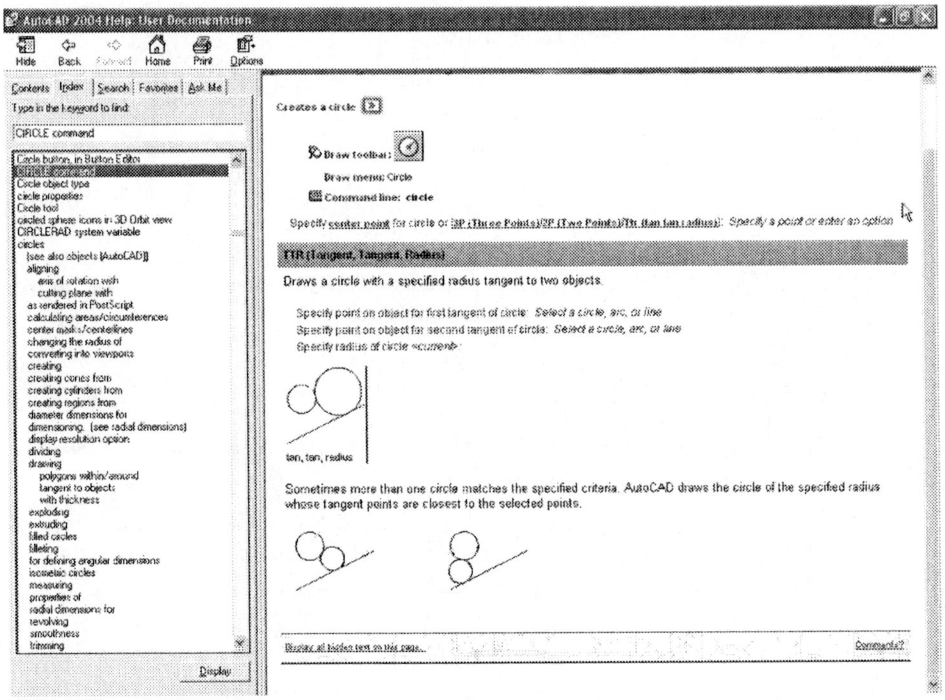

Figure 2.11

⌖ **To exit HELP, click on the close button, the x in the upper right corner of the Help window.**

This terminates the HELP command and brings you back to the command prompt. The HELP feature is a great resource. You are encouraged to access it at any time to expand your knowledge of AutoCAD 2004.

2.7 USING THE ERASE COMMAND

AutoCAD allows for many different methods of editing and even allows you to alter some of the basics of how edit commands work. Fundamentally, there are two different sequences for using most edit commands. These are called the Noun/Verb and the Verb/Noun methods.

In earlier versions of AutoCAD, most editing was carried out in a verb/noun sequence. That is, you would enter a command, such as ERASE (the verb), then select objects (the nouns), and press enter to carry out the command. This method is still effective, but AutoCAD also allows you to reverse the verb/noun sequence. You can use either method as long as "Noun/Verb" selection is enabled in your drawing.

In this section we will explore the traditional verb/noun sequence and then introduce the noun/verb or "pick first" method along with some of the many methods for selecting objects.

2.7.1 Verb/Noun Editing

⌗ **To begin this task you should have the six circles on your screen, as shown previously in Figure 2.8.**

We will use verb/noun editing to erase the two outer circles.

⌗ **Type "e" or select the Erase tool from the Modify toolbar, as shown in Figure 2.12.**

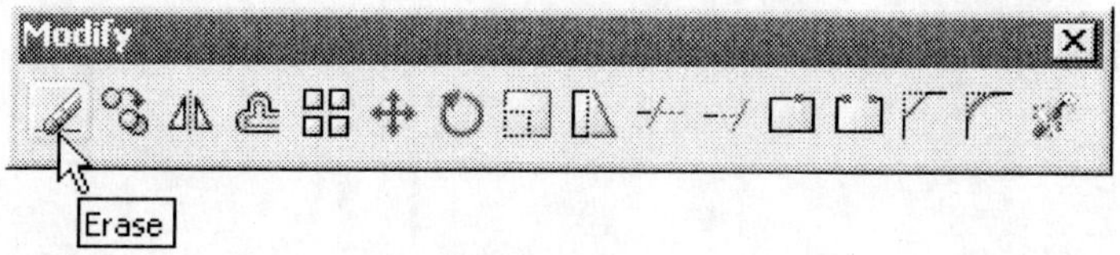

Figure 2.12

Erase can also be found on the Modify menu, but the other methods are more efficient.

The cross hairs will disappear, but the pickbox will still be on the screen and will move when you move your cursor.

Also notice the command area. It should be showing this prompt:

Select objects:

This is a very common prompt. You will find it in all edit commands and many other commands as well.

⌗ **Move your cursor so that the outer circle crosses the pickbox.**

TIP: In many situations you may find it convenient or necessary to turn snap off (F9) while selecting objects, since this gives you more freedom of motion.

⌗ **Press the pickbutton.**

The circle will be highlighted (dotted). This is how AutoCAD indicates that an object has been selected for editing. It is not yet erased, however. You can go on and add more objects to the selection set and they, too, will become dotted.

⌗ **Use the box to pick the second circle moving in toward the center.**

It too should now be dotted.

⌗ **Press enter, the space bar, or the right button on your pointing device to carry out the command.**

This is typical of the verb/noun sequence in most edit commands. Once a command has been entered and a selection set defined, a press of the enter key is required to complete the command. At this point the two outer circles should be erased.

TIP: In Verb/Noun edit command procedures where the last step is to press enter to complete the command, it is good heads-up practice to use the right button on your mouse in place of the space bar or enter key. It will carry out your command in exactly the same way but is more convenient. There will be no intervening shortcut menu.

2.7.2 Noun/Verb Editing

Now let's try the noun/verb sequence.

- **Type "u" to undo the ERASE and bring back the circles.**
- **Use the pickbox to select the outer circle.**

  The circle will be highlighted, and your screen should now resemble Figure 2.13. Those little blue boxes are called "grips." They are part of AutoCAD's autoediting system, which we will begin exploring in Chapter 3. For now you can ignore them.

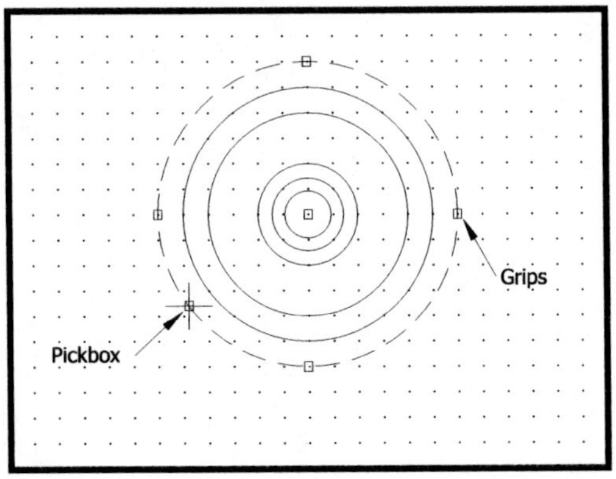

Figure 2.13

- **Pick the second circle in the same fashion.**

  The second circle will also become dotted, and more grips will appear.

- **Type "e" or select the Erase tool from the Modify toolbar.**

  Your two outer circles will disappear as soon as you press enter or pick the tool. Note that in this sequence the right mouse button calls a shortcut menu, so you should avoid it unless you have use for the options on the menu.

The two outer circles should now be gone. As you can see, there is not a lot of difference between the two sequences. One difference that is not immediately apparent is that there are numerous selection methods available in the verb/noun system that cannot be activated when you pick objects first. We will get to other object selection methods momentarily, but first try out the OOPS command.

2.7.3 OOPS!

- **Type "oops" and watch the screen.**

  If you have made a mistake in your erasure, you can get your selection set back by typing "oops." OOPS is to ERASE as REDO is to UNDO. You can use OOPS to undo an ERASE command, as long as you have not done another ERASE in the meantime. In other words, AutoCAD only saves your most recent ERASE selection set.

  You can also use U to undo an ERASE, but notice the difference: U simply undoes the last command, whatever it might be; OOPS works specifically with ERASE to recall the last set of erased objects. If you have drawn other objects in the meantime, you can still use OOPS to recall a previously erased set. But if you tried to use U, you would have to backtrack, undoing any newly drawn objects along the way.

2.7.4 Other Object Selection Methods

You can select individual entities on the screen by pointing to them one by one, as we have done previously, but in complex drawings this will often be inefficient. AutoCAD offers a variety of other methods, all of which have application in specific drawing circumstances. In this exercise we will select circles by the "windowing" and "crossing" methods, by indicating "last" or "L," meaning the last entity drawn, and by indicating "previous" or "P" for the previously defined set. There are also options to add or remove objects from the selection set and other variations on windowing and crossing. We suggest that you study Figure 2.14 to learn about other methods. The number of selection

OBJECT SELECTION METHOD	DESCRIPTION	ITEMS SELECTED
(W) WINDOW	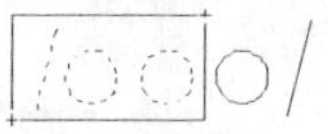	The entities within the box.
(C) CROSSING	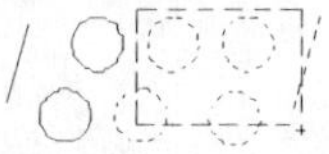	The entities crossed by or within the box.
(P) PREVIOUS	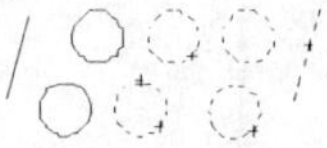	The entities that were previously picked.
(L) LAST		The entity that was drawn last.
(R) REMOVE	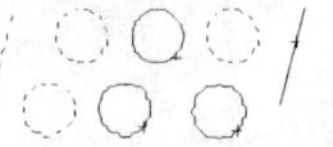	Removes entities from the items selected so they will not be part of the selected group.
(A) ADD	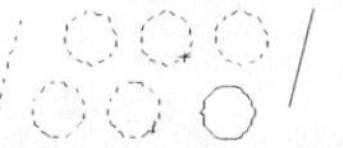	Adds entities that were removed and allows for more selections after the use of remove.
ALL		All the entities currently visible on the drawing.
(F) FENCE	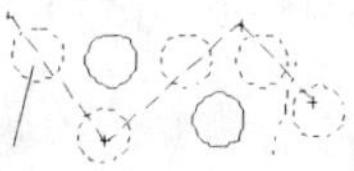	The entities crossed by the fence.
(WP) WPOLYGON	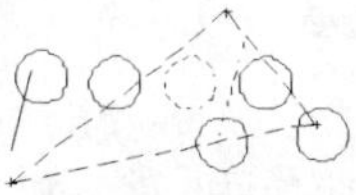	All the entities completely within the window of the polygon.
(CP) CPOLYGON	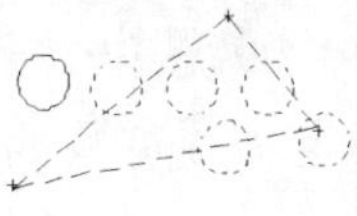	All the entities crossed by the polygon.

Figure 2.14

options available may seem a bit overwhelming at first, but time learning them will be well spent. These same options appear in many AutoCAD editing commands (MOVE, COPY, ARRAY, ROTATE, MIRROR) and should become part of your CAD vocabulary.

2.7.5 Selection by Window

The object selection window was demonstrated previously. Now we will put it to use. Window and crossing selections, like individual object selection, can be initiated without entering a command. In other words, they are available for noun/verb selection. Whether you select objects first or enter a command first, you can force a window or crossing selection simply by picking points on the screen that are not on objects. AutoCAD will assume you want to select by windowing or crossing and will ask for a second point.

Let's try it. We will show AutoCAD that we want to erase all of the inner circles by throwing a temporary selection window around them. The window will be defined by two points moving left to right that serve as opposite corners of a rectangle. Only entities that lie completely within the window will be selected. See Figure 2.15.

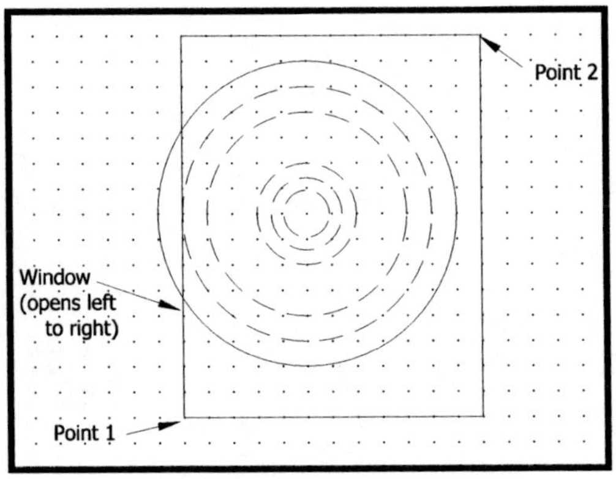

Figure 2.15

⌗ **Pick point 1 at the lower left of the screen, as shown. Any point in the neighborhood of (3.5, 1) will do.**

AutoCAD will prompt for another corner:

Specify opposite corner:

⌗ **Pick point 2 at the upper right of the screen, as shown.**

Any point in the neighborhood of (9.5, 8.5) will do. To see the effect of the window, be sure that it crosses the outside circle, as in Figure 2.16.

⌗ **Type "e" or select the Erase tool.**

The inner circles should now be erased.

⌗ **Type "oops" to retrieve the circles once more. Since ERASE was the last command, typing "U" or selecting the Undo tool will also work.**

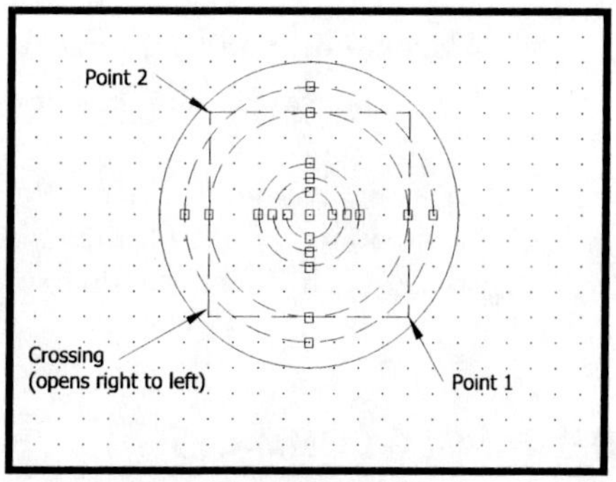

Figure 2.16

2.7.6 Selection by Crossing Window

Crossing is an alternative to windowing that is useful in many cases where a standard window selection could not be performed. The selection procedure is the same, but a crossing box opens to the left instead of to the right and all objects that cross the box will be chosen, not just those that lie completely inside the box.

We will use a crossing box to select the inside circles.

⌖ **Pick point 1 close to (8.0, 3.0), as in Figure 2.16.**

AutoCAD prompts:

Specify opposite corner:

⌖ **Pick a point near (4.0, 7.0).**

This point selection must be done carefully to demonstrate a crossing selection. Notice that the crossing box is shown with dashed lines, whereas the window box was shown with solid lines.

Also, notice how the circles are selected: those that cross and those that are completely contained within the crossing box, but not those that lie outside.

At this point we could enter the ERASE command to erase the circles, but instead we will demonstrate how to use the Esc key to cancel a selection set.

⌖ **Press the Esc key on your keyboard.**

This will cancel the selection set. The circles will no longer be highlighted and the grips disappear.

2.7.7 Selecting the "Last" Entity

AutoCAD remembers the order in which new objects have been drawn during the course of a single drawing session. As long as you do not close the drawing, you can select the last drawn entity using the "last" option.

⌖ **Type "e" or select the Erase tool.**

Notice that there is no way to specify "last" before you enter a command. This option is only available as part of a command procedure. In other words, it only works in a verb/noun sequence.

⌖ **Type "L."**

The inner circle should be highlighted.

☩ **Press enter to carry out the command.**

The inner circle should be erased.

There are several more object selection methods, all of which may be useful to you in a given situation. Some of the most useful options are described and illustrated in Figure 2.14, which you should study before moving on.

2.8 USING THE RECTANGLE COMMAND

Now that you have created object selection windows, the RECTANGLE command will come naturally. Creating a rectangle in this way is just like creating an object selection window.

☩ **To prepare for this exercise, erase all objects from your screen.**

☩ **Select the Rectangle tool from the Draw toolbar, as shown in Figure 2.17.**

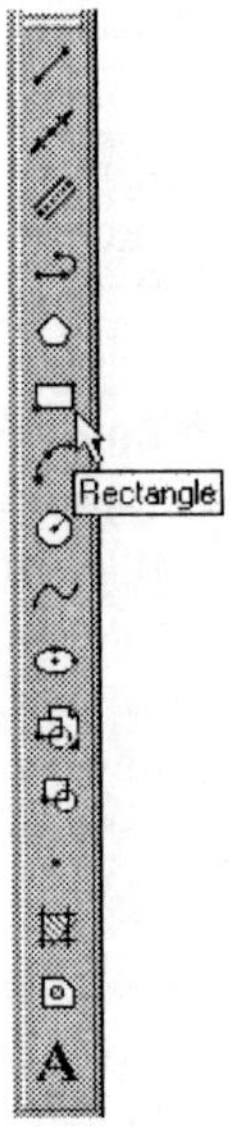

Figure 2.17

AutoCAD will prompt for a corner point:

Specify first corner point or

[Chamfer/Elevation/Fillet/Thickness/Width]:

You can ignore the options for now and proceed with the defaults.

☩ **Pick (3.00, 3.00) for the first corner point, as shown in Figure 2.18.**

AutoCAD will prompt for another point:

Specify other corner point:

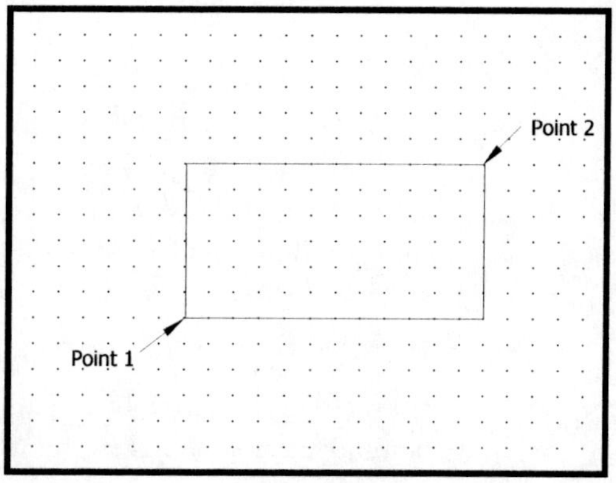

Figure 2.18

⌖ **Pick (9.00, 6.00) for a second corner point, as shown in Figure 2.18.**

As soon as you enter the second corner, AutoCAD draws a rectangle between the two corner points and returns you to the command prompt. This is a faster way to draw a rectangle than drawing it line by line.

Leave the rectangle on your screen for the plotting demonstration in Section 2.9.

2.9 PLOTTING OR PRINTING A DRAWING

AutoCAD 2004's printing and plotting capabilities are extensive and complex. In this book we will introduce you to them a little at a time. As usual we will try to keep you moving and get your drawing on paper as efficiently as possible.

Plotting and printing in AutoCAD requires that you understand the relationships among model space, paper space, plot styles, page setups, and layouts. All of these concepts will be introduced as you need them. In this chapter, we will perform the simplest type of plot, going directly from your current model space objects to a sheet of drawing paper, changing only one or two plot settings. One of the difficulties is that different types of plotters and printers work somewhat differently. This introductory procedure assumes that you do not have to change devices or configuration details. It should work adequately for all plotters and printers and the drawings in this chapter. We will use a Window selection to define a plot area and observe how this affects the plot scale.

⌖ **Select Plot... from the File menu, or the Plot tool from the Standard toolbar, as shown in Figure 2.19.**

Figure 2.19

Either of these methods will call up the Plot dialog box illustrated in Figure 2.20. You will become very familiar with it as you work through this book. It is one of the most important working spaces in AutoCAD. It contains many options, but for now we are going to look at only two settings.

As you look over the Plot dialog you will see the following panels. At the top are two panels devoted to Layouts and Page Setups. These allow you to save plot configurations and to use them in other drawings. Below this there are two tabs, one for Plot Device and one for Plot Settings.

⌖ **If Plot Settings is not on top, click the tab to bring it up.**

On the Plot Settings tab are panels for Paper size and paper units, Drawing orientation, Plot area, Plot scale, Plot offset, and Plot options.

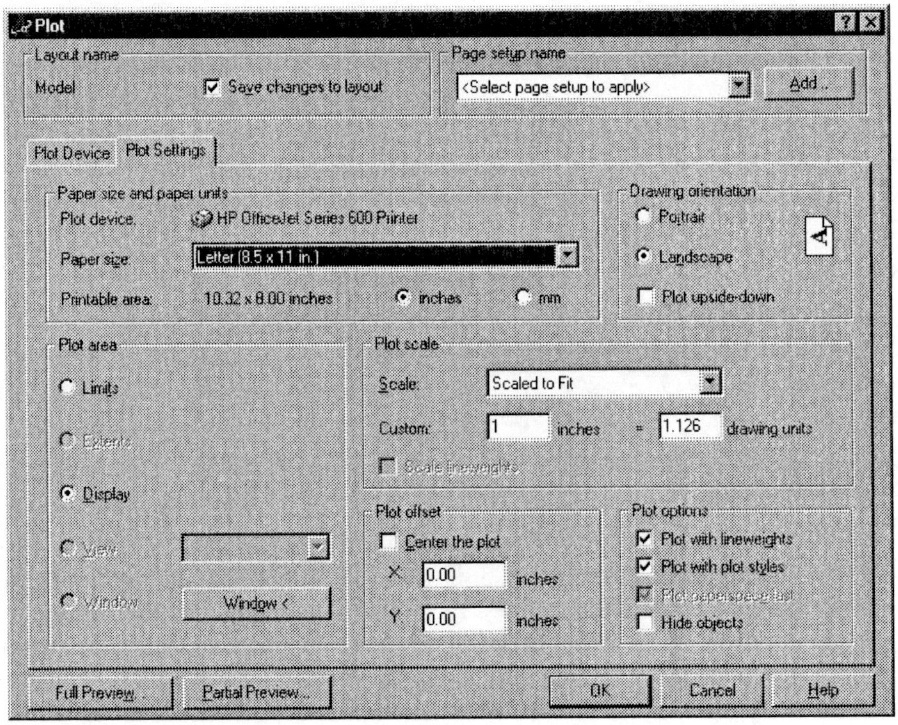

Figure 2.20

2.9.1 Dialog Box Radio Buttons

Look at the panel labeled "Plot area" on the left. The list of options in the panel make use of radio buttons. Unlike check boxes, radio buttons are mutually exclusive. In a list of radio buttons, only one button can be on at a time. This list of radio buttons allows you to tell AutoCAD what part of your drawing you want to plot. Right now you will see that only Display and Limits are accessible. The Window option will become available after you have defined a window in the drawing. Windowing allows you to plot any portion of a drawing simply by defining the window. AutoCAD will base the size and placement of the plot on the window you define.

Before creating the plot area window, look at the Plot scale panel on the right of the dialog box. In the Scale list box, you should see the words "Scaled to fit." If your plot scale is configured as scaled to fit, as it should be by default, then AutoCAD will plot your drawing at maximum size based on paper size and the window you specify.

⌖ **If for any reason "Scaled to fit" is not in the Scale list box, open the list and select it.**

On the Custom line below Plot scale, you should see edit boxes with numbers something like 1 = 1.126. Right now the plot area is based on the outer limits of your grid. When you use a window to create a plot area that is somewhat smaller, these scale numbers will change automatically.

⌖ **Click on "Window<" at the bottom of the Plot area panel.**

The Plot dialog box will disappear temporarily, giving you access to the drawing. You will see the cross hairs, but the pickbox will be absent. AutoCAD will prompt for point selection:

Specify window for printing:

⌖ **Select the point (1.00, 1.00), as shown in Figure 2.21**

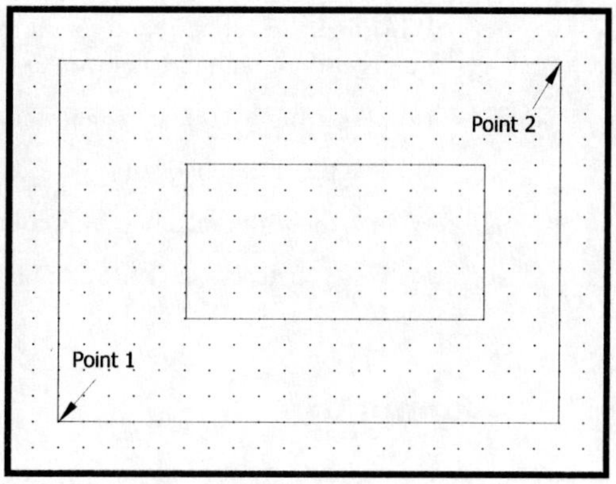

Figure 2.21

AutoCAD will prompt:

Specify opposite corner:

⌖ **Select the point (11.00, 8.00), as shown in Figure 2.21.**

As soon as you have picked the second point, AutoCAD will display the Plot dialog box again. There will be two changes. First, the Window radio button will now be accessible. Second, the Custom scale ratio will change to something like 1 = .9533. We use the phrase "something like" because there may be minor variations depending on your plotter.

You are now ready to plot.

⌖ **If you want to plot or print the rectangle, prepare your plotter and then click on OK. Otherwise, click on Cancel.**

Clicking OK sends the drawing information out to be printed. You can sit back and watch the plotting device at work. If you need to cancel for any reason, click on the Cancel button.

For now, that's all there is to it. If your plot does not look perfect—if it is not centered on your drawing sheet, for example—don't worry, you will learn all you need to know about plotting in later chapters.

2.10 REVIEW MATERIAL

Questions

1. Which is likely to have the smaller setting, GRID or SNAP? Why? What happens if the settings are reversed?
2. Why do some dialog box panels use check boxes while others use radio buttons?
3. How do you switch from decimal units to architectural units?
4. Where is 0 degrees located in AutoCAD's default units setup? Where is 270 degrees? Where is −45 degrees?
5. How do you enter the CIRCLE command?
6. Why does the rubber band touch the circumference of the circle when you are using the radius option, but not when you are using the diameter option?
7. How does AutoCAD know when you want a crossing selection instead of a window selection?
8. What is the difference between a "Last" selection and a "Previous" selection?
9. What is the difference between noun/verb and verb/noun editing?
10. How do you access the AutoCAD HELP index?

Commands

CIRCLE	DDRMODES	ERASE
GRID	HELP	OOPS
PLOT	RECTANGLE	SNAP
UNITS		

2.11 DRAWING PROBLEMS

1. Leave the grid at 0.50 and set snap to 0.25.
2. Use the 3P option to draw a circle that passes through the points (2.25, 4.25), (3.25, 5.25), and (4.25, 4.25).
3. Using the 2P option, draw a second circle with a diameter from (3.25, 4.25) to (4.25, 4.25).
4. Draw a third circle centered at (5.25, 4.25) with a radius of 1.00.
5. Draw a fourth circle centered at (4.75, 4.25) with a diameter of 1.00.

PROFESSIONAL SUCCESS

Ensuring Your File Is Compatible With All AutoCAD Releases

Imagine this scenario: You work all night at home on an important AutoCAD assignment, which must be plotted and turned in the following day. In the computer lab, you access AutoCAD, and try to load your file from the floppy disk you used at home. You panic when you're unable to load your file, and wonder what has gone wrong.

Chances are that you are using two different releases of AutoCAD: one at home, and another, older one in the computer lab. While all versions of AutoCAD are downward compatible (files created on older versions can be opened and interpreted by newer releases), files created using the most recent releases of AutoCAD may not open on older versions. Luckily, there is a solution: Save your file using the "Save As" command, and choose the appropriate older format in the pop-up dialog box. You should never face the scenario described if you choose a format compatible with the oldest release of AutoCAD that you are using.

This issue is not unique to AutoCAD. Many other popular software packages, including Microsoft Office, allow you to save files in various formats, so that they can be read and modified by older releases of the software. It is good practice to always keep track of which software releases you are using, and to make sure that you save your files in a format compatible with all of them. This precaution will increase the chances that your files will open whenever you try to access them.

DRAWING 1

Aperture Wheel

This drawing will give you practice creating circles using the center point, radius method. Refer to the table below the drawing for radius sizes. With snap set at 0.25, some of the circles can be drawn by pointing and dragging. Other circles have radii that are not on a snap point. These circles can be drawn by typing in the radius.

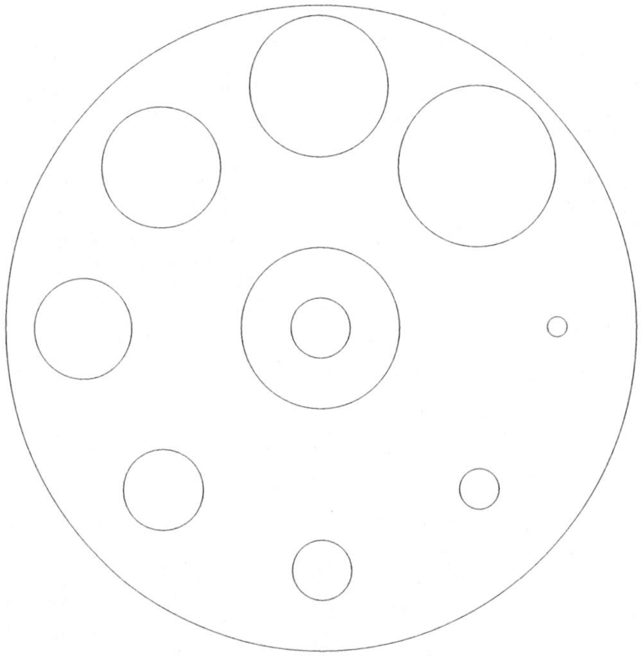

Drawing Suggestions

GRID = 0.50

SNAP = 0.25

- A good sequence for doing this drawing would be to draw the outer circle first, followed by the two inner circles (h and c). These are all centered on the point (6.00, 4.50). Then begin at circle a and work around clockwise, being sure to center each circle correctly.
- Notice that there are two circles c and two h. The two circles having the same letter are the same size.
- Remember, you may type any value you like and AutoCAD will give you a precise graphic image, but you cannot always show the exact point you want with a pointing device. Often it is more efficient to type a few values than to turn snap off or change its setting for a small number of objects.

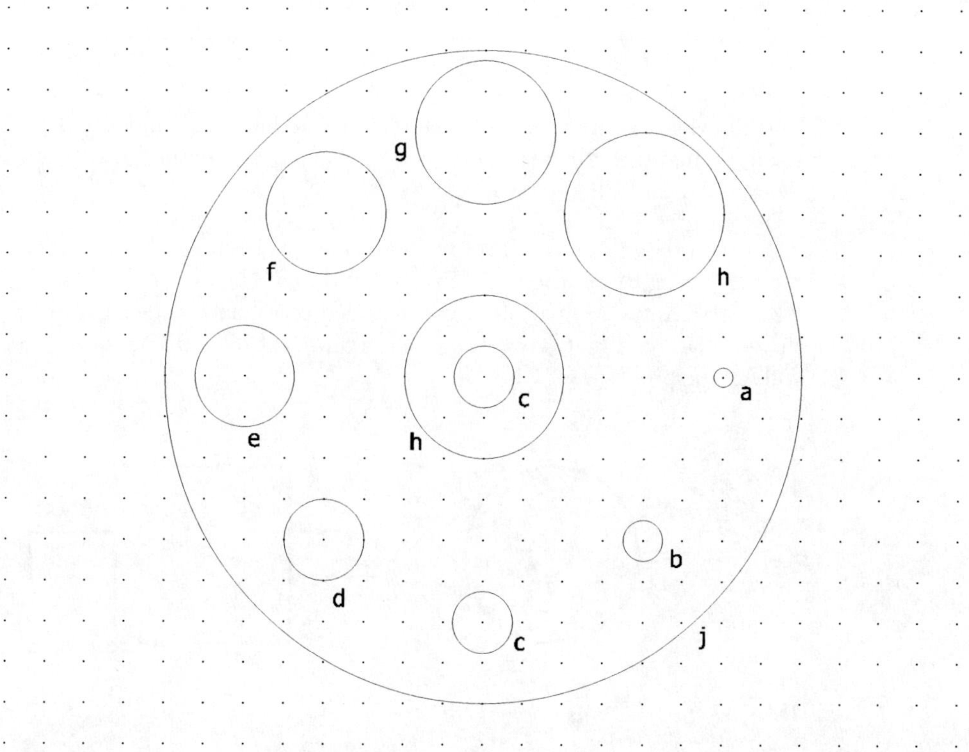

LETTER	a	b	c	d	e	f	g	h	j
RADIUS	.12	.25	.38	.50	.62	.75	.88	1.00	4.00

APERTURE WHEEL

DRAWING 2

Roller

This drawing will give you a chance to combine lines and circles and to use the center point, diameter method. It will also give you some experience with smaller objects, a denser grid, and a tighter snap spacing.

TIP: Even though units are set to show only two decimal places, it is important to set the snap using three places (0.125) so that the grid is on a multiple of the snap (0.25 = 2 × 0.125). AutoCAD will show you rounded coordinate values, like 0.13, but will keep the graphics on target. Try setting snap to either 0.13 or 0.12 instead of 0.125, and you will see the problem for yourself.

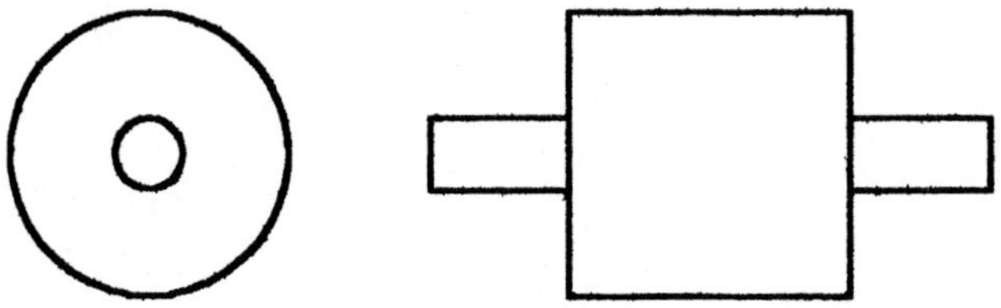

Drawing Suggestions

GRID = 0.25

SNAP = 0.125

- The two views of the roller will appear fairly small on your screen, making the snap setting essential. Watch the coordinate display as you work and get used to the smaller range of motion.
- Choosing an efficient sequence will make this drawing much easier to do. Since the two views must line up properly, we suggest that you draw the front view first, with circles of diameter 0.25 and 1.00, and then use these circles to position the lines in the right side view.
- The circles in the front view should be centered in the neighborhood of (2.00, 6.00). This will put the upper left-hand corner of the 1 × 1 square at around (5.50, 6.50).

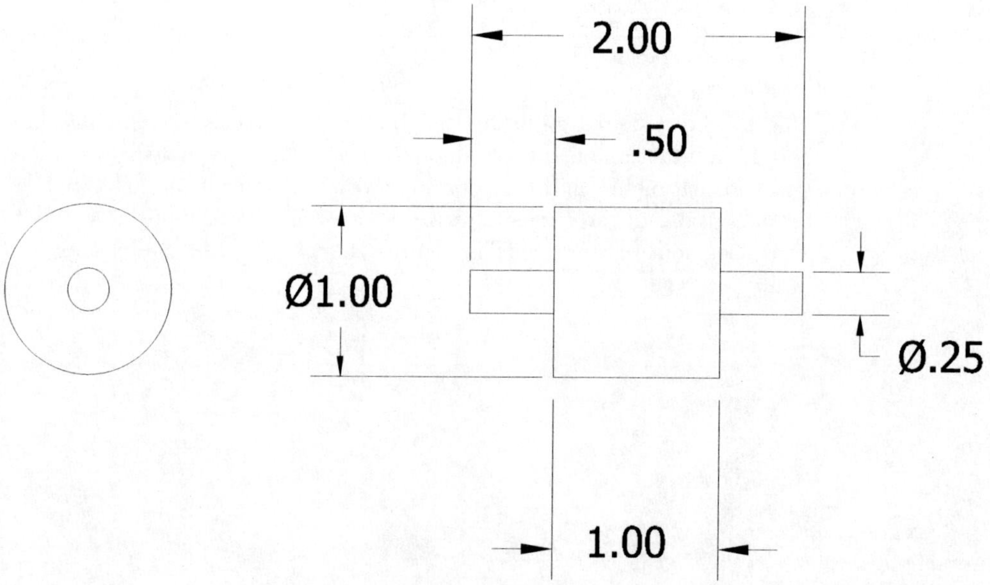

ROLLER

DRAWING 3

Switch Plate

This drawing is similar to the last one, but the dimensions are more difficult, and a number of important points do not fall on the grid. The drawing will give you practice using grid and snap points and the coordinate display. Refer to the table below the drawing for dimensions of the circles, squares, and rectangles inside the 7 x 10 outer rectangle. The placement of these smaller figures is shown by the dimensions on the drawing itself.

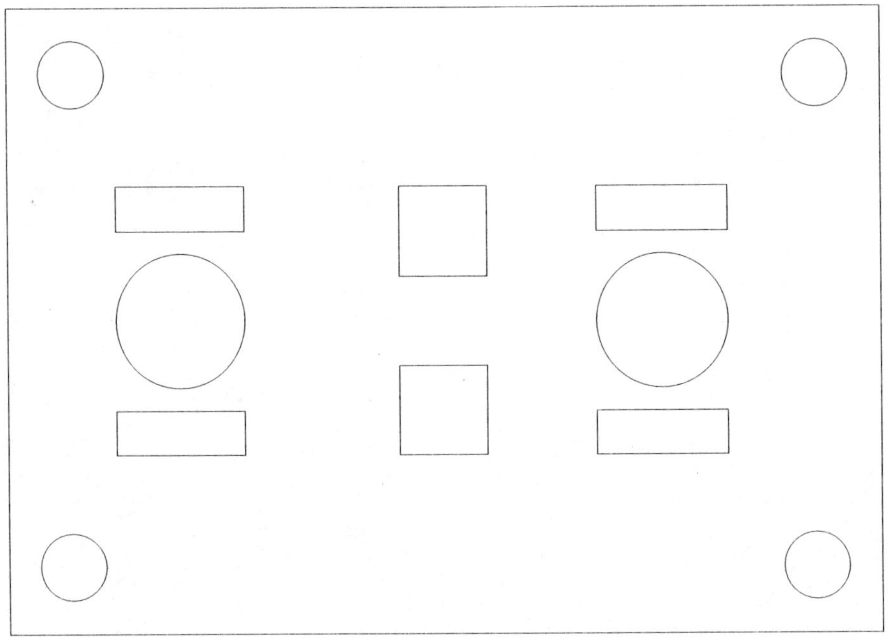

Drawing Suggestions

GRID = 0.50

SNAP = 0.25

- Turn ortho or polar snap on to do this drawing.
- A starting point in the neighborhood of (1, 1) will keep you well positioned on the screen.

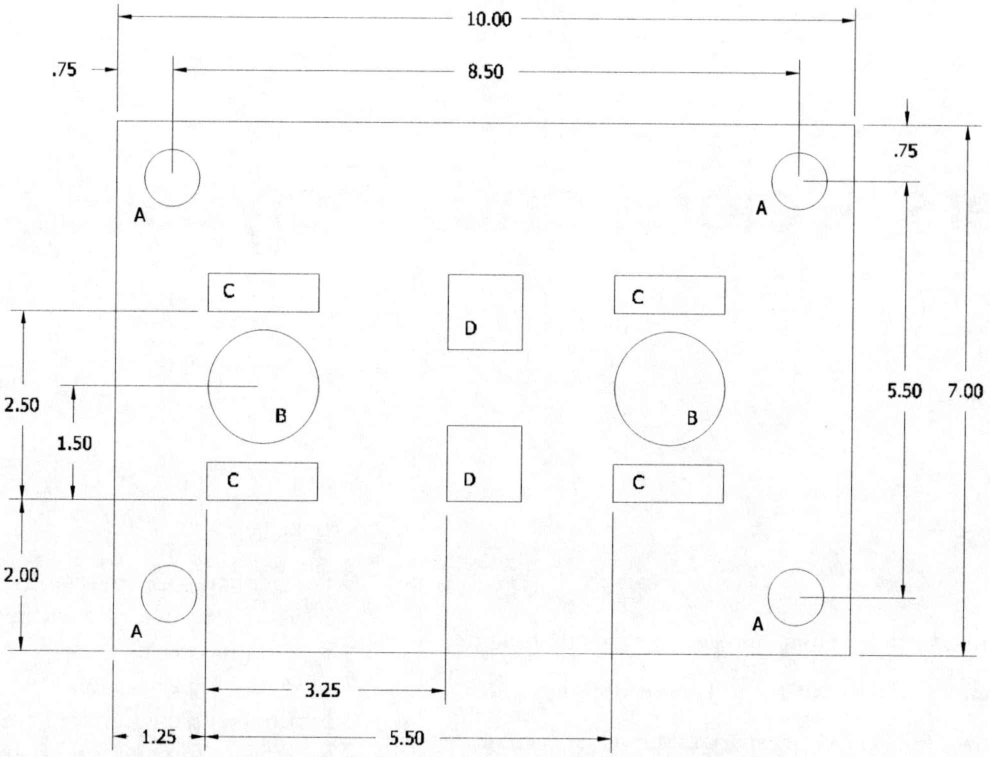

HOLE	SIZE
A	Ø.75
B	Ø1.50
C	.50 H x 1.50 W
D	1.00 SQ

SWITCH PLATE

3

Layers, Colors, and Linetypes

OVERVIEW

CAD is much more than a computerized way to do drafting. CAD programs have many powerful features that have no real correlation in manual drawing. Layering is a good example. Layers exist in the same space and the same drawing, but can be set up and controlled individually, allowing for greater control, precision, and flexibility. In the first two chapters all of your drawings were done on a single layer called "0." In this chapter, you will create and use three new layers, each with its own associated color and linetype.

The ZOOM command is another bit of CAD magic, allowing your drawings to accurately represent real world detail at the largest and smallest scales within the same drawing. In this chapter you will also learn to FILLET and CHAMFER the corners of previously drawn objects and to move between adjacent portions of a drawing with the PAN command. You will gain further control of the PLOT command by using partial and full previews. All of these new techniques will add considerably to the professionalism of your developing CAD technique.

SECTIONS

OBJECTIVES

After reading this chapter, you should be able to:

- Create new layers.
- Assign colors to layers.
- Assign linetypes to layers.
- Change the current layer.
- FILLET the corners of a square.
- CHAMFER the corners of a square.
- ZOOM in and out using Window, Previous, and All.
- Use realtime PAN and ZOOM.
- Use the Plot Preview feature.
- Draw a Mounting Plate.
- Draw a Bushing.
- Draw a Half Block.

3.1 CREATING NEW LAYERS

Layers allow you to treat specialized groups of entities in your drawing separately from other groups. For example, all of the dimensions in this book were drawn on a special dimension layer so that we could turn them on and off at will. We turned off the dimension layer to prepare the reference drawings, which are shown without dimensions. When a layer is turned off, all the objects on that layer become invisible, though they are still part of the drawing database and can be recalled at any time. In this way, layers can be viewed, edited, manipulated and plotted independently.

It is common practice to put dimensions on a separate layer, but there are many other uses of layers as well. Fundamentally, layers are used to separate colors and linetypes, and these, in turn, take on special significance depending on the drawing application. It is standard drafting practice, for example, to use small, evenly spaced dashes to represent objects or edges that would, in reality, be hidden from view. On a CAD system, these hidden lines can also be given their own color to make it easy for the designer to remember what layer he or she is working on.

In this book we will use a simple layering system, most of which will be presented in this chapter. You should remember that there are countless possibilities. AutoCAD allows a full range of colors and as many layers as you like.

You should also be aware that linetypes and colors are not restricted to being associated with layers. It is possible to mix linetypes and colors on a single layer. But while this may be useful for certain applications, we do not recommend it at this point.

⌖ **Open a new drawing using the Start from Scratch option to ensure that you are using the same defaults as those used in this chapter.**

3.1.1 The Layer Properties Manager Dialog Box

The creation and specification of layers and layer properties in AutoCAD is handled through the Layer Properties Manager dialog box. This dialog box consists of a table of layers. Clicking in the appropriate row and column will change a setting or take you to another dialog where a setting may be changed.

⌖ **Select the Layer tool from the Object Properties toolbar, as shown in Figure 3.1, or select "Layer..." from the Format pull-down menu.**

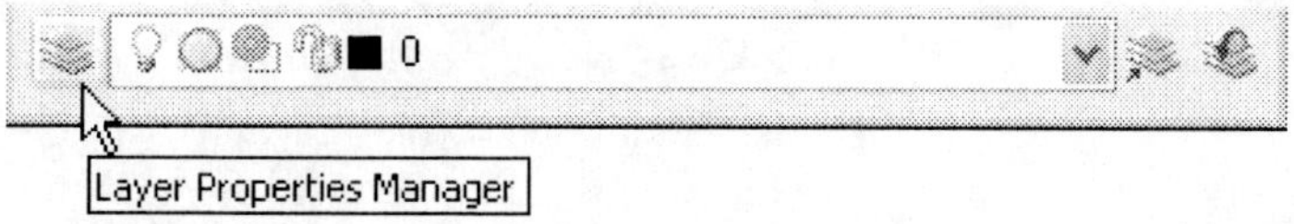

Figure 3.1

Either method will call the Layer Properties Manager dialog box illustrated in Figure 3.2. The large open space in the middle shows the names and properties of all layers defined in the current drawing. Layering systems can become very complex, and for this reason there is a system to limit or "filter" the layer names shown on the layer list. This is controlled by the box at the top left, which currently says "Show all layers." This is an unusual list box with the added feature of an ellipse button, which calls a Named Layers Filter dialog box. From this dialog you can specify

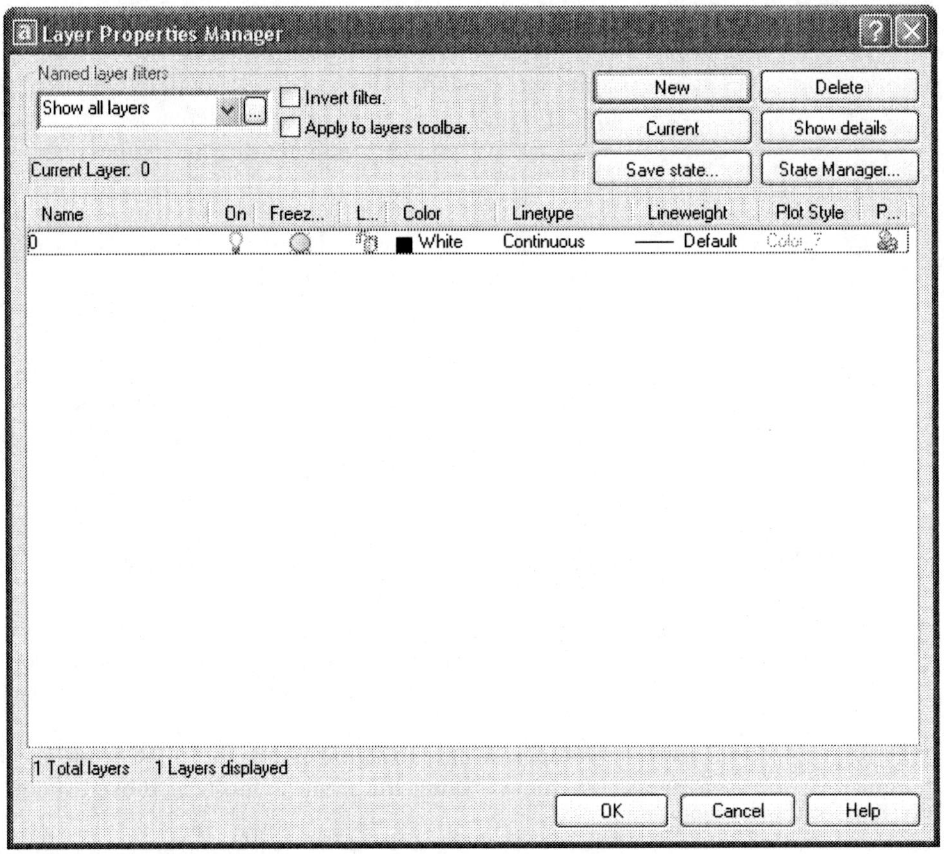

Figure 3.2

features to use as filters. You could, for example, only show layers of a certain color. Since we will be working with a small set of layers, we will not need to do filtering.

In the layer name list window, you will see that "0" is the only defined layer. The icons on the line after the layer name show the current state of various properties of that layer. We will get to these shortly.

Now we will create three new layers. AutoCAD makes this easy.

⌖ **Click on "New," to the right of the Named layers filter list.**

A newly defined layer, "Layer1," will be created immediately and added to the layer name window. You will see that the new layer is given the characteristics of Layer 0. We will alter these in Section 3.2. But first, we will give this layer a new name and then define three more layers.

Layer names may be long or short. We have chosen single-digit numbers as layer names because they are easy to type and we can match them to AutoCAD's color numbering sequence.

⌖ **Type "1" for the layer name.**

"Layer1" will change to simply "1." It is not necessary to press enter after typing the name.

⌖ **Click on "New" again.**

A second new layer will be added to the list. It will again have the default name "Layer1." Change it to "2."

- **Type "2" for the second layer name.**
- **Click on "New" again.**
- **Type "3" for the third layer name.**

At this point your layer name list should show Layers 0, 1, 2, and 3, all with identical properties.

3.2 ASSIGNING COLORS TO LAYERS

We now have four layers, but they are all pretty much the same. Obviously, we have more changes to make before our new layers will have useful identities.

It is common practice to leave Layer 0 defined the way it is. We will begin our changes on Layer 1.

- **(If for any reason you have left the Layer Properties Manager dialog box, reenter it by selecting the Layers tool from the Object properties toolbar or "Layers..." from the Format menu.)**
- **Move the cursor arrow to the Layer 1 line and click on the white square under "Color."**

Clicking on the white square in the color column of Layer 1 selects Layer 1 and opens the Select Color dialog box illustrated in Figure 3.3. The three tabs in this

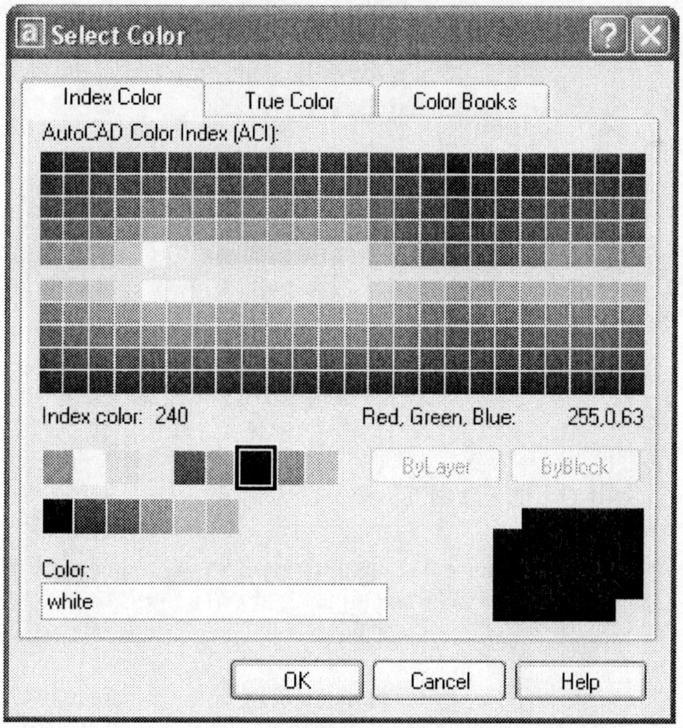

Figure 3.3

dialog box show three ways in which colors can be defined in AutoCAD. By default, the Index color tab is probably selected, as shown in Figure 3.3. The index color system is a simple numbered selection of 255 colors and shades. The True Color and Color Books systems are standard color systems commonly used by graphic designers. In this book we confine ourselves to the Index Color tab.

⌖ **If necessary, click on the Index Color tab.**

The Index Color tab shows the complete selection of 255 colors. At the top is a full palette of shades 10 through 249. Below that are the nine standard colors, numbered 1 through 9, followed by gray shades, numbered 250 through 255.

⌖ **Move your cursor freely inside the dialog box.**

When your cursor is on a color, it is highlighted with a white box.

⌖ **Let your cursor rest on any color.**

Notice that the number of the color is registered under the palette next to the words Index color. This is the AutoCAD index color number for the color currently highlighted.

⌖ **Left click to select any color in the palette.**

When a color is selected, it is outlined with a black box and a preview "patch" is displayed on the bottom right of the dialog box against a patch of the current color for comparison. The color is not actually selected in the drawing until you click OK to exit the dialog box. For our purposes, we want to select standard red, color number 1 on the strip in the middle of the dialog box.

⌖ **Move the white cursor box to the red box, the first of the nine standard colors in the middle of the box.**

Notice that this is index color number 1, pure red.

⌖ **Select the red box.**

You should see the word red and the color red shown in the edit box preview area at the bottom of the dialog box. Note that you can also select colors by typing names or numbers directly in this edit box. Typing "red" or the number 1 (for color #1) is the same as selecting the red color box from the chart.

⌖ **Click on OK.**

You will now see that Layer 1 is defined with the color red in the layer name list box.

Next we will assign the color yellow to Layer 2.

⌖ **Click on the white square under Color in the Layer 2 line and assign the color yellow to layer 2 in the Select Color dialog box.**

⌖ **Click on OK.**

⌖ **Select Layer 3 and set this layer to green.**

Look at the layer list. You should now have Layers 0, 1, 2, and 3 defined with the colors white, red, yellow, and green.

3.3 ASSIGNING LINETYPES

AutoCAD has a standard library of linetypes that can be assigned easily to layers. There are 45 standard types in addition to continuous lines. In addition to continuous lines, we will be using hidden and center lines. We will put hidden lines in yellow on Layer 2 and center lines in on Layer 3.

The procedure for assigning linetypes is almost identical to the procedure for assigning colors, except that you will have to load linetypes into the drawing before they can be used.

- **(If for any reason you have left the Layer Properties Manager, reenter it by selecting the Layer tool from the Object Properties toolbar.)**

- **Click on "Continuous" in the Linetype column of the Layer 2 line.**

NOTE: Make sure that you actually click on the word "Continuous." If you click on one of the icons in the Layer 2 line, you may turn the layer off or freeze it so that you cannot draw on it. These properties are discussed at the end of Section 3.5

This will select Layer 2 and call up the Select Linetype dialog box illustrated in Figure 3.4. The box containing a list of loaded linetypes currently only shows the continuous linetype. We can fix this by selecting the "Load..." button at the bottom of the dialog box.

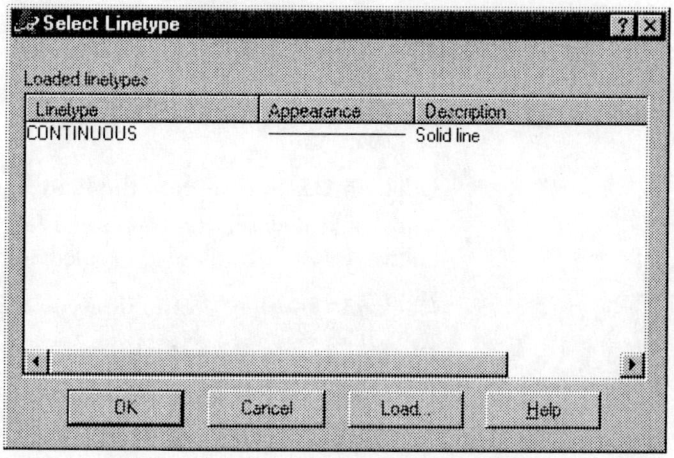

Figure 3.4

- **Click on "Load...."**

This will call a second dialog box, the Load or Reload Linetypes box illustrated in Figure 3.5. Here you can pick from the list of linetypes available from the standard "acad" file or from other files containing linetypes, if there are any on your system. You also have the option of loading all linetypes from any given file at once. The linetypes are then defined in your drawing, and you can assign a new linetype to a layer at any time. This makes things easier. It does, however, use up more memory.

For our purposes we will load only the hidden and center linetypes we are going to be using.

- **Scroll down until you see the Center linetype.**

- **Click on "Center" in the Linetype column at the left.**

- **Scroll down again until you see the "Hidden" linetype on the list.**

- **Hold down the Ctrl key and click on "Hidden" in the Linetype column.**

The Ctrl key lets you highlight two separated items in a list.

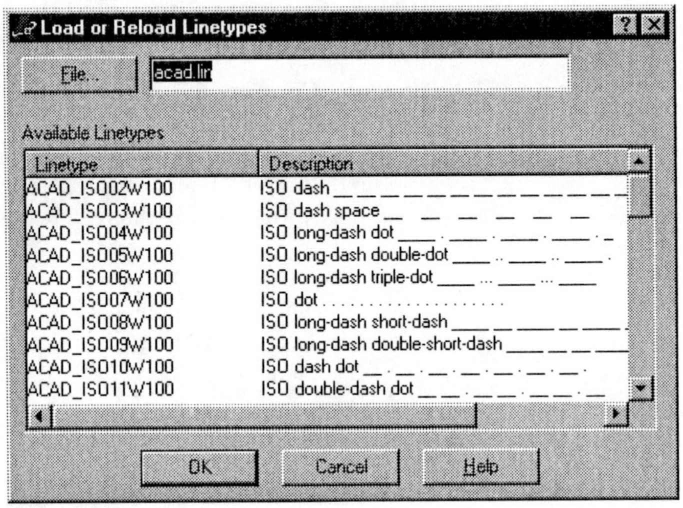

Figure 3.5

- **Click on OK to complete the loading process.**

  You should now see the center and hidden linetypes added to the list of loaded linetypes. Now that these are loaded, we can assign them to layers.

- **Click on "Hidden" in the linetype column.**
- **Click on OK to close the box.**

  You should see that Layer 2 now has the hidden linetype.

  Next assign the center linetype to Layer 3.

- **Click on "Continuous" in the linetype column of the Layer 3 line.**
- **In the Select Linetype dialog box, select the Center linetype.**
- **Click on OK.**

  Examine your layer list again. It should show Layer 2 with the hidden linetype and Layer 3 with the center linetype. Before exiting the Layer Properties Manager, we will create one additional layer to demonstrate AutoCAD's lineweight feature.

3.4 ASSIGNING LINEWEIGHT

Lineweight refers to the thickness of lines as they are displayed and plotted. All lines are initially given a default lineweight. Lineweights are assigned by layer and will be displayed only if the LWT button on the status bar is in the On position. In this section we will create a new layer and give it a much larger lineweight for demonstration purposes.

- **(If for any reason you have left the Layer Properties Manager dialog box, reenter it by selecting the Layers tool from the Object Properties toolbar.)**

  First we will create a new layer, since we do not want to change our previous layers from the default lineweight setting.

⌗ **If Layer 3 is not highlighted, highlight it by pointing to the name "3" and pressing the pickbutton.**

⌗ **Click on the New button in the dialog box.**

Notice that the new layer takes the characteristics of the previously highlighted layer. Our last action was to give Layer 3 the center linetype, so your new layer should have green center lines and the other characteristics of Layer 3.

⌗ **Type "4" for the new layer name.**

⌗ **Click on "default" in the Lineweight column of Layer 4.**

This will open the Lineweight dialog box, shown in Figure 3.6. We will use a rather large lineweight to create a clear demonstration.

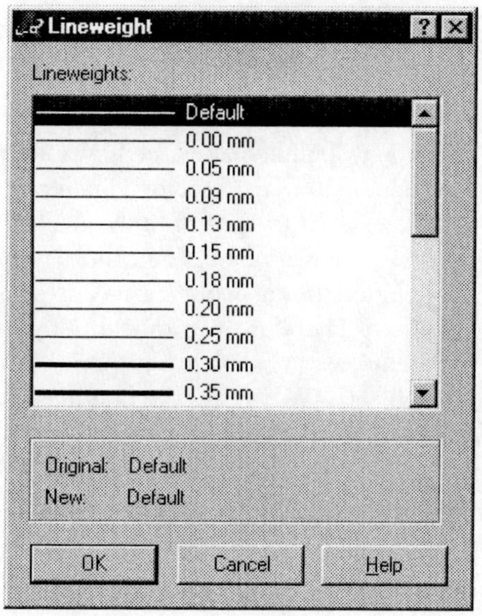

Figure 3.6

⌗ **Scroll down until you see "0.50 mm" on the list.**

⌗ **Highlight the 0.50 mm line.**

Below the list you will see that the original specification for this layer was the default, and is now being changed to 0.50 mm.

⌗ **Click on OK to return to the Layer Properties Manager.**

It is now time to leave the dialog and see what we can do with our new layers.

⌗ **Click on OK to exit Layer Properties Manager.**

NOTE: Do not exit the dialog box by clicking the close button. Exit only by clicking OK. If you use the close button, or if you cancel the dialog, all of your changes, new layers, and so forth will be lost.

Before proceeding, you should be back in your drawing window with your new layers defined in your drawing. To verify that you have successfully defined new layers, open the layer list on the Object Properties toolbar, as shown in Figure 3.7.

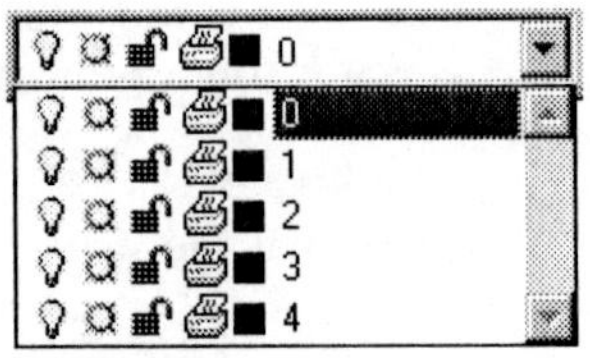

Figure 3.7

⌖ **To open the layer list, click anywhere in the list box.**
Your list should resemble the one in Figure 3.7.

3.5 CHANGING THE CURRENT LAYER

In this section we will make each of your new layers current and draw objects on them. You will immediately see how much power you have added to your drawing by the addition of new layers, colors, linetypes, and lineweight.

To draw new entities on a layer, you must make it the currently active layer. Previously drawn objects on other layers that are turned on will be visible also and will be plotted, but new objects will go on the current layer.

There are two quick methods to establish the current layer. The first works the same as any dialog box pop-down list. The second makes use of previously drawn objects. We will use the first method to draw the objects in Figure 3.8.

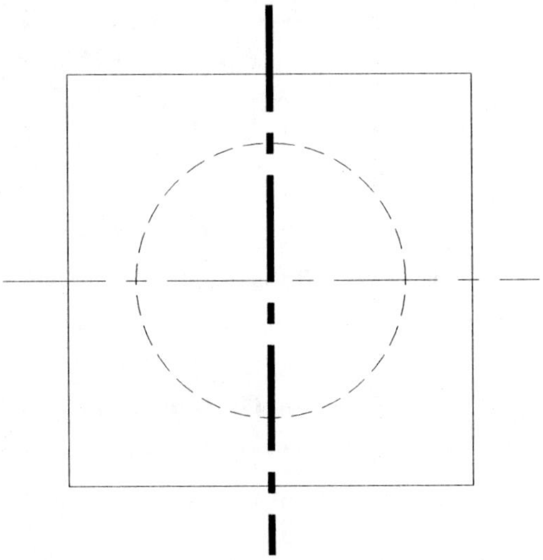

Figure 3.8

⌖ **Click anywhere in the current layer list box on the Object Properties toolbar.**
This will open the list, as shown in Figure 3.7.

⌖ **Select Layer 1, by clicking on the layer name "1" in the pop-down list.**

Layer 1 will replace Layer 0 as the current layer on the Object Properties toolbar.

⌖ **Using the Rectangle command, draw the 6 × 6 square shown in Figure 3.8, with the first corner at (3,2) and the other corner at (9,8).**

Your rectangle should show the red, continuous lines of Layer 1.

⌖ **Click anywhere in the Layer Control box on the Object Properties toolbar.**

⌖ **Click on the layer name "2."**

Layer 2 will become the current layer.

⌖ **With Layer 2 current, draw the hidden circle in Figure 3.8, centered at (6,5) with radius 2.**

Your circle should appear in yellow hidden lines.

⌖ **Make Layer 3 current and draw a horizontal center line from (2,5) to (10,5).**

This line should appear as a green center line.

⌖ **Click on the LWT button on the status line so that it is in the On position.**

⌖ **Make Layer 4 current and draw a vertical line from (6,1) to (6,9).**

This line should appear as a green center line with noticeable thickness.

⌖ **Click the LWT button again to put it in the Off position.**

With LWT off, the lineweight of the horizontal center line will not be displayed.

3.5.1 Making an Object's Layer Current

Finally, we will use another method to make Layer 1 current before moving on.

⌖ **Select the Make Object's Layer Current tool from the Object Properties toolbar, as shown in Figure 3.9.**

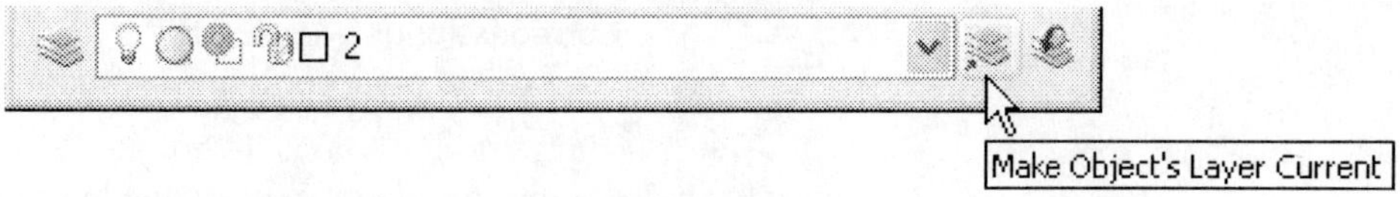

Figure 3.9

This tool allows us to make a layer current by selecting any object on that layer. AutoCAD will show this prompt:

Select object whose layer will become current:

⌖ **Select the red rectangle drawn on Layer 1.**

Layer 1 will replace Layer 4 in the current layer box.

3.6 EDITING CORNERS USING FILLET

Now that you have a variety of linetypes to use, you can begin to do more realistic mechanical drawings. All you will need is the ability to create filleted (rounded) and chamfered (cut) corners. The two work similarly, and AutoCAD makes them easy. Fillets may also be created between circles and arcs, but the most common usage is the type of situation demonstrated here.

We will only be working with the square in this exercise, but instead of erasing the other objects, turn them off, as follows:

- **If you have not already done so, set Layer 1 as the current layer.**
- **Open the layer list on the Object Properties toolbar, and click the light bulb icons on Layers 2, 3, and 4 so that they turn from yellow to gray, indicating that they are off.**
- **Click anywhere outside the list box to close it.**

  When you are done you should see only the square. The other objects are still in your drawing and may be recalled at anytime simply by turning their layers on again.

  We will use the square to practice fillets and chamfers.

- **Type "f" or select the Fillet tool from the Modify toolbar, as shown in Figure 3.10.**

  Fillet is also on the Modify menu, but it is near the bottom of a lengthy list, so the alias or the toolbar selection is quicker.

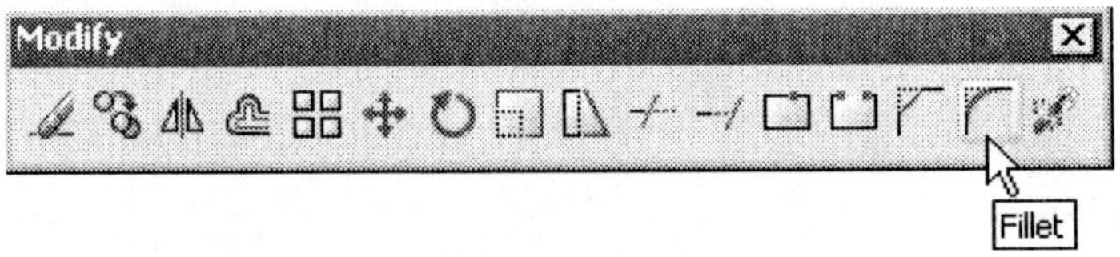

Figure 3.10

A prompt with options will appear as follows:

Current settings: Mode = TRIM, Radius = 0.50
Select first object or [Polyline/Radius/Trim]:

The first thing you must do is determine the degree of rounding you want. Since fillets are really arcs, they can be defined by a radius.

- **Type "r."**

  AutoCAD prompts:

  Enter fillet radius <0.50>:

  The default is 0.50.

- **Type "0.75" or show two points 0.75 units apart.**

  You have set 0.75 as the current fillet radius for this drawing. You can change it at any time. Changing will not affect previously drawn fillets.

- **Press Enter or the space bar to repeat FILLET.**

  The prompt is the same as before, but the radius value has changed:

  Current settings: Mode = TRIM, Radius = 0.75
  Select first object or [Polyline/Radius/Trim]:

  You will notice that you have the pickbox on the screen now without the cross hairs.

- **Use the pickbox to select two lines that meet at any corner of your square.**

Behold! A fillet! You did not even have to press Enter. AutoCAD knows that you are done after selecting two lines.

⌖ **Press Enter or the space bar to repeat FILLET. Then fillet another corner.**

⌖ **Proceed to fillet all four corners.**

When you are done, your screen should resemble Figure 3.11.

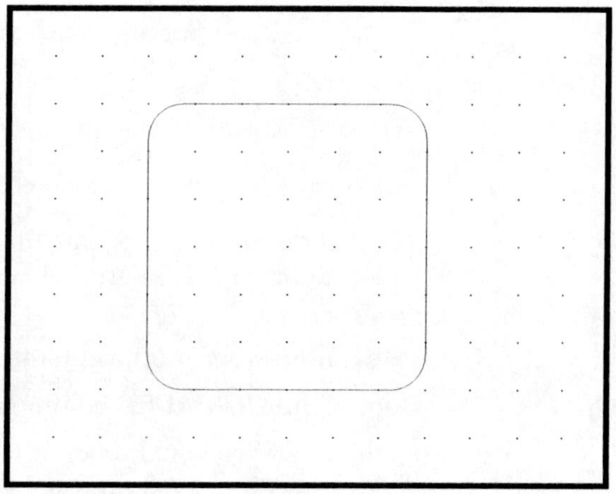

Figure 3.11

3.7 EDITING CORNERS USING CHAMFER

The CHAMFER command sequence is almost identical to the FILLET command, with the exception that chamfers may be uneven. That is, you may cut back farther on one side of a corner than on the other. To do this you must give AutoCAD two distances instead of one.

In this exercise we will draw even chamfers on the four corners of the square. By using the Polyline option, we will chamfer all four corners at once. We will also take the opportunity to use a new cursor menu.

⌖ **Select the Chamfer tool, as shown in Figure 3.12.**

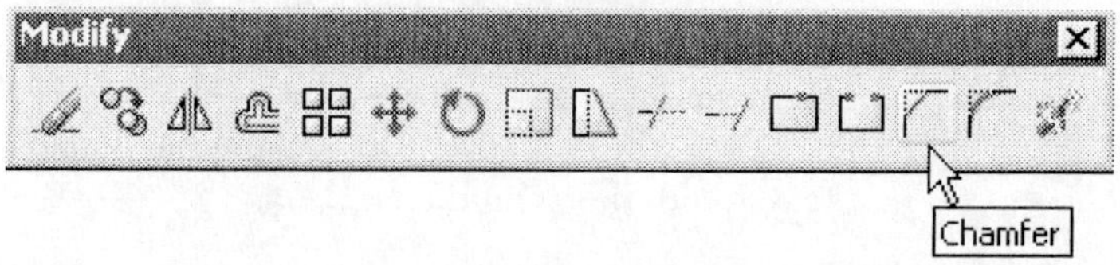

Figure 3.12

AutoCAD prompts:

(TRIM mode) Current chamfer Dist1 = 0.50, Dist2 = 0.50
Select first line or [Polyline/Distance/Angle/Trim/Method]:

You can type a letter to select an option, but there is also a shortcut menu.

- **Right click anywhere in the drawing area.**

This will call a cursor menu with the Polyline, Distance, Angle, Trim, and Method options in the middle panel.

- **Select "Distance."**

The next prompt will be

Specify first chamfer distance <0.50>:

- **Type "1."**

AutoCAD asks for another distance:

Specify second chamfer distance <1.00>:

The first distance has become the default and most of the time it will be used. If you want an asymmetric chamfer, enter a different value for the second distance.

- **Press enter to accept the default, making the chamfer distances symmetrical.**
- **Repeat the CHAMFER command.**

At this point you could proceed to chamfer each corner of the square independently. However, if you drew the square using the RECTANGLE command you have a quicker option. The RECTANGLE command draws a polyline rectangle. A polyline is a single entity comprised of several lines and arcs. If you have drawn a closed polyline and specify the Polyline option in the CHAMFER or FILLET commands, AutoCAD will edit all corners of the object.

- **Type "p" or open the shortcut menu and select Polyline.**

AutoCAD prompts:

Select 2D polyline:

- **Answer the prompt by pointing to any part of the square.**

You should have four neat chamfers on your square, replacing the fillets from the previous section.

3.8 ZOOMING WINDOW, PREVIOUS, AND ALL

The capacity to zoom in and out of a drawing is one of the more impressive benefits of working on a CAD system. When drawings get complex, it often becomes necessary to work in detail on small portions of the drawing space. Especially with a small monitor, the only way to do this is by making the detailed area larger on the screen. This is done easily with the ZOOM command.

- **You should have a square with chamfered corners on your screen from the previous exercise.**

We will demonstrate zooming using the window, all, previous, and realtime options.

- **Type "z" or select the Zoom Window tool from the Standard toolbar, as illustrated in Figure 3.13.**

Figure 3.13

The prompt that follows includes the following options:

Specify corner of window, enter a scale factor (nX or nXP), or
[All/Center/Dynamic/Extents/Previous/Scale/Window] <realtime>:

If you have used the Zoom Window tool, the Window option will be entered automatically. As in ERASE and other edit commands, you can force a window selection by typing "w" or selecting "Window." However, this is unnecessary. The windowing action is automatically initiated if you pick a point on the screen after entering ZOOM.

Pick a point just below and to the left of the lower left-hand corner of your square (Point 1 in Figure 3.14).

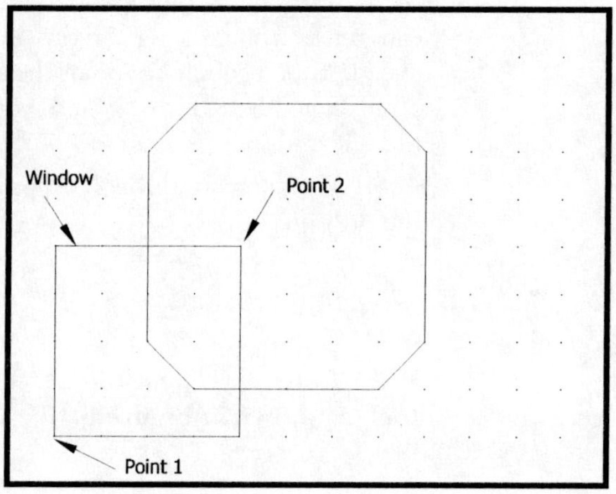

Figure 3.14

AutoCAD asks for another point:

Specify opposite corner:

You are being asked to define a window, just as in the ERASE command. This window will be the basis for what AutoCAD displays next. Since you are not going to make a window that conforms exactly to the screen size and shape, AutoCAD will interpret the window this way: Everything in the window will be shown, plus whatever additional area is needed to fill the screen. The center of the window will become the center of the new display.

Pick a second point near the center of your square (Point 2 in the figure).

The lower left corner of the square should now appear enlarged on your screen, as shown in Figure 3.15.

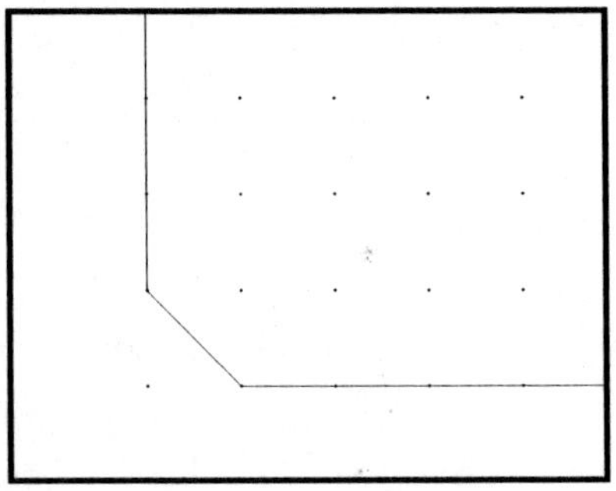

Figure 3.15

⌗ **Using the same method, try zooming up further on the chamfered corner of the square. If snap is on, you may need to turn it off (F9).**

Remember that you can repeat the ZOOM command by pressing Enter or the space bar.

At this point, most people cannot resist seeing how much magnification they can get by zooming repeatedly on the same corner or angle of a chamfer. Go ahead. After a couple of zooms the angle will not appear to change. An angle is the same angle no matter how close you get to it. But what happens to the spacing of the grid and snap as you move in?

When you are through experimenting with window zooming, try zooming to the previous display.

3.8.1 Zoom Previous

⌗ **Press Enter to repeat the ZOOM command, or select the Zoom Previous tool, as shown in Figure 3.16.**

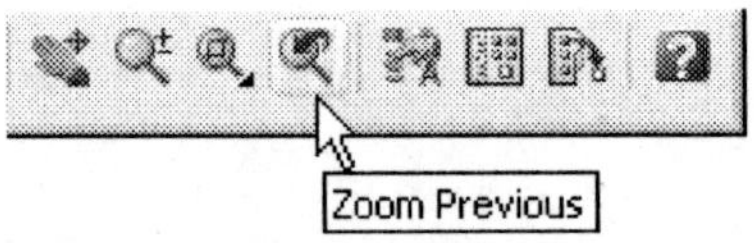

Figure 3.16

⌗ **If you repeated the command by pressing enter, type "p."**

You should now see your previous display.

AutoCAD keeps track of up to 10 previous displays.

⌗ **ZOOM "Previous" as many times as you can until you get a message that says**

No previous display saved.

3.8.2 Zoom All

ZOOM All zooms out to display the whole drawing. It is useful when you have been working in a number of small areas of a drawing and are ready to view the whole scene. You do not want to have to wade through previous displays to find your way back. ZOOM All will take you there in one jump.

To see it work, you should be zoomed in on a portion of your display before executing ZOOM All.

- **Press Enter or type "z" to repeat the ZOOM command and zoom in on a window within your drawing.**
- **Press Enter or type "z" to repeat ZOOM again.**
- **Type "a" for the All option.**

NOTE: The Zoom Window tool also has a flyout that includes tools for all of the ZOOM command options, including ZOOM All, as shown in Figure 3.17. Flyouts are toolbar features that make additional tools available. Any tool button that has a small black triangle in one corner will open a flyout. To open a flyout, hold down the pickbutton while the arrow is on the tool. Then run down or across the flyout to the tool you want. When the tool button is "down," release the pickbutton.

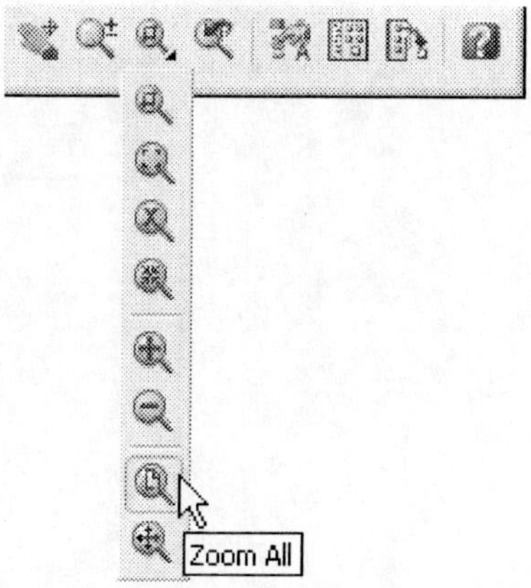

Figure 3.17

3.9 USING REALTIME ZOOM AND PAN

Realtime ZOOM and PAN allow you to see changes in display and magnification dynamically as you make adjustments. As soon as you start to use ZOOM, you are likely to need PAN as well. While ZOOM allows you to magnify portions of your drawing, PAN allows you to shift the area you are viewing in any direction.

You also have the option of panning with the scroll bars at the edges of the drawing area, but the PAN command allows more flexibility. In particular, it allows diagonal motion. We will use the PAN Realtime tool first and then the ZOOM Realtime tool.

- **Type "p" or select the Pan Realtime tool from the Standard toolbar (as illustrated in Figure 3.18).**

With either method, you will see the PAN command cursor representing a hand with which you can move objects on the screen. When the mouse button is not depressed, the hand will move freely across the screen. When you move the mouse with the pickbutton held down, the complete drawing display will move along with the hand.

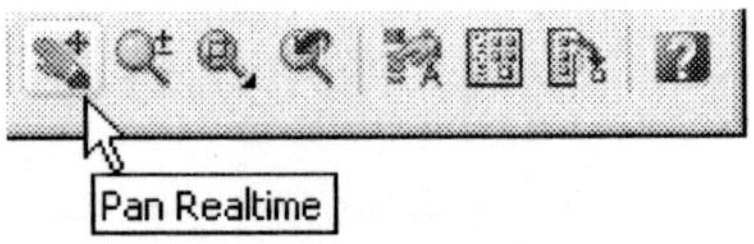

Figure 3.18

- **Move the hand near the middle of the screen without holding down the pickbutton.**
- **Hold down the pickbutton and move the cursor diagonally up and to the right, as illustrated in Figure 3.19.**
- **Release the pickbutton to complete the PAN procedure.**

Experiment with Realtime PAN, moving objects up, down, left, right, and diagonally. Watch the scroll bars respond as you PAN across the drawing area.

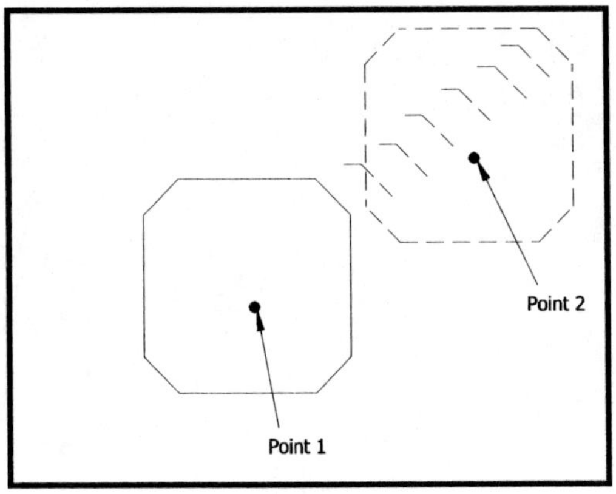

Figure 3.19

3.9.1 Realtime ZOOM

When you are in either the ZOOM or PAN command, you can access a shortcut menu by right clicking anywhere on the screen. Try it.

- **Without leaving PAN, press the right button on your mouse.**

This will call up the shortcut menu illustrated in Figure 3.20. This menu will allow you to switch quickly between realtime PAN and realtime ZOOM.

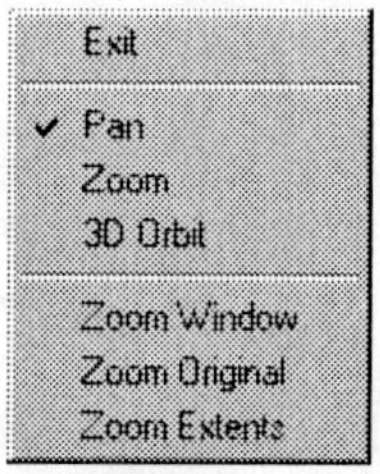

Figure 3.20

- **Select Zoom from the shortcut menu.**

  The menu will vanish and the realtime ZOOM cursor will appear. As illustrated in Figure 3.21, this represents a magnifying glass with a + sign above and a − sign below.

Figure 3.21

- **Without pressing the pickbutton, move the zoom cursor near the bottom of the screen.**

  As with the PAN cursor, you will be able to move freely when the pickbutton is not held down.

- **Press the pickbutton and move the cursor upward.**

  With the pickbutton down, upward motion will increase magnification, enlarging objects on the screen.

- **Move up and down to see the effects of zoom cursor movement.**
- **Release the pickbutton to complete the process.**

  When you release the button you will not exit the command. This is important because it may take several trips up or down the screen to indicate the amount of magnification you want. Moving the cursor halfway up the screen will produce a 100% magnification.

- **Continue to experiment with Realtime ZOOM and PAN until you feel comfortable.**
- **To exit, press ESC, the space bar, or the enter key.**

  You can also right click to open the shortcut menu and then select Exit.

3.10 USING PLOT PREVIEW

Plot preview is an essential tool in carrying out efficient plotting and printing. Plot configuration is complex, and the odds are good that you will waste time and paper by printing drawings directly without first previewing them on the screen. AutoCAD has previewing tools that assist you in knowing exactly what to expect when your drawing reaches a sheet of drawing paper.

In this section we are still significantly limited in our use of plot settings, but learning to use the plot preview will make all of your future work with plotting and printing more effective. We suggest that you work through this section now with the objects on your screen, and refer to it as necessary after you have done any of the drawings at the end of this chapter.

⌖ **To begin this task you should have objects or a drawing on your screen ready to preview.**

⌖ **Type Ctrl-P, or select the Plot tool from the Standard toolbar or Plot from the File menu.**

This will open the Plot dialog box, familiar from the last chapter. The two preview options are at the bottom left of the dialog box. A partial preview will show you an outline of the effective plotting area in relation to the paper size but will not show an image of the plotted drawing. A full preview will display an image of the objects in your drawing on a sheet of drawing paper.

NOTE: We will address paper sizes in the next chapter. For now, we will assume that your plot configuration is correctly matched to the paper in your printer or plotter. If you do not get good results with this task, the problem may very well lie here.

3.10.1 Partial Preview

Partial previews are quick and should be accessed frequently as you specify plot settings that affect how paper will be used and oriented to print your drawing. Partial previews give you specific information on how your settings translate into areas on your drawing sheet. Full previews give you less detailed information, but let you see how your drawing will actually appear on paper.

We will look at a partial preview first.

⌖ **Click on Partial Preview.**

You will see a preview image similar to the one shown in Figure 3.22. The exact image will depend on your plotting device, so it may be different from the one shown here. The elements of the preview will be the same, however. The white rectangle represents your drawing paper. It may be oriented in landscape (horizontally) or portrait (vertically). Typically, printers are in portrait, and plotters in landscape. Below the preview image you will see the dimensions of this area listed as Paper size.

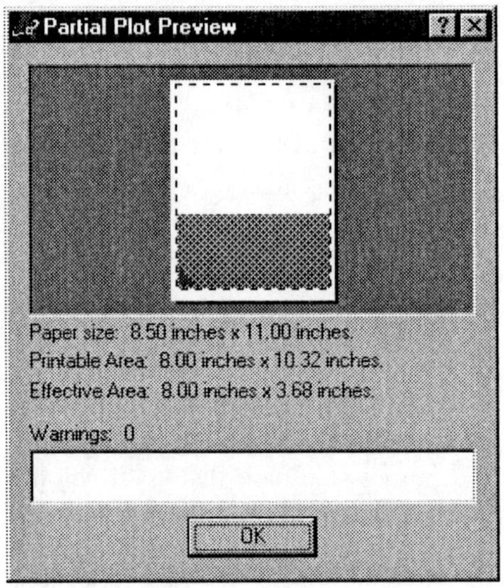

Figure 3.22

The blue-dotted-line rectangle inside the white area illustrates the printable plotting area. Its dimensions are listed as Printable area.

The area in blue cross hatching represents the effective plotting area, the size and shape of the area that AutoCAD can actually use given the shape and orientation of the drawing area in relation to the size and orientation of the paper. Its dimensions are listed as Effective area. The effective area is dependent on many things, as you will see. We will leave it as is for now and return to it later when you begin to alter the plot configuration.

In one corner of the preview image you will see a small red triangle. This is the rotation icon. It shows the corner of the plotting area where the plotter will begin plotting (the origin).

⌖ **Click on OK to exit the preview box.**

3.10.2 Full Preview

⌖ **Click on the Full preview button.**

The dialog box will disappear temporarily and you will see a preview image similar to the one in Figure 3.23. This image represents your drawing on paper as it is now configured for printing. The ZOOM Realtime cursor appears to allow you to zoom in or out on aspects of the preview. By clicking on the right button, you can access the zoom and pan pop-up list demonstrated earlier in this chapter. Panning and zooming in the preview has no effect on the plot parameters. You may want to experiment with this feature now.

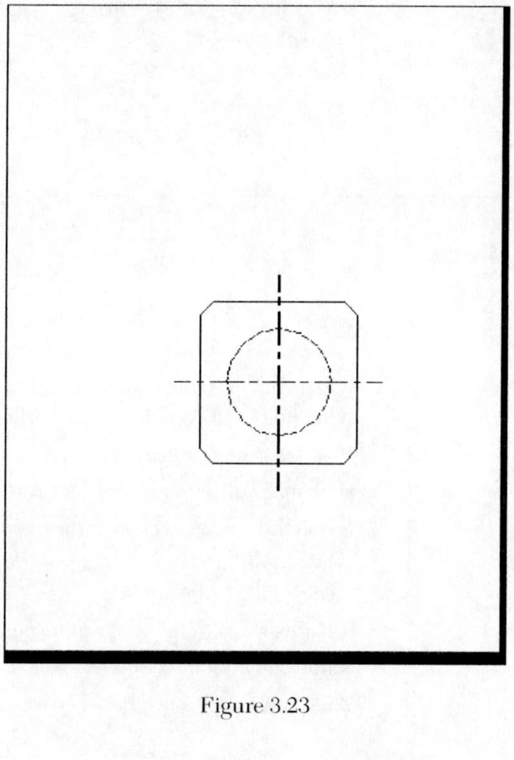

Figure 3.23

✤ **When you are done experimenting with Zoom and Pan, press ESC or the enter key or space bar to return to the Plot dialog box.**

This ends our initial preview of your drawing. In ordinary practice, if everything looked right in the preview you would move on to plot or print your drawing now by clicking on OK. In the chapters that follow, we will explore more features of the plot dialog box and will use full and partial plot previews extensively as we change plot parameters. For now, get used to using plot preview. If things are not coming out quite the way you want, you will be able to fix them soon.

✤ **Click OK to plot or print your drawing, or Cancel to exit without printing.**

3.10.3 Using Print Preview

AutoCAD also has a Print preview tool on the Standard toolbar, as illustrated in Figure 3.24. This tool looks like the preview tool in other Windows applications and performs the same function as the Full preview option in the Plot dialog box. It will give you a quick look at your drawing positioned on a drawing sheet, but you will have to go to the Plot dialog if you want to make changes in plot configuration. Try it.

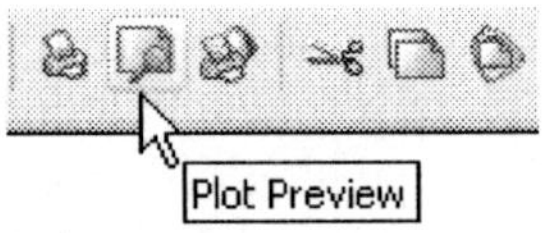

Figure 3.24

✤ **Click the Print preview tool, as illustrated in Figure 3.24.**

You will see a full preview of your printed drawing, as shown previously in Figure 3.23.

3.11 REVIEW MATERIAL

Questions

1. What function(s) can be performed directly from the Layer list on the Object Properties toolbar? What functions can be performed from the Layer Properties Manager?
2. What linetype is always available when you start a drawing from scratch in AutoCAD? What must you do to access other linetypes?
3. How many colors are available in AutoCAD's Index Color System?
4. How many different layers does AutoCAD allow you to create?
5. Name three ways to change the current layer.
6. Why is it often necessary to enter the FILLET and CHAMFER commands twice to create a single fillet or chamfer?
7. What happens to the grid when you zoom way out on a drawing?
8. Name one limitation of scroll bars that the PAN command does not have.
9. What is the difference between a partial and a full plot preview?

Commands

CHAMFER	FILLET	LAYER
LTSCALE	PAN	REGEN
ZOOM		

3.12 DRAWING PROBLEMS

1. Make Layer 3 current and draw a green center line cross with two perpendicular lines, each two units long and intersecting at their midpoints.
2. Make Layer 2 current and draw a hidden line circle centered at the intersection of the cross drawn in step 1, with a diameter of two units.
3. Make Layer 1 current and draw a red square two units on a side centered on the center of the circle. Its sides will run tangent to the circle.
4. Use a window to zoom in on the objects drawn in steps 1, 2, and 3.
5. Fillet each corner of the square with a 0.125 radius fillet.

DRAWING 1

Mounting Plate

This drawing will give you experience using center lines and chamfers. Since there are no hidden lines, you will have no need for Layer 2, but we will continue to use the same numbering system for consistency. Draw the continuous lines in red on Layer 1 and the center lines in green on Layer 3.

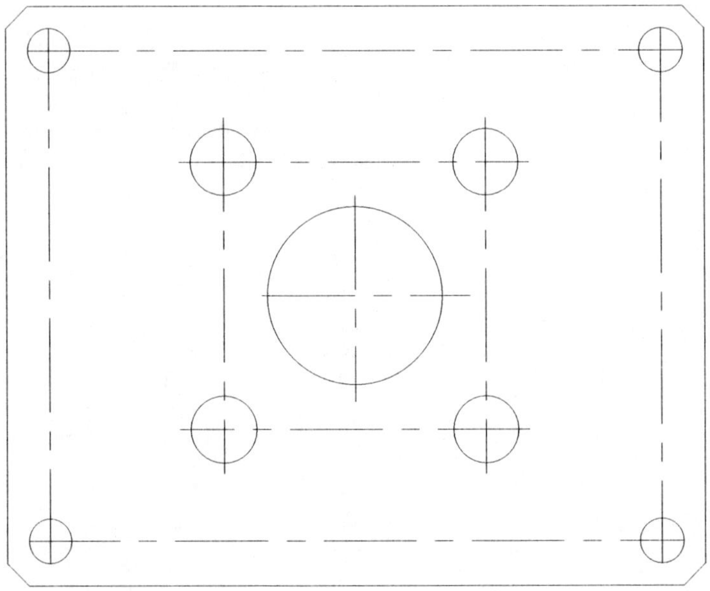

Drawing Suggestions

GRID = 0.5

SNAP = 0.25

LTSCALE = 0.5

LTSCALE The size of the individual dashes and spaces that make up center lines, hidden lines, and other linetypes is determined by a global setting called "LTSCALE." By default it is set to a factor of 1.00. In smaller drawings this setting will be too large and will cause some of the shorter lines to appear continuous regardless of what layer they are on.

To remedy this, change LTSCALE as follows:

1. Type "lts."
2. Enter a value.

For the drawings in this chapter use a setting of 0.50.

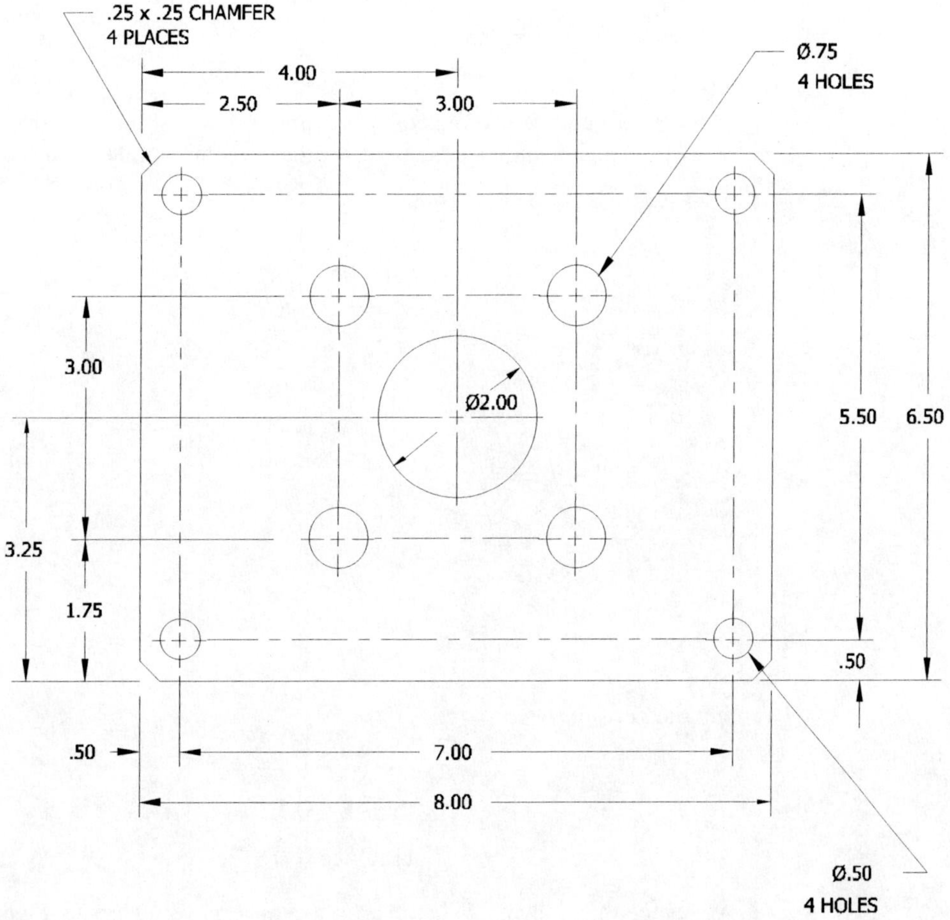

MOUNTING PLATE

DRAWING 2

Bushing

This drawing will give you practice with chamfers, layers, and zooming. Notice that because of the smaller dimensions here, we have recommended a smaller LTSCALE setting.

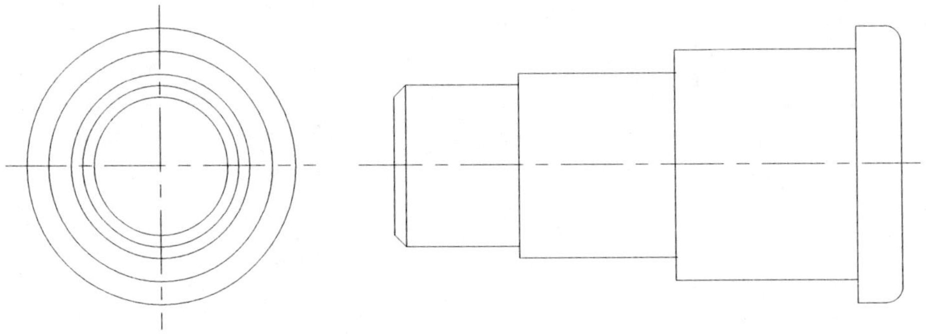

Drawing Suggestions

GRID = 0.25

SNAP = 0.125

LTSCALE = 0.25

- Since this drawing will appear quite small on your screen, it would be a good idea to ZOOM in on the actual drawing space you are using and PAN if necessary.
- Notice that the two 0.25-diameter screw holes are 1.50 apart. This puts them squarely on grid points that you will have no trouble finding.

Regen When you zoom you may find that your circles turn into many-sided polygons. AutoCAD does this to save drawing regeneration time. These time savings are not noticeable now, but when you get into larger drawings they become significant. If you want to see a proper circle, type "Regen." This command will cause your drawing to be regenerated more precisely from the data you have given.

You may also notice that REGENs happen automatically when certain operations are performed, such as changing the LTSCALE setting after objects are already on the screen.

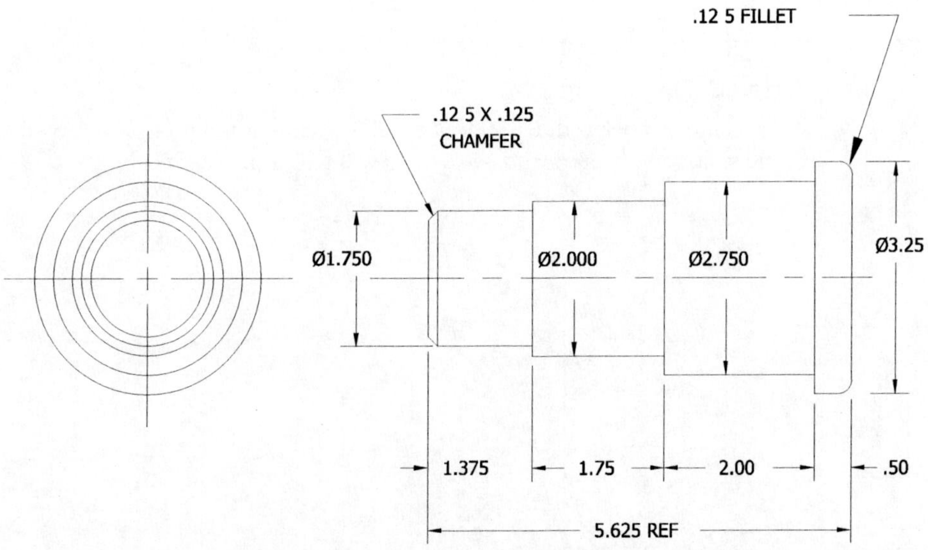

STEPPED SHAFT

DRAWING 3

Half Block

This cinder block is the first project using architectural units in this book. Set units, grid, and snap as indicated, and everything will fall into place nicely.

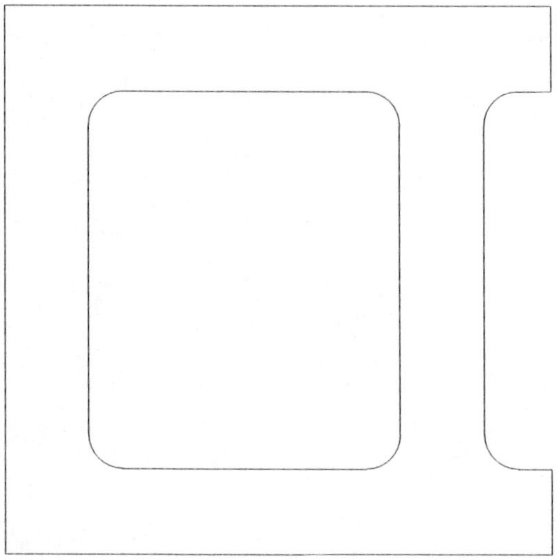

Drawing Suggestions

UNITS =Architectural
smallest fraction = 4 ($\frac{1}{4}$")

GRID = $\frac{1}{4}$"

SNAP = $\frac{1}{4}$"

- Start with the lower left corner of the block at the point (0'–1", 0'–1") to keep the drawing well placed on the display.
- Set the FILLET radius to $\frac{1}{2}$" or 0.5. Notice that you can use decimal versions of fractions. The advantage is that they are easier to type.

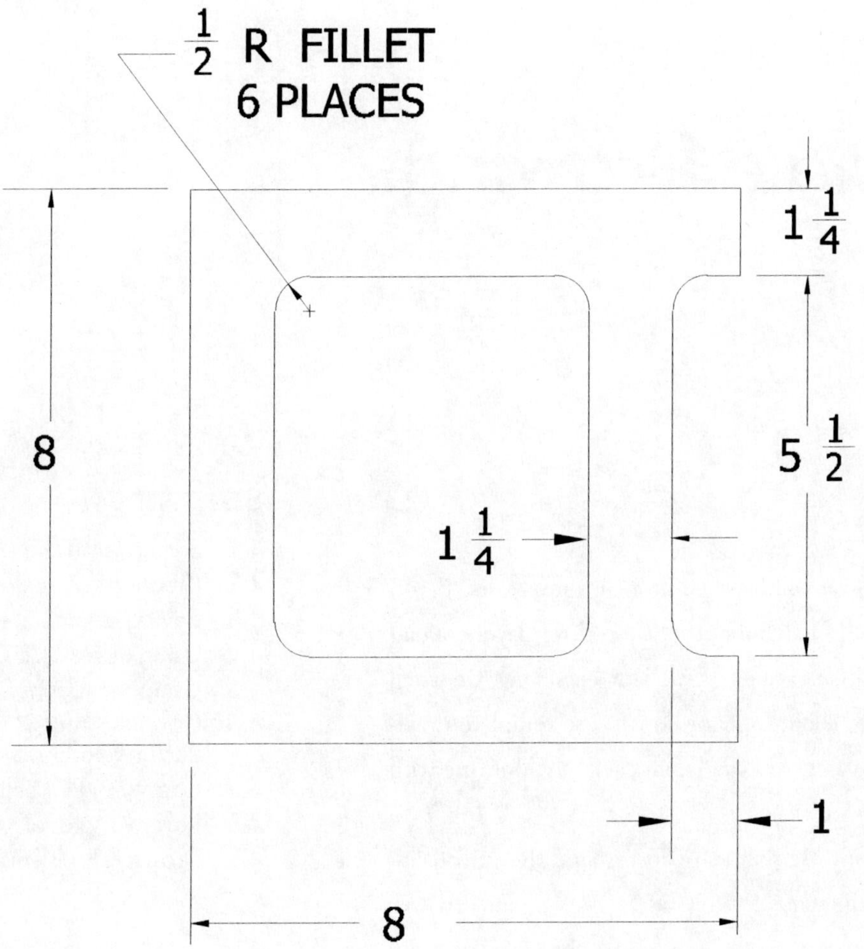

HALF BLOCK

4

Template Drawings

Overview

In this chapter you will learn some real time savers. If you have grown tired of defining the same three layers, along with units, grid, snap, and ltscale, for each new drawing, read on. You are about to learn how to use template drawings. With templates, you can begin each new drawing with whatever setup you want.

In addition, you will learn to reshape the grid using the LIMITS command and to COPY, MOVE, and ARRAY objects on the screen so that you do not have to draw the same thing twice. We will begin with LIMITS, since we will want to change the limits as part of defining your first template.

Sections

Objectives

After reading this chapter, you should be able to:

- Change the shape of the grid using the Advanced Setup Wizard and the LIMITS command.
- Create a template drawing.
- Select your drawing as the template.
- MOVE an object in a drawing.
- COPY an object in a drawing.
- Create a rectangular array.
- Change Plot Configuration parameters.
- Draw a grill.
- Draw a test bracket.
- Draw a floor frame.

4.1 SETTING LIMITS

You have changed the density of the screen grid many times, but always within the same 12 × 9 space, which basically represents an A-size sheet of paper. Now you will learn how to change the shape by setting new limits to emulate other sheet sizes or any other space you want to represent. But first, a word about model space and paper space.

4.1.1 Model Space and Paper Space

Model space is an AutoCAD concept that refers to the imaginary space in which we create and edit objects. In model space, objects are always drawn full scale (1 screen unit = 1 unit of length in the real world). The alternative to model space is paper space, in which screen units represent units of length on a piece of drawing paper. You will encounter paper space when you begin to use AutoCAD's layout features. A layout is like an overlay on your drawing in which you specify a sheet size and other paper-related options. Layouts also allow you to create multiple views of the same model space objects. To avoid confusion and keep your learning curve on track, however, we will avoid using layouts for the time being.

In this exercise we will reshape our model space to emulate different drawing sheet sizes. This will not be necessary in later practice. With AutoCAD you can scale your drawing to fit any drawing sheet size when it comes time to plot. Model space limits should be determined by the size and shapes of objects in your drawing, not by the paper you are going to use when you plot.

4.1.2 The Advanced Setup Wizard

Limits can be set from within a drawing using the LIMITS command. When you are beginning a new drawing, however, a quick way is to use a drawing setup wizard which will set up units at the same time. Wizards are standard Windows features that guide you through setup functions in all kinds of applications. We will use the Advanced Setup Wizard to begin this drawing and set 18 × 12 limits.

⌖ **Start AutoCAD or begin a new drawing.**

If the Create New Drawing dialog box is not showing, open the File menu and select New, or select the New tool from the Standard toolbar.

⌖ **In the Create New Drawing dialog box click the Use a Wizard icon, the one on the right.**

This will open the Select a Wizard box with the two options "Advanced Setup" and "Quick Setup."

⌖ **Highlight Advanced Setup in the Select a Wizard box.**

How do you like that? You are already into advanced options! The Quick Setup Wizard will also allow you to set limits, but does not allow for units setup.

⌖ **Click on OK.**

This will bring up the Advanced Setup dialog box illustrated in Figure 4.1. The list on the left shows you the steps the Wizard will take you through: Units, Angle, Angle Measure, Angle Direction, and Limits. The first four are familiar from the UNITS command. Limits is new. In the first four steps you will set up 2 place decimal units, 0 place angles measured in degrees, starting with 0 on the right horizontal and moving counterclockwise. Then you will set limits at 18 × 12.

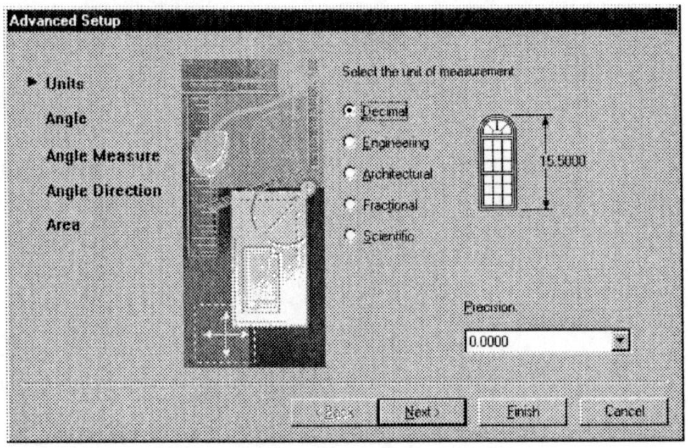

Figure 4.1

- **If the Decimal radio button is not selected, select it.**
- **Open the Precision box at the bottom right and select 0.00.**
- **Click Next to move on to the next step, Angle units.**

  The wizard will show a second set of dialog box options. Here again you can choose an option for units and an option for precision.
- **Check to see that the Decimal degrees radio button is selected and that the precision is set to 0.**
- **Click Next to move on to Angle Measure.**

  The only options here are the four points of the compass. This will allow you to determine which compass point is 0 degrees. East is the standard setting.
- **Check to see that the East radio button is selected, then click Next to move on to Angle Direction.**

  Here you have only two options, clockwise or counterclockwise. Counterclockwise is the usual AutoCAD direction for measuring and specifying angles.
- **Check to see that Counterclockwise is selected, then click Next to move on to Area.**

  This, at last, is where you set the limits of your new drawing, using the edit boxes and icon shown in Figure 4.2. The number in the width box should read 12.00. The number in the length box should show 9.00.

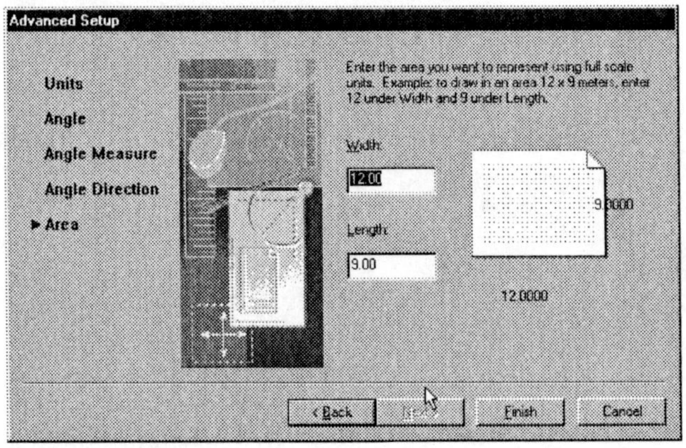

Figure 4.2

At the right you will see a preview image of a sheet of drawing paper with the 12 × 9 limits. We will change to an 18 × 12 area.

⌖ **Double click in the Width box and type "18."**

⌖ **Double click in the Length box and type "12."**

The width box and the preview image will show 18 × 12.

⌖ **Click Finish to exit the Advanced Setup Wizard.**

Upon returning to the drawing area you will see that the grid now covers your screen. To see the complete new area, however, you will need to ZOOM All.

⌖ **Type "z" to enter the ZOOM command and then "a" for the "All" option.**

Your screen should resemble Figure 4.3, showing an 18 × 12 grid.

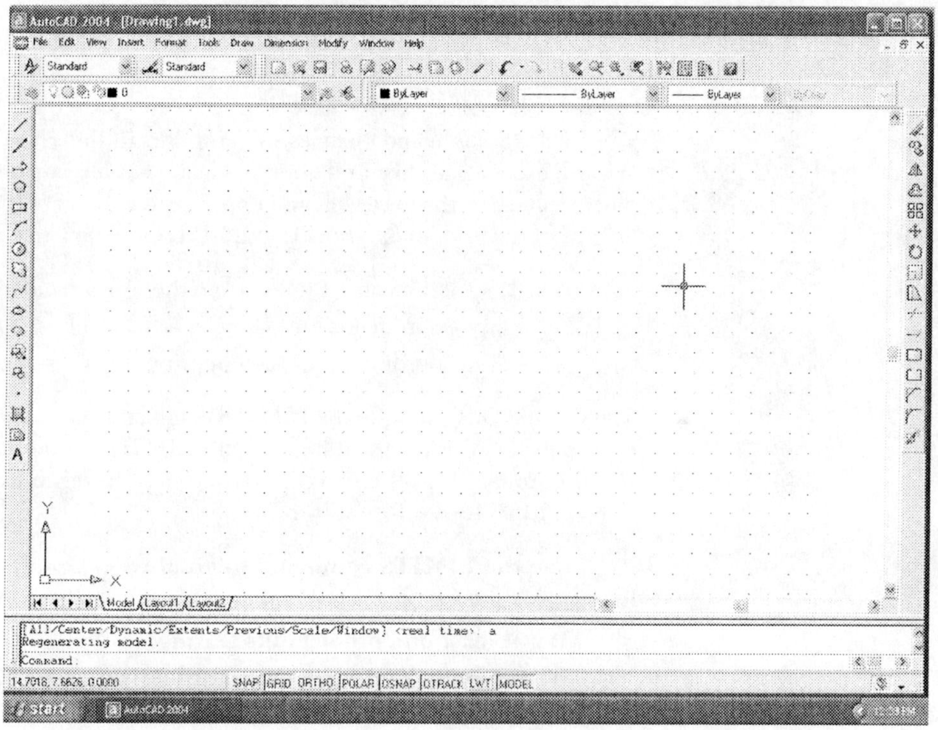

Figure 4.3

After we are finished exploring the LIMITS command, we will create the other new settings we want and save this drawing as your B-size template.

We suggest that you continue to experiment with setting limits and that you try out the Quick Setup Wizard, as well as the LIMITS command, which is described next. Try some of the possibilities listed in Figure 4.4, which is a table of sheet sizes.

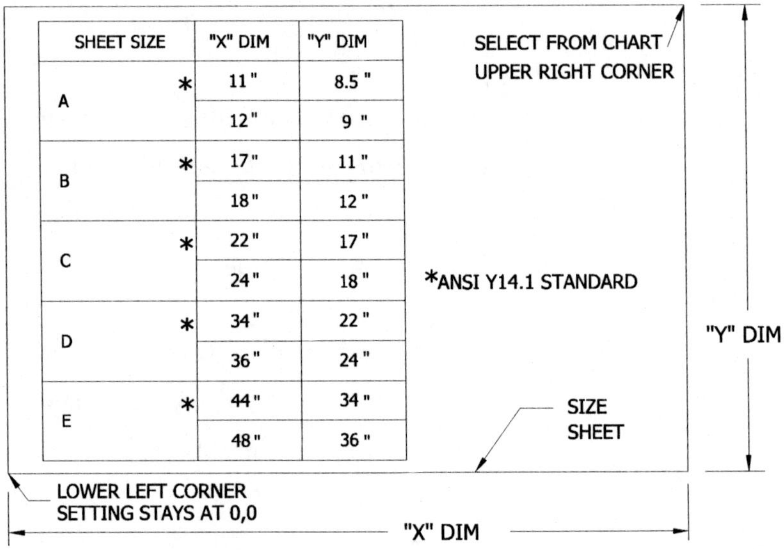

SHEET SIZE		"X" DIM	"Y" DIM
A	*	11"	8.5"
		12"	9"
B	*	17"	11"
		18"	12"
C	*	22"	17"
		24"	18"
D	*	34"	22"
		36"	24"
E	*	44"	34"
		48"	36"

Figure 4.4

4.1.3 The LIMITS command

The LIMITS command changes the grid area in the same way as the Advanced Setup Wizard, except that it is used after a drawing has already been opened and it uses coordinate values for the lower left and upper right corners of the grid in place of widths and lengths of the grid boundaries. To use LIMITS, follow this procedure:

1. Select "Drawing Limits" from the Format menu.
2. Type coordinates for the lower left corner—for example, "0, 0."
3. Type coordinates for the upper right corner—for example, "18, 12."

The Off and On options in the LIMITS command control what happens when you try to draw outside of the defined limits. With LIMITS off, nothing will happen. With LIMITS on, AutoCAD will not accept any attempt to begin an entity outside of limits. By default, LIMITS is off.

⌖ **Use the LIMITS command to create a C size drawing area.**

Remember to ZOOM All after changing limits.

⌖ **Try at least one other limits setting.**

⌖ **When you are done experimenting, return LIMITS to (0, 0) and (18, 12), using the LIMITS command, and then ZOOM All.**

You are now in the drawing that we will use for your template, so it is not necessary to begin a new drawing for the next section.

4.2 CREATING A TEMPLATE

To make your own template, so that new drawings will begin with the settings you want, all you have to do is create a drawing that has those settings and then tell AutoCAD that this is a drawing you want to use to define an initial drawing setup. The first part should be easy for you now, since you have been doing your own drawing setup for each new drawing in this book.

⌖ **Make changes to the present drawing as follows:**

GRID:	1.00 ON	(F7)COORD:	ON (F6)
SNAP:	0.25 ON	(F9)LTSCALE:	.5
UNITS:	2-place decimal	LIMITS:	(0, 0) (18, 12)

Also, ensure that the Snap, Grid, and Model buttons on the status line are on, and that Ortho, Polar, Osnap, Otracking, and LWT are off.

⌖ **Load all linetypes from the ACAD file using the following procedure.**

1. Open the Linetype dialog box from the Format menu.
2. Click on Load… to open the Load dialog box.
3. Highlight the first linetype on the list.
4. Scroll down to the end of the list.
5. Hold down the shift key as you highlight the last linetype on the list.
6. With all linetypes highlighted, click on OK.
7. Click on OK in the Linetype dialog box.

⌖ **Create layers and associated colors, linetypes, and settings to match those in Figure 4.5.**

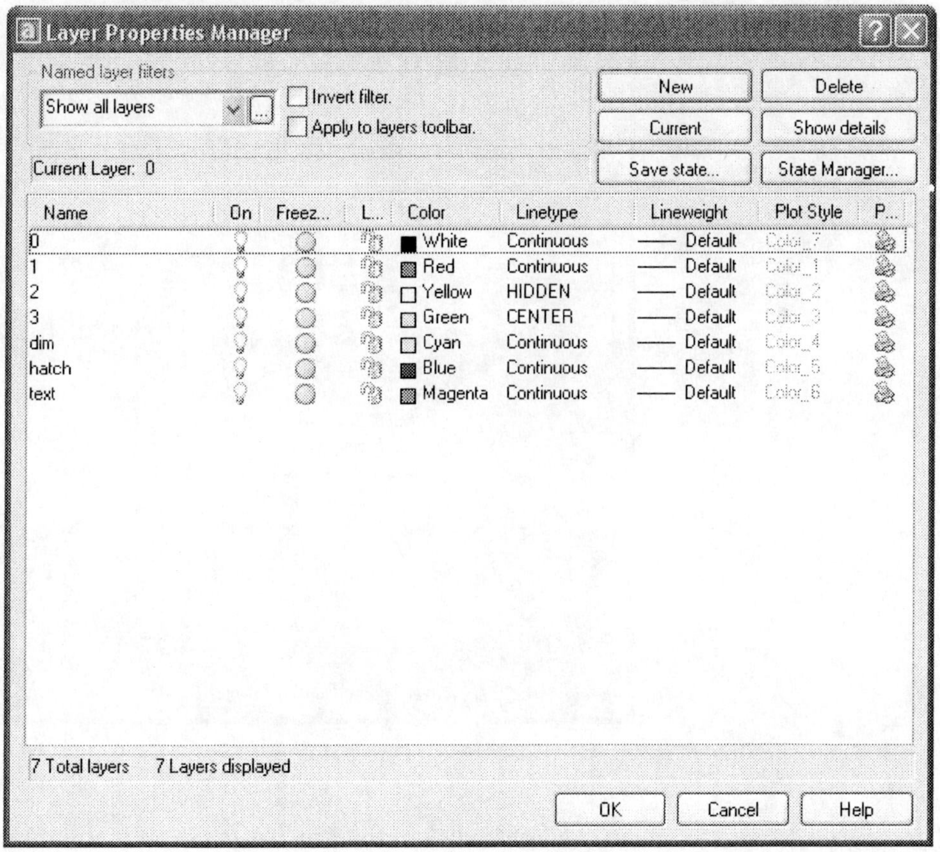

Figure 4.5

Remember that you can make changes to your template at any time. The layers called "text," "hatch," and "dim" will not be used now, but creating them here will save time and avoid confusion later.

At this point your drawing is on file and ready to be saved as a template, which is the focus of the next section.

NOTE: Do not leave anything drawn on your screen or it will come up as part of the template each time you open a new drawing. For some applications this is quite useful. For now we want a blank template.

4.3 SAVING A TEMPLATE DRAWING

A drawing becomes a template when it is saved as a template. Template files are given a .dwt extension and placed in the template file folder.

⌗ **To begin this task you should be in the drawing created in the last section. All the drawing changes should be made as described previously.**

⌗ **Open the File menu and select Save As... .**

This will call up the familiar Save Drawing As dialog box shown in Figure 4.6. The edit box in the middle holds the name of the current drawing. If you have not named the drawing, it will be called "Drawing1."

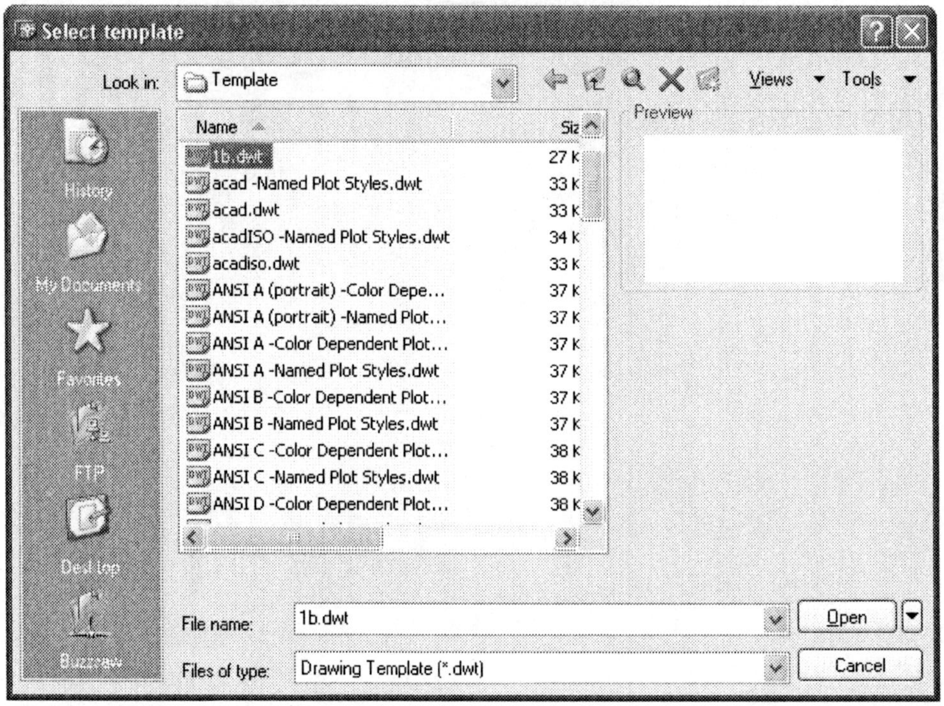

Figure 4.6

⌗ **Double click in the File name box to highlight the drawing name.**

⌗ **Type "1B" for the new name.**

TIP: Since template files are listed alphabetically in the file list, it is convenient to start your template file name with a number so that it appears before the Acad and Ansii standard templates that come with the AutoCAD software. Numbers precede letters in the alphanumeric sequence, so your numbered template file will appear at the top of the list and save you the trouble of scrolling down to find it.

Below the file name box is the Save As type box. This box will list options for saving the drawing. AutoCAD Drawing Template File is fourth on the list.

⌖ **Highlight "AutoCAD Drawing Template File (*.dwt)," and click on it so that it shows up in the list box.**

This will also open the Template file folder automatically. You will see that there are many templates already there. These are supplied by AutoCAD and may be useful to you later. At this point it is more important to learn how to make your own.

Once your drawing name ("1B") is in the name box and the Save As type box shows AutoCAD Drawing Template File, you are ready to save.

⌖ **Click on Save.**

This will call up a Template Description box, as illustrated in Figure 4.7. Here you can specify a description that will appear in the Create New Drawing dialog box whenever this template is used.

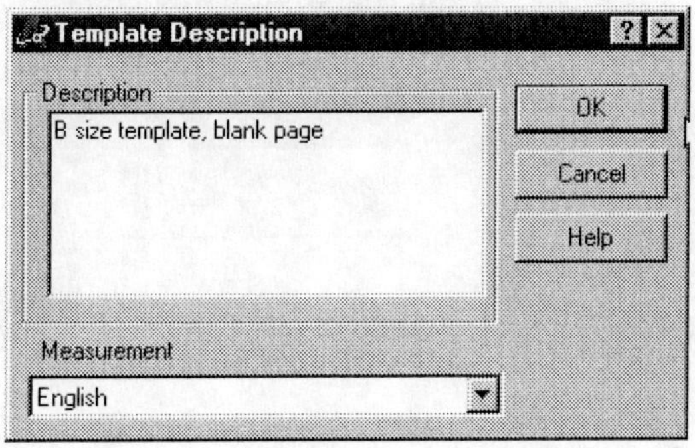

Figure 4.7

⌖ **Type "B size template, blank page."**

This will indicate that this is your B template and that there is no title block or other object drawn in the template.

⌖ **Click on OK.**

The task of creating the drawing template is now complete. All that remains is to create a new drawing using the template to see how it works.

4.4 USING THE MOVE COMMAND

The ability to copy and move objects on the screen is one of the great advantages of working on a CAD system. It can be said that CAD is to drafting as word processing is to typing. Nowhere is this analogy more appropriate than in the cut-and-paste capacities that the COPY and MOVE commands give you.

⌖ **Draw a circle with a radius of 1 near the center of the screen (9, 6), as shown in Figure 4.8.**

Figure 4.8

AutoCAD allows you to pick objects before or after entering an edit command. In this exercise we will use MOVE both ways, beginning with the verb/noun method. We will use the circle you have just drawn, but be aware that the selection set could include as many entities as you like and that a group of entities can be selected with a window or crossing box.

⌗ **Type "m," select Move from the Modify menu, or select the Move tool from the Modify toolbar, as shown in Figure 4.9.**

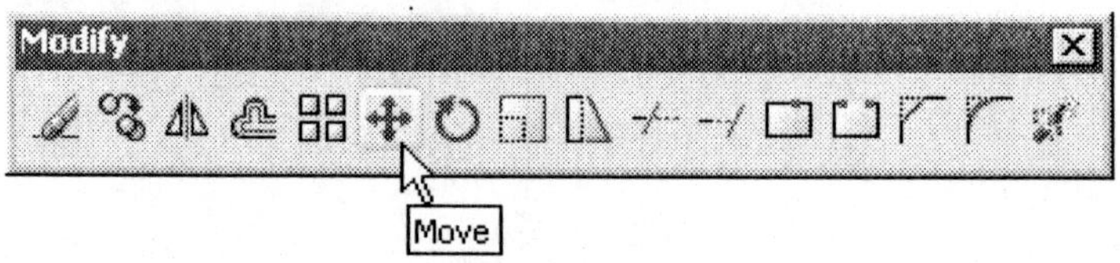

Figure 4.9

You will be prompted to select objects to move.

⌗ **Point to the circle.**

As in the ERASE command, your circle will become dotted.

In the command area, AutoCAD will tell you how many objects have been selected and prompt you to select more. When you are through selecting objects you will need to press Enter to move on.

⌗ **Right click to end object selection.**

AutoCAD prompts:

Specify base point or displacement:

Most often you will show the movement by defining a vector that gives the distance and direction you want the object to be moved. To define movement with a vector, all AutoCAD needs is a distance and a direction. Therefore, the base point does not have to be on or near the object you are moving. Any point will do, as long as you can use it to show how you want your objects moved. This may seem strange at first, but it will soon become natural. Of course, you may choose a point on the object if you wish. With a circle, the center point may be convenient.

⌗ **Point to any location not too near the right edge of the screen.**

AutoCAD will give you a rubber band from the point you have indicated and will ask for a second point:

Specify second point of displacement or < use first point as displacement>:

As soon as you begin to move the cursor, you will see that AutoCAD also gives you a circle to drag so you can immediately see the effect of the movement you are indicating. An example of how this may look is shown in Figure 4.10. Let's say you want to move the circle 3.00 to the right. Watch the coordinate display and stretch the rubber band out until the display reads "3.00 < 0,0" (press F6 or double click on the coordinate display to get polar coordinates).

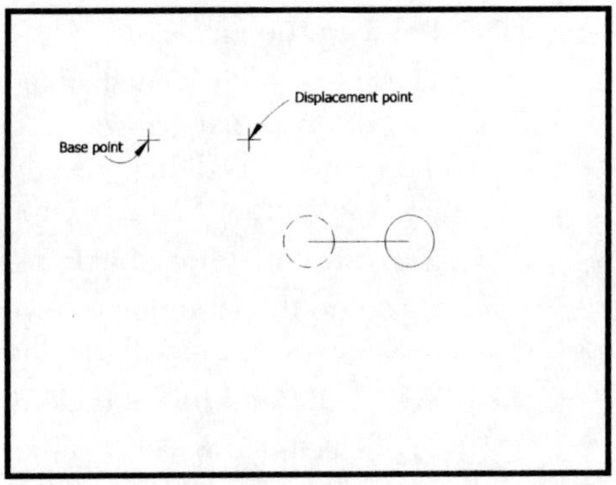

Figure 4.10

- **Pick a point 3.00 to the right of your base point.**

The rubber band and your original circle disappear, leaving you a circle in the new location.

Now, if ortho is on, turn it off (F8) and try a diagonal move.

- **Type "m," or select the Move tool, or press the space bar to repeat the command.**

AutoCAD follows with the "Select objects:" prompt.

- **Reselect the circle.**
- **Right click to end the object selection process.**
- **Select a base point.**
- **Move the circle diagonally in any direction you like.**

Figure 4.11 is an example of how this might look.

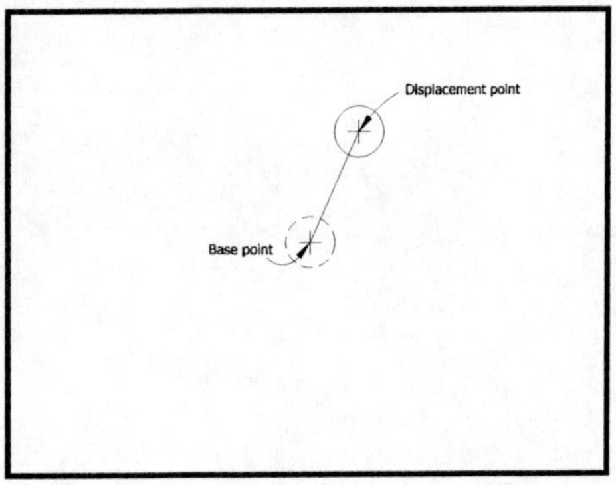

Figure 4.11

Try moving the circle back to the center of the screen.

It may help to choose the center point of the circle as a base point this time, and choose a point at or near the center of the grid for your second point.

4.4.1 Moving with Grips

You can use grips to perform numerous editing procedures without ever entering a command. This is probably the simplest of all editing methods, called autoediting. It does have some limitations, however. In particular, you can only select by pointing, windowing, or crossing.

Point to the circle.

The circle will become highlighted and grips will appear.

Notice that grips for a circle are placed at quadrants and at the center. In more involved editing procedures the choice of which grip or grips to use for editing is significant. In this exercise you will do fine with any of the grips.

Move the pickbox slowly over one of the grips.

If you do this carefully you will notice that the pickbox "locks onto" the grip as it moves over it. You will see this more clearly if snap is off (F9).

When the pickbox is locked on a grip, press the pickbutton.

The selected grip will become filled and change colors (from blue to red).
In the command area you will see this:

** STRETCH **
Specify stretch point or [Base point/Copy/Undo/eXit]:

Stretching is the first of a series of five autoediting modes that you can activate by selecting grips on objects. The word "stretch" has many meanings in AutoCAD, and they are not always what you would expect. For now, we will bypass stretch and use the MOVE mode.

AutoCAD has a convenient shortcut menu for use in grip editing.

Click the right button on your mouse.

This will call up the shortcut menu shown in Figure 4.12. It contains all of the grip edit modes plus several other options.

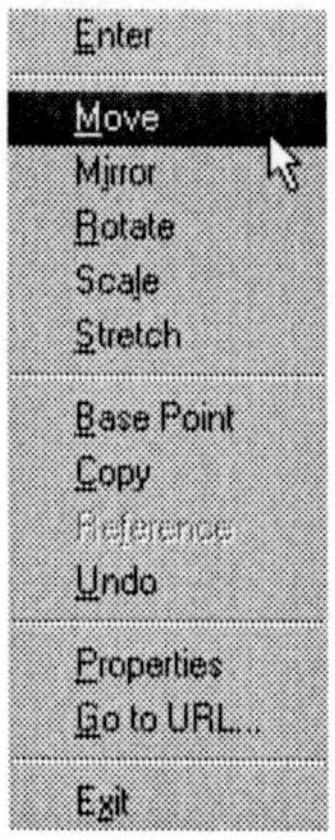

Figure 4.12

Select Move on the shortcut menu.

The pop-up list will disappear and you will be in Move mode. Move the cursor and you will see a rubber band from the selected grip to the same position on a dragged circle. Notice that the prompt has changed to:

** MOVE **
Specify move point or [Base point/Copy/Undo/eXit]:

Pick a point anywhere on the screen.

The circle will move where you have pointed.

4.5 USING THE COPY COMMAND

The COPY command works so much like the MOVE command that you should find it easy to learn at this point, and we will give you fewer instructions. The main difference is that the original object will not disappear when the second point of the displacement vector is given. There is the additional option of making multiple copies of the same object, which we will explore in a moment.

First, we suggest that you try making several copies of the circle in various positions on the screen. Try using both noun/verb and verb/noun sequences.

To initiate COPY, type "co," select Copy from the Modify menu, or select the Copy Object tool from the Modify toolbar, as shown in Figure 4.13.

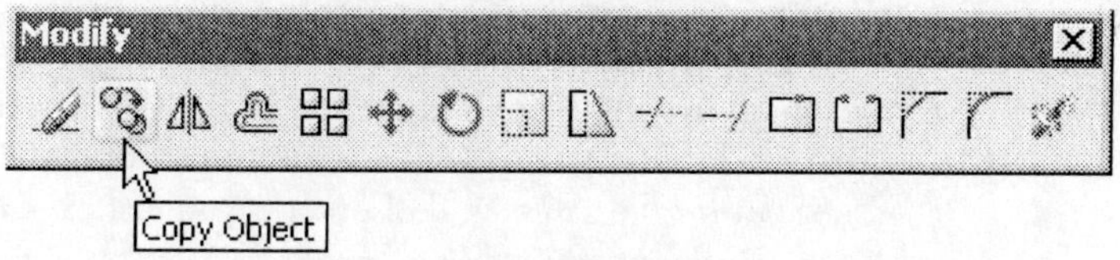

Figure 4.13

Notice that "c" is not an alias for COPY. Also notice that there is a Copy to Clipboard tool on the Standard toolbar that initiates the COPYCLIP command. This tool has a very different function. It is used to copy objects to the Windows Clipboard and then into other applications or drawings. It has no effect on objects within your current drawing, other than to save them on the clipboard.

Make several copies of the circle at different points on the screen, as shown in Figure 4.14.

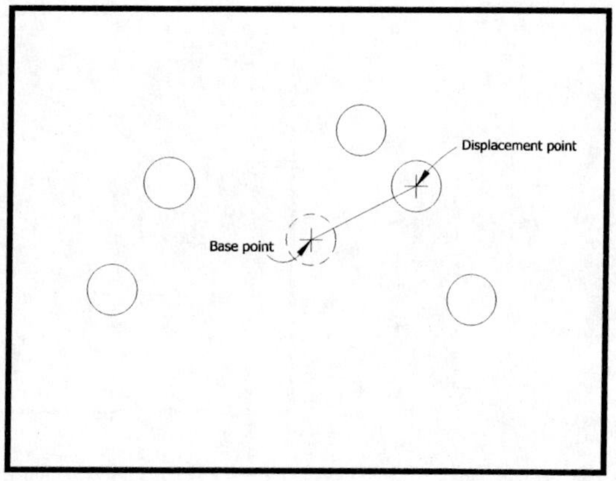

Figure 4.14

When you are satisfied that you know how to use the basic COPY command, move on to the Multiple copy option.

4.5.1 The Multiple Copy Option

This option allows you to show a series of vectors starting at the same base point, with AutoCAD placing copies of your selection set accordingly.

- **Select the Copy tool from the Modify toolbar.**
- **Point to one of the circles on your screen.**
- **Right click to end the selection process.**
- **Type "m" for the Multiple option.**
- **Show AutoCAD a base point.**
- **Show AutoCAD a second point.**

  You will see a new copy of the circle. Notice also that the prompt to "Specify second point of displacement" has returned in the command area. AutoCAD is waiting for another vector, using the same base point as before.
- **Show AutoCAD another second point.**

  Repeat as many times as you wish. If you get into this you may begin to feel like a magician pulling rings out of thin air and scattering them across the screen.

4.5.2 Copying with Grips

The grip editing system includes a variety of special techniques for creating multiple copies in all five modes. The function of the Copy option will differ depending on the grip edit mode. For now we will use the Copy option with the Move mode, which provides a shortcut for the same kind of process you just executed with the COPY command.

Since you should have several circles on your screen now, we will take the opportunity to demonstrate how you can use grips on more than one object at a time. This can be very useful if your drawing contains two or more objects that maintain the same relationship with each other at different locations in your drawing.

- **Pick any two circles.**

  The circles you pick should become highlighted, and grips should appear on both, as illustrated in Figure 4.15.

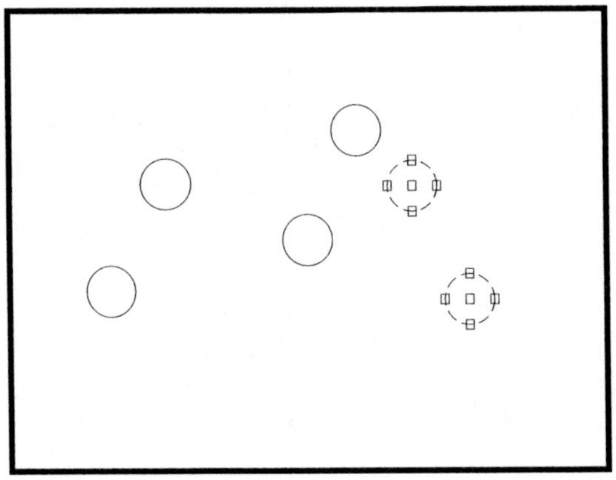

Figure 4.15

- **Pick any grip on either of the two highlighted circles.**

  The grip should change colors. This time we will not use the pop-up menu. In the command area you will see the grip edit prompt for the Stretch mode:

  ** STRETCH **
  Specify stretch point or [/Base point/Copy/Undo/eXit]:

- **Press the space bar.**

  This will bring you to the MOVE mode prompt:

  ** MOVE**
  Specify move point or [/Base point/Copy/Undo/eXit]:

- **Type "c" to initiate copying.**

  The prompt will change to

  ** MOVE (multiple) **
  Specify move point or [/Base point/Copy/Undo/eXit]:

  You will find that all copying in the grip editing system is multiple copying. Once in this mode AutoCAD will continue to create copies wherever you press the pick-button until you exit by typing "x" or pressing the space bar.

- **Move the cursor and observe the two dragged circles.**
- **Pick a point to create copies of the two highlighted circles, as illustrated in Figure 4.16.**

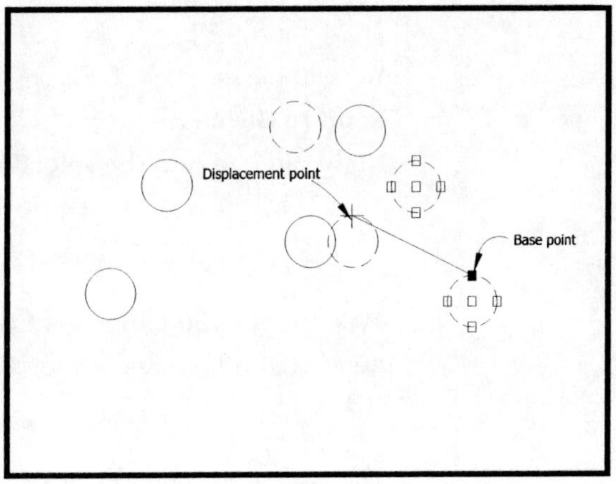

Figure 4.16

- **Pick another point to create two more copies.**
- **When you are through, press Enter or the space bar to exit the grip editing system.**
- **Press Esc twice to remove grips.**

4.6 USING THE ARRAY COMMAND—RECTANGULAR ARRAYS

The ARRAY command gives you a powerful alternative to simple copying. An array is the repetition of an image in matrix form. This command takes an object or group of objects and copies it a specific number of times in mathematically defined, evenly spaced locations.

There are two types of arrays. Rectangular arrays are linear and defined by rows and columns. Polar arrays are angular and based on the repetition of objects around the circumference of an arc or circle. The dots on the grid are an example of a rectangular array; the lines on any circular dial are an example of a polar array. Both types are common. We will explore rectangular arrays in this chapter and polar arrays in the next.

In preparation for this exercise, erase all the circles from your screen. This is a good opportunity to try the ERASE All option.

- **Type "e" or select the Erase tool from the Modify toolbar.**
- **Type "all."**
- **Press Enter.**
- **Now draw a single circle, radius 0.5, centered at the point (2, 2).**
- **Type "Ar" or select Array from the Modify menu, or the Array tool from the Modify toolbar, as shown in Figure 4.17.**

Figure 4.17

You will see the "Select objects" prompt.

- **Point to the circle.**
- **Right click to end the selection process.**

AutoCAD will ask which type of array you want:

Enter the type of array [Rectangular/Polar]<R>:

- **Type "r," or you can press Enter if R is the default.**

AutoCAD will prompt you for the number of rows in the array.

Enter the number of rows (---) <1>:

The (---) is to remind you of what a row looks like (i.e., it is horizontal). The default is 1. So if you press Enter you will get a single row of circles. The number of circles in the row will depend, then, on the number of columns you specify. We will ask for three rows instead of just one.

- **Type "3."**

AutoCAD now asks for the number of columns in the array:

Enter the number of columns (| | | |) <1>:

Using the same format (|||), AutoCAD reminds you that columns are vertical. The default is 1 again. What would an array with three rows and only one column look like?

We will construct a five-column array.

- **Type "5."**

Now AutoCAD needs to know how far apart to place all these circles. There will be 15 of them in this example—three rows with five circles in each row. AutoCAD prompts

Enter the distance between rows or specify unit cell (---):

"Unit cell" means that you can respond by showing two corners of a window. The horizontal side of this window would give the space between columns; the vertical side would give the space between rows. You could do this exercise by showing a 1 × 1 window. We will use the more basic method of typing values for these distances. The distance between rows will be a vertical measure.

Type "1."

AutoCAD now asks for the horizontal distance between columns:

Specify the distance between columns (|||):

Type "1" again.

You should have a 3 × 5 array of circles, as shown in Figure 4.18.

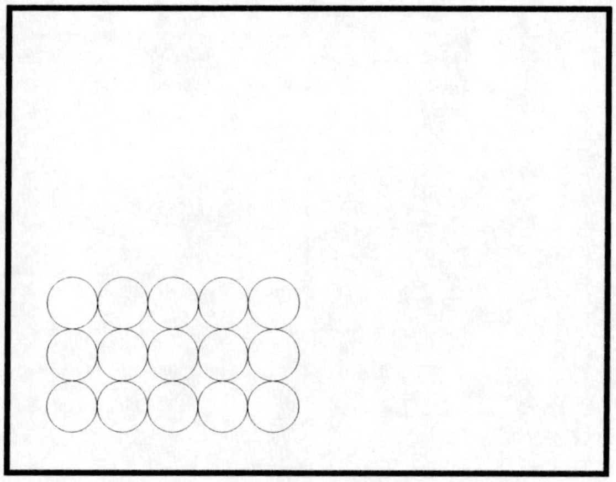

Figure 4.18

Notice that AutoCAD builds arrays up and to the right. This is consistent with the coordinate system, which puts positive values to the right on the horizontal x axis, and upward on the vertical y axis. Negative values can be used to create arrays in other directions.

4.7 CHANGING PLOT SETTINGS

In the previous chapter you began using full and partial plot previews. In this chapter we will complete the exploration of many of the basic options in the Plot dialog box. There is a lot of information here, so walk through the material carefully and try out the options and previews as suggested. We have used no specific drawing for illustration. Now that you know how to use plot preview, you can observe the effects of changing plot parameters with any drawing you like and decide at any point whether you actually want to print out the results. We will continue to remind you to look at a plot preview after making changes. Plot previewing will save you a lot of time, paper, and will speed up your learning curve.

⌖ **To begin this exploration, you should have a drawing or drawn objects on your screen so that you can observe the effects of various changes you will be making. The drawing you are in should use the 1B template so that Limits are set to 18 × 12.**

⌖ **Select Plot... from the File pull-down menu, or the Plot tool from the Standard toolbar.**

This will open up the Plot dialog box.

4.7.1 The Plot Device Tab

We will begin by looking into the Plot Device tab before we return to conclude the discussion of plot settings.

⌖ **Click on the Plot Device tab.**

This will call the dialog box shown in Figure 4.19. The first panel within this tab will show whatever plotter or printer is currently selected in your system and will probably be different from ours.

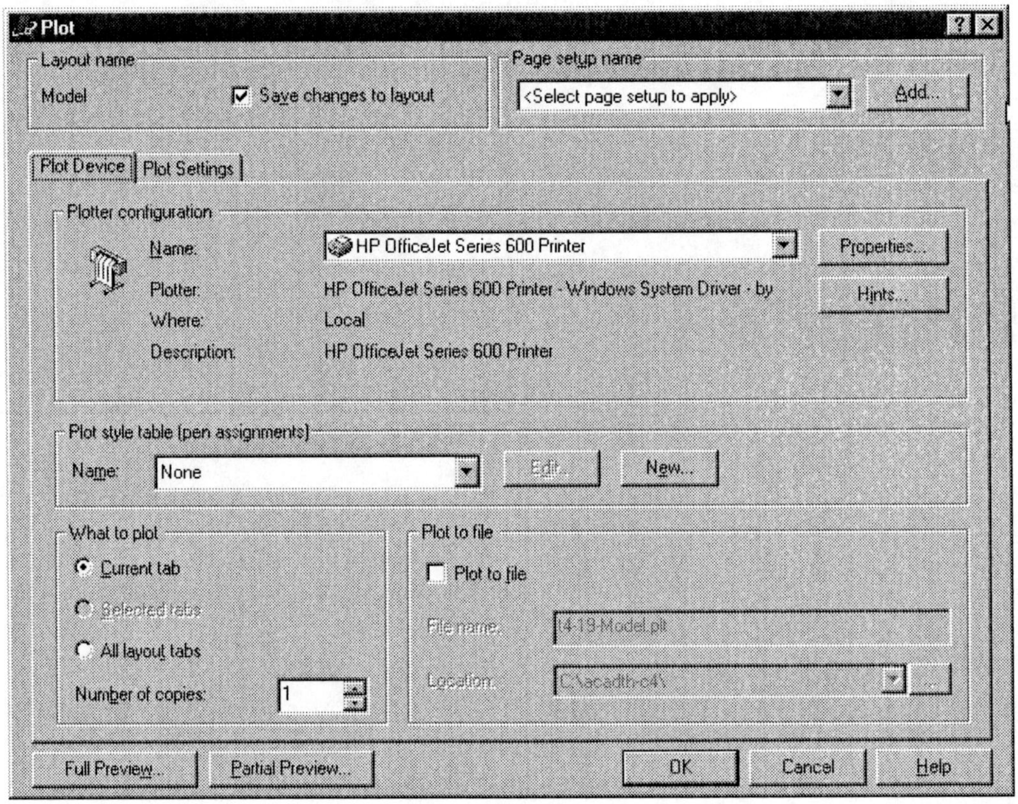

Figure 4.19

⌖ **Click on the arrow at the right to open the plotter name list.**

The list you see will depend on your system and may include printers, plotters, and any faxing devices you have, along with AutoCAD's DWF Classic and Eplot utilities, which may be used to send plotting information to the Internet.

4.7.2 The Add A Plotter Wizard

For a thorough exploration of AutoCAD plotting it will be important that you have at least one plotter available. If you have only a printer, you will probably be somewhat limited in the range of drawing sheets available. You may not have a B-size option, for example. For the exercises in this book, you can use the DWF ePlot utility to simulate a plotter, or you can use the Add A Plotter Wizard to install one of the AutoCAD standard plotter drivers, even if you actually have no such plotter on your system. To add a plotter, follow this procedure:

1. Close the Plot dialog box
2. From the File menu, select Plotter Manager....
3. From the Plotters box, select the Add A Plotter Wizard....
4. Click Next on the Introduction page.
5. Check to see that My Computer is selected on the Add Plotter-Begin page, then click Next.
6. On the Plotter Model page, select a manufacturer and a model, then click Next.
7. Click Next on the Import Pcp or Pc2 page.
8. Click Next on the Ports page.
9. Click Next on the Plotter Name page.
10. Click Finish on the Finish page.

When the Wizard is done, the new plotting device will be added to your list of plotting devices.

⌖ **If you have left the Plot dialog to install a plotter driver, reenter it by selecting the plot tool from the Standard toolbar. Click the Plot Device tab if necessary, then open the list of plotting devices.**

⌖ **From the list of plotting devices, select a plotter or the DWF ePlot utility to simulate a plotter.**

NOTE: Whenever you change plotting devices, it is likely that you will see a warning that says "The paper size in the layout is not supported by the selected plotting device. The layout will use the paper size specified by the plotting device." Click OK to move on.

4.7.3 Plot Styles

Below the Plotter Configuration panel of the Plot Device tab you will see the Plot Style table area. Most of the time you will not need to work with a plot style because plotters and printers are configured to produce colors, linetypes, and lineweights just as they appear on your screen. Plot styles come into play when you want to present your drawing in a manner different from the way you have drawn it. Plot styles essentially override the color, linetype, and lineweight setting of objects and layers in your drawing. This allows you to completely change the presentation of objects in your drawing without changing anything in the drawing itself. Since plot styles can be named and saved, you can use several different plot styles with a single drawing to create a variety of different presentations. Plot styles can also be saved and transferred from one drawing to another so that a wide variety of presentation styles may be quickly applied with a few clicks of the mouse and without actually changing the drawing. Plot styles offer a lot of power and flexibility, but can be ignored most of the time when you are creating your drawing in the way you want it to appear.

4.7.4 What to Plot

At the bottom left of the Plot Device dialog you will see a panel labeled "What to plot." The choices are Current tab, Selected tab, or All layout tabs. The tabs referred to are those at the bottom of your drawing area, to the left of the horizontal scroll bar, labeled "Model" and "Layout1." At this time we are making use of only the Model tab, which will also be the current tab as long as you are in model space. Once you have more than one tab active in your drawing you can choose to plot them one at a time or all at once using these options. You also have the option of printing multiple copies.

4.7.5 Plot to File

To the right of "What to plot" you will see the "Plot to file" panel. AutoCAD plot information may be sent to a plot file so that it can be plotted at a later time or sent to another site for plotting. Plots saved to a file are given the same name as the drawing but with a .plt extension.

We will now return to the Plot Settings tab to complete our exploration of the PLOT dialog box.

⌗ **Click on the Plot Settings tab.**

You should now have a plotter selected that will give you a number of paper size options.

⌗ **From the Paper size list, below the plotter name list, select a B size drawing sheet.**

The exact size will depend on the plotter you have selected. An ANSII B (17 × 11) sheet will be a common choice.

4.7.6 Drawing Orientation

There are basically two options for drawing orientation, Portrait, in which the short edge of the paper is across the bottom, and Landscape, in which the long edge is across the bottom. Portrait is typical of a letter or printed sheet of text, Landscape is typical of a drawing sheet. Your plotting device has a default orientation, but you can print either way using the radio buttons. Drawing orientation will obviously have a major impact on how the plotting area of the page is used, so be sure to check out the partial preview any time you switch orientations. Try this:

⌗ **Do a partial preview to see how your current drawing orientation is interpreted.**

⌗ **Switch from Landscape to Portrait, or vice versa.**

⌗ **Do a second partial preview to see how drawing orientation changes the plot.**

TIP: On some plotters you will have a choice of different paper orientations. You may have an 11 × 17 and a 17 × 11 option, for example. In this case there should be a correlation between the paper you choose and the drawing orientation. If you are plotting in Landscape, select the 17 × 11, in Portrait, select the 11 × 17. Otherwise your paper setting will be 90° off from your drawing orientation and things will get confusing.

⌗ **For this task, check to see that your drawing orientation is set to Landscape.**

This will be the default for most plotters.

4.7.7 Plot Area

Look at the Plot area panel at the left of the Plot settings dialog. This is a crucial area of the dialog box that allows you to specify the portion of your drawing to be plotted. Other options include Limits, Extents, Display, and View. Changes here will have a significant impact on the effective plotting area. Be sure to use plot preview any time you make changes in these parameters.

The radio buttons on the left show the options for plotting area. "Limits," as you know, are specified using the LIMITS command or a setup Wizard. If you are using our standard B-size template, and the Limits radio button is selected, the plot area will be 18 × 12. "Extents" refers to the actual drawing area in which you have drawn objects. It may be larger or smaller than the limits of the drawing. "Display" will create a plot using whatever is actually on the screen. If you used the ZOOM command to enlarge a portion of the drawing before entering PLOT and then selected this option, AutoCAD would plot whatever is showing in your drawing window. "View" will be accessible only after you have defined named views in the drawing using the VIEW command. "Window" will not be accessible until you define a window, as you have done previously in other drawings.

⌗ **Try switching among Limits, Extents, Display, and Window selections and use plot preview to see the results. Use both partial and full previews to ensure that you clearly see what is happening.**

Whenever you make a change, also observe the changes in the boxes showing inches = drawing Units. Assuming that "Scaled to Fit" is checked, you will see significant changes in these scale ratios as AutoCAD adjusts scales according to the area it is being asked to plot.

4.7.8 Plot Scale

Plot scale has many options, but most of the time you will only need two very simple settings. In model space you will usually use "Scaled to fit." In paper space you will use 1:1.

When you are plotting from model space you will use "Scaled to fit" since there may be no logical relation between model space units, which are determined by the real world size of objects, and the size of the paper you are using. The most important consideration will be fitting the drawing to the drawing sheet, which is best accomplished using the "Scaled to fit" option. If you have a need for a precise drawing unit to paper unit ratio, you can find many options on the Scale list, or type in a custom option. In all cases, the scale ratio will be given with the paper unit first followed by the drawing unit. For example, 1:2 will mean that 1 inch on the drawing sheet will represent two drawing units.

⌗ **Try changing the scale selection to 1:2 and observe the effect in a partial preview. Try other options if you like and then return to "Scaled to fit."**

4.7.9 Plot Offset

The Plot offset panel is at the bottom middle of the Plot Settings dialog. Plot offset determines the way the Plot area is positioned on the drawing sheet. Specifically, it determines where the plot origin is placed. To understand plot offset, it is best to use Partial preview and observe the location of the red triangle which marks the plot origin. The default locates the origin point (0, 0) at the lower left of the plotted area and determines other locations from there. If you enter a different offset specification, (2, 3) for example, then the origin point of the drawing area will be positioned at this point instead, and plot locations determined from there. This will have a dramatic effect on the placement of objects on paper.

The other option in Plot offset is to Center the plot. In this case AutoCAD will position the drawing so that the center point of the plot area coincides with the center point of the drawing sheet. Try this:

⌗ **Try various plot offset combinations, including "Center the plot," and use plot preview to see the results.**

Be sure to use partial previews and observe the red origin triangle to ensure that you clearly see what is happening.

4.7.10 Plot Options

This last area of the Plot settings tabs has four settings that can be turned on or off. Plot with lineweights determines whether lineweights that have been specified in your drawing will be used in plotting, or if all lines will be given the same default weight. This is just like the LWT button on the taskbar, but it is for plotting rather than screen display. Depending on your application, you may want to keep to the default lineweights in early drafts of a drawing and save the full lineweight plot for final versions.

Similarly, plot styles may be ignored in early drafts and turned on later when you want to create a specific presentation effect. Plot styles are essentially tables of plotting characteristics which can be defined, named, saved, and attached to objects or layers. They override layer specifications and can therefore be used to create very different plots of the same drawing.

"Plot paperspace last" will not be accessible until you have defined at least one paper space layout. We will continue to plot from model space for now, but later this option will cause your plotter to draw the model space objects in your drawing before it draws the titles, text, and annotation objects that may exist in your paperspace layout.

This completes our discussion of basic model space plotting options. With a little practice you should be able to plot any area of any drawing in model space and position it on any size drawing sheet so that it is well presented.

4.8 REVIEW MATERIAL

Questions

1. What command is automated through the first four steps of the Advanced Setup Wizard?
2. Name at least five settings that would typically be included in a Template drawing.
3. Where are template drawings stored in a standard AutoCAD file configuration? What extension is given to template file names?
4. What is the value of using a template drawing?
5. What is the main difference between the command procedure for MOVE and that for COPY?
6. What is the main limitation of grip editing?
7. What do you have to do to remove grips from an object once they are displayed?
8. How do you access the grip edit shortcut menu?
9. Explain how arrays are a special form of copying.
10. What is a rectangular array? What is a polar array?
11. Why is it important to do a partial plot preview after changing plot area or plot offset?

Commands

ARRAY (rectangular)	COPY	LIMITS
MOVE		

PROFESSIONAL SUCCESS

What is the Correct Procedure?

A group of twenty students given an AutoCAD assignment would be expected to produce drawings that are nearly identical to each other. It would be surprising, however, if any of them used the exact same sequence of commands to produce their drawings.

It is very important to understand that AutoCAD is a means to an end—that is, it is the appearance and precision of the final drawing that matters, and not the specific sequence of commands used to produce it. For example, there are at least twelve possible command sequences that can be used to draw a rectangle:

Lines may be used to draw the four sides separately. The LINE command may be chosen from either the pull-down menus or the toolbox, or it may be typed directly into the command area.

The complete rectangle may be drawn at once by using any of the above three methods to invoke the RECTANGLE command.

Coordinates necessary to complete either the LINE or RECTANGLE commands may either be typed in on the command line, or specified directly via the mouse or tablet.

4.9 DRAWING PROBLEMS

1. Create a C-size drawing template using an ANSI standard sheet size, layers, and other settings as shown in this chapter. Start with your 1B template settings to make this process easier.
2. Open a drawing with your new C-size template and draw a circle with a two-unit radius centered at (11, 8).
3. Using grips, make four copies of the circle, centered at (15, 8), (11, 12), (7, 8), and (11, 4).
4. Switch to Layer 2 and draw a 1×1 square with lower left corner at (1, 1).
5. Create a rectangular array of the square with 14 rows and 20 columns, one unit between rows, and one unit between columns.

DRAWING 1

Grill

This drawing should go very quickly if you use the ARRAY command.

Drawing Suggestions

GRID = 0.5

SNAP = 0.25

- Begin with a 4.75 × 4.75 square.
- Move in 0.25 all around to create the inside square.
- Draw the rectangle in the lower left-hand corner first; then use the ARRAY command to create the rest.

Also remember that you can undo a misplaced array using the U command.

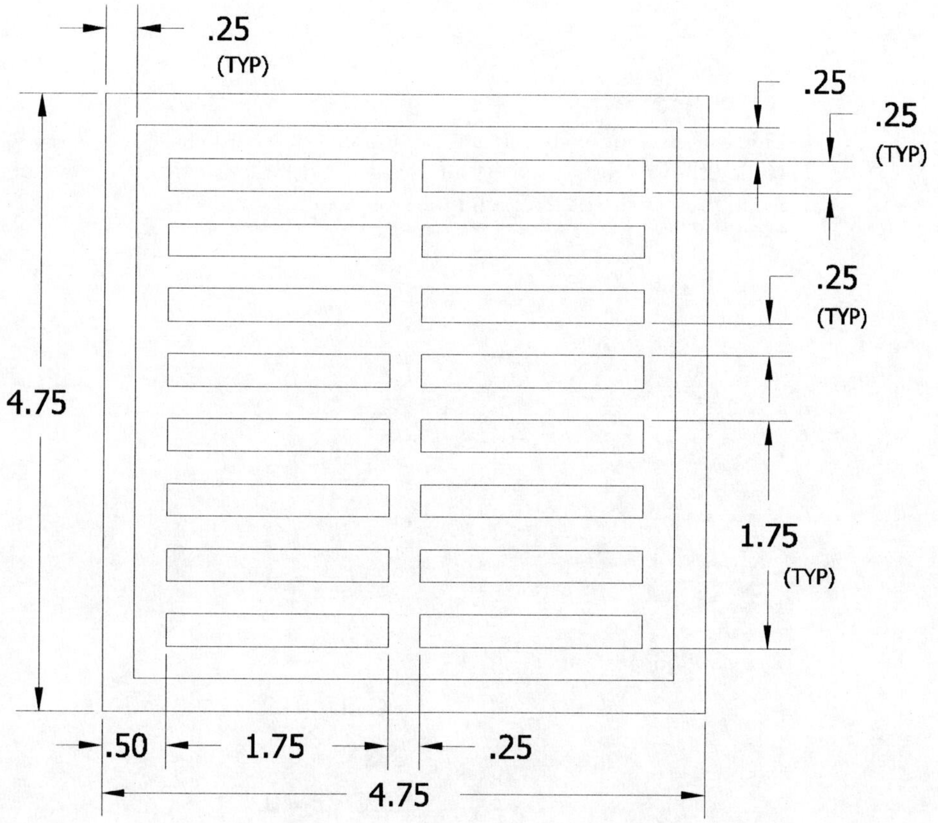

GRILL

DRAWING 2

Test Bracket

This is a great drawing for practicing much of what you have learned up to this point. Notice the suggested snap, grid, ltscale, and limit settings, and use the ARRAY command to draw the 25 circles on the front view.

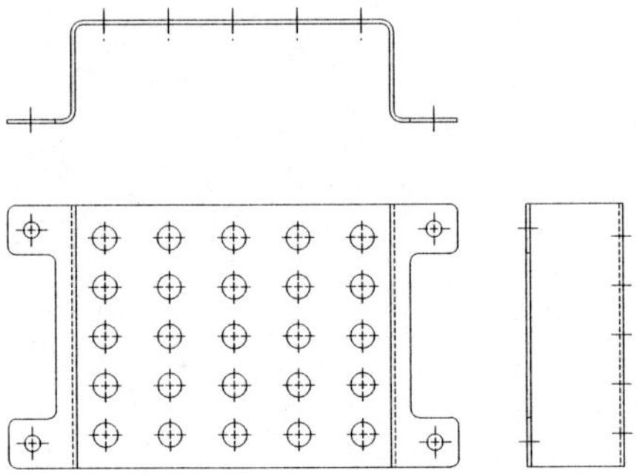

Drawing Suggestions

GRID = 0.25

SNAP = 0.125

LTSCALE = 0.50

LIMITS = (0,0) (24,18)

- Be careful to draw all lines on the correct layers, according to their linetypes.
- Draw center lines through circles before copying or arraying them; otherwise you will have to go back and draw them on each individual circle or repeat the array process.
- A multiple copy will work nicely for the four 0.50-diameter holes. A rectangular array is definitely desirable for the twenty-five 0.75-diameter holes.

Creating Center Marks With the Dimcen System Variable There is a simple way to create the center marks and center lines shown on all the circles in this drawing. It involves changing the value of a dimension variable called "dimcen" (dimension center). The following procedure will work nicely in this drawing.

1. Type "dimcen." The default setting for dimcen is 0.09, which will cause AutoCAD to draw a simple cross as a center mark. Changing it to −0.09 will tell AutoCAD to draw a cross that reaches across the circle.
2. Type "−.09."
3. After drawing your first circle, and before arraying it, type "dim." This will put you in the dimension command.
4. Type "cen," indicating that you want to draw a center mark. This is a very simple dimension feature.
5. Point to the circle.
6. Press the Esc key to quit the DIM command.

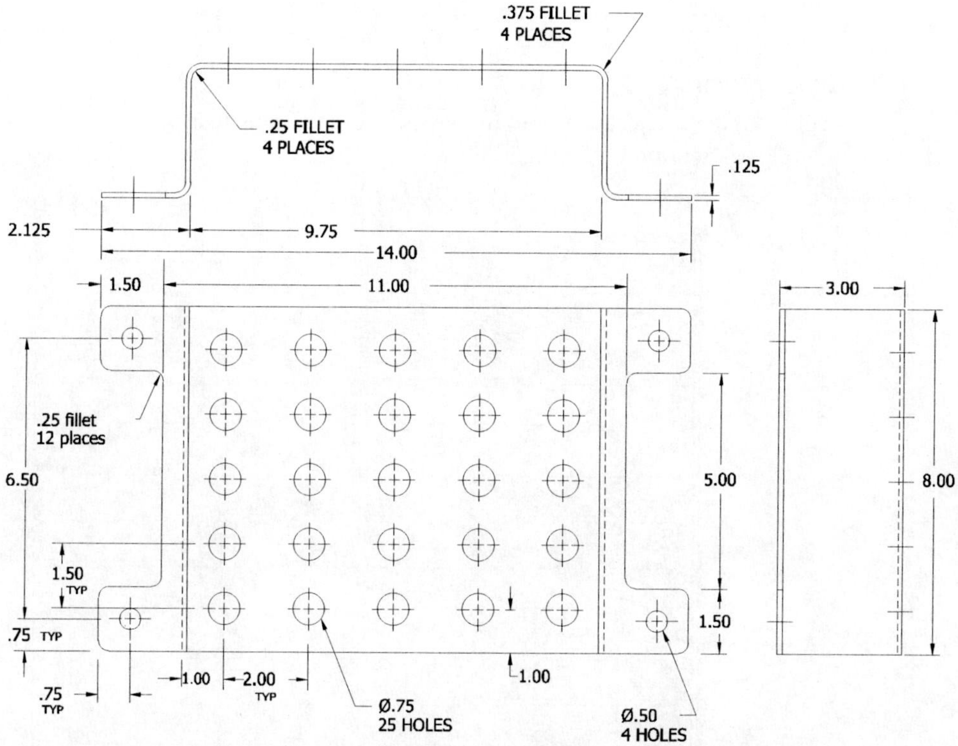

TEST BRACKET

DRAWING 3

Floor Framing

This architectural drawing will require changes in many features of your drawing setup. Pay close attention to the suggested settings.

Drawing Suggestions

UNITS = Architectural, smallest fraction = 1"

LIMITS = 36", 24"

GRID = 1'

SNAP = 2"

LTSCALE = 12

- Be sure to use foot (') and inch (") symbols when setting limits, grid, and snap (but not ltscale).
- Begin by drawing the 20' × 17'-10" rectangle, with the lower left corner somewhere in the neighborhood of (4', 4').
- Complete the left and right 2 × 10 joists by copying the vertical 17'-10" lines 2" in from each side. You may find it helpful to use the arrow keys when working with such small increments.
- Draw a 19'-8" horizontal line 2" up from the bottom and copy it 2" higher to complete the double joists.
- Array the inner 2 × 10 in a 14" row by 1-column array, with 16" between rows.
- Set to Layer 2 and draw the three 17'-4" hidden lines down the center.

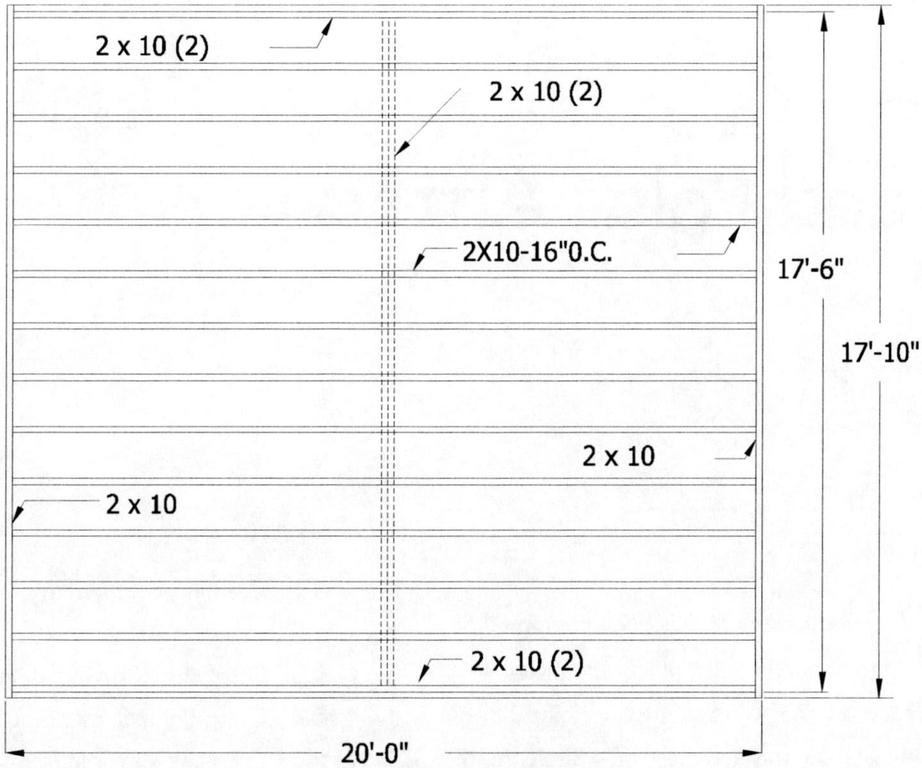

FLOOR FRAMING

5

Arcs and Polar Arrays

OVERVIEW

So far, every drawing you have done has been composed of lines and circles. In this chapter you will learn a third major entity, the ARC. In addition, you will expand your ability to manipulate objects on the screen. You will learn to ROTATE objects and create their MIRROR images. You will learn to save Plot settings as named Page setups. But first, we will pick up where we left off in Chapter 4 by showing you how to create polar arrays.

SECTIONS

OBJECTIVES

After reading this chapter, you should be able to:

- Create three polar arrays.
- Draw arcs in eight different ways.
- Rotate a previously drawn object.
- Use polar tracking at Any angle.
- Create mirror images of previously drawn objects.
- Change page setups.
- Draw dials
- Draw an alignment wheel.
- Draw a hearth.

5.1 CREATING POLAR ARRAYS

The procedure for creating polar arrays is lengthy and requires some explanation. The first two steps are the same as in rectangular arrays. Step 3 is also the same, except that you respond with "p" instead of "r." From here on the steps will be new. First you will pick a center point, and then you will have several options for defining the array.

There are three qualities that define a polar array, but two are sufficient. A polar array is defined by two of the following: (1) a certain number of items, (2) an angle that these items span, and (3) an angle between each item and the next. However you define your polar array, you will have to tell AutoCAD whether or not to rotate the newly created objects as they are copied.

- **Begin a new drawing using the 1B template.**
- **In preparation for this exercise, draw a vertical 1.00 line at the bottom center of the screen, near (9.00, 2.00), as shown in Figure 5.1.**

Figure 5.1

We will use a 360 degree polar array to create Figure 5.2.

Figure 5.2

- **Type "Ar," select Array from the Modify menu, or select the Array tool from the Modify toolbar, as illustrated in Figure 5.3.**

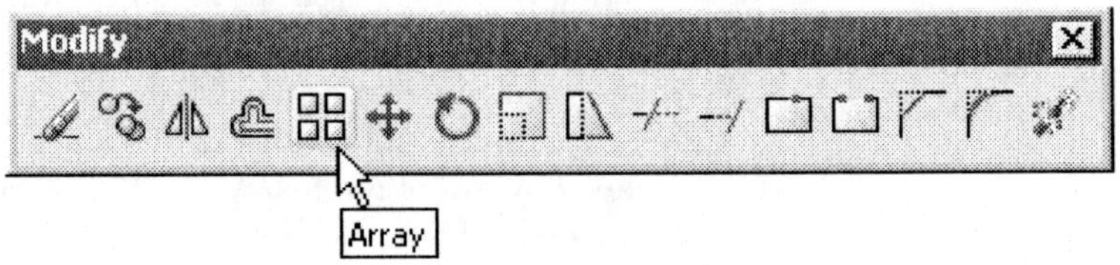

Figure 5.3

- **Select the line.**

So far, so good. Nothing new up to this point.

- **Type "p."**

Now you have a prompt that looks like this:

Specify center point of array:

Rectangular arrays are not determined by a center, so we did not encounter this prompt before. Polar arrays, however, are built by copying objects around the circumferences of circles or arcs, so we need a center to define one of these. We will also need to specify whether objects should be rotated as they are copied.

- **Pick a point directly above the line and somewhat below the center of the screen.**

Something in the neighborhood of (9.00, 4.50) will do. The next prompt is

Enter the number of items in the array:

Remember that we have a choice of two out of three among number of items, angle to fill, and angle between items. This time we will give AutoCAD the first two.

- **Type "12."**

Now that AutoCAD knows that we want 12 items, all it needs is either the angle to fill with these, or the angle between the items. It will ask first for the angle to fill:

Specify the angle to fill (+=ccw,−=cw) <360>:

The symbols in parentheses tell us that if we give a positive angle, the array will be constructed counterclockwise; if we give a negative angle, it will be constructed clockwise. Get used to this; it will come up frequently.

The default is 360 degrees, meaning an array that fills a complete circle.

If we did not give AutoCAD an angle (that is, if we responded with a "0"), we would be prompted for the angle between. This time around we will give 360 as the angle to fill.

- **Press Enter to accept the default, a complete circle.**

AutoCAD now has everything it needs, except that it doesn't know whether we want our lines to retain their vertical orientation or to be rotated along with the angular displacement as they are copied. AutoCAD prompts:

Rotate arrayed objects [Yes/No] <Y>:

Notice the default, which we will accept.

⌗ **Press Enter or type "y."**
Your screen should resemble Figure 5.2.

This ends our discussion of polar arrays. With the options AutoCAD gives you, there are many possibilities that you may want to try out. As always, we encourage experimentation. When you are satisfied, erase everything on the screen in preparation for learning the ARC command.

5.2 DRAWING ARCS

Learning AutoCAD's ARC command is an exercise in geometry. In this section we will give you a firm foundation for understanding and drawing arcs so that you will not be confused by all the options that are available. The information we give you will be more than enough to do the drawings in this chapter and most drawings you will encounter elsewhere. Refer to the AutoCAD Command Reference and the chart at the end of this section (Figure 5.4) if you need additional information.

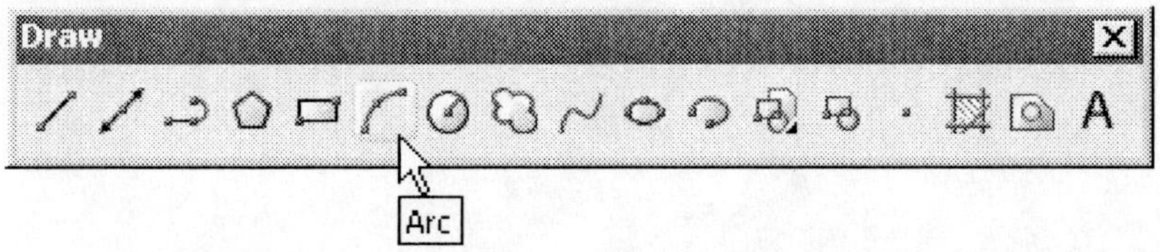

Figure 5.4

AutoCAD gives you eight distinct ways to draw arcs, eleven if you count variations in order. Every option requires you to specify three pieces of information: where to begin the arc, where to end it, and what circle it is theoretically a part of.

We will begin by drawing an arc using the simplest method, which is also the default the three-points option. The geometric key to this method is that any three-points not on the same line determine a circle or an arc of a circle. AutoCAD uses this in the CIRCLE command (the 3P option) as well as in the ARC command.

⌗ **Type "a" or select the Arc tool from the Draw toolbar, as shown in Figure 5.4.**
AutoCAD's response will be this prompt:

Specify start point of arc or [Center]:

Accepting the default by specifying a point will leave open all those options in which the start point is specified first.

If you instead type a "c," AutoCAD will prompt for a center point and follow with those options that begin with a center.

⌗ **Select a starting point near the center of the screen.**
AutoCAD prompts:

Specify second point of arc or [Center/End]:

We will continue to follow the default three-point sequence by specifying a second point. You may want to refer to the chart (Figure 5.5) as you draw this arc.

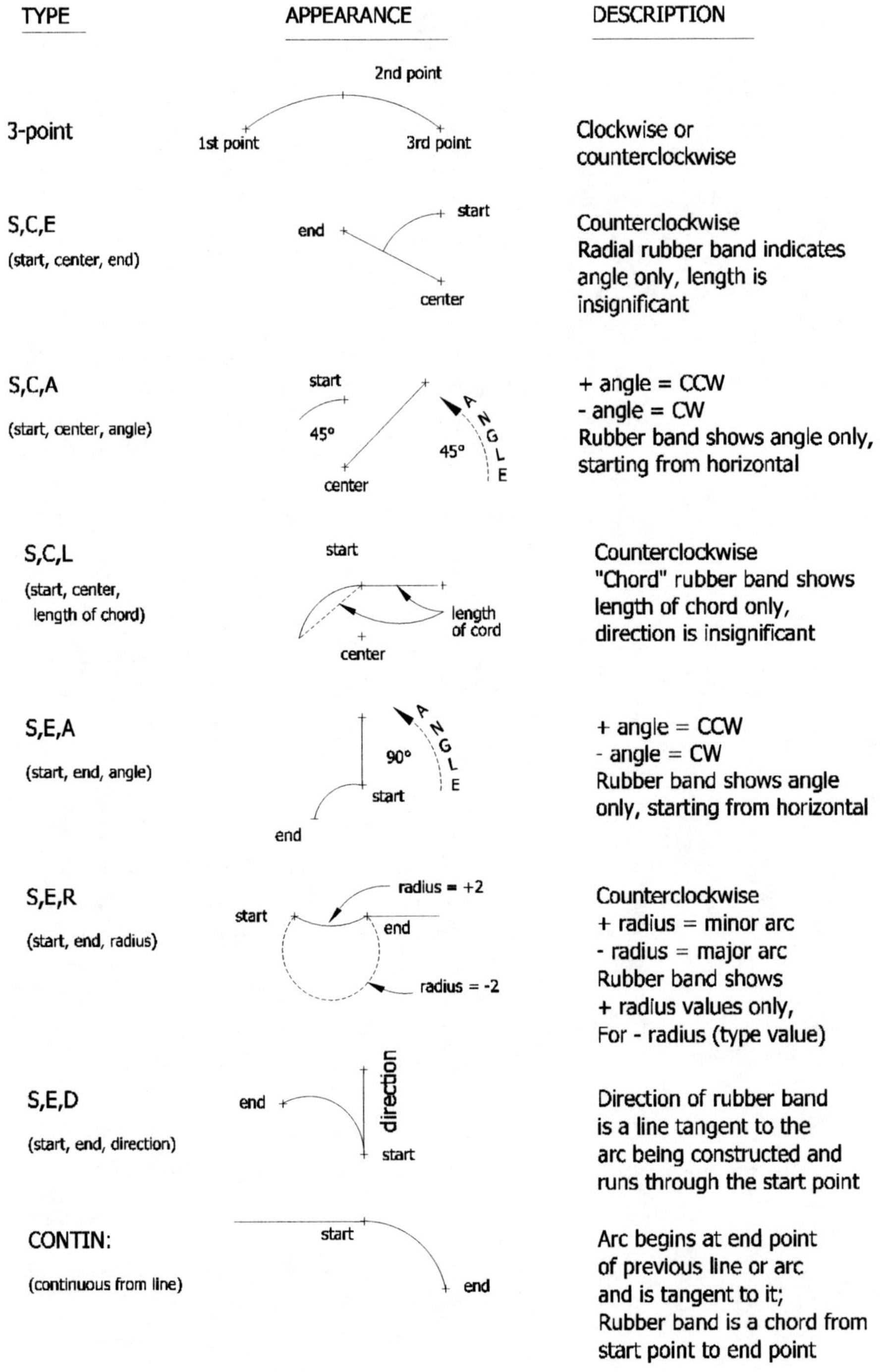

Figure 5.5

⌖ **Select any point one or two units away from the previous point. Exact coordinates are not important.**

Once AutoCAD has two points, it gives you an arc to drag. By moving the cursor slowly in a circle and in and out, you can see the range of what the third point will produce.

AutoCAD also knows now that you have to provide an endpoint to complete the arc, so the prompt has only one option:

Specify endpoint of arc:

Any point you select will do, as long as it produces an arc that fits on the screen.

⌖ **Pick an endpoint.**

As you can see, three-point arcs are easy to draw. It is much like drawing a line, except that you have to specify three points instead of two. In practice, however, you do not always have three points to use this way. This necessitates the broad range of options in the ARC command. The dimensions you are given and the objects already drawn will determine what options are useful to you.

Next, we will create an arc using the start, center, end method, the second option illustrated in Figure 5.5.

⌖ **Type "U" to undo the three-point arc.**

⌖ **Type "a" or select the Arc tool.**

⌖ **Select a point near the center of the screen as a start point.**

The prompt that follows is the same as for the three-point option, but we will not use the default this time:

Specify second point of arc or [Center/End]:

We will choose the Center option.

TIP: If you choose options from the Draw menu, you will find some steps automated. If you select "Start, Center, End," for example, the "c" will be entered automatically.

⌖ **Type "c," if necessary.**

This tells AutoCAD that we want to specify a center point next, so we see this prompt:

Specify center point of arc:

⌖ **Select any point roughly one to three units away from the start point.**

The circle from which the arc is to be cut is now clearly determined. All that is left is to specify how much of the circle to take, which can be done in one of three ways, as the prompt indicates:

Specify end point of arc or [Angle/ chord Length]:

We will specify an endpoint by typing coordinates or pointing. But first, move the cursor slowly in a circle and in and out to see how the method works. As before, there is an arc to drag, and now there is a radial direction rubber band as well. If you pick a point anywhere along this rubber band, AutoCAD will assume that you want the point where it crosses the circumference of the circle.

NOTE: Here, as in the polar arrays in this chapter, AutoCAD is building arcs counterclockwise, consistent with its coordinate system.

⌖ **Select an endpoint to complete the arc.**

Now that you have tried three of the basic methods for constructing an arc, we strongly suggest that you study the chart in Figure 5.5 and then try out the other options. The notes in the right-hand column will serve as a guide to what to look for.

The differences in the use of the rubber band from one option to the next can be confusing. You should understand, for instance, that in some cases the linear rubber band is only significant as a distance indicator; its angle is of no importance and is ignored by AutoCAD. In other cases it is just the reverse; the length of the rubber band is irrelevant, while its angle of rotation is important.

TIP: One additional trick you should try out as you experiment with arcs is as follows: If you press Enter or the space bar at the "Specify start point [Center]:" prompt, AutoCAD will use the endpoint of the last line or arc you drew as the new starting point and construct an arc tangent to it. This is the same as the Continue option on the pull-down menu.

This completes the present discussion of the ARC command. Constructing arcs, as you may have realized, can be tricky. Another option that is available and often useful is to draw a complete circle and then use the TRIM or BREAK commands to cut out the arc you want. BREAK and TRIM are introduced in the next chapter.

5.3 USING THE ROTATE COMMAND

ROTATE is a fairly straightforward command, and it has some uses that might not be apparent immediately. For example, it frequently is easier to draw an object in a horizontal or vertical position and then ROTATE it rather than drawing it in a diagonal position.

In addition to the ROTATE command, there is a rotate mode in the grip edit system, which we will introduce later in this section.

⌖ **In preparation for this exercise, clear your screen and draw a three-point arc using the points (8, 4), (11.5, 2), and (15, 4), as in Figure 5.6.**

Figure 5.6

We will begin by rotating the arc to the position shown in Figure 5.7.

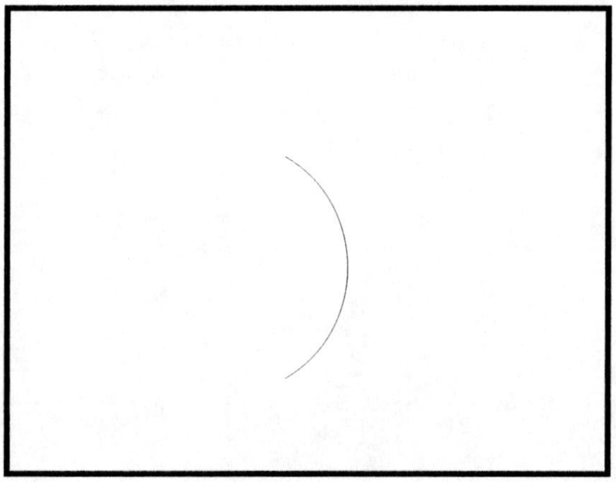

Figure 5.7

- **Select the arc.**
- **Type "Ro," select Rotate from the Modify menu, or select the Rotate tool from the Modify toolbar, as shown in Figure 5.8.**

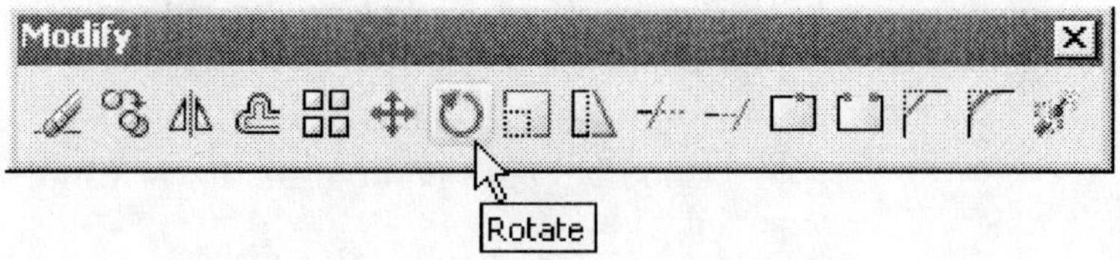

Figure 5.8

You will be prompted for a base point:

Specify base point:

This will be the point around which the object is rotated. The results of the rotation, therefore, are dramatically affected by your choice of base point. We will choose a point at the left tip of the arc.

- **Point to the left tip of the arc.**

The prompt that follows looks like this:

Specify rotation angle or [Reference]:

The default method is used to indicate a rotation angle directly. The object will be rotated through the angle specified and the original object will be deleted.

Move the cursor in a circle and you will see that you have a copy of the object to drag into place visually. If ortho or snap are on, turn them off to see the complete range of rotation.

- **Type "90" or point to a rotation of 90 degrees (use F6 if your coordinate display is not showing polar coordinates).**

The results should resemble Figure 5.7.

Notice that when specifying the rotation angle directly like this, the original orientation of the selected object is taken to be 0 degrees. The rotation is figured counterclockwise from there. However, there may be times when you want to refer to the coordinate system in specifying rotation. This is the purpose of the "Reference" option. To use it, all you need to do is specify the present orientation of the object relative to the coordinate system, and then tell AutoCAD the orientation you want it to have after rotation. Look at Figure 5.9. To rotate the arc as shown, you either can indicate a rotation of −45 degrees or tell AutoCAD that it is presently oriented to 90 degrees and you want it rotated to 45 degrees. Try this method for practice.

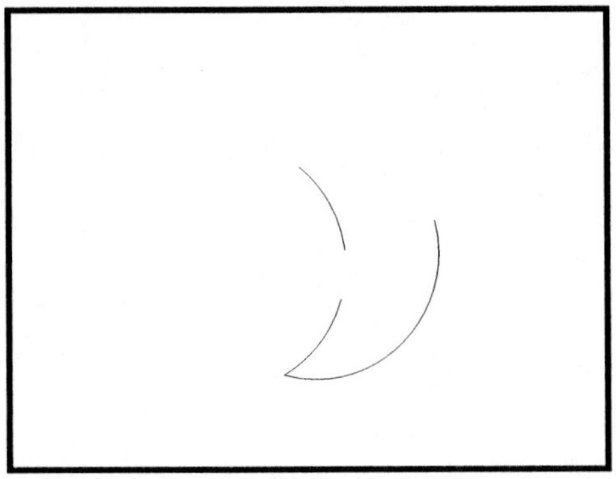

Figure 5.9

- **Repeat the ROTATE command.**
- **Select the arc.**
- **Right click to end selection.**
- **Choose a base point at the lower tip of the arc.**
- **Type "r."**

  AutoCAD will prompt for a reference angle:

  Specify the reference angle <0>:

- **Type "90."**

  AutoCAD prompts:

  Specify the new angle:

- **Type "45."**

  Your arc should now resemble the solid arc in Figure 5.9.

5.3.1 Rotating with Grips

Rotating with grips is simple, and there is a useful option for copying, but your choice of object selection methods is limited, as always, to pointing and windowing. Try this:

- **Pick the arc.**

  The arc will become highlighted and grips will appear.

- **Pick the center grip.**
- **Right click to open the grip shortcut menu.**
- **Select Rotate.**

  Move your cursor in a circle and you will see the arc rotating around the grip at the center of the arc.

- **Now type "b" or right click again and select Base point from the menu.**

  Base point will allow you to pick a base point other than the selected grip.

- **Pick a base point above and to the left of the grip, as shown in Figure 5.10.**

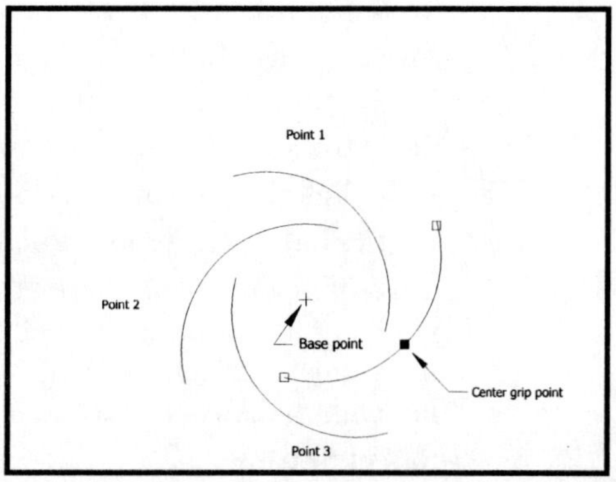

Figure 5.10

Move your cursor in circles again. You will see the arc rotating around the new base point.

- **Type "c," or open the shortcut menu and select Copy.**

  Notice the Command area prompt, which indicates that you are now in a rotate and multiple copy mode.

- **Pick a point showing a rotation angle of 90 degrees, as illustrated by the top arc in Figure 5.10.**
- **Pick a second point showing a rotation angle of 180 degrees, as illustrated by the arc at the left in the figure.**
- **Pick Point 3 at 270 degrees to complete the design shown in Figure 5.10.**
- **Press enter or the space bar to exit the grip edit mode.**

This capacity to create rotated copies is very useful, as you will find when you do the drawings at the end of this chapter.

5.4 USING POLAR TRACKING AT ANY ANGLE

You may have noticed that using Ortho or Polar Tracking to force or snap to the 90, 180, and 270 degree angles in the last exercise would make the process more efficient. In AutoCAD you can extend this concept to include angular increments other than the standard 90 degree orthogonal angles. This feature combined with the Rotate Copy technique will facilitate the creation of rotated copies at regular angles. As an example, we will use this process to create Figure 5.11.

Figure 5.11

- **To begin this task, Erase or Undo all but one arc on your screen.**
- **Move the arc to the center of your screen.**

We are going to rotate and copy this arc as before, but first we will set Polar Tracking to track at 30-degree angles. This is done in the Drafting Settings dialog box.

- **Left click on the Polar button on the status bar so that Polar tracking is on.**
- **Right click on the same Polar button.**

This will open a small shortcut menu with three options: On, Off, and Settings.... On and Off are not very useful since you can turn the Polar button on and off more quickly by left clicking. But Settings... will open the Drafting Settings dialog box with the Polar Tracking tab selected.

- **Select Settings.... .**

You will see the Drafting Settings dialog box as shown in Figure 5.12. This is the same dialog box used to specify Snap and Grid settings, but now the Polar Tracking tab is selected. In the next chapter we will use the third tab, Object Snap.

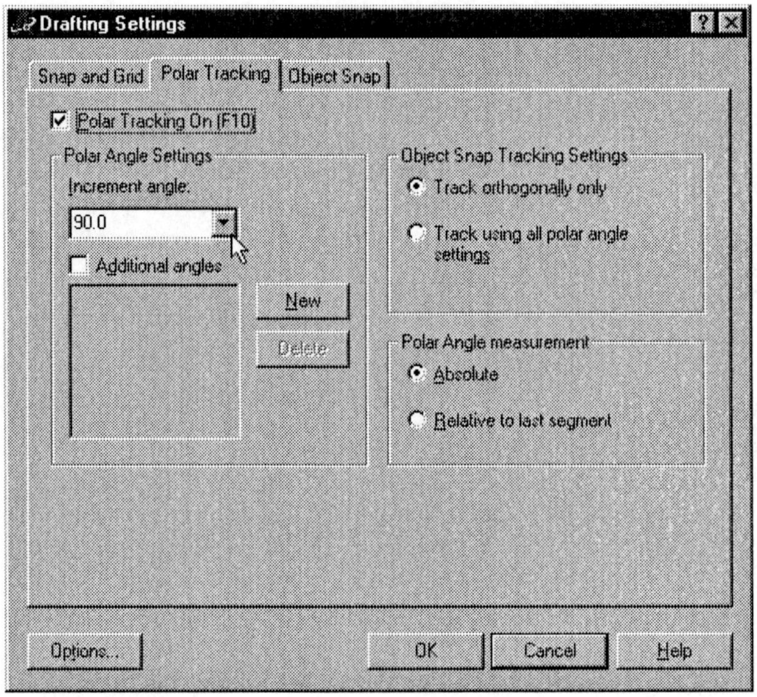

Figure 5.12

If you are using AutoCAD default settings, the increment angle will be 90 degrees. Otherwise, you will see whatever increment was set last in your AutoCAD system.

- **Open the Increment angle pop-down list.**

Notice the standard selections, from 90 at the top to 5 at the bottom. Notice also that you can add custom angles by checking the Additional Angles box, clicking on New and typing in a new value.

- **Select 30 from the list.**

Thirty will replace 90 as the current increment angle. We will not use the other two panels yet. The first panel sets the relationship between Object Snap Tracking settings and Polar Tracking. This will be covered in Chapter 6. The second panel gives you the option of measuring angles from the last line segment drawn instead of measuring from the 0 point of the screen coordinate system (absolute).

- **With 30 showing as the current increment angle, click on OK.**
- **Select the arc.**
- **Click on the grip in the center of the arc.**
- **Right click to open the grip shortcut menu.**
- **Select Rotate.**
- **Slowly move the cursor in a wide circle around the selected grip.**

You will see that Polar Tracking now tracks and snaps to every 30 degree angular increment.

- **Right click to open the shortcut menu again.**
- **Select Copy.**
- **Carefully create a copy at every 30 degree angle until you have created a design similar to Figure 5.11.**

If your design is not exactly like ours, in particular if the ends of the arcs overlap or do not meet, it is because you have used an arc that is not the same as the one we used.

5.5 CREATING MIRROR IMAGES OF OBJECTS ON THE SCREEN

There are two main differences between the command procedures for Mirror and Rotate. First, to mirror an object you will have to define a mirror line; second, you will have an opportunity to indicate whether you want to retain the original object or delete it. In the Rotate sequence the original is always deleted.

There is also a mirror mode in the grip edit system, which we will explore later in this section.

- **To begin this exercise, Erase or Undo all but one arc on your screen.**
- **Rotate the arc and move it so that you have a bowl-shaped arc placed left of the center of your screen, as in Figure 5.13.**

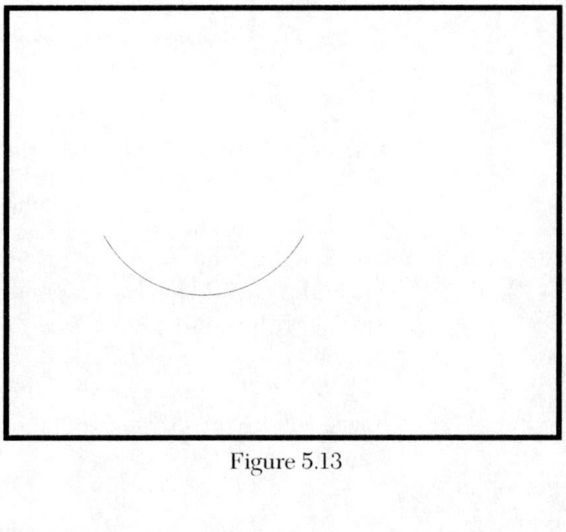

Figure 5.13

- **Keep Polar tracking on to do this exercise.**
- **Select the arc.**
- **Type "Mi", select Mirror from the Draw menu, or select the Mirror tool from the Modify toolbar, as shown in Figure 5.14.**

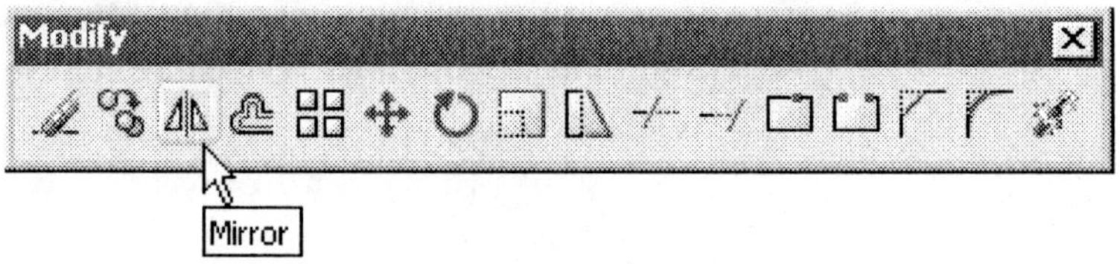

Figure 5.14

Now AutoCAD will ask you for the first point of a mirror line:

Specify first point of mirror line:

A mirror line is just what you would expect; the line serves as the "mirror," and all points on your original object will be reflected across the line at an equal distance and opposite orientation.

We will show a mirror line even with the top of the arc, so that the endpoints of the mirror images will be touching.

- **Select a point even with the left endpoint of the arc, as in Figure 5.15.**

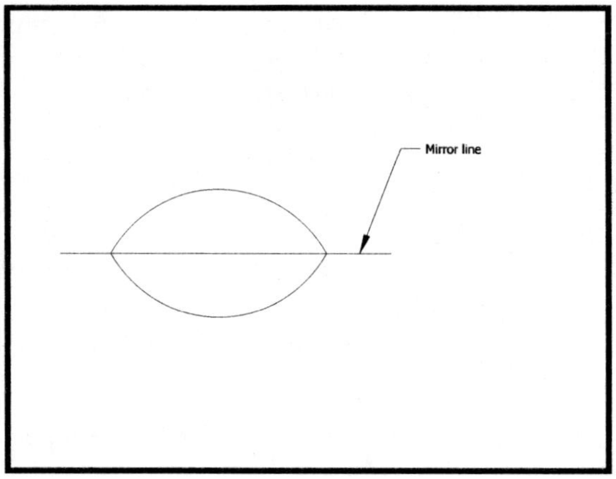

Figure 5.15

You are prompted to show the other endpoint of the mirror line:

Specify second point of mirror line:

The length of the mirror line is not important. All that matters is its orientation. Move the cursor slowly in a circle, and you will see an inverted copy of the arc moving with you to show the different mirror images that are possible, given the first point you have specified.

We will select a point at 0 degrees from the first point, so that the mirror image will be directly above the original arc and touching at the endpoints, as in Figure 5.15.

⌖ **Select a point directly to the right (0 degrees) of the first point.**

The dragged object will disappear until you answer the next prompt, which asks if you want to delete the original object or not.

Delete source objects [Yes/No]? <N>:

This time around we will not delete the original.

⌖ **Press Enter to retain the old object.**

Your screen will look like Figure 5.15, without the mirror line in the middle.

5.5.1 Mirroring with Grips

The Mirror grip edit mode works exactly like the rotate mode, except that the rubber band will show you a mirror line instead of a rotation angle. The option to retain or delete the original is obtained through the copy option, just as in the Rotate mode. Try it.

⌖ **Select the two arcs on your screen by pointing or windowing.**

The arcs will be highlighted and grips will be showing.

⌖ **Pick any of the grips.**

⌖ **Right click and then select Mirror from the shortcut menu.**

Move the cursor and observe the dragged mirror images of the arcs. Notice that the rubber band operates as a mirror line, just as in the Mirror command.

⌖ **Type "b" or right click again and select Base point.**

This frees you from the selected grip and allows you to create a mirror line from any point on the screen. Notice the "Specify base point:" prompt in the command area.

⌖ **Type "c" or right click and select Copy from the shortcut menu.**

As in the Rotate mode, this is how you retain the original in a grip edit mirroring sequence.

⌖ **Pick a base point slightly below the arcs.**

⌖ **Pick a second point to the right of the first.**

Your screen should resemble Figure 5.16.

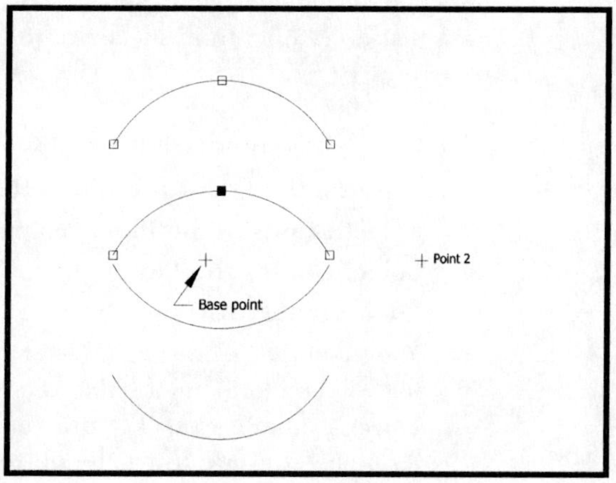

Figure 5.16

⌖ **Press enter or the space bar to exit grip edit mode.**

5.6 CREATING PAGE SETUPS

In this chapter and the next you will move to another level in your exploration of AutoCAD plotting. So far we have confined ourselves to plot configurations tied directly to objects visible in your model space drawing area. In the last chapter we went through many of the remaining options of the PLOT dialog box. In this chapter we will continue to plot from model space, but will introduce the concept and technique of Page Setups. With page setups you can name and save different plot configurations so that one drawing may produce several different page setups. We will define two simple page setups. You will not need to learn any new options, but all of the options you have learned so far can be saved and reused as part of a page setup.

⌖ **To begin this task you should be in an AutoCAD drawing using the 1B template.**

Any drawing will do. We will continue using the objects drawn in Section 5.5.

5.6.1 The Page Setup Dialog Box

A page setup is nothing more than a group of plot settings. The only difference is that you will give the configuration a name and save it on a list of setups. Once named, the plot settings can be restored by selecting the name and can even be exported to other drawings.

You can define a page setup from the Plot dialog box or from the Page Setup dialog box, accessible from the File menu. There is little difference between the two dialogs. One important difference, however, is that Page Setup does not have preview options. For this reason alone, we will continue to use the Plot dialog box.

⌖ **Select the Plot tool from the Standard toolbar.**

You should now be in the familiar Plot dialog box with the Plot settings tab on top. We will make a few changes in parameters and then give this page setup a name.

We will create a portrait setup and a landscape setup. Besides the difference in orientation the only difference in settings between the two will be that the portrait setup will be centered, while the landscape setup will be plotted from the origin. Remember, however, that everything from sheet size to the plotter you are using can be included in a page setup.

⌖ **Open the paper size list and select an A size (8.50 × 11.00) sheet.**

⌖ **Click on the Portrait radio button in the Drawing Orientation panel.**

⌖ **Select Limits in the Plot area panel.**

⌖ **Select Center the Plot.**

⌖ **Do a partial preview.**

You should see a preview similar to the one in Figure 5.17, showing that the drawing will be plotted in a reduced area in the middle of the portrait-oriented page. Pause a minute to make sure you understand why the preview looks this way. Assuming you are using the objects drawn in this chapter, or another drawing using the 1B template, you have model space limits set to 18 × 12. You are plotting to an 8.5 × 11 sheet of paper. The 18 × 12 limits have been positioned in portrait orientation, placed across the effective area of the drawing sheet, scaled to fit, and centered on the paper.

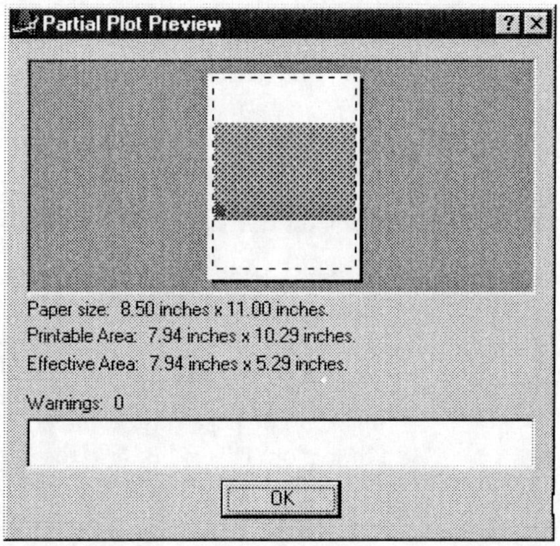

Figure 5.17

Now we will name this page setup.

☩ **Click on the Add... button at the upper right of the dialog box next to the Page setup name box.**

This will open the User Defined Page Setups box shown in Figure 5.18.

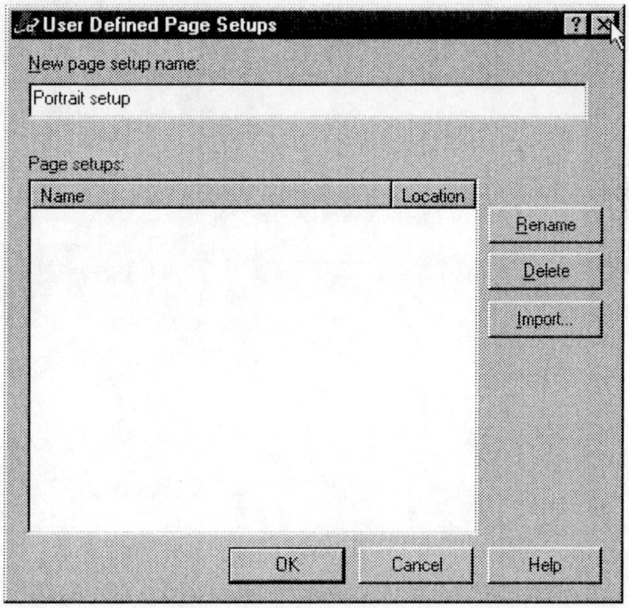

Figure 5.18

☩ **Type "Portrait setup" as the page setup name.**

☩ **Click on OK.**

This will bring you back to the Plot dialog. "Portrait setup" will now be entered in the Page setup name box. That's all there is to it. The Portrait page setup is now part of the current drawing.

Next we will define a landscape page setup and put it on the list as well. The only difference in this setup will be that it is in landscape orientation and plotted from the origin rather than centered.

- **Click on the Landscape radio button in the Drawing Orientation panel.**
- **Deselect Center the plot.**
- **Do a partial preview.**

You should see a preview similar to the one in Figure 5.19, showing that the drawing will be plotted from the corner of the landscape-oriented page. Notice that the image of the page stays in the portrait position even though the plot will be a landscape plot. This is because the sheet size is 8.5×11. If we wanted to rotate this image to the horizontal we would need to select an 11×8.5 sheet. So, now you have the 18×12 limits aligned with the left edge of the page, positioned at the origin of the effective area, and scaled to fit. Let's give this setup a name.

- **Click on the Add... button again.**
- **Type "Landscape setup" in the User Defined Page Setups box.**
- **Click on OK.**

Back in the Plot dialog again you will see that "Landscape setup" has been entered as the current page setup. You should now restore the portrait settings.

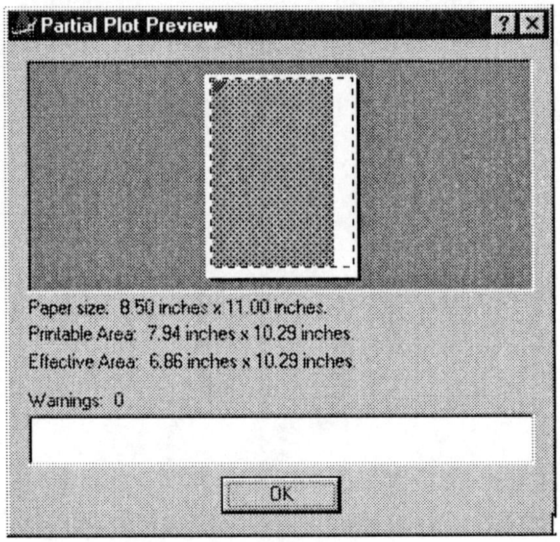

Figure 5.19

- **Open the list and select "Portrait setup."**

Your portrait settings, including the "portrait radio" button and "center the plot" will be restored.

- **Click on Full preview.**

You should see a preview similar to Figure 5.20.

Figure 5.20

- **Press Esc to return to the dialog box.**
- **Open the list again and select "Landscape setup."**

  Your landscape settings will be restored.
- **Click on Full preview.**

  You should see a preview similar to Figure 5.21. Notice that AutoCAD turns the paper image to landscape orientation in the full preview.

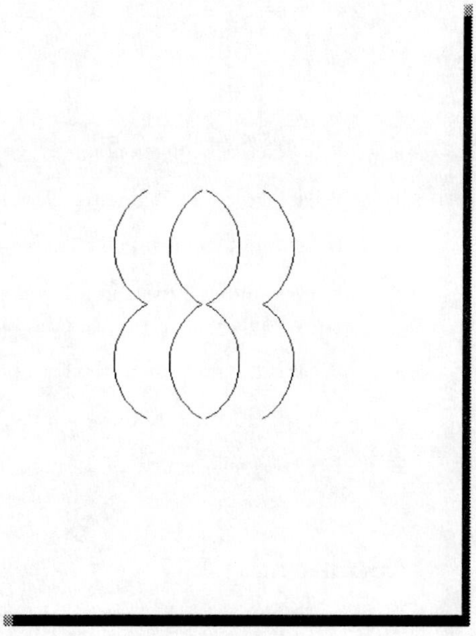

Figure 5.21

This is a simple demonstration, but remember that everything from sheet size to the plotter you are using can be included in a named page setup.

5.6.2 Importing Page Setups

A powerful feature of page setups is that they can be exchanged between drawings using the PSETUPIN command. This is accomplished by importing page setups from a known drawing into the current drawing. The procedure is as follows:

1. From a drawing into which you would like to import a page setup, type "psetupin" at the command line.
2. In the Select File box enter the name and path of the drawing file from which you would like to import a page setup, or open the folder containing the file and select the file name.
3. In the Import user defined page setups box, select the name of the page setup you want to import.
4. Enter the Plot or Page Setup dialog box and open the Page setup name list. The imported page setup should be there.

NOTE: Page setups are defined in either model space or paper space as part of a layout. If you have created a page setup in model space and then go into a paper space layout, you will not see it on your list. Also if you define a page setup as part of a layout you will not see it if you begin a plot from model space.

5.7 REVIEW MATERIAL

Questions

1. What factors define a polar array? How many are needed to define an array?
2. What factors define an arc? How many are needed for any single method?
3. How would you use Polar Tracking instead of Polar ARRAY to create Figure 5.5?
4. How would you use the reference option to rotate a line from 60 degrees to 90 degrees? How would you accomplish the same rotation without using reference?
5. What is the purpose of the base point option in the grip edit Rotate mode?
6. Why does Mirror require a mirror line where Rotate only requires a single point?
7. How do you create a landscape plot if your printer prints in portrait orientation?

Commands

ARC	ARRAY (polar)	MIRROR
ROTATE		

5.8 DRAWING PROBLEMS

1. Draw an arc starting at (10, 6) and passing through (12, 6.5) and (14, 6).
2. Create a mirrored copy of the arc across the horizontal line passing through (10, 6).
3. Rotate the pair of arcs from Step 2, 45 degrees around the point (9, 6).
4. Create a mirrored copy of the pair of arcs mirrored across a vertical line passing through (9, 6).
5. Create mirrored copies of both pairs of arcs mirrored across a horizontal line passing through (9, 6).
6. Erase any three of the four pairs of arcs on your screen and recreate them using a polar array.

DRAWING 1

Dials

This is a relatively simple drawing that will give you some good practice with polar arrays and the ROTATE and COPY commands.

Notice that the needle drawn at the top of the next page is only for reference; the actual drawing includes only the plate and the three dials with their needles.

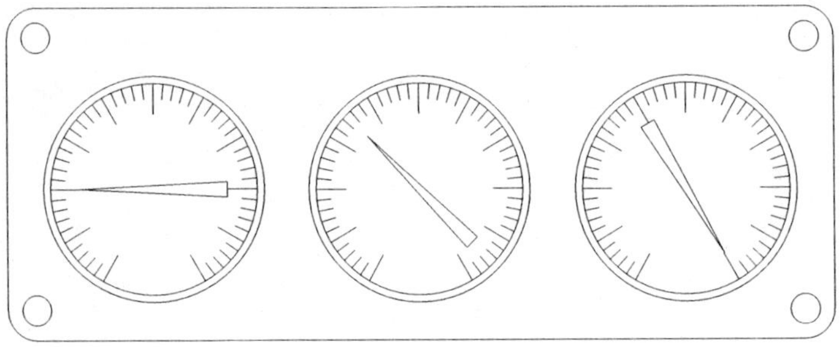

Drawing Suggestions

GRID = 0.25

SNAP = 0.125

LTSCALE = 0.50

LIMITS = (0, 0) (18, 12)

- After drawing the outer rectangle and screw holes, draw the leftmost dial, including the needle. Draw a 0.50 vertical line at the top and array it to the left (counterclockwise—a positive angle) and to the right (negative) to create the 11 larger lines on the dial. Question: How many lines in each of these left and right arrays do you need in order to end up with 11?
- Draw a 0.25 line on top of the 0.50 line at the top of the dial. Then use right and left arrays with a Last selection to create the 40 small markings. How many lines in these two arrays?
- Complete the first dial and then use a multiple copy to produce two more dials at the center and right of your screen. Be sure to use a window to select the entire dial.
- Finally, use the ROTATE command to rotate the needles as indicated on the new dials. Use a window to select the needle, and rotate it around the center of the dial.

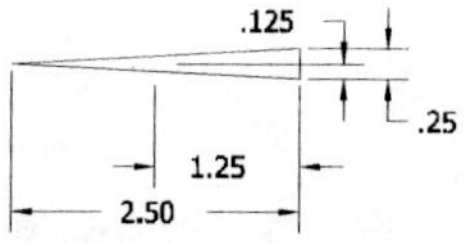

Detail of pointer

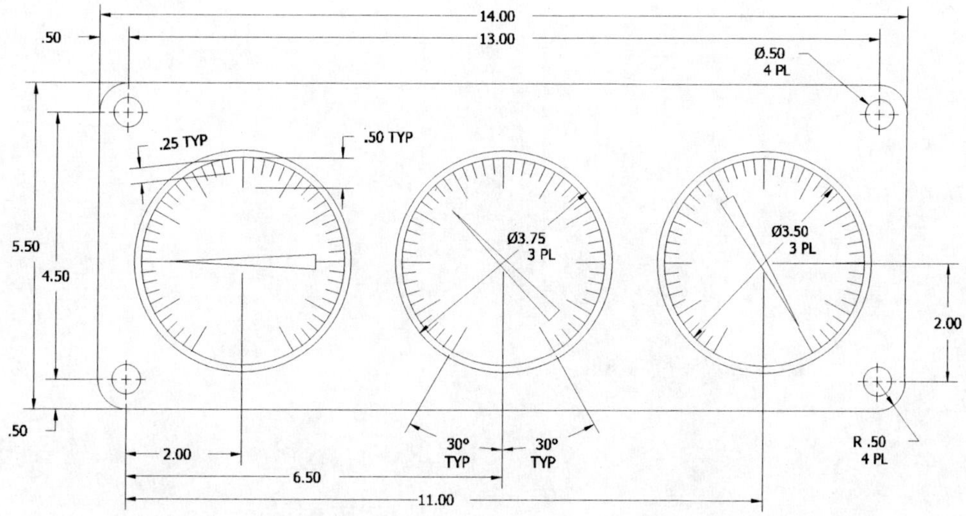

DIALS

DRAWING 2

Alignment Wheel

This drawing shows a typical use of the MIRROR command. Carefully mirroring sides of the symmetrical front view will save you from duplicating some of your drawing efforts. Notice that you will need a small snap setting to draw the vertical lines at the chamfer.

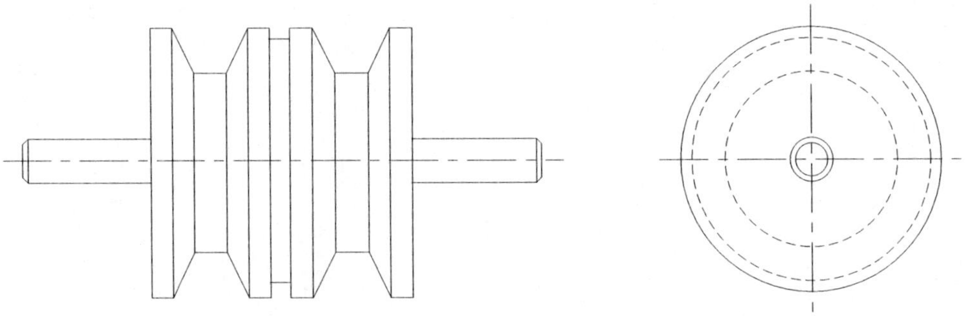

Drawing Suggestions

GRID = 0.25

SNAP = 0.125

LTSCALE = 0.50

LIMITS = (0, 0) (12, 9)

- There are numerous ways to use Mirror in drawing the front view. As the reference shows, there is top–bottom symmetry as well as left–right symmetry. The exercise for you is to choose an efficient mirroring sequence.
- Whatever sequence you use, consider the importance of creating the chamfer and the vertical line at the chamfer before this part of the object is mirrored.
- Once the front view is drawn, the right-side view will be easy. Remember to change layers for center and hidden lines and to line up the small inner circle with the chamfer.

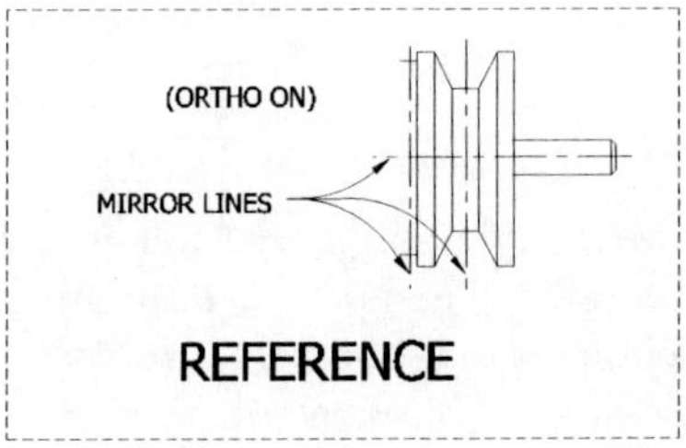

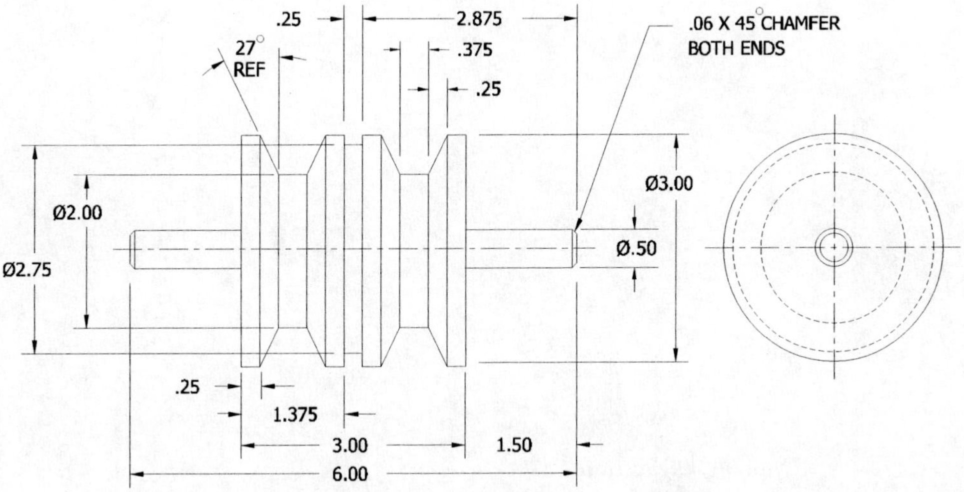

ALIGNMENT WHEEL

DRAWING 3

Hearth

Once you have completed this architectural drawing as it is shown, you might want to experiment with filling in a pattern of firebrick in the center of the hearth. The drawing itself is not complicated, but little errors will become very noticeable when you try to make the row of 4 × 8 bricks across the bottom fit with the arc of bricks across the top, so work carefully.

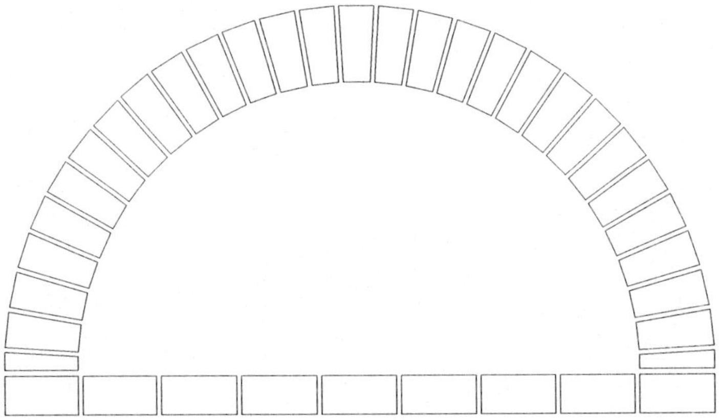

Drawing Suggestions

UNITS = Architectural
Smallest fraction = 8 (1/8")

LIMITS = (0, 0) (12', 9')

GRID = 1'

SNAP = 1/8"

- Zoom in to draw the wedge-shaped brick indicated by the arrow on the right of the dimensioned drawing. Draw half of the brick only and mirror it across the center line as shown. (Notice that the center line is for reference only.) It is very important that you use Mirror so that you can erase half of the brick later.
- Array the brick in a 29-item, 180-degree polar array.
- Erase the bottom halves of the end bricks at each end.
- Draw a new horizontal bottom line on each of the two end bricks.
- Draw a 4 × 8 brick directly below the half brick at the left end.
- Array the 4 × 8 brick in a one-row, nine-column array, with 8.5" between columns.

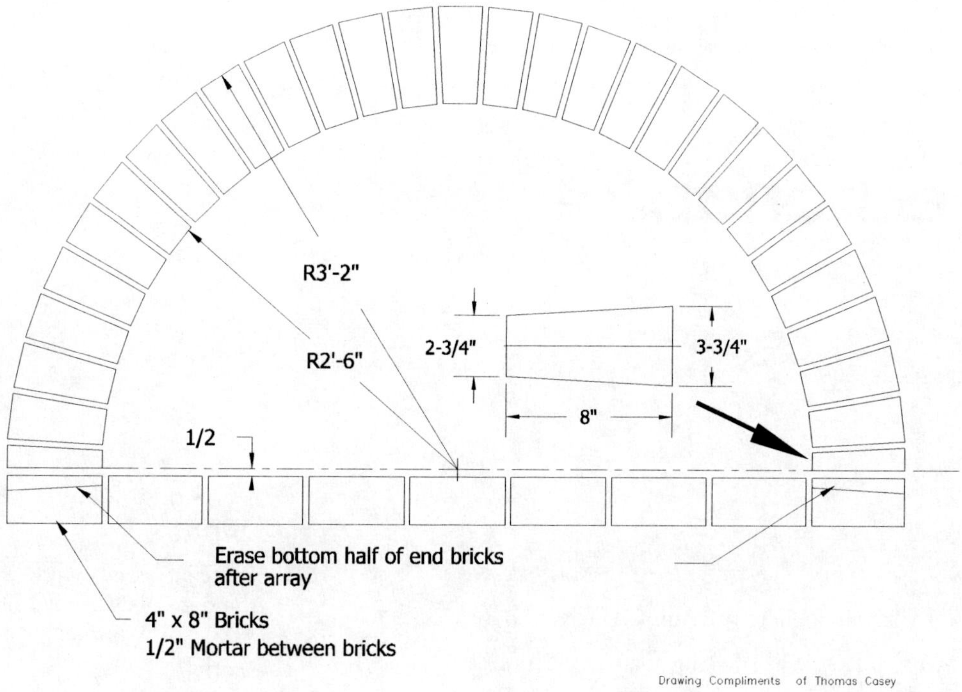
R3'-2"
R2'-6"
2-3/4"
3-3/4"
8"
1/2
Erase bottom half of end bricks after array
4" x 8" Bricks
1/2" Mortar between bricks
Drawing Compliments of Thomas Casey

HEARTH

6

Object Snap

OVERVIEW

In this chapter you will begin to use AutoCAD's very powerful Object Snap and Object Tracking features. These will take you to a new level of accuracy and efficiency as a CAD operator. You will also learn to BREAK entities on the screen into pieces so that they may be manipulated or erased separately, to shorten objects at intersections with other objects using the TRIM command, or to lengthen them with the EXTEND command.

SECTIONS

OBJECTIVES

After reading this chapter, you should be able to:

- Select points with Object Snap (single-point override).
- Select points with OSNAP (running mode).
- Use object snap tracking.
- Create parallel objects with OFFSET.
- BREAK previously drawn objects.
- Shorten objects with the TRIM command.
- Extend objects with the EXTEND command.
- Draw an Archimedes spiral.
- Draw spiral designs.
- Draw a grooved hub.

6.1 SELECTING POINTS WITH OBJECT SNAP (SINGLE-POINT OVERRIDE)

Some drawings push the limits of what you can accomplish accurately on a CAD system with incremental snap alone. Object snap is a related tool that works in a very different manner. Instead of snapping to points defined by the coordinate system, it snaps to geometrically specifiable points on objects that you already have drawn. There are 13 different varieties of object snap, and each may be used as a one-time option for selecting a point (single-point override) or turned on to affect all point selection (running object snap). In this section we will introduce the single-point method and then move on to the running mode in the next section.

Let's say you want to begin a new line at the endpoint of one that is already on the screen. If you are lucky, the endpoint may be on a snap point, but it is just as likely not to be. Turning snap off and moving the cursor to the apparent endpoint may appear to work, but when you zoom in you probably will find that you have missed the point. Using object snap is the only precise way, and it is as precise as you could want. Let's try it.

The Osnap button and the Snap button should be off for this exercise.

To prepare for this exercise, draw a 6 × 6 box with a circle inside, as in Figure 6.1.

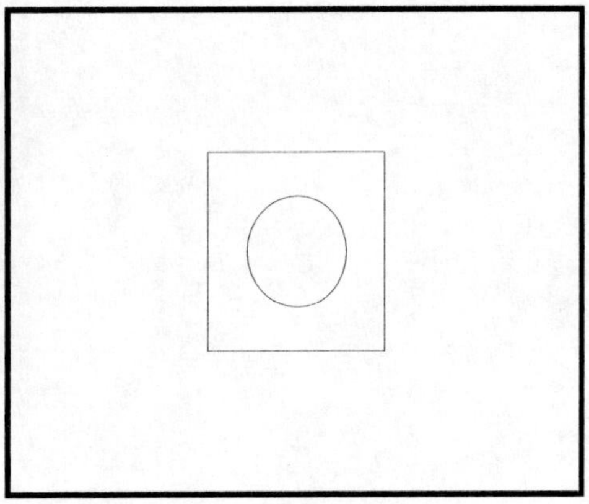

Figure 6.1

Exact sizes and locations are not important; however, the circle should be centered within the square.

Now enter the LINE command (type "L" or select the Line tool).

We are going to draw a line from the lower left corner of the square to a point on a line tangent to the circle, as shown in Figure 6.2. This task would be extremely difficult without object snap. The corner is easy to locate, since you probably have drawn it on snap, but the tangent may not be.

We will use an endpoint object snap to locate the corner and a tangent object snap to locate the tangent point. When AutoCAD asks for a point, you can select an object snap mode from the object snap shortcut menu.

At the "Specify first point:" prompt, instead of specifying a point, hold down the Shift or Ctrl key and press the right button on your mouse.

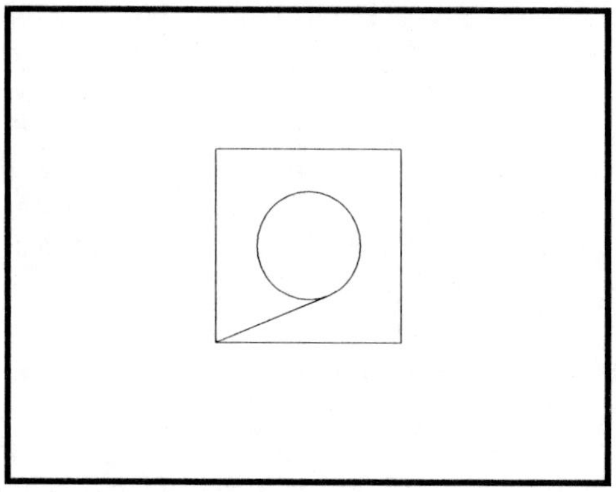

Figure 6.2

This will open the shortcut menu illustrated in Figure 6.3.

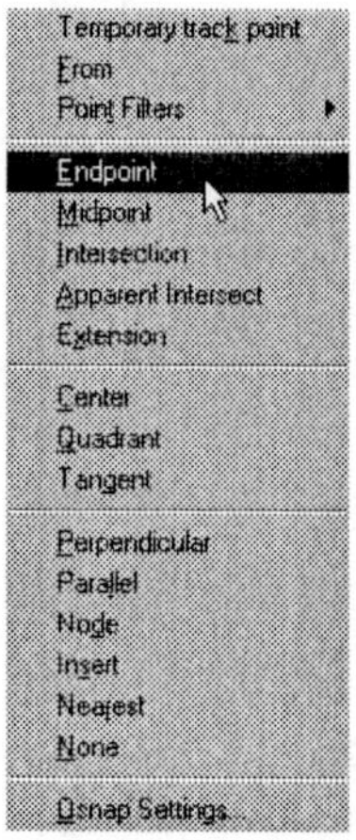

Figure 6.3

- **Select "Endpoint."**

This tells AutoCAD that you are going to select the start point of the line by using an endpoint object snap rather than by direct pointing or entering coordinates.

Now that AutoCAD knows that we want to begin at the endpoint of a previously drawn entity, it needs to know which one.

- **Move the cursor near the lower left corner of the square.**

When you are close to the corner, AutoCAD will recognize the endpoint of the lines there and indicate this with a yellow box surrounding the endpoint. This object snap symbol is called a marker. There are different-shaped markers for each type of object snap. If you let the cursor rest here for a moment, a tooltip-like label will appear, naming the type of object that has been recognized, as shown in Figure 6.4. This label is called a snap-tip. Also notice that if the cross hairs are inside the marker, they will lock onto the endpoint. This action can be turned on or off and is called the magnet setting. You do not have to be locked on to the endpoint, however. As long as the endpoint marker is showing, the endpoint will be selected.

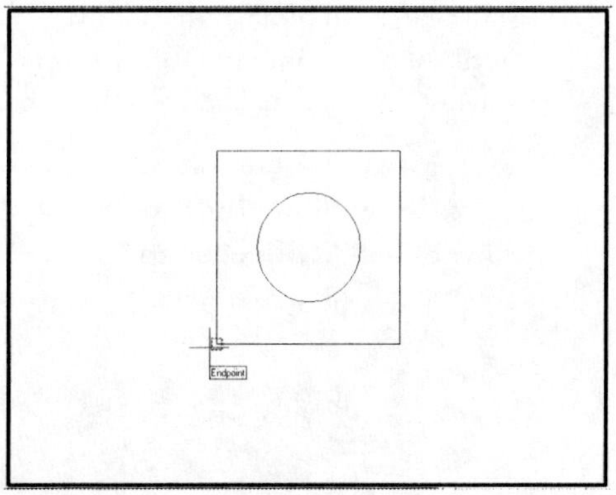

Figure 6.4

⌗ **With the endpoint object snap marker showing, press the pickbutton.**

The yellow endpoint box and the snap-tip will disappear, and there will be a rubber band stretching from the lower left corner of the square to the cursor position. In the command area you will see the Specify next point prompt.

We will use a tangent object snap to select the second point.

⌗ **At the "Specify next point or [Undo]:" prompt, select "Tangent" from the shortcut menu (shift + right click).**

⌗ **Move the cursor to the right and position the cross hairs so that they are near the lower right side of the circle.**

When you approach the tangent area, you will see the yellow tangent marker, as shown in Figure 6.5. Here again, if you let the cursor rest you will see a snap-tip.

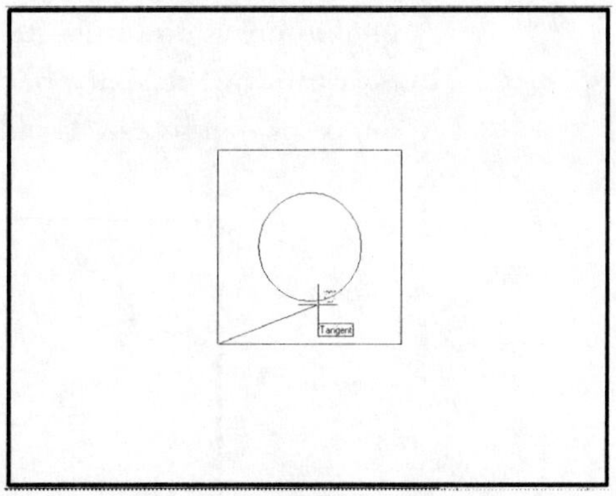

Figure 6.5

⌗ **With the tangent marker showing, press the pickbutton.**

AutoCAD will locate the tangent point and draw the line. Notice the power of being able to precisely locate the tangent point in this way.

⌖ **Press Enter to exit the LINE command.**

Your screen should now resemble Figure 6.2.

We will repeat the process now, but start from the midpoint of the bottom side of the square instead of its endpoint. Also, this time we will use the object snap toolbar instead of the shortcut menu. Object snap is so important a feature that you may find yourself leaving this toolbar open much of the time.

⌖ **Move the cursor over any toolbar on your screen and right click to open the toolbar shortcut menu.**

⌖ **Select "Object snap."**

This will open the Object snap toolbar shown in Figure 6.6.

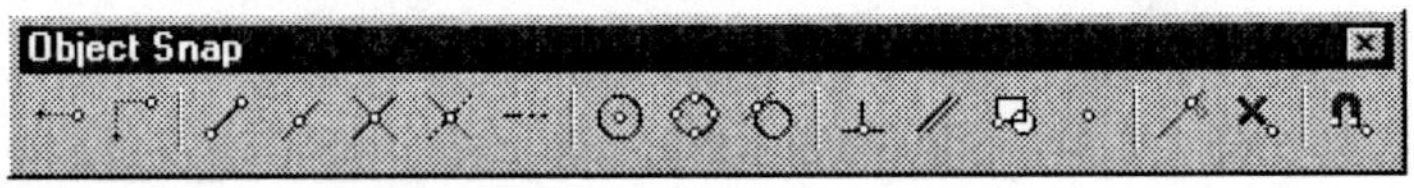

Figure 6.6

⌖ **Move the toolbar anywhere out of the way, or dock it along one side.**

⌖ **Enter the LINE command.**

⌖ **At the prompt for a point, select the Snap to Midpoint tool from the toolbar.**

All of the Osnap modes have fairly obvious icons. Snap to Midpoint is the second tool in the second panel.

⌖ **Position the aperture anywhere along the bottom side of the square so that a yellow triangle, the snap to midpoint marker, appears at the midpoint of the line.**

⌖ **Press the pickbutton.**

⌖ **At the prompt for a second point, select the Snap to Tangent tool from the toolbar.**

Snap to Tangent is the third tool in the third panel.

⌖ **Position the aperture along the right side of the circle so that the tangent symbol appears and then press the pickbutton.**

⌖ **Press Enter or the space bar to exit the LINE command.**

At this point your screen should resemble Figure 6.7.

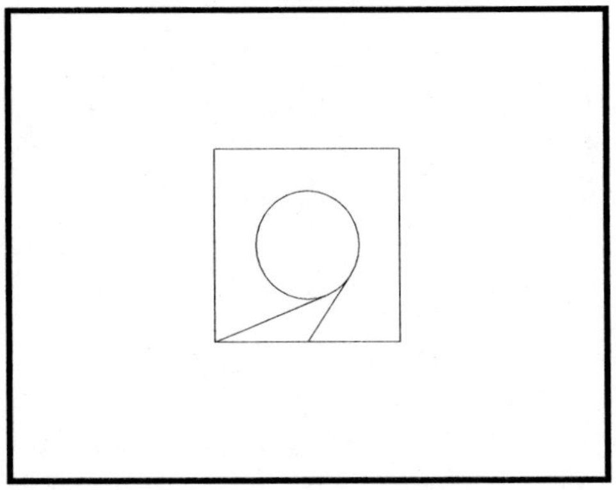

Figure 6.7

That's all there is to it. Remember the steps: (1) Enter a command; (2) when AutoCAD asks for a point, specify an object snap mode; (3) position the cross hairs near an object to which the mode can be applied and let AutoCAD find the point.

NOTE: Both the shortcut menu and the toolbar are efficient methods of specifying a single point object snap. But you can also type the name of any object snap method when AutoCAD asks for a point. All modes have aliases that are the first three letters of the mode, "end" for endpoint, "tan" for tangent, and so forth.

6.2 SELECTING POINTS WITH OSNAP (RUNNING MODE)

So far we have been using object snap one point at a time. Since object snap is not constantly in use for most applications, this single-point method is common. But often you will find that you are going to be using one or a number of object snap types repeatedly, and will not need to select many points without them. In this case, you can keep object snap modes on so that they affect all point selection. This is called running object snap. We will use this method to complete the drawing shown in Figure 6.8. Notice how each line is drawn from a midpoint or corner to a tangent point on the circle. This is done easily with running object snaps.

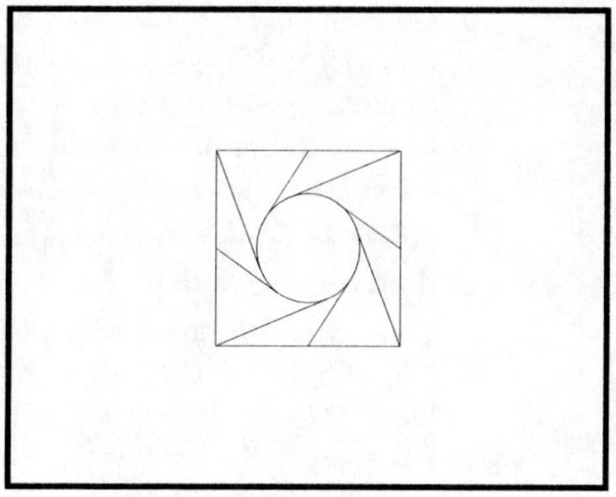

Figure 6.8

⌖ **Click the Osnap button on the status bar so that it is on.**

When the Osnap button is on, you will be in running object snap mode. The modes that will be in effect depend on the AutoCAD default settings, or whatever settings were last selected. To change settings or see what settings are on, we open the Drafting Settings dialog box.

⌖ **Right click on the status bar Osnap button.**

This will open a small shortcut menu with three options: On, Off, and Settings.... On and Off are redundant since you can turn Osnap on and off more easily by left clicking as usual. But Settings is very useful.

⌖ **Select Settings.**

⌖ **This will open the Drafting Settings dialog box with the Object Snap tab on top, as shown in Figure 6.9.**

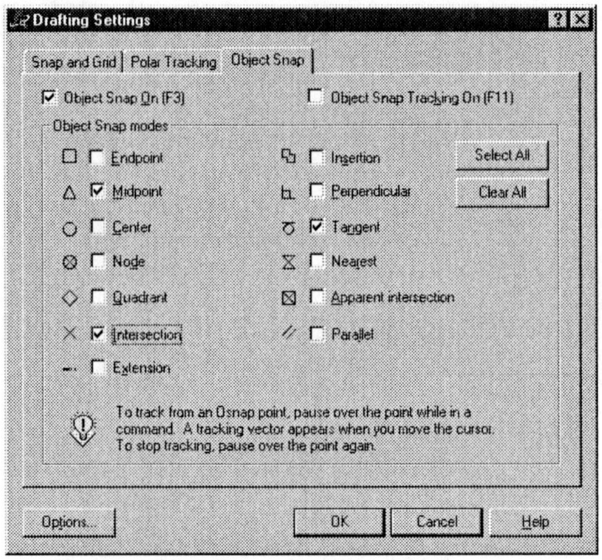

Figure 6.9

You will find a description of all of the object snap modes on the chart in Figure 6.10, but for now we will be using three: Midpoint, Intersection, and Tangent. Midpoint and tangent you already know. Intersection snaps to the point where two entities meet or cross. We will use intersect instead of endpoint to select the remaining three corners of the square. Endpoint could be used instead.

Select Midpoint, Intersection, and Tangent, and deselect any other modes that are checked.

When you are done, your dialog box should resemble Figure 6.9. Notice that Object Snap On (F3) is checked at the top of the box, and Object Snap Tracking On (F11) is not checked.

Click OK.

Enter the LINE command.

Position the aperture so that the lower right corner is within the box.

A yellow X, the intersection marker, will appear.

With the intersection marker showing, press the pickbutton.

AutoCAD will select the intersection of the bottom and the right sides and give you the rubber band and the prompt for the next point.

Move the cross hairs up and along the right side of the circle until the tangent marker appears.

With the tangent marker showing, press the pickbutton.

AutoCAD will construct a new tangent from the lower right corner to the circle.

Press the space bar to complete the command sequence.

Press the space bar again to repeat LINE so you can begin with a new start point.

We will continue to move counterclockwise around the circle. This should begin to be easy now.

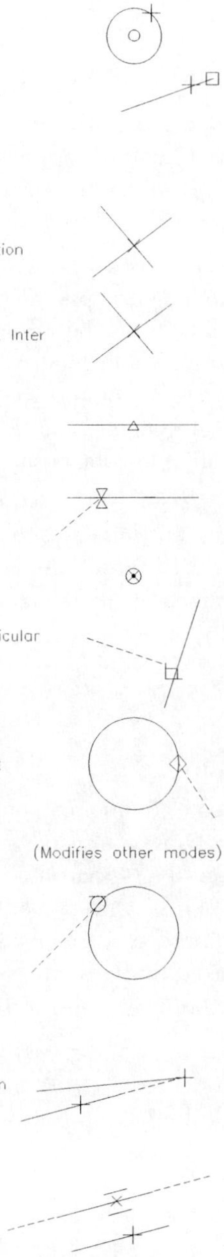

TYPE	APPEARANCE	DESCRIPTION
CENter		Snaps to the center of an arc, circle, ellipse, or elliptical arc.
ENDpoint		Snaps to the closest endpoint of an arc, elliptical arc, line, mline, polyline, ray, or to the closest corner of a trace, solid or 3D face.
INSertion		Snaps to the insertion point of a block, attribute, shape or text.
INTersection		Snaps to crossing or meeting point of arcs, lines, circles, ellipses, elliptical arcs, mlines, polylines, rays, splines, or xlines.
APParent Inter		Snaps to apparent crossing or meeting point of arcs, lines, circles, ellipses, elliptical arcs, mlines, polylines, rays, splines, or xlines. If apparent intersection and intersection are on at the same time, varying results may occur.
MIDpoint		Snaps to the midpoint of an arc, circle, ellipse, elliptical arc, line, mline, polyline, solid, spline, or xline.
NEArest		Snaps to the nearest point on an arc, circle, ellipse, elliptical arc, line, mline point, polyline, spline or xline.
NODe		Snaps to a point object.
PERpendicular		Snaps to a point on an arc, circle, ellipse, elliptical arc, line, mline, ray, solid, spline or xline.
QUAdrant		Snaps to nearest quadrant point of an arc, circle ellipse, or elliptical arc. 0, 90, 180, or 270 degrees
QUIck	(Modifies other modes)	Snaps to the first snap point found. Quick must be used in conjunction with other objects snap modes.
TANgent		Snaps to the tangent of an arc, circle ellipse, or elliptical arc.
EXTension		Snaps to the extension point of an object. Establish an extension path by moving the cursor over the endpoint of an object. A marker is placed on the endpoint. While the endpoint is marked, the cursor snaps to the extension path of the endpoint.
PARallel		Snaps to an extension parallel with an object. When the cursor is moved over the endpoint of an object, the endpoint is marked and the cursor snaps to the parallel alignment path to that object. The alignment path is calculated from the current "from point" of the command.

Figure 6.10

⌗ **Position the aperture along the right side of the square so that the midpoint triangle marker appears.**

⌗ **With the midpoint marker showing, press the pickbutton.**

AutoCAD snaps to the midpoint of the side.

- **Move up along the upper right side of the circle so that the tangent marker appears.**
- **With the tangent marker showing, press the pickbutton.**
- **Press the space bar to exit LINE.**
- **Press the space bar again to repeat LINE and continue around the circle drawing tangents like this: upper right corner to top of circle, top side midpoint to top left of circle, upper left corner to left side, left side midpoint to lower left side.**

Remember that running osnap modes should give you both speed and accuracy, so push yourself a little to see how quickly you can complete the figure.

Your screen should now resemble Figure 6.8. Before going on you should study the Object Snap chart, Figure 6.10. Before you can effectively analyze situations and look for opportunities to use object snap and object snap tracking, you will need to have a good acquaintance with all of the object snap modes.

TIP: Occasionally you may encounter a situation where there are several possible object snap points in a tight area. If AutoCAD does not recognize the one you want, you can cycle through all choices by pressing the tab key repeatedly.

6.3 OBJECT SNAP TRACKING

Object Snap tracking creates temporary construction lines from designated object snap points. Once you are in a Draw command, such as LINE, any object snap point that can be identified in an active object snap mode can be "acquired." An acquired point is highlighted with a yellow cross. Once a point is acquired, object snap tracking will automatically throw out temporary construction lines from this point. Construction lines are dotted lines like those used by Polar tracking. They extend to the edge of the display and are drawn along the horizontal and vertical from the acquired point, or along polar tracking angles. Try this:

- **To begin this task the Osnap button should be on with the Endpoint mode in effect; all other modes from the last exercise should be turned off.**

  As a reminder:

  1. Right click on the Osnap button.
  2. Select Settings....
  3. Check Endpoint, and uncheck everything else.
  4. Click on OK.

- **Click the Otrack button on the status bar so that it is in the on position.**
- **Enter the LINE command.**
- **Select a first point to the left of the square and circle even with the top of the square, as shown by Point 1 in Figure 6.11.**

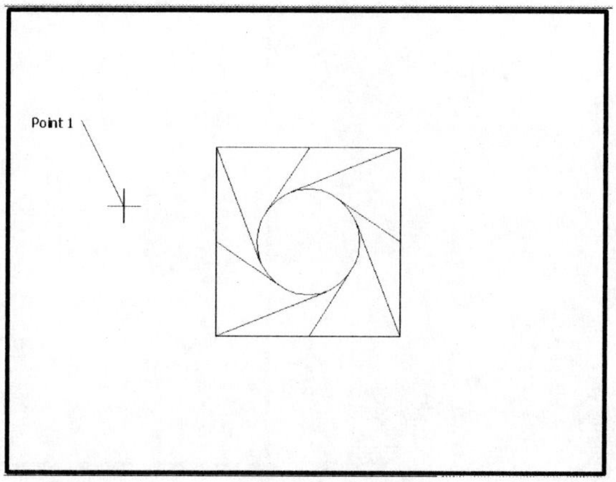

Figure 6.11

6.3.1 Point Acquisition

To take the next step, you will need to learn a new technique called point acquisition. Before a point can be used for object snap tracking it must be acquired, which is a form of selection. To acquire a point, move the cursor over it so that the object snap marker shows, and pause for about a second without clicking. Try it.

⌗ **Move the cursor over the lower left corner of the square, Point 2 in Figure 6.12, so that the endpoint marker appears.**

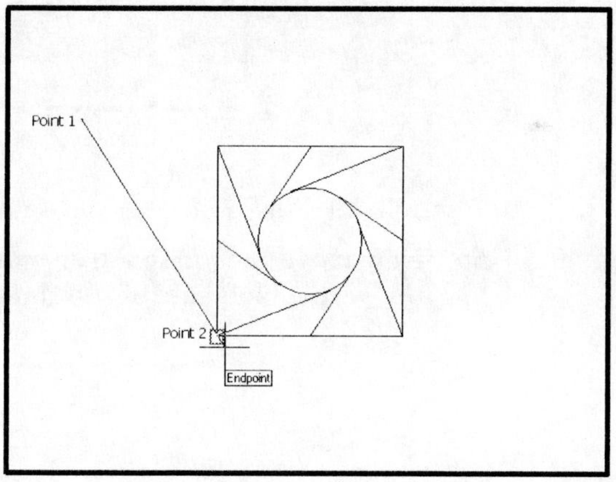

Figure 6.12

⌗ **Pause.**

⌗ **Now move the cursor away from the corner.**

If you have done this correctly, a small yellow cross will appear at the corner intersection, as shown in Figure 6.13, indicating that this point has been acquired for object snap tracking. (Repeating this procedure over the same point will remove the cross.)

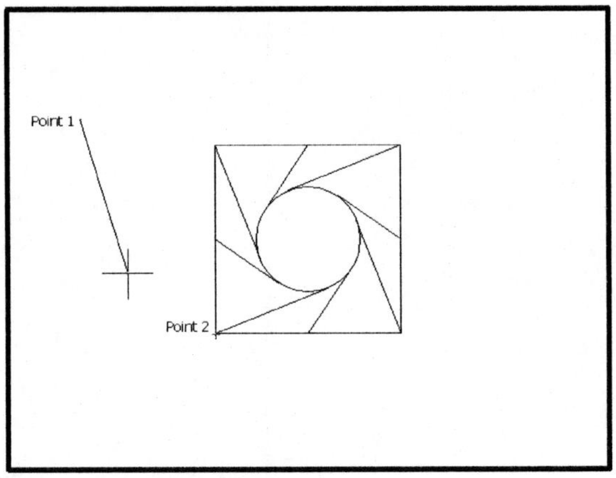

Figure 6.13

⌖ **Move the cursor to a position left of Point 2 and even with the horizontal lower side of the square, as shown in Figure 6.14.**

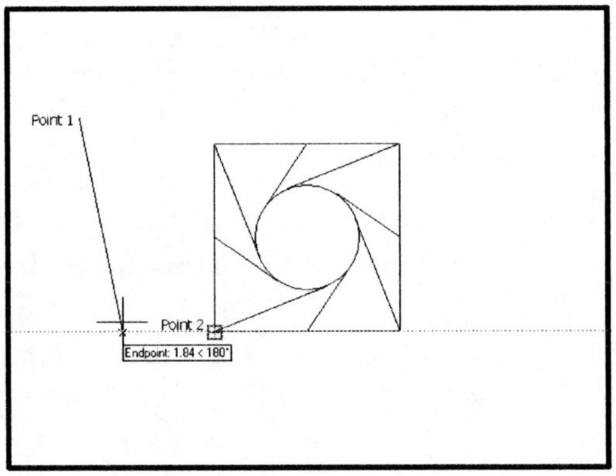

Figure 6.14

You will see a construction line and a tracking tip like those in Figure 6.14.

⌖ **Now move the cursor over and down to a position even with and below the vertical left side of the square, as shown in Figure 6.15.**

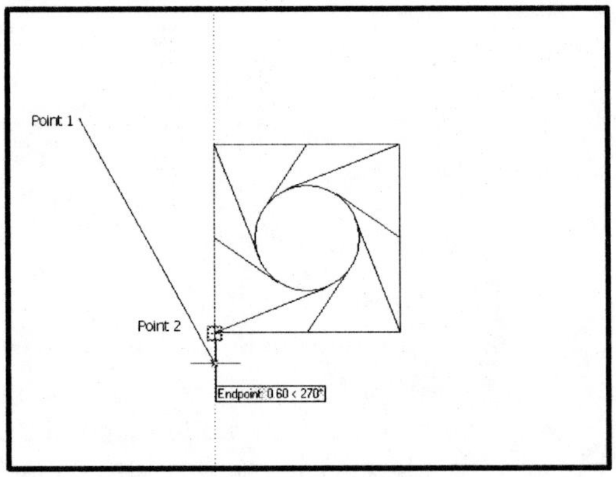

Figure 6.15

You will see a different construction line and tracking tip, like those in Figure 6.15.

These construction lines are interesting, but they do not accomplish a great deal since your square is probably constructed on grid snap points anyway. So let's try something more difficult and a lot more interesting. Here we will use two acquired points to locate a point that currently is not specifiable either in object snap or incremental snap.

Move the cursor up and acquire Point 3, as shown in Figure 6.16.

Point 3 is the endpoint of the line drawn from the midpoint of the top side of the square to a point tangent to the circle. You should now have two acquired points, with two yellow crosses showing, one at Point 2 and one at Point 3.

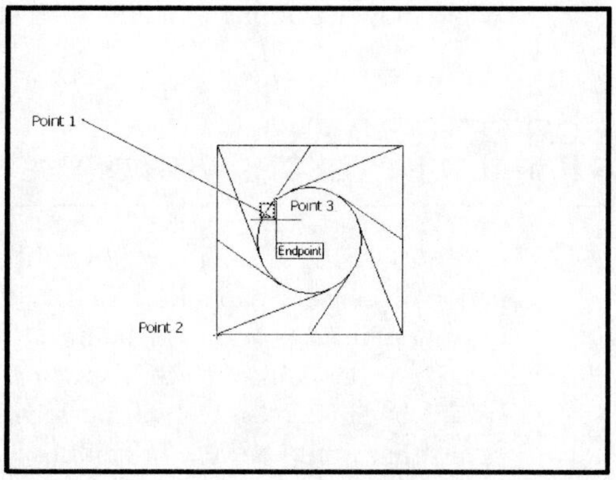

Figure 6.16

Move the cursor slowly up along the left side of the square.

You are looking for Point 4, the point where the vertical tracking line from Point A intersects the horizontal tracking line from Point B. When you near it your screen should resemble Figure 6.17. Notice the double tracking tip "Endpoint: less than 90, Endpoint: less than 180."

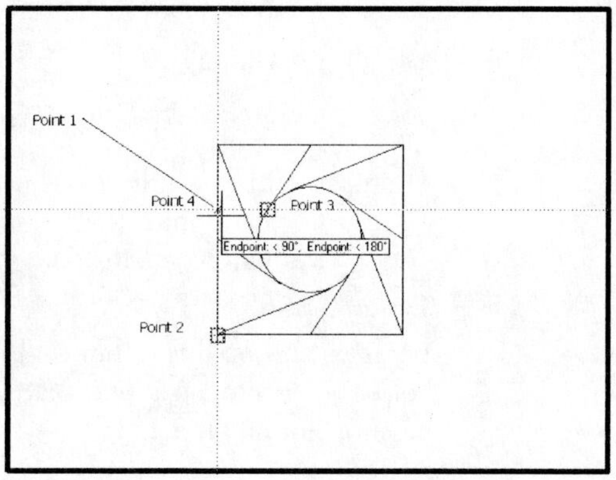

Figure 6.17

⌖ **With the double tracking tip and the two tracking lines showing, press the pickbutton.**

A line will be drawn from Point 1 to Point 4.

Before going on, we need to turn off the running osnap to endpoint mode.

⌖ **Click the Osnap button or press F3 to turn off running Osnap modes.**

If you have followed this exercise closely, you have already increased greatly the power of your understanding of CAD technique. You will find many opportunities to use Object Snap and Object Snap Tracking from now on.

Next we will move on to a very powerful editing command called OFFSET. Before leaving Object Snap, be sure that you have studied the chart in Figure 6.10, which shows examples of all the Object Snap modes.

6.4 USING THE OFFSET COMMAND (CREATING PARALLEL OBJECTS WITH OFFSET)

OFFSET is one of the most powerful editing commands in AutoCAD. With the combination of Object Snap and the OFFSET command you can become completely free of incremental snap and grid points. Any point in the drawing space can be precisely located. Essentially, OFFSET creates parallel copies of lines, circles, arcs, or polylines. In this brief exercise we will perform an offset operation to draw some lines through points that would be very difficult to locate without OFFSET.

⌖ **Select Offset from the Modify menu, or the Offset tool from the Modify toolbar, as shown in Figure 6.18.**

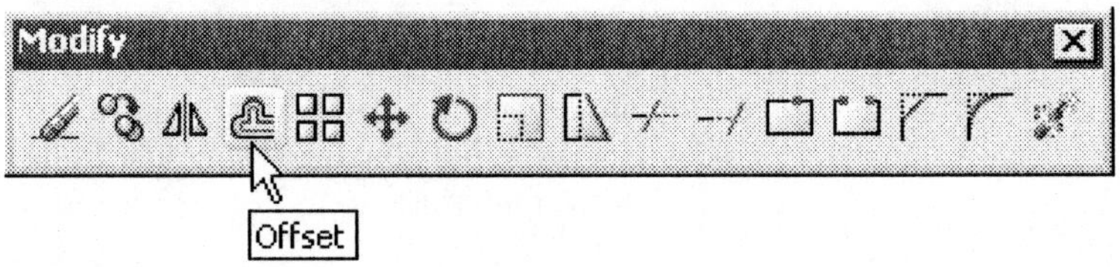

Figure 6.18

AutoCAD prompts:

Specify offset distance or [Through]:

There are three methods. You can type a distance, show a distance with two points, or pick a point that you want the new copy to run through (the through option). We will type a distance.

⌖ **Type "0.258."**

We have chosen this rather odd number to make the point that this command can help you locate positions that would be difficult to find otherwise. AutoCAD prompts for an object:

Select object to offset or <exit>:

⌖ **Type "l" for last, or select the diagonal line drawn in the last exercise.**

AutoCAD now needs to know whether to create the offset image above or below the line:

Specify point on side to offset:

⌖ **Pick a point anywhere below the line.**

Your screen should now resemble Figure 6.19. AutoCAD continues to prompt for objects to offset using the same offset distance. You can continue to create offset objects at the same offset distance by pointing and clicking.

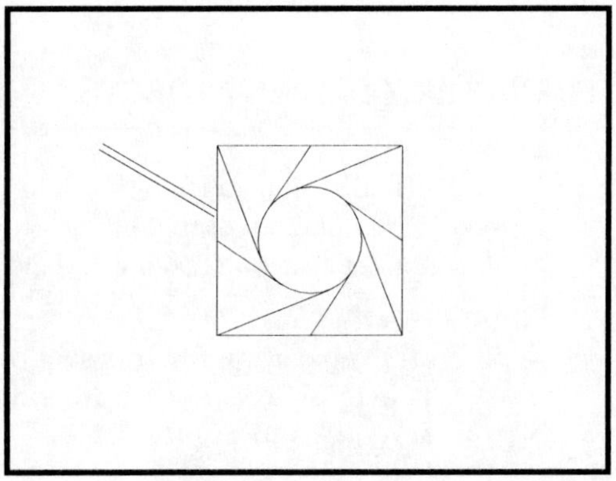

Figure 6.19

⌖ **Pick the line just created.**

⌖ **Pick any point below the line.**

A second offset line will be added, as shown in Figure 6.20. As long as you stay within the OFFSET command you can select any object to offset using the same offset distance.

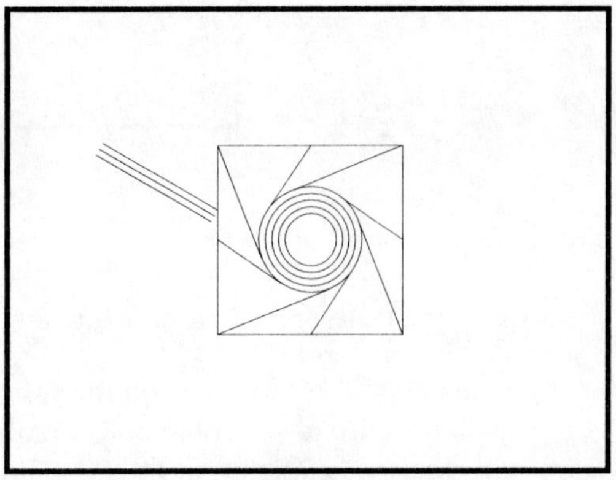

Figure 6.20

⌖ **Pick the circle in the square.**

⌖ **Pick any point inside the circle.**

An offset circle will be added, as shown in Figure 6.20.

- **Continue pointing and clicking to create additional offset circles, as shown in Figure 6.20.**
- **Press Enter to exit the OFFSET command.**

  When you exit OFFSET, the offset distance will be retained as the default, so you can return to the command and continue using the same distance.

Next we will turn to three useful commands that allow you to shorten and lengthen objects: BREAK, TRIM, and EXTEND.

6.5 BREAKING PREVIOUSLY DRAWN OBJECTS

The BREAK command allows you to break an object on the screen into two entities, or to cut a segment out of the middle or off the end. The command sequence is similar for all options. The action taken will depend on the points you select for breaking.

- **In preparation for this section, clear your screen of objects left over from previous tasks and draw a 5.0 horizontal line across the middle of your screen, as in Figure 6.21.**

Figure 6.21

Exact lengths and coordinates are not important. Also, be sure to turn off object snap.

AutoCAD allows for four different ways to break an object, depending on whether the point you use to select the object is also to be considered a break point. You can break an object at one point or at two points, and you have the choice of using your object selection point as a break point.

We begin by breaking the line you have just drawn into two independent lines using a single break point, which is also the point used to select the line.

- **Type "br," select the Break tool from the Modify menu, or select the Break tool from the Modify toolbar, as shown in Figure 6.22.**

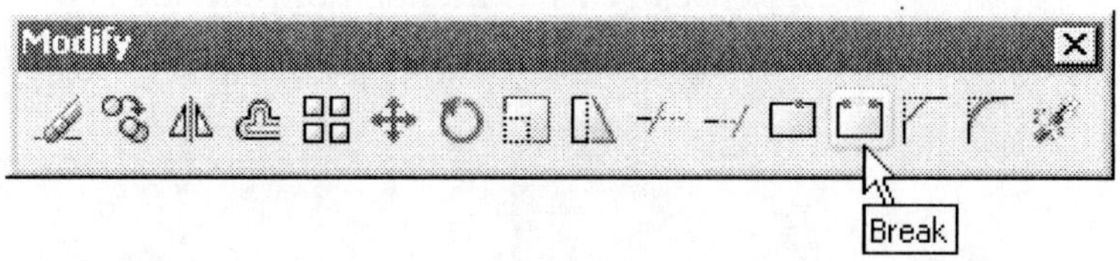

Figure 6.22

Be aware that the noun/verb or pick-first sequence does not work with BREAK. AutoCAD will prompt you to select an object to break:

Select object:

You may select an object in any of the usual ways, but notice that you can only break one object at a time. If you try to select more—with a window, for example—AutoCAD will highlight only one. Because of this you will best indicate the object you want to break by pointing to it.

TIP: Object snap modes work well in edit commands such as BREAK. If you wish to break a line at its midpoint, for example, you can use the midpoint object snap mode to select the line and the break point.

⌖ **Select the line by picking any point near its middle. (The exact point is not critical; if it were, we would use a midpoint object snap.)**

The line has now been selected for breaking, and since there can be only one object, you do not have to press Enter to end the selection process, as you often do in other editing commands.

The break is complete. To demonstrate that the line is really two lines now, we will select the right half of it for our next break.

⌖ **Press Enter or the space bar to repeat the BREAK command.**

⌖ **Point to the line on the right side of the last break.**

The right side of the line should be highlighted, as in Figure 6.23. Clearly, the original line is now being treated as two separate entities.

Figure 6.23

We will shorten the end of this dotted section of the line. Assume that the point you just used to select the object is the point where you want it to end; now all you need to do is to select a second point anywhere beyond the right end of the line.

⌖ **Select a second point beyond the right end of the line.**

Your line should now be shortened, as in Figure 6.24.

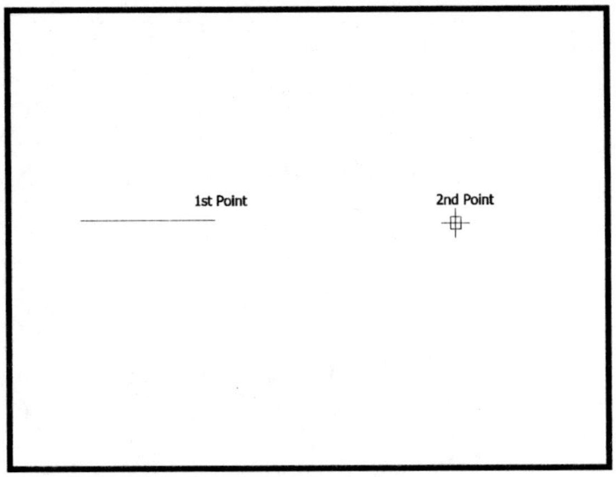

Figure 6.24

BREAK is a useful command, but there are times when it is cumbersome to shorten objects one at a time. The TRIM command has some limitations that BREAK does not have, but it is much more efficient in situations where you want to shorten objects at intersections.

6.6 SHORTENING OBJECTS WITH THE TRIM COMMAND

The TRIM command works wonders in many situations where you want to shorten objects at their intersections with other objects. It will work with lines, circles, arcs, and polylines. The only limitation is that you must have at least two objects and they must cross or meet. If you are not trimming to an intersection, use BREAK.

⌖ **In preparation for exploring TRIM, clear your screen and then draw two horizontal lines crossing a circle, as in Figure 6.25. Exact locations and sizes are not important.**

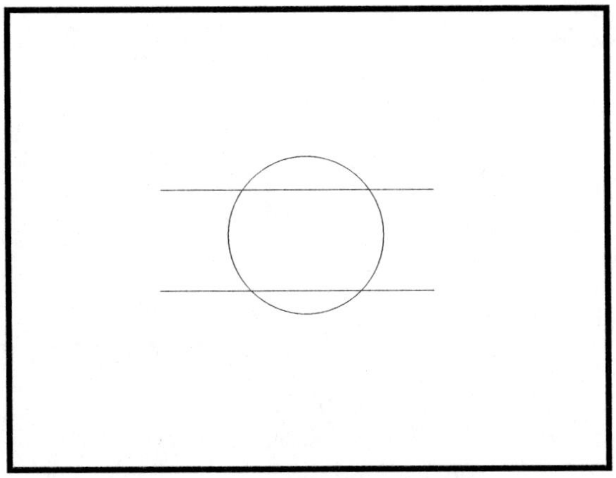

Figure 6.25

First we will use the TRIM command to go from Figure 6.25 to Figure 6.26.

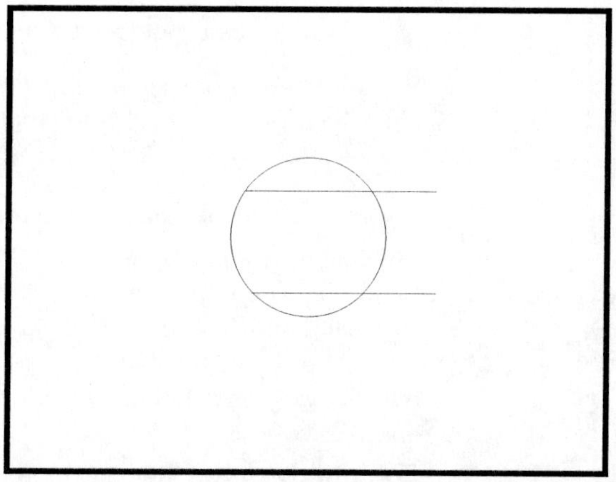

Figure 6.26

⌖ **Type "Tr" or select Trim from the Modify menu or the Trim tool from the Modify toolbar, as shown in Figure 6.27.**

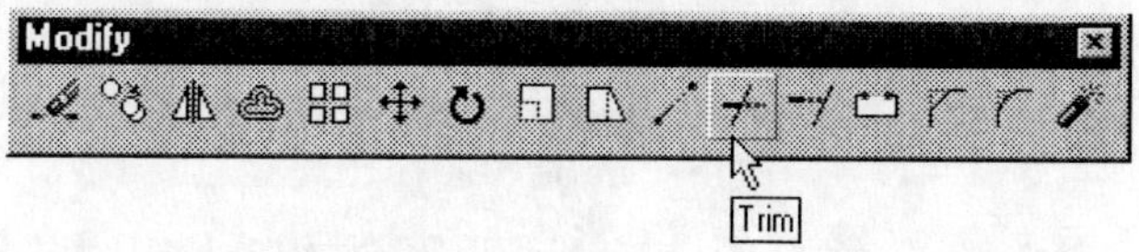

Figure 6.27

The first thing AutoCAD will want you to specify is at least one cutting edge. A cutting edge is an entity you want to use to trim another entity. That is, you want the trimmed entity to end at its intersection with the cutting edge.

Current settings: Projection = UCS, Edge = None
Select cutting edges...
Select objects:

The current settings are relevant to 3D drawing and need not concern you at this point. (For your information, Projection and Edge refer to system variables that determine the way AutoCAD will interpret boundaries and intersections in 3D space.) The second line reminds you that you are selecting edges first—the objects you want to trim will be selected later. The option of selecting more than one edge is a useful one, as we will demonstrate shortly.

For now we will select the circle as an edge and use it to trim the upper line.

⌖ **Point to the circle.**

The circle becomes dotted and will remain so until you leave the TRIM command. AutoCAD will prompt for more objects until you indicate that you are through selecting edges.

⌖ **Right click to end the selection of cutting edges.**

You will be prompted for an object to trim:

Select object to trim or [Project/Edge/Undo]:

We will trim off the segment of the upper line that lies outside the circle on the left. The important thing is to point to the part of the object you want to remove, as shown in Figure 6.26.

⌖ **Point to the upper line to the left of where it crosses the circle.**

The line is trimmed immediately, but the circle is still dotted, and AutoCAD continues to prompt for more objects to trim. Note how this differs from the BREAK command, in which you could only break one object at a time.

Also notice that you have an undo option, so that if the trim does not turn out the way you wanted, you can back up without having to leave the command and start over.

⌖ **Point to the lower line to the left of where it crosses the circle.**

Now you have trimmed both lines.

⌖ **Press Enter or the space bar to end the TRIM operation.**

Your screen should resemble Figure 6.26.

This has been a very simple trimming process, but more complex trimming is just as easy. The key is that you can select as many edges as you like and that an entity may be selected as both an edge and an object to trim, as we will demonstrate.

⌖ **Repeat the TRIM command.**

⌖ **Select both lines and the circle as cutting edges.**

This can be done with a window or with a crossing box.

⌖ **Right click or press the space bar to end the selection of edges.**

⌖ **Point to each of the remaining two line segments that lie outside the circle on the right, and to the top and bottom arcs of the circle to produce the bandaid-shaped object in Figure 6.28.**

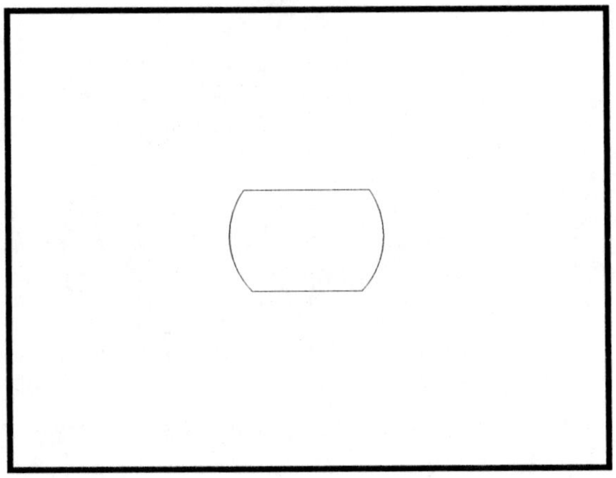

Figure 6.28

⌖ **Press Enter to exit the TRIM command.**

6.7 EXTENDING OBJECTS WITH THE EXTEND COMMAND

If you compare the procedures of the EXTEND command and the TRIM command, you will notice a remarkable similarity. Just substitute the word "boundary" for "cutting edge" and the word "extend" for "trim" and you've got it. These two commands are conceptually related and are so efficient that it is sometimes good practice to draw a temporary cutting edge or boundary on your screen and erase it after trimming or extending.

⌖ **Leave Figure 6.28, the bandaid, on your screen, and draw a vertical line to the right of it, as in Figure 6.29.**

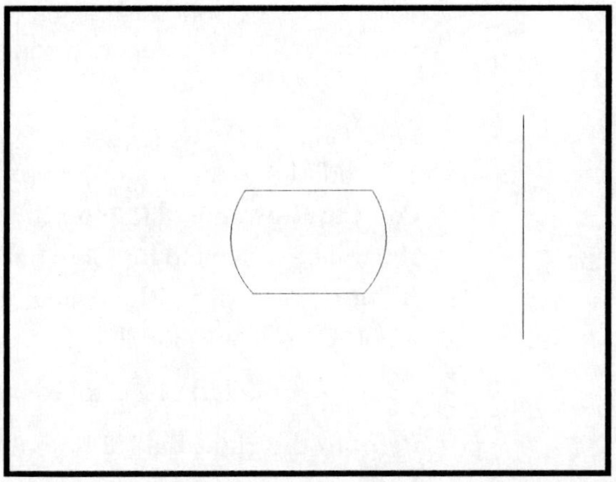

Figure 6.29

We will use this line as a boundary to which to extend the two horizontal lines, as in Figure 6.30.

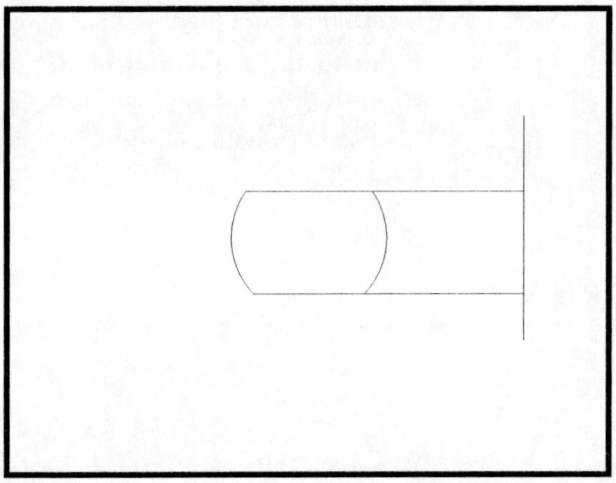

Figure 6.30

⌖ **Type "Ex" or select Extend from the Modify menu or the Extend tool from the Modify toolbar, as shown in Figure 6.31.**

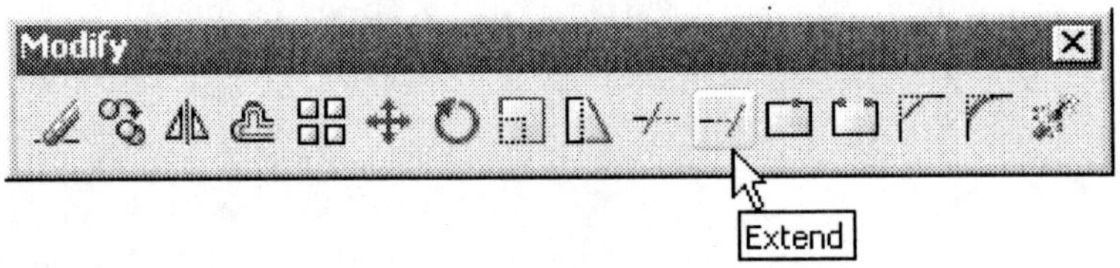

Figure 6.31

You will be prompted for objects to serve as boundaries:

```
Current settings: Projection = UCS, Edge = None
Select boundary edges...
Select objects:
```

Look familiar? As with the TRIM command, any of the usual selection methods will work. For our purposes, simply point to the vertical line.

- **Point to the vertical line on the right.**

You will be prompted for more boundary objects until you exit object selection.

- **Right click or press the space bar to end the selection of boundaries.**

AutoCAD now asks for objects to extend:

```
Select object to extend or [Project/Edge/Undo]:
```

- **Point to the right half of one of the two horizontal lines.**

Notice that you have to point to the line on the side closer to the selected boundary. Otherwise AutoCAD will look to the left instead of the right and give you the following message:

```
Object does not intersect an Edge
```

Note also that you only can select objects to extend by pointing. Windowing, crossing, or last selections will not work. Also be aware that arcs and polylines can be extended in the same manner as lines.

- **Point to the right half of the other horizontal line. Both lines should be extended to the vertical line.**

Your screen should resemble Figure 6.30.

- **Press the space bar to exit the EXTEND command.**

6.8 REVIEW MATERIAL

Questions

1. What is the difference between the pickbox and the object snap aperture?
2. At what point in a command procedure would you use an object snap single-point override? How would you signal the AutoCAD program that you want to use an object snap?
3. How do you access the Object Snap shortcut menu?
4. What is an acquired point?
5. How do you use BREAK to shorten a line at one end? When would you use this procedure instead of the TRIM command?

Commands

BREAK	EXTEND	OFFSET
OSNAP	TRIM	

6.9 DRAWING PROBLEMS

1. Draw a line from (6, 2) to (11, 6). Draw a second line perpendicular to the first starting at (6, 6).
2. Break the first line at its intersection with the second.
3. There are now three lines on the screen. Draw a circle centered at their intersection and passing through the midpoint of the line going up and to the right of the intersection.
4. Trim all the lines to the circumference of the circle.
5. Erase what is left of the line to the right of the intersection and trim the portion of the circle to the left, between the two remaining lines.

DRAWING 1

Archimedes Spiral

This drawing and the next go together as an exercise you should find interesting and enjoyable. These are not technical drawings, but they will give you valuable experience with important CAD commands. You will be creating a spiral using a radial grid of circles and lines as a guide. Once the spiral is done, you will use it to create the designs in the next drawing, 6.2, "Spiral Designs."

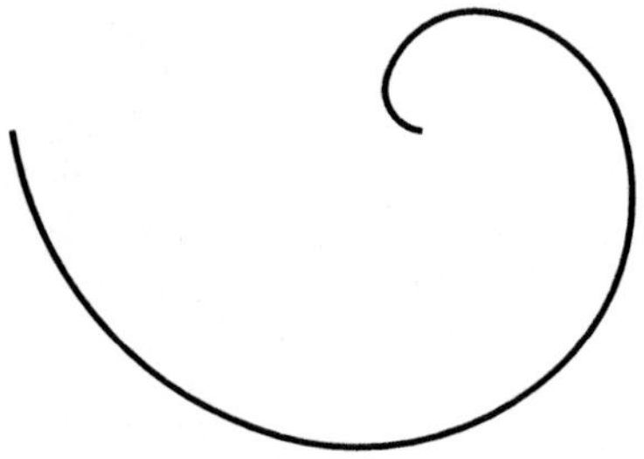

Drawing Suggestions

GRID = 0.5

SNAP = 0.25

LIMITS = (0,0) (18,12)

LTSCALE = 0.5

- The alternating continuous and hidden lines work as a drawing aid. If you use different colors and layers, they will be more helpful. Since all circles are offset 0.50, you can draw one continuous and one hidden circle, then use the OFFSET command to create all the others.
- Begin by drawing one of the continuous circles on Layer 0, centered near the middle of your display, then offset all the other continuous circles.
- Draw the continuous horizontal line across the middle of your six circles and then array it in a three-item polar array.
- Set to Layer 2, draw one of the hidden circles, then offset the other hidden circles.
- Draw a vertical hidden line and array it as you did the horizontal continuous line.
- Set to Layer 1 for the spiral itself.
- Turn on a running object snap to Intersection mode and construct a series of three-point arcs. Be sure to turn off any other modes that may get in your way. Start points and endpoints will be on continuous line intersections; second points always will fall on hidden line intersections.
- When the spiral is complete, turn off Layers 0 and 2. There should be nothing left on your screen but the spiral itself. Save it or go on to Drawing 6.2.

Grouping Objects

Here is a good opportunity to use the GROUP command. GROUP defines a collection of objects as a single entity so that they may be selected and modified as a unit. The spiral you have just drawn will be used in the next drawing, and it will be easier to manipulate if you GROUP it.

1. Type "g."
2. In the Object Grouping dialog box, type "Spiral" for a group name.
3. Click on "New <."
4. Select the six arcs with a window.
5. Right click to end selection.
6. Click on OK.

The spiral can now be selected, moved, rotated, and copied as a single entity.

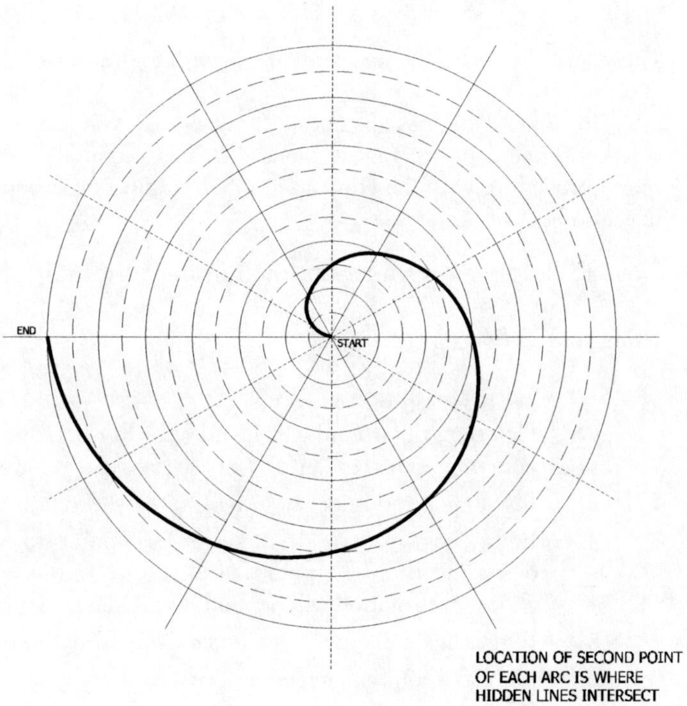

SOLID CIRCLE RADII	HIDDEN CIRCLE RADII
0.50	0.25
1.00	0.75
1.50	1.25
2.00	1.75
2.50	2.25
3.00	2.75

ARCHIMEDES SPIRAL

DRAWING 2

Spiral Designs

These designs are different from other drawings in this book. There are no dimensions, and you will use only edit commands now that the spiral is drawn. Below the designs is a list of the edit commands you will need. Don't be too concerned with precision. Some of your designs may come out slightly different from ours. When this happens, try to analyze the differences.

Drawing Suggestions

LIMITS = (0, 0) (34, 24)

These large limits will be necessary if you wish to draw all of these designs on the screen at once.

In some of the designs and in Drawing 6.3, you will need to rotate a copy of the spiral and keep the original in place. You can accomplish this by using the grip edit rotate procedure with the copy option. Setting up Polar snap to track at various angles may also be useful.

How To Rotate An Object and Retain the Original

Using Grip Edit

1. Select the spiral.
2. Pick the grip around which you want to rotate, or any of the grips if you are not going to use the grip as a base point for rotation.
3. Right click and select Rotate from the shortcut menu.
4. Right click and type "b" or select Base point from the shortcut menu, if the design needs a base point not on a grip. In this exercise the base point you choose for rotation will depend on the design you are trying to create.
5. Right click and type "c" or select Copy from the shortcut menu.
6. Show the rotation angle(s).
7. Press the space bar to exit the grip edit system

SPIRAL DESIGNS

DRAWING 3

Grooved Hub

This drawing includes a typical application of the rotation technique just discussed. The hidden lines in the front view must be rotated 120 degrees and a copy retained in the original position. There are also good opportunities to use MIRROR, Object Snap, Object Snap tracking, and TRIM.

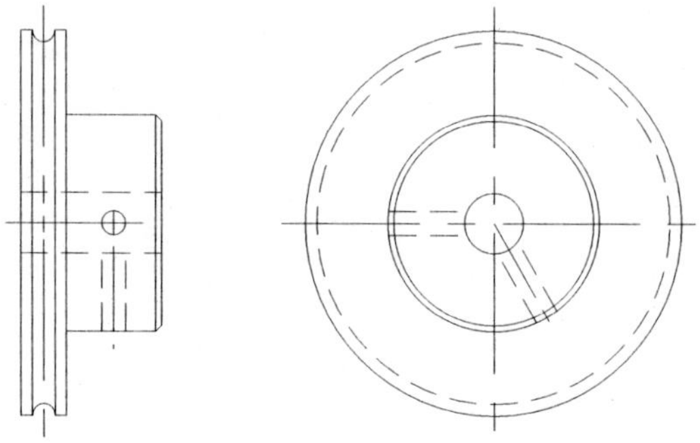

Drawing Suggestions

GRID = 0.5
SNAP = 0.0625
LIMITS = (0,0) (12,9)
LTSCALE = 1

- Draw the circles in the front view and use these to line up the horizontal lines in the left side view. This is a good opportunity to use Object Snap tracking. By acquiring the quadrant of a circle in the front view, you can track along the horizontal construction lines to the left side view.
- There are several different planes of symmetry in the left side view, which suggests the use of mirroring. We leave it up to you to choose an efficient sequence.
- A quick method for drawing the horizontal hidden lines in the left-side view is to acquire the upper and lower quadrants points of the 0.625 diameter circle in the front view to track horizontal construction lines. Draw the lines in the left side view longer than actual length and then use TRIM to erase the excess on both sides of the left-side view.
- The same method can be used to draw the two horizontal hidden lines in the front view. A slightly different method which does not use object tracking is to Snap lines directly to the top and bottom quadrants of the 0.25 diameter circle in the left side view as a guide, and draw them all the way through the front view. Then trim to the 2.25 diameter circle and the 0.62 diameter circle.
- Once these hidden lines are drawn, rotate them, retaining a copy in the original position.

Creating the Multiple View Layout

Use this drawing to create the multiple view layout shown below the dimensioned drawing. Exact dimensions of the viewports are not given. You should create them depending on the paper size you wish to use. What should remain consistent is the scale relationships among the three viewports. On an A sheet, for example, if the largest viewport is zoomed 0.5xp, then the left close up is 1.0xp and the top close up is 1.5xp. These ratios will have to be adjusted for other sheet sizes.

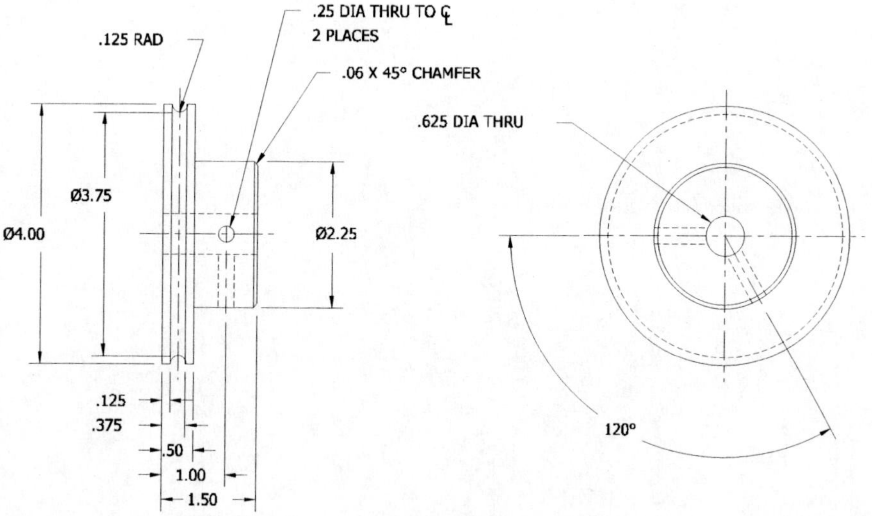
.25 DIA THRU TO ℄
2 PLACES
.125 RAD
.06 X 45° CHAMFER
.625 DIA THRU
Ø3.75
Ø4.00
Ø2.25
.125
.375
.50
1.00
1.50
120°

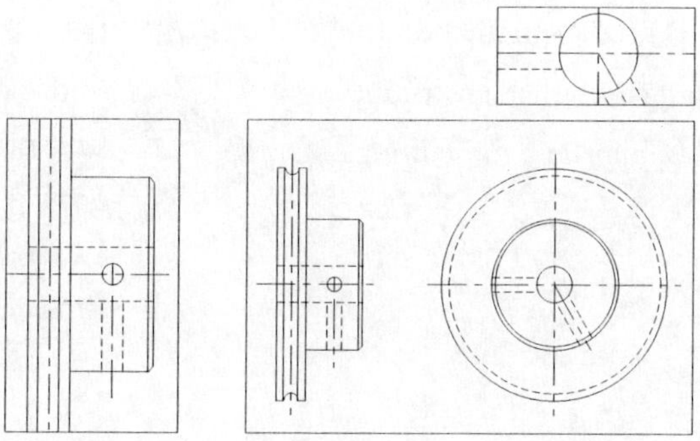

GROOVED HUB

7

Text

Overview

Now it's time to add text to your drawings. In this chapter you will learn to use AutoCAD's DTEXT command. In addition, you will learn editing commands that are often used with text but that are equally important for editing other objects.

Sections

Objectives

After reading this chapter, you should be able to:

- Enter standard text using the DTEXT command.
- Enter standard text using different justification options.
- Check spelling of text in a drawing.
- Change fonts and styles.
- Change properties with MATCHPROP.
- Use SCALE to change the size of objects on the screen.
- Draw a title block.
- Draw gauges.
- Draw a control panel.

7.1 ENTERING LEFT-JUSTIFIED TEXT USING DTEXT

AutoCAD provides two commands for entering text in a drawing. DTEXT (also called TEXT) allows you to enter single lines of text and displays them as you type. You can backspace through lines to make corrections if you do not leave the command. MTEXT allows you to type multiple lines of text in a dialog box and positions them in a windowed area in your drawing. Both commands have numerous options for placing text, and a variety of fonts to use and styles that can be created from them. In the first task we will focus on the basic placement features of the DTEXT command, sticking with the standard style and font.

⌖ **To prepare for this exercise, open a new drawing using the B template and draw a 4.00 horizontal line beginning at (1, 1). Then create a six-row by one-column array with 2.00 between rows, as shown in Figure 7.1.**

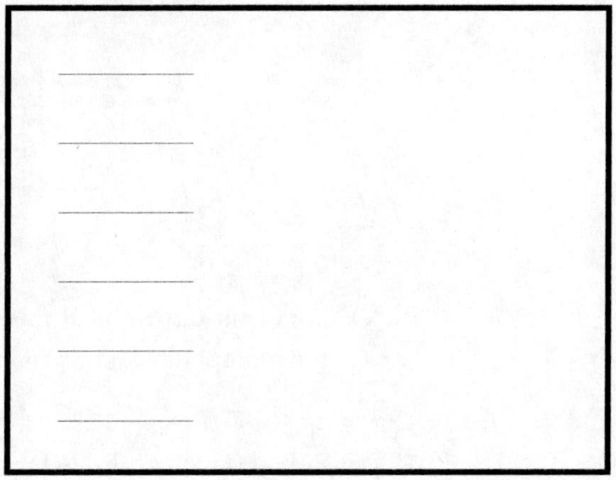

Figure 7.1

These lines are for orientation in this exercise only; they are not essential for drawing text.

⌖ **Type "dt" or open the Draw menu, highlight Text, and then select Single-Line Text, as shown in Figure 7.2.**

There is a Text tool on the Draw toolbar, but it enters the MTEXT command.

Either of the methods here will enter the DTEXT command, and you will see a prompt with three options:

Current text style: "STANDARD" Text height: 0.20
Specify start point of text or [Justify/Style]:

"Style" will be explored in Section 7.5 In this section we will be looking at different options for placing text in a drawing. These are all considered text justification methods and will be listed if you choose the "Justify" option at the command prompt.

First we will use the default method by picking a start point. This will give us left-justified text, inserted left to right from the point we pick.

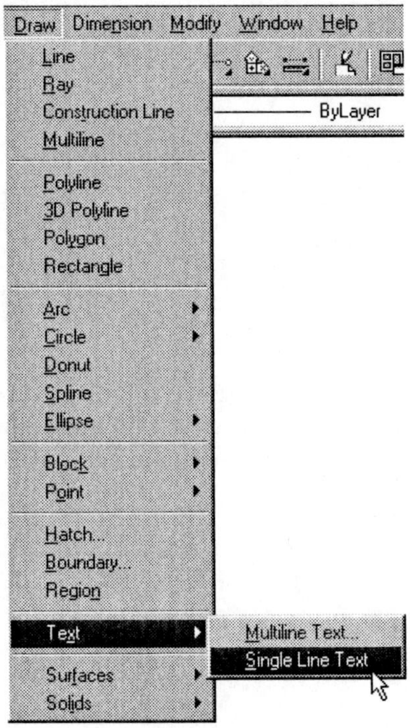

Figure 7.2

⌖ **Pick a start point at the left end of the upper line.**

Look at the prompt that follows and be sure that you do not attempt to enter text yet:

Specify height <0.20>:

This gives you the opportunity to set the text height. The number you type specifies the height of uppercase letters in the units you have specified for the current drawing. For now we will accept the default height.

⌖ **Press Enter to accept the default height (0.20).**

The prompt that follows allows you to place text in a rotated position.

Specify rotation angle of text <0>:

The default of 0 degrees orients text in the usual horizontal manner. Other angles can be specified by typing a degree number relative to the polar coordinate system or by showing a point. If you show a point, it will be taken as the second point of a baseline along which the text string will be placed. For now we will stick to horizontal text.

⌖ **Press Enter to accept the default angle (0).**

Now, at last, it is time to enter the text itself. AutoCAD prompts

Enter text:

Notice that a small text cursor has appeared at the start point on your screen. Move your cross hairs away from this point and you will see the cursor clearly. This shows where the first letter you type will be placed. For our text we will type the word "Left," identifying this as an example of left-justified text. Watch the screen as you type and you will see the text drawn as you type.

- **Type "Left" and press Enter.**

  (Remember, you cannot use the space bar in place of the enter key when entering text.) Notice that the text cursor jumps down below the line when you hit Enter. Also notice that you are given a second "Enter text:" prompt in the command area.
- **Type "Justified" and press Enter.**

  The text cursor jumps down again and another "Enter text:" prompt appears. This is how DTEXT allows for easy entry of multiple lines of text directly on the screen in a drawing. To exit the command, you need to press Enter at the prompt.
- **Press Enter to exit DTEXT.**

  This completes the process and returns you to the command prompt.

Figure 7.3 shows the left-justified text you have just drawn, along with other options that we will demonstrate in the next section.

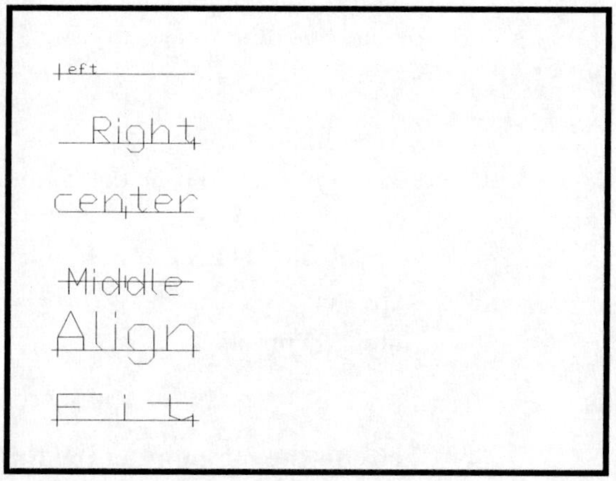

Figure 7.3

7.2 USING OTHER TEXT JUSTIFICATION OPTIONS

We will now proceed to try out some of the other text placement options, beginning with right-justified text, as shown on the second line of Figure 7.3. We will also specify a change in height.

7.2.1 Right-Justified Text

Right-justified text is constructed from an endpoint backing up, right to left.

- **Repeat the DTEXT command.**

  You will see the same prompt as before.
- **Type "r" for right-justified text.**

  Now AutoCAD prompts for an endpoint instead of a start point:

  Specify right endpoint of text baseline:

  We will choose the right end of the second line.
- **Point to the right end of the second line.**

This time we will change the height to 0.50. Notice that AutoCAD gives you a rubberband from the endpoint. It can be used to specify height and rotation angle by pointing, if you like.

- **Type "0.5" or show a height of 0.50 by pointing.**
- **Press Enter to retain 0 degrees of rotation.**

You are now prompted to enter text.

- **Type "Right" and press Enter.**

Here you should notice an important fact about the DTEXT command. Initially, DTEXT ignores your justification choice, entering the letters you type from left to right as usual. The justification will be carried out only when you exit the command.

At this point you should have the word "Right" showing to the right of the second line. Watch what happens when you press Enter a second time to exit the command.

- **Press Enter.**

The text will jump to the left, onto the line. Your screen should now include the second line of text in right-justified position, as shown in Figure 7.3.

7.2.2 Centered Text

Centered text is justified from the bottom center of the text.

- **Repeat the DTEXT command.**
- **Type "c."**

AutoCAD prompts

Specify center point of text:

- **Point to the midpoint of the third line.**
- **Press Enter to retain the current height, which is now set to 0.50.**
- **Press Enter to retain 0 degrees of rotation.**
- **Type "Center" and press Enter.**

Notice again how the letters are displayed on the screen in the usual left-to-right manner.

- **Press Enter again to complete the command.**

The word "Center" should now be centered, as shown in Figure 7.3.

7.2.3 Middle, Aligned, and Fit Text

Looking at the bottom three lines of Figure 7.3 you will see middle text, aligned text, and text stretched to fit on the line. You can try these options using the procedures just described. Repeat Dtext, type in an option, and pick a point or points on the line.

Middle text (type "m") is justified from the middle of the text horizontally and vertically, rather than from the bottom.

Aligned text (type "a") is placed between two specified points. The height of the text is calculated proportional to the distance between the two points and the text is drawn along the line between two points.

The Fit option (type "f") is similar to the Aligned option, except that the specified text height is retained. Text will be stretched horizontally to fill the line without a change in height.

7.2.4 Other Justification Options

There are additional justification options that are labeled with various combinations of top, middle, bottom, left, and right. The letter options are shown in Figure 7.4. As shown in the figure and the screen menu, T is for top, M is for middle, and B is for bottom. L, C, and R stand for left, center, and right. All of these options work the same way. Just enter DTEXT and the one or two letters of the option.

TEXT JUSTIFICATION	
START POINT TYPE ABBREVIATION	TEXT POSITION +INDICATES START POINT or PICK POINT
A	ALIGN
F	FIT
C	CENTER
M	MIDDLE
R	RIGHT
TL	TOP LEFT
TC	TOP CENTER
TR	TOP RIGHT
ML	MIDDLE LEFT
MC	MIDDLE CENTER
MR	MIDDLE RIGHT
BL	BOTTOM LEFT
BC	BOTTOM CENTER
BR	BOTTOM RIGHT

Figure 7.4

7.3 USING THE SPELL COMMAND

AutoCAD's SPELL command is simple to use and will be very familiar to anyone who has used spell checkers in word processing programs. We will use SPELL to check the spelling of all the text we have drawn so far.

⌗ **Type "sp" or select Spelling from the Tools menu.**

You will see a "Select objects:" prompt on the command line. At this point you could point to individual objects. Any object may be selected, although no checking will be done if you select a line, for example.

For our purposes we will use an "All" option to check all the spelling in the drawing.

- **Type "all."**

AutoCAD will continue to prompt for object selection until you press Enter.

- **Press Enter to end object selection.**

Assuming you have no mispelled words in your drawing you will see a message box that says:

Spelling check complete

If there are mispelled words, you will see the Check Spelling dialog box shown in Figure 7.5. This example shows that the AutoCAD spell check would treat the word "Mtext" as a mispelling and often "Text" as a suggested change. Look at the options that are available. You can ignore a word the checker does not recognize, or change it. You can change a single instance of a word, or change all instances in the currently selected text. You can add a word to a customized dictionary or you can change to another dictionary.

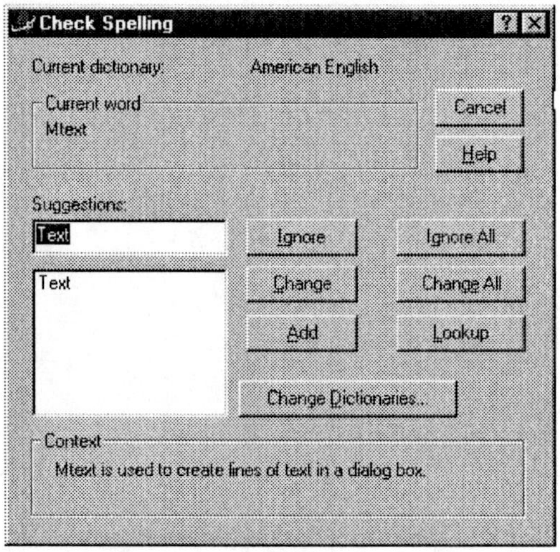

Figure 7.5

- **Click on "OK" to end the spell check.**

If you have made any corrections in spelling, they will be incorporated into your drawing at this point.

7.4 CHANGING FONTS AND STYLES

By default, the current text style in any AutoCAD drawing is one called "STANDARD." It is a specific form of a font called "txt" that comes with the software. All the text you have entered so far has been drawn with the standard style of the "txt" font.

Changing fonts is a simple matter. However, there is room for confusion in the use of the words "style" and "font." Fonts are the basic patterns of character and symbol shapes that can be used with the DTEXT and MTEXT commands. Styles are variations in the size, orientation, and spacing of the characters in those fonts. It is possible to create your own fonts, but for most of us this is an esoteric activity. In contrast, creating your own styles is easy and practical.

We will begin by creating a variation of the STANDARD style you have been using.

⌗ **Type "st" or select Text Style... from the Format menu.**

Either method will open the Text Style dialog box shown in Figure 7.6. You will probably see STANDARD listed in the Style name box. However, it is possible that there will be other styles listed. In this case you should open the list with the arrow on the right and select STANDARD, the AutoCAD default style. We will create our own variation of the STANDARD style and call it "VERTICAL." It will use the same "txt" character font, but will be drawn down the display instead of across.

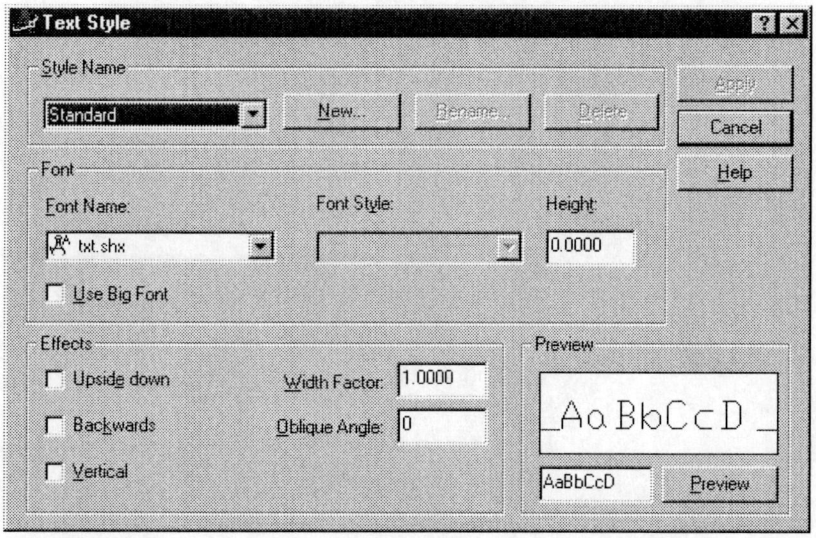

Figure 7.6

⌗ **Click in the "Vertical" check box.**

We will also give this style a fixed height and a width factor. Notice that the current height is 0.00. This does not mean that your characters will be drawn 0.00 units high. It means that there will be no fixed height, so you will be able to specify a height whenever you use this style. STANDARD currently has no fixed height, so VERTICAL has inherited this setting. Try giving our new "VERTICAL" style a fixed height.

⌗ **Double click in the Height edit box and then type "0.5."**

⌗ **Double click in the Width Factor box and type "2."**

⌗ **Click on "New."**

AutoCAD opens a smaller dialog box that asks for a name for the new text style.

⌗ **Type "vertical".**

⌗ **Click on OK.**

This brings you back to the Text Style dialog box, with the new style listed in the style name area.

⌗ **Click on Close to exit the Text Style dialog.**

The new VERTICAL style is now current. To see it in action you will need to enter some text.

⌗ **Type "dt" or open the Draw menu, highlight Text, and then highlight Single Line text.**

⌗ **Pick a start point, as shown by the placement of the letter "V" in Figure 7.7.**

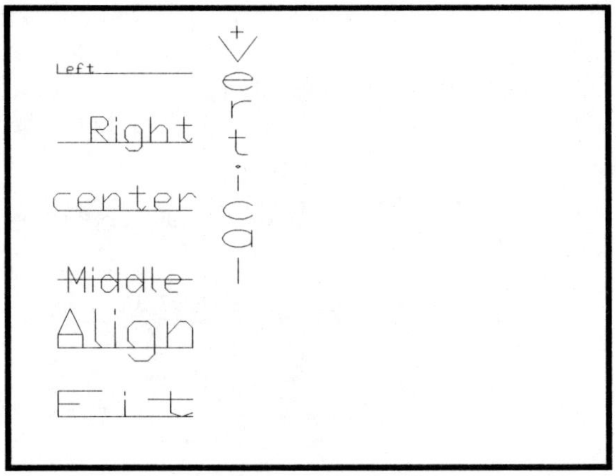

Figure 7.7

Notice that you are not prompted for a height because the current style has height fixed at 0.50.

⌗ **Press Enter to retain 270 degrees of rotation.**

⌗ **Type "Vertical".**

⌗ **Press Enter to end the line.**

Before going on, notice that the DTEXT text placement box has moved up to begin a new column of text next to the word "vertical."

⌗ **Press Enter to exit DTEXT.**

Your screen should resemble Figure 7.7.

There are now two text styles in the current drawing. Both use the txt font. Next we will create a third style using a different font and some of the other style options.

⌗ **Type "st" or select Text Style... from the Format menu.**

⌗ **Open the Font name list by clicking on the arrow.**

⌗ **Scroll to "Romand.shx" and stop.**

Romand stands for "Roman Duplex," an AutoCAD font.

⌗ **Click on "romand.shx" to place it in the font name box.**

⌗ **Click in the Vertical box to remove the check.**

⌗ **Set the text height to 0.00.**

⌗ **Set the width factor to 1.**

⌗ **Set Obliquing angle to 45.**

This will cause your text to be slanted 45 degrees to the right. For a left slant, you would type a negative number.

⌗ **Click on New to give the style a name.**

⌗ **In the New text style dialog box, give the style the name "Slanted."**

⌗ **Click on OK to close the New Text Style box.**

⌗ **Click on Close to exit the Text Style box.**

Now enter some text to see how this slanted Roman Duplex style looks.

⌗ **Enter the DTEXT command and answer the prompts to draw the words "Roman Duplex" with a 0.50 height, as shown in Figure 7.8.**

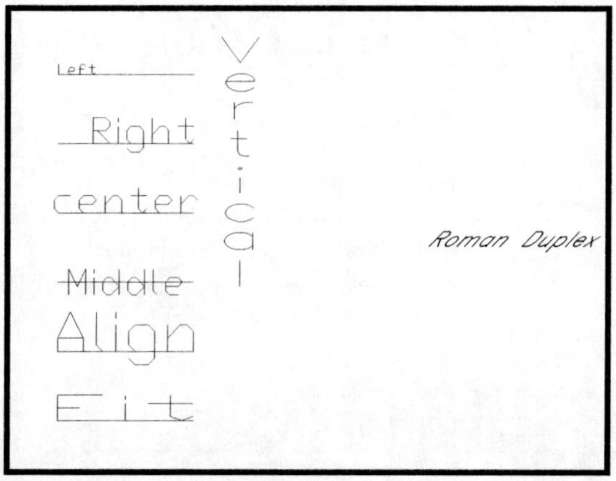

Figure 7.8

7.4.1 Switching the Current Style

There are now two styles defined in your drawing. All new text is created in the current style. The style of previously drawn text can be changed, as we will show later. Once you have a number of styles defined in a drawing, you can switch from one to another by using the Style option of the DTEXT and MTEXT commands or by selecting a text style from the Text Style dialog box.

NOTE: If you change the definition of a text style, all text previously drawn in that style will be regenerated with the new style specifications.

7.5 CHANGING PROPERTIES WITH MATCHPROP

MATCHPROP is a very efficient command that lets you match all or some of the properties of an object to those of another object. Properties that can be transferred from one object to another, or to many others, include layer, linetype, color, and linetype scale. These settings are common to all AutoCAD entities. Other properties that only relate to specific types of entities are thickness, text style, dimension style, and hatch style. In all cases the procedure is the same.

Here we will use MATCHPROP to change some previously drawn text to the new "Slanted" style.

⌗ **Select the Match Properties tool from the Standard toolbar, as shown in Figure 7.9.**

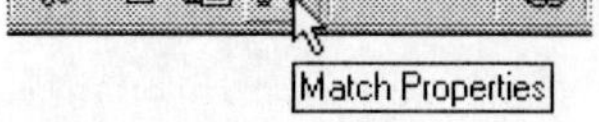

Figure 7.9

You can also type "ma" or select Match Properties from the Modify toolbar.
AutoCAD will prompt:

Select Source Object:

You can have many destination objects but only one source object.

Select the text "Roman Duplex," drawn in the last section in the Slanted style.

AutoCAD switches to the Match Properties cursor, shown in Figure 7.10, and displays a list of active settings and prompts:

Current active settings: Color Layer Ltype Ltscale Lineweight Thickness PlotStyle Text Dim Hatch
Select destination object(s) or [Settings]:

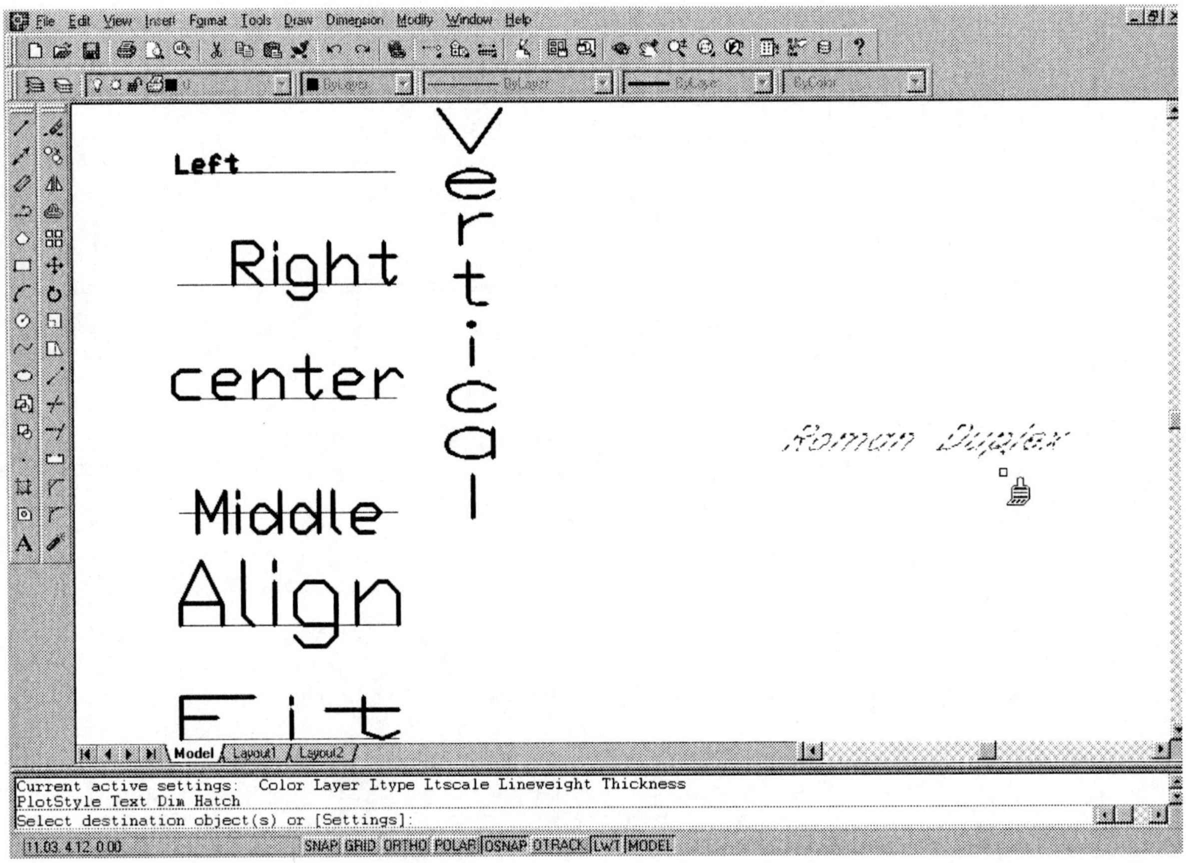

Figure 7.10

At this point you can limit the settings you want to match by typing "s" for settings, or you can select destination objects, in which case all properties will be matched.

Type "s."

This opens the Property Settings dialog box, shown in Figure 7.11. The Basic properties panel shows properties that can be changed and the settings that will be used based on the source object you have selected.

At the bottom you will see Dimension, Text, and Hatch in the Special Properties panel. These refer to dimension, text, and hatch styles that have been defined in your drawing. If any of these is deselected, then Match Properties will ignore style definitions and will only match the basic properties checked.

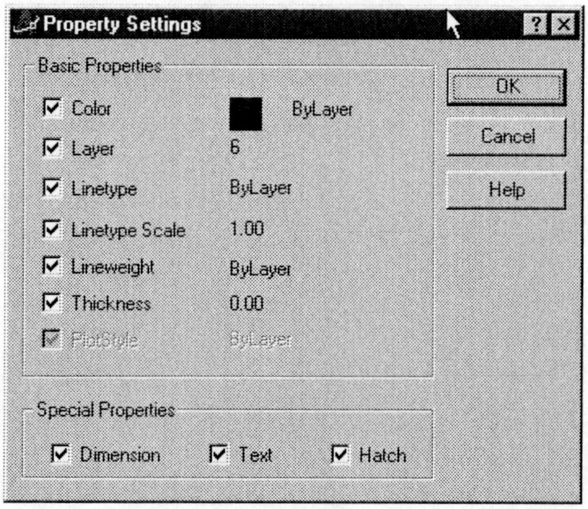

Figure 7.11

⌖ **Click on OK to exit the dialog.**

AutoCAD returns to the screen with the same prompt as before.

⌖ **Select the words "Align" and "Vertical."**

These two words will be redrawn in the Slanted style, as shown in Figure 7.12.

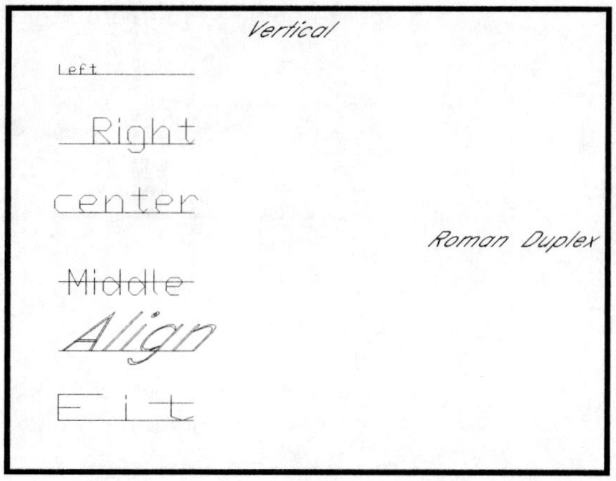

Figure 7.12

7.5.1 The CHANGE Command

The CHANGE command is an older AutoCAD command that has been largely replaced by other editing commands. CHANGE works at the command line and allows you to modify all of the basic text properties, including insertion point, style, height, rotation angle, and text content. You can select as many objects as you like and CHANGE will cycle through them. In addition, CHANGE can be used to alter the end points of lines and the size of circles. With lines, CHANGE will perform a function similar to the EXTEND command, but without the necessity of defining an extension boundary. CHANGE will cause circles to be redrawn so that they pass through a designated "change point." The effects of change points on lines and circles are shown in Figure 7.13. Notice in particular the way lines will react to a change point with ortho on.

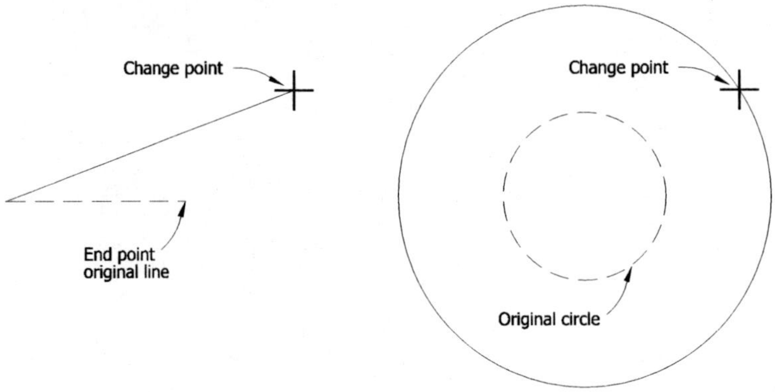

Figure 7.13

7.6 SCALING PREVIOUSLY DRAWN ENTITIES

Any object or group of objects can be scaled up or down using the SCALE command or the grip edit scale mode. In this exercise we will practice scaling some of the text and lines that you have drawn on your screen. Remember, however, that there is no special relationship between SCALE and text and that other types of entities can be scaled just as easily.

⌖ **Select the Scale tool from Modify toolbar, as shown in Figure 7.14.**

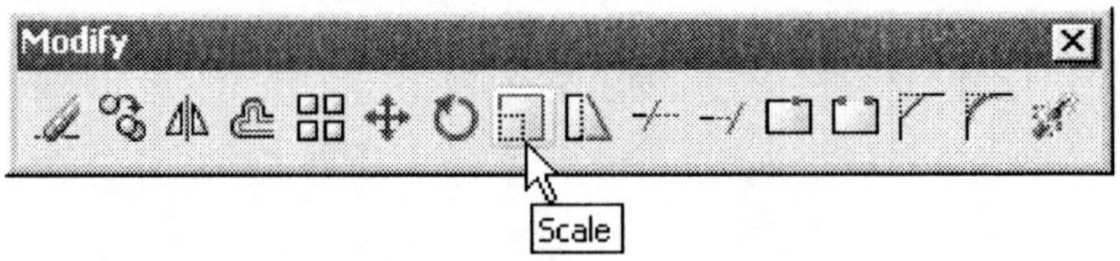

Figure 7.14

You can also type "sc" or select Scale from the Modify menu.

AutoCAD will prompt you to select objects.

⌖ **Use a crossing box (right to left) to select the set of six lines and text drawn in Section 7.1**

⌖ **Press Enter to end selection.**

You will be prompted to pick a base point:

Specify base point:

The concept of a base point in scaling is critical. Imagine for a moment that you are looking at a square and you want to shrink it using a scale-down procedure. All the sides will be shrunk the same amount, but how do you want this to happen? Should the lower left corner stay in place and the whole square shrink toward it? Or should everything shrink toward the center? Or toward some other point on or off the square (see Figure 7.15)? This is what you will tell AutoCAD when you pick a base point.

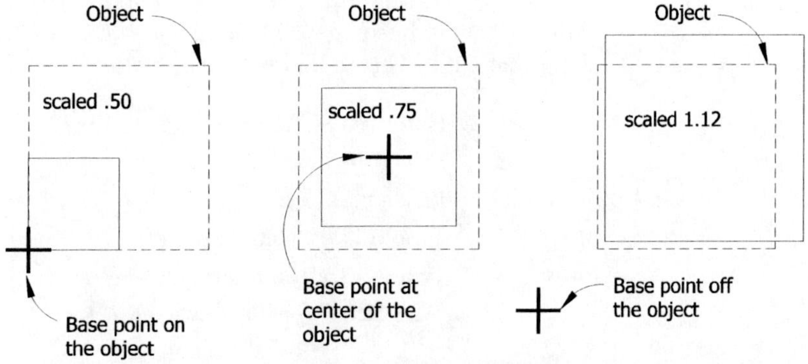

Figure 7.15

Pick a base point at the left end of the bottom line of the selected set (shown as Base point in Figure 7.16).

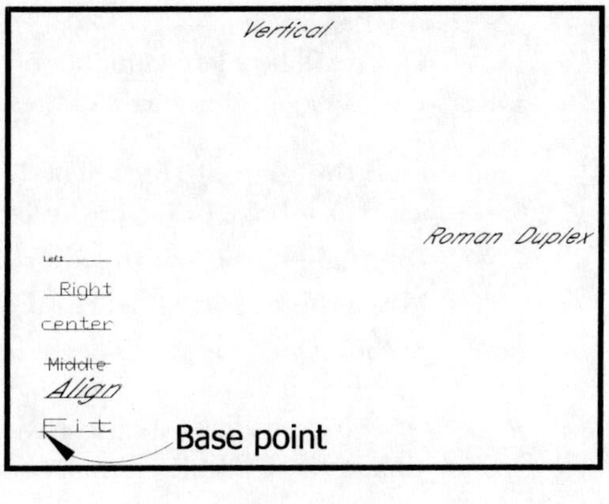

Figure 7.16

AutoCAD now needs to know how much to shrink or enlarge the objects you have selected:

Specify scale factor or [Reference]:

We will get to the reference method in a moment. When you enter a scale factor, all lengths, heights, and diameters in your set will be multiplied by that factor and redrawn accordingly. Scale factors are based on a unit of 1. If you enter 0.5, objects will be reduced to half their original size. If you enter 2, objects will become twice as large.

Type "0.5" and press Enter.

Your screen should now resemble Figure 7.16.

7.6.1 Scaling by Reference

This option can save you from doing the arithmetic to figure out scale factors. It is useful when you have a given length and you know how large you want that length to become after the scaling is done. For example, we know that the lines we just scaled are now 2.00 (they were 4.00 and we scaled them down by 0.50). Let's say that we want to scale them again to become 2.33 long (a scale factor of 1.165, but who wants to stop and figure that out?). This could be done using the following procedure:

1. Enter the SCALE command.
2. Select the lines.
3. Pick a base point.
4. Type "r" or select "reference."
5. Type "2" for the reference length.
6. Type "2.33" for the new length.

NOTE: You can also perform reference scaling by pointing. In the preceding procedure, you could point to the ends of the 2.00 line for the reference length and then show a 2.33 line for the new length.

7.6.2 Scaling with Grips

Scaling with grips is very similar to scaling with the SCALE command. To illustrate this, try using grips to return the text you just scaled back to its original size.

Use a window or crossing box to select the six lines and the text drawn in Section 7.1 again.

There will be a large number of grips on the screen, three on each line and two on most of the text entities. Some of these will overlap or duplicate each other.

- **Pick the grip at the lower left corner of the word "Fit," the same point used as a base point in the last scaling procedure.**
- **Right click to open the shortcut menu and then select Scale.**
- **Move the cursor slowly and observe the dragged image.**

  AutoCAD will use the selected grip point as the base point for scaling unless you specify that you want to pick a different base point.

  Notice that you also have a reference option as in the SCALE command. Unlike the SCALE command, you also have an option to make copies of your objects at different scales.

  As in SCALE, the default method is used to specify a scale factor by pointing or typing.
- **Type "2" or show a length of 2.00 for the scale factor.**

  Your text will return to its original size, and your screen will resemble Figure 7.12 again.
- **Press Esc twice to clear grips.**

7.7 REVIEW MATERIAL

Questions

1. You have drawn two lines of text using DTEXT and have left the command to do some editing. You discover that a third line of text should have been entered with the first two lines. What procedure will allow you to add the third line of text efficiently so that it is spaced and aligned with the first two, as if you had never left DTEXT?

2. What is the difference between center-justified text and middle-justified text?
3. What is the purpose of MATCHPROP?
4. How do you check all the spelling in your drawing at once?
5. What is the difference between a font and a style?
6. What can happen if you choose the wrong base point when using the SCALE command?
7. How would you use SCALE to change a 3.00 line to 2.75?

Commands

CHANGE	DTEXT	MATCHPROP
SCALE	SPELL	STYLE

7.8 DRAWING PROBLEMS

1. Draw a 6 × 6 square. Draw the word "Top," on top of the square, 0.4 units high, centered on the midpoint of the top side of the square.
2. Draw the word "Left," 0.4 units high, centered on the left side of the square.
3. Draw the word "Right," 0.4 units high, centered on the right side of the square.
4. Draw the word "Bottom," 0.4 units high, below the square so that the top of the text is centered on the midpoint of the bottom side of the square.
5. Draw the words "This is the middle," inside the square, 0.4 units high, so that the complete text wraps around within a 2-unit width and is centered on the center point of square.

DRAWING 1

Title Block

This title block will give you practice in using a variety of text styles and sizes. You may want to save it and use it as a title block for future drawings.

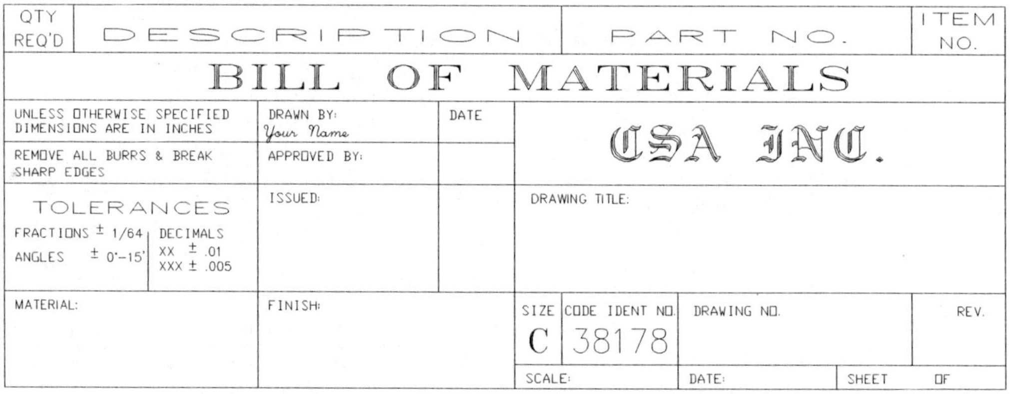

Drawing Suggestions

GRID = 1

SNAP = 0.0625

- Make ample use of TRIM as you draw the line patterns of the title block. Take your time and make sure that at least the major divisions are in place before you start entering text into the boxes.
- Set to the "text" layer before entering text.
- Use DTEXT with all the STANDARD, 0.09, left-justified text. This will allow you to do all of these in one command sequence, moving the cursor from one box to the next and entering the text as you go.
- Remember that once you have defined a style, you can make it current in the DTEXT command. This will save you from having to restyle more than necessary.
- Use "%%D" for the degree symbol and "%%P" for the plus or minus symbol.

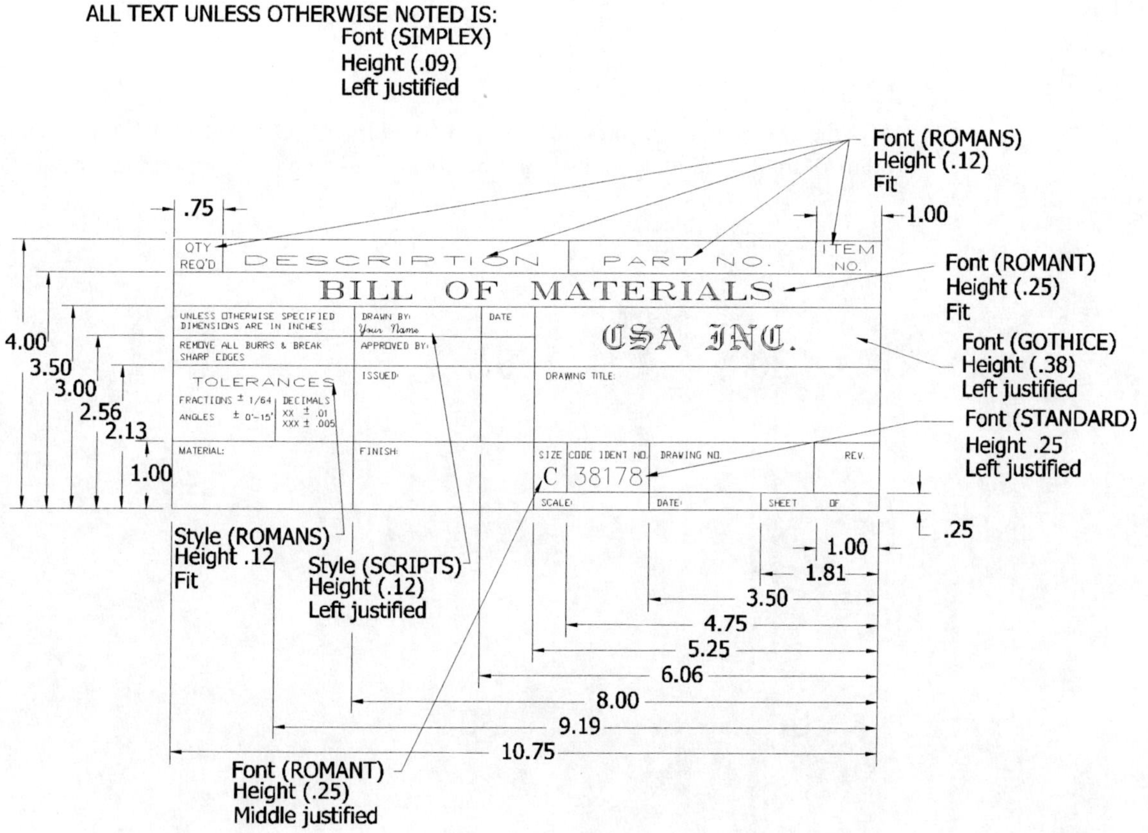
ALL TEXT UNLESS OTHERWISE NOTED IS:
Font (SIMPLEX)
Height (.09)
Left justified
Font (ROMANS)
Height (.12)
Fit
.75
1.00
QTY REQ'D
DESCRIPTION
PART NO.
ITEM NO.
BILL OF MATERIALS
Font (ROMANT)
Height (.25)
Fit
UNLESS OTHERWISE SPECIFIED DIMENSIONS ARE IN INCHES
DRAWN BY:
Your Name
DATE
CSA INC.
Font (GOTHICE)
Height (.38)
Left justified
REMOVE ALL BURRS & BREAK SHARP EDGES
APPROVED BY:
TOLERANCES
ISSUED:
DRAWING TITLE:
FRACTIONS ± 1/64
DECIMALS
ANGLES ± 0°-15'
XX ± .01
XXX ± .005
Font (STANDARD)
Height .25
Left justified
MATERIAL:
FINISH:
SIZE
CODE IDENT NO.
DRAWING NO.
REV.
C
38178
SCALE:
DATE:
SHEET
OF
4.00
3.50
3.00
2.56
2.13
1.00
.25
Style (ROMANS)
Height .12
Fit
Style (SCRIPTS)
Height (.12)
Left justified
1.00
1.81
3.50
4.75
5.25
6.06
8.00
9.19
10.75
Font (ROMANT)
Height (.25)
Middle justified

TITLE BLOCK

DRAWING 2

Gauges

This drawing will teach you some typical uses of the SCALE and DDEDIT commands. Some of the techniques used will not be obvious, so read the suggestions carefully.

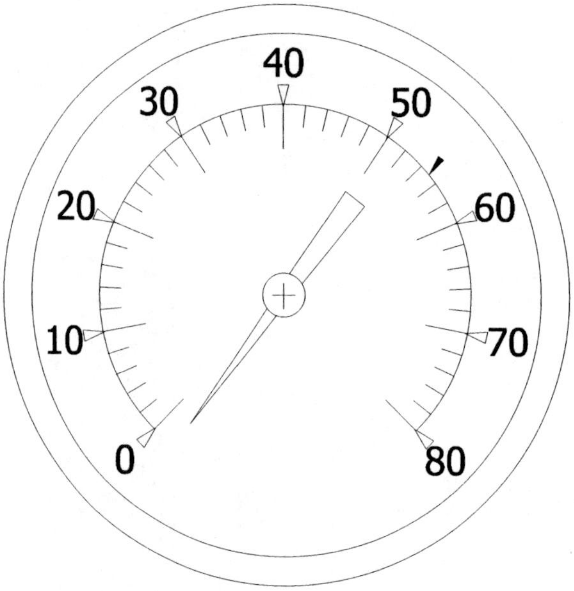

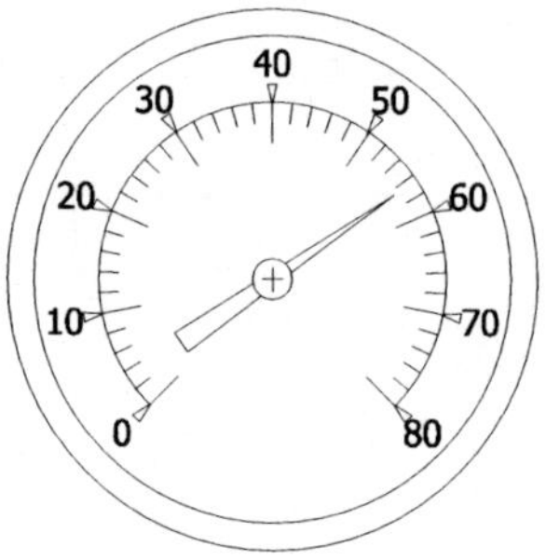

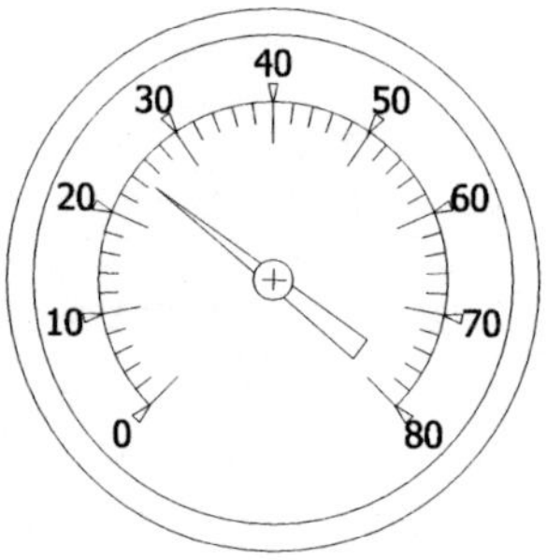

Drawing Suggestions

GRID = 0.5

SNAP = 0.125

- Draw three concentric circles at diameters of 5.0, 4.5, and 3.0. The bottom of the 3.0 circle can be trimmed later.
- Zoom in to draw the arrow-shaped tick at the top of the 3.0 circle. Then draw the 0.50 vertical line directly below it and the number "40" (middle-justified text) above it.
- These three objects can be arrayed to the left and right around the perimeter of the 3.0 circle using angles of +135 and −135 as shown.
- Use DDEDIT to change the arrayed numbers into 0, 10, 20, 30, etc. You can do all of these without leaving the command.
- Draw the 0.25 vertical tick directly on top of the 0.50 mark at top center and array it left and right. There will be 20 marks each way.
- Draw the needle horizontally across the middle of the dial.
- Make two copies of the dial; use SCALE to scale them down as shown. Then move them into their correct positions.
- Rotate the three needles into positions as shown.

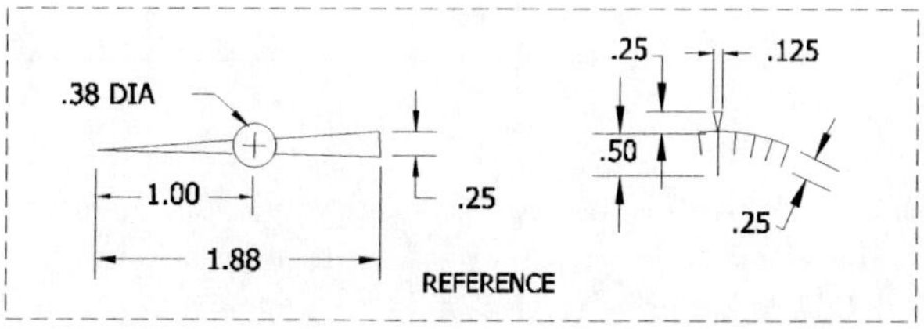
.38 DIA
1.00
1.88
.25
REFERENCE
.25
.125
.50
.25

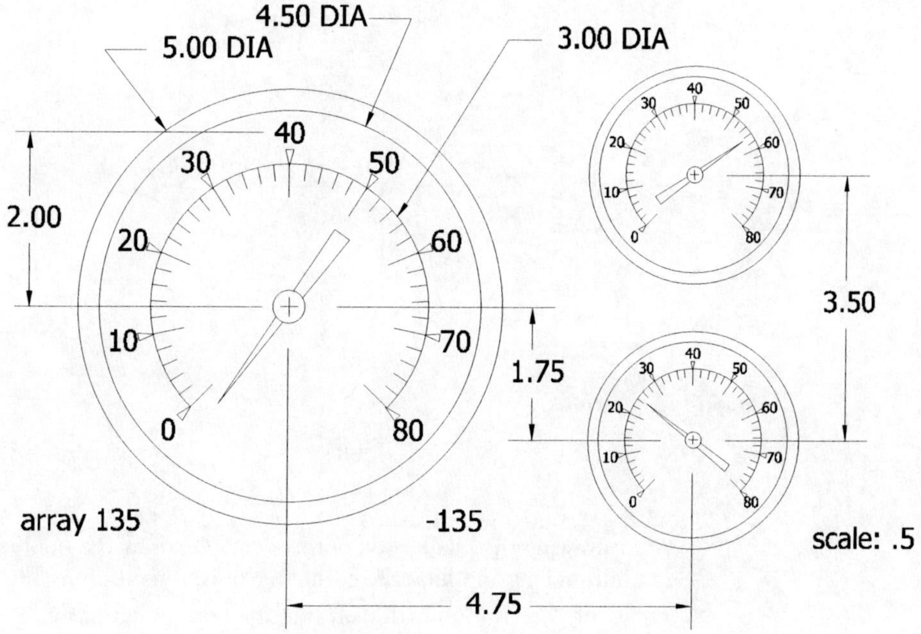
4.50 DIA
5.00 DIA
3.00 DIA
2.00
40
30
50
20
60
10
70
0
80
1.75
3.50
array 135
-135
scale: .5
4.75

GAUGES

DRAWING 3

Control Panel

Done correctly, this drawing will give you a good feel for the power of the commands you now have available to you. Be sure to take advantage of combinations of ARRAY and DDEDIT as described. Also, read the suggestion on moving the origin before you begin. Moving the origin in this drawing will make it easier to read the dimensions, which are given in ordinate form measured from the (0, 0) point at the lower left corner of the object.

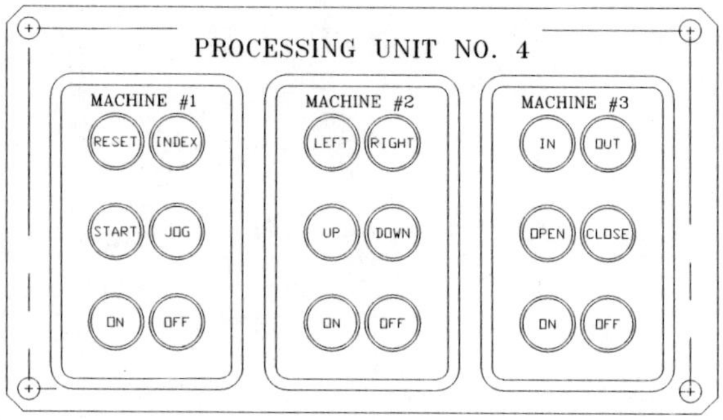

Drawing Suggestions

GRID = 0.50

SNAP = 0.0625

- After drawing the chamfered outer rectangle, draw the double outline of the left button box, and fillet the corners. Notice the different fillet radii.
- Draw the "on" button with its text at the bottom left of the box. Then array it 2 × 3 for the other buttons in the box.
- Use DDEDIT to change the lower right button text to "off" and draw the MACHINE # text at the top of the box.
- ARRAY the box 1 × 3 to create the other boxes.
- Use DDEDIT to change text for other buttons and machine numbers as shown.

Moving The Origin With the UCS Command The dimensions of this drawing are shown in ordinate form, measured from a single point of origin in the lower left-hand corner. In effect, this establishes a new coordinate origin. If we move our origin to match this point, then we will be able to read dimension values directly from the coordinate display. This could be done by setting the lower left-hand limits to (−1, −1). But it may be done more efficiently using the UCS command to establish a User Coordinate System with the origin at a point you specify. For now, here is a simple procedure:

1. From the Tools menu, select Move UCS.
2. Point to the new origin.

That's all there is to it. Move your cursor to the new origin and watch the coordinate display. It should show "0.00,0.00,0.00," and all values will be measured from there.

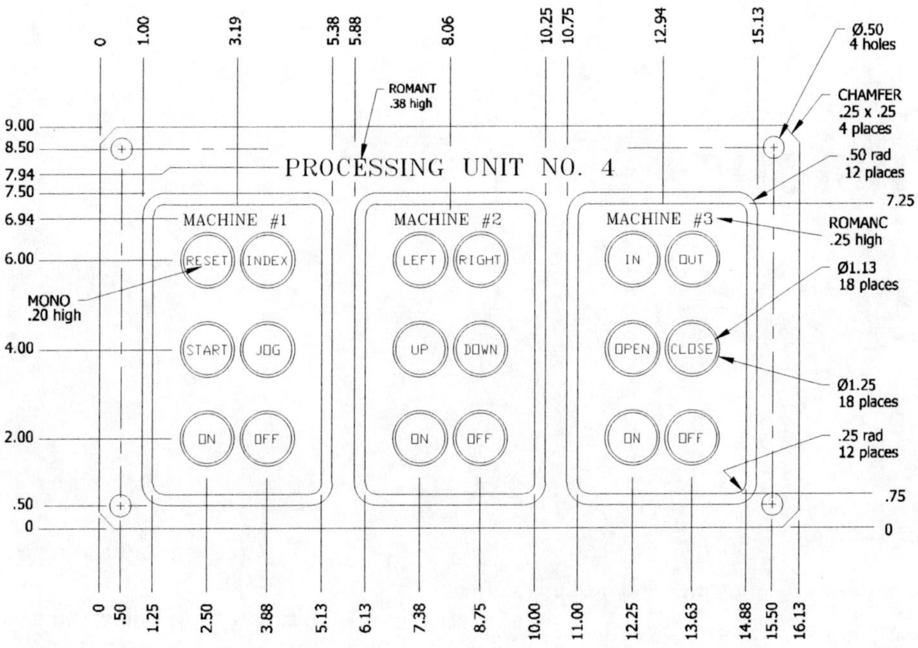

CONTROL PANEL

8

Dimensions

OVERVIEW

The ability to dimension your drawings and add crosshatch patterns will greatly enhance the professional appearance and utility of your work. AutoCAD's dimensioning features form a complex system of commands, subcommands, and variables that automatically measure objects and draw dimension text and extension lines. With AutoCAD's dimensioning tools and variables, you can create dimensions in a wide variety of formats, and these formats can be saved as styles. The time saved through not having to draw each dimension object line by line is among the most significant advantages of CAD. AutoCAD even has a command, QDIM, which can be used to create multiple dimension objects at once.

SECTIONS

OBJECTIVES

After reading this chapter, you should be able to:

- Define and save a dimension style.
- Draw linear dimensions (horizontal, vertical, and aligned).
- Draw baseline and continued linear dimensions.
- Draw angular dimensions.
- Draw center marks and diameter and radius dimensions.
- Add crosshatching to previously drawn objects.
- Draw a flanged wheel.
- Draw a shower head.
- Draw a plot plan.

8.1 CREATING AND SAVING A DIMENSION STYLE

Dimensioning in AutoCAD is highly automated and very easy compared to manual dimensioning. To achieve a high degree of automation while still allowing for the broad range of flexibility required to cover all dimension styles, the AutoCAD dimensioning system is necessarily complex. In the exercises that follow we will guide you through the system, show you some of what is available, and give you a good foundation for understanding how to get what you want out of AutoCAD dimensioning. We will create a basic dimension style and use it to draw standard dimensions and tolerances. We will leave it to you to explore the many variations that are possible.

In AutoCAD it is best to begin by naming and defining a dimension style. A dimension style is a set of dimension variable settings that control the text and geometry of all types of AutoCAD dimensions. In older versions of AutoCAD, the default styles for most dimensions would use the drawing units set through the Units Control dialog box or the UNITS command. Now dimension units must be set separately. We recommend that you create the new dimension style in your template drawing and save it. Then you will not have to make these changes again when you start new drawings.

⌗ **To begin this exercise, open the 1B template drawing.**

Remember to look for this file in the Template folder and that it will have a .tmp file extension. We will make changes in dimension style settings in the template drawing so that all dimensions showing distances will be presented with two decimal places and angular dimensions will have no decimals. This will become the default dimension setting in any drawing created using the 1B template.

⌗ **Type "d," select Dimension style from the Format menu, or select Style from the Dimension menu, or open the Dimension toolbar and select the Dimension Style tool (see Figure 8.1).**

Figure 8.1

TIP: Dimensioning is a good example of a case where you may want to open a toolbar and leave it open for a while. Since dimensioning is often saved for last in a drawing and may be done all at once, bringing up the toolbar and keeping it on your screen while you dimension may be most efficient.

Any of the preceding methods will call the Dimension Style Manager shown in Figure 8.2. You will see that the current dimension style is called "Standard." Among other things, the AutoCAD Standard dimension style uses four-place decimals in all dimensions, including angular dimensions.

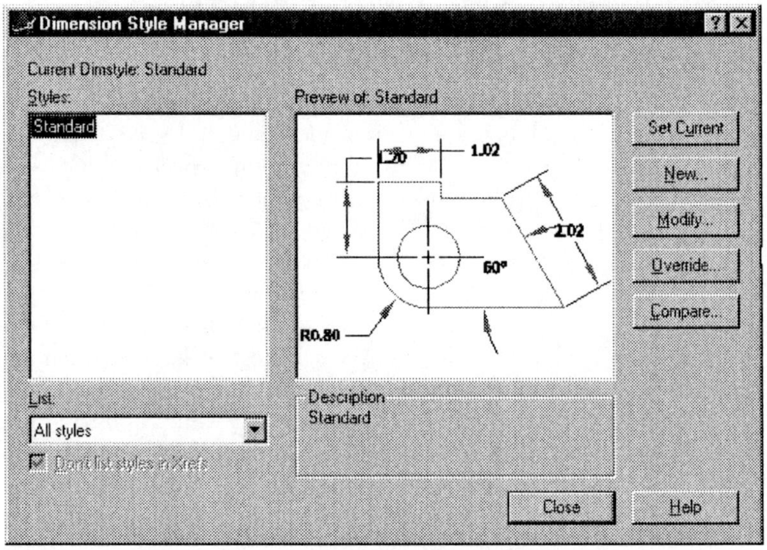

Figure 8.2

To the right of the Styles box is a preview image that will show you many of the Standard settings. The preview image will be updated immediately any time you make a change in a dimension setting.

To the right of the preview is a set of five buttons, the second of which is New....

⊕ **Click on the New... button.**

This will open the small Create New Dimension style dialog box shown in Figure 8.3.

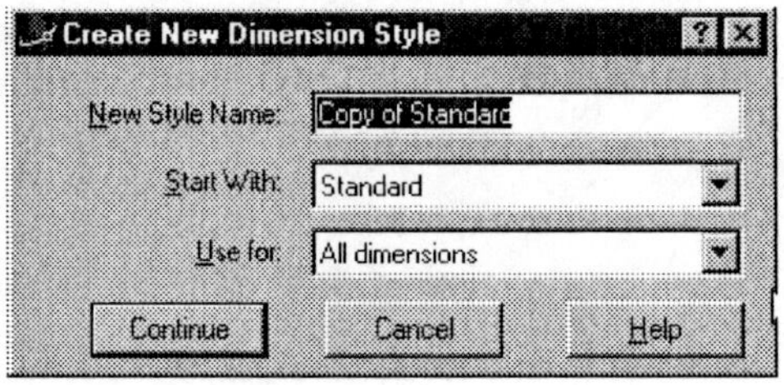

Figure 8.3

⊕ **Double click in the New Style Name: edit box to highlight the word "Standard."**

Note that the new style is based on the current Standard style. It will start with all of the Standard settings. Anything we don't change will be the same as in the Standard style.

⊕ **Type "1B."**

Any name will do. We chose this one to go with the template file name.

⊕ **Click on Continue....**

This will create the new dimension style and take us into the New Dimension Style dialog box, shown in Figure 8.4. Here there are six tabbed cards that will allow us to make many changes in dimension Lines and Arrows, Text, Fit, Primary Units, Alternate Units, and Tolerance.

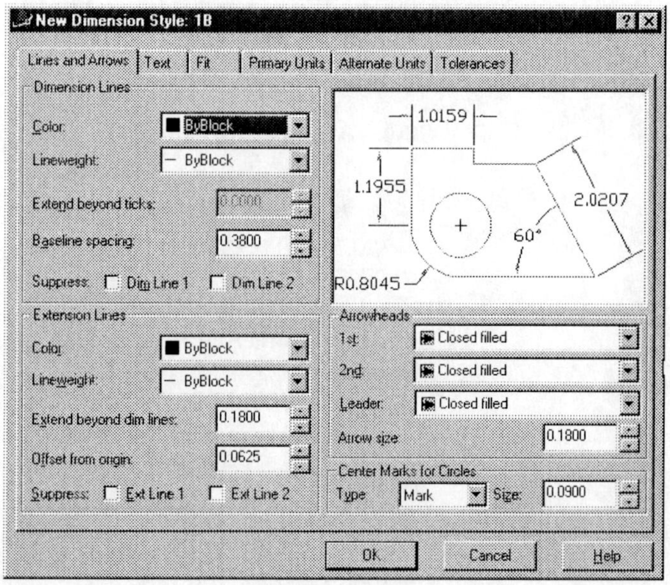

Figure 8.4

⌗ **Click on the Primary Units tab.**

This will bring up the Primary Units card, as shown in Figure 8.5. There are adjustments available for linear and angular units. The lists under Units and Angles are similar to the lists used in the Drawing Units dialog box. In the Linear dimension panel, Units format should show "Decimal," and in the Angular dimensions panel Units format should show "Decimal Degrees." If for any reason these are not showing in your box, you should make these changes now. For our purposes all we need to change is the number of decimal places showing in the Dimension Precision box. By default it will be 0.0000. We will change it to 0.00.

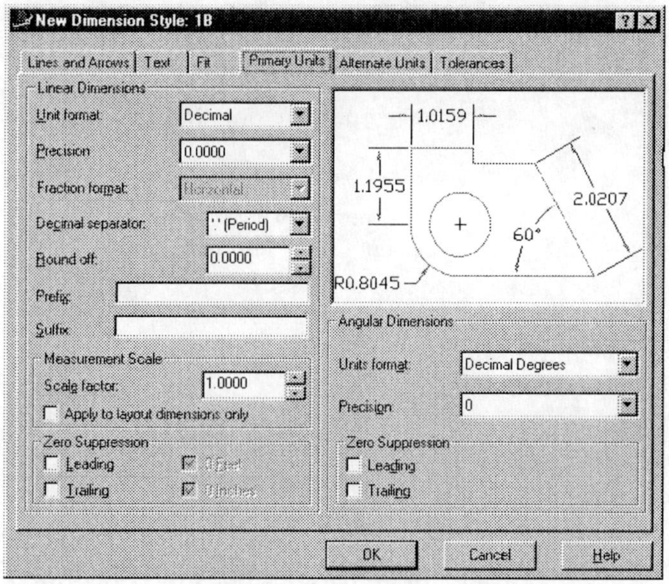

Figure 8.5

- **Click on the arrow to the right of the Precision box in the Linear dimensions panel.**

  This will open a list of precision settings ranging from 0 to 0.00000000.

- **Click on 0.00.**

  This will close the list box and show 0.00 as the selected precision. Notice the change in the preview image, which now shows two place decimals. At this point we are ready to complete this part of the procedure by returning to the Dimension Style Manager.

  Before leaving the New Dimension Style dialog box, we recommend that you open the other tabs and take a look at the large variety of dimension features which can be adjusted. Each of the many options changes a dimension variable setting. For example, in the Lines and Arrows tab you will find options for changing the size and positioning of dimension geometry. Dimension variables have names and can be changed at the command line by typing in the name and entering a new value, but in AutoCAD the dialog box makes the process much easier and the preview images give you immediate visual feedback.

- **Click on OK to exit the New Dimension Style dialog box.**

  Back in the Dimension Style Manager dialog you will see that 1B has been added to the list of styles. At this point you should have at least the Standard and 1B dimension styles defined in your drawing. 1B should be selected. The preview image shows the selected style.

NOTE: When a dimension style is selected in the Dimension Style Manager it is not necessarily the current style in the drawing. To make a style current you also need to click the Set Current button. You can tell which style is current by looking at the Override button. It will be accessible when the current style is selected and grayed out otherwise. This also indicates that you can temporarily override settings in the current style only.

- **Click on Set Current to set 1B as the current dimension style.**

- **Click on Close to exit the Dimension Styles dialog box.**

- **Save template drawing 1B.**

- **Select New and open a new drawing using the 1B template.**

  If the new drawing is opened with the 1B template, the 1B dimension style will be current for the next task.

8.2 DRAWING LINEAR DIMENSIONS

AutoCAD has many commands and features that aid in the drawing of dimensions, as evidenced by the fact that there is an entire pull-down menu for dimensioning only. In this exercise you will create some basic linear dimensions in the now-current 1B style.

- **To prepare for this exercise, draw a triangle (ours is 3.00, 4.00, 5.00) and a line (6.00) above the middle of the display, as shown in Figure 8.6.**

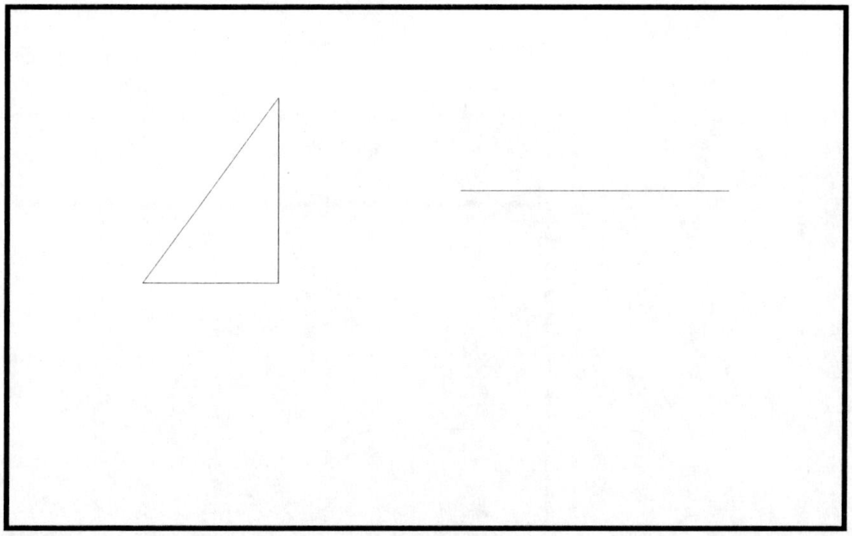

Figure 8.6

Exact sizes and locations are not critical. We will begin by adding dimensions to the triangle.

The dimensioning commands are streamlined and efficient. Their full names, however, are all rather long. They all begin with "dim" and are followed by the name of a type of dimension (for example, DIMLINEAR, DIMALIGNED, and DIMANGULAR). Use the Dimensioning menu or the Dimensioning toolbar to avoid typing these names.

We begin by placing a linear dimension below the base of the triangle.

⌖ **Select Linear from the Dimension menu, or select the Linear Dimension tool from the Dimension toolbar, as shown in Figure 8.7.**

Figure 8.7

This will initiate the DIMLINEAR command, with the following prompt appearing in the command area:

Specify first extension line origin or <select object>:

There are two ways to proceed at this point. One is to show where the extension lines should begin, and the other is to select the object you want to dimension and let AutoCAD position the extension lines. In most simple applications the latter method is faster.

⌖ **Press Enter to indicate that you will select an object.**

AutoCAD will replace the cross hairs with a pickbox and prompt for your selection:

Select object to dimension:

Select the horizontal line at the bottom of the triangle, as shown by Point 1 in Figure 8.8.

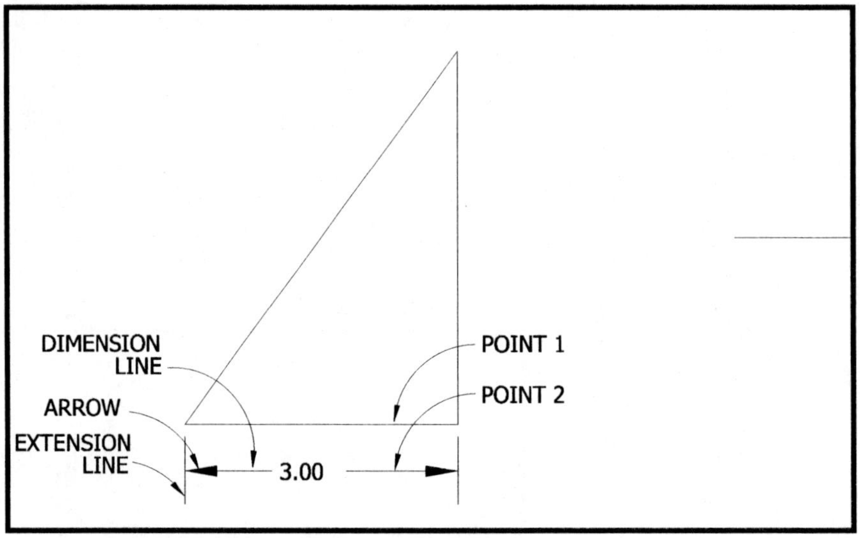

Figure 8.8

AutoCAD immediately creates a dimension, including extension lines, dimension line, and text, that you can drag out away from the selected line. AutoCAD will place the dimension line and text where you indicate but will keep the text centered between the extension lines. The prompt is as follows:

Specify dimension line location or
[MText/Text/Angle/Horizontal/Vertical/Rotated]:

In the default sequence, you will simply show the location of the dimension. If you wish to alter the text content, you can do so using the "Mtext" or "Text" options, or you can change it later with a command called DIMEDIT. "Angle," "Horizontal," and "Vertical" allow you to specify the orientation of the text. Horizontal text is the default for linear text. "Rotated" allows you to rotate the complete dimension so that the extension lines move out at an angle from the object being dimensioned (text remains horizontal).

NOTE: If the dimension variable "dimsho" is set to 0 (off), you will not be given an image of the dimension to drag into place. The default setting is 1 (on), so this should not be a problem. If, however, it has been changed in your drawing, type "dimsho" and then "1" to turn it on again.

Pick a location about 0.50 below the triangle, as shown by Point 2 in Figure 8.8.

Bravo! You have completed your first dimension. (Notice that our figure and others in this chapter are shown zoomed in on the relevant object for the sake of clarity. You may zoom or not as you like.)

At this point, take a good look at the dimension you have just drawn to see what it consists of. As in Figure 8.8, you should see the following components: two extension lines, two "arrows," a dimension line on each side of the text, and the text itself.

Notice also that AutoCAD has automatically placed the extension line origins a short distance away from the triangle base (you may need to zoom in to see this). This distance is controlled by a dimension variable called "dimexo," which can be changed in the Modify Dimension Style dialog, Lines and Arrows tab in the Extension lines panel. The setting is called Offset from origin.

Next, we will place a vertical dimension on the right side of the triangle. You will see that DIMLINEAR handles both horizontal and vertical dimensions.

Repeat the DIMLINEAR command.

You will be prompted for extension line origins as before:

Specify first extension line origin or <select object>:

This time we will show the extension line origins manually.

Pick the right-angle corner at the lower right of the triangle, Point 1 in Figure 8.9. AutoCAD will prompt for a second point:

Specify second extension line origin:

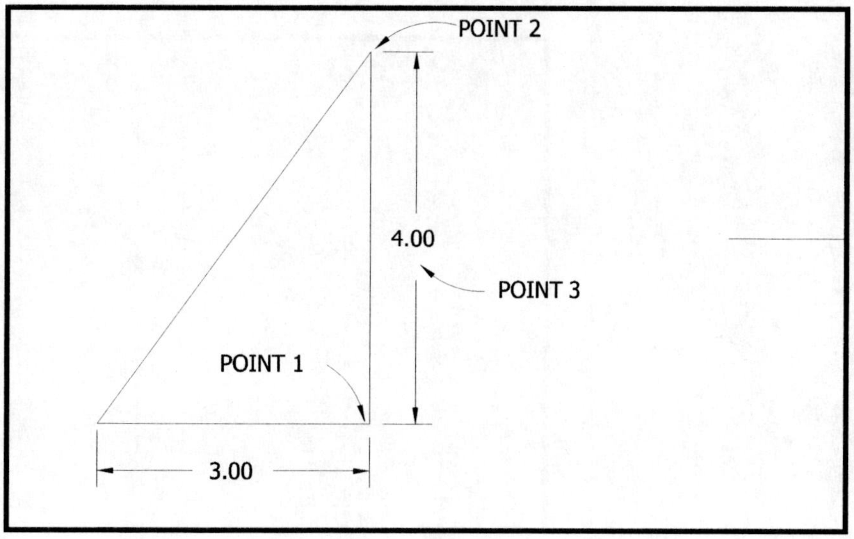

Figure 8.9

Even though you are manually specifying extension line origins, it is not necessary to show the exact point where you want the line to start. AutoCAD will automatically set the dimension lines slightly away from the line as before, according to the setting of the dimexo dimension variable.

Pick the top intersection of the triangle, Point 2 in Figure 8.9.

From here on, the procedure will be the same as before. You should have a dimension to drag into place, and the following prompt:

Specify dimension line location or
[Mtext/Text/Angle/Horizontal/Vertical/Rotated]:

- **Pick a point 0.50 to the right of the triangle, Point 3 in Figure 8.9.**

Your screen should now include the vertical dimension, as shown in Figure 8.9.

Now let's place a dimension on the diagonal side of the triangle. For this we will need the DIMALIGNED command.

- **Select Aligned from the Dimension menu, or the Aligned Dimension tool from the Dimension toolbar, as shown in Figure 8.10.**

Figure 8.10

- **Press Enter, indicating that you will select an object.**

AutoCAD will give you the pickbox and prompt you to select an object to dimension.

- **Select the hypotenuse of the triangle.**
- **Pick a point approximately 0.50 above and to the left of the line.**

Your screen should resemble Figure 8.11. Notice that AutoCAD retains horizontal text in aligned and vertical dimensions as the default.

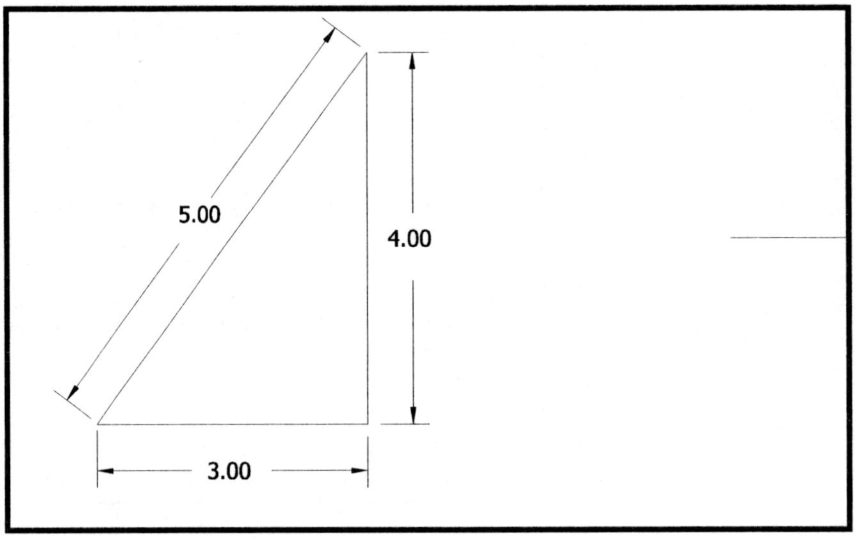

Figure 8.11

8.3 DRAWING MULTIPLE LINEAR DIMENSIONS—QDIM

QDIM is a miracle-working AutoCAD command that automates the creation of certain types of multiple dimension formats. With this command you can create a whole series of related dimensions with a few mouse clicks. To introduce QDIM we will create a continuous dimension series dimensioning the bottom of the triangle, the space between the triangle and the line, and the length of the line itself. Then we will edit the series to show several points along the line. Finally we will change the dimensions on the line from a continuous series to a baseline series.

- **To begin this task, erase the dimension from the bottom of the triangle.**

Notice that you can select the complete dimension, including extension lines, dimension lines, text and arrows with a single pick. The dimension is, like text and other objects, a complex object, made up of many simple objects.

- **Select the bottom of the triangle and the 6.00 line to the right of the triangle.**

Noun/verb editing allows you to select objects before entering QDIM. Your selected lines will be highlighted and have grips showing.

- **Select QDIM from the Dimension menu, or the Quick Dimension tool from the Dimension toolbar, as shown in Figure 8.12.**

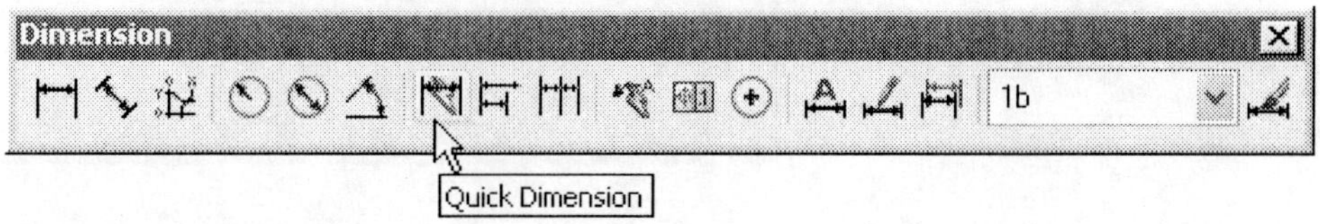

Figure 8.12

AutoCAD prompts:

Specify dimension line position, or
[Continuous/Staggered/Baseline/Ordinate/Radius/Diameter/datumPoint/Edit]
<Continuous>:

The options here are various forms of multiple dimensions. Continuous, staggered, baseline, and ordinate are all linear styles. Radius and Diameter are for dimensioning circles and arcs. Datum Point is used to change the point from which a set of linear dimensions is measured and Edit has several functions we will explore in a moment.

Continuous dimensions are the AutoCAD default, but this may have changed if someone else has used QDIM on your system, since the last option used is retained as the default.

- **If necessary, type "c" for the Continuous option.**

Continuous dimensions are positioned end to end, as shown in Figure 8.13. AutoCAD creates three linear dimensions at once, and positions them end to end.

- **Select a point about 1.0 unit below the triangle, as shown in Figure 8.13.**

Next we will edit the dimension on the right, so that the line length is measured to several different lengths.

- **Repeat QDIM.**
- **Select the dimension at the right, below the 6.00 line.**

Notice that this dimension can be selected independently. The three continuous dimensions just created are separate objects, even though they were created simultaneously.

NOTE: The objects selected for the QDIM command can be dimensions or objects to be dimensioned. If you select objects, QDIM will create new dimensions for these objects, if you select dimensions, QDIM will edit or recreate these dimensions depending on the options you select.

- **Right click to end object selection.**

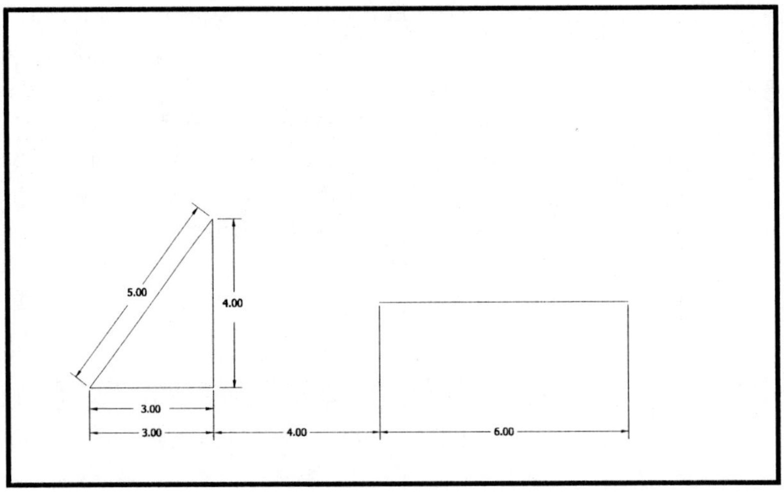

Figure 8.13

AutoCAD will give you a single dimension to drag into place. If you pick a point now the selected 6.00 dimension will be recreated at the point you choose. We will do something more interesting.

⌖ **Type "e" for the Edit option.**

QDIM prompts:

Indicate dimension point to remove, or [Add/eXit] <eXit>:

We will add dimension points.

⌖ **Type "a" for the Add option.**

Small white x's are added at the endpoints of the line. These indicate the current dimension points. The prompt changes slightly.

Indicate dimension point to Add, or [Remove/eXit] <eXit>:

⌖ **Pick Point 1, as shown in Figure 8.14.**

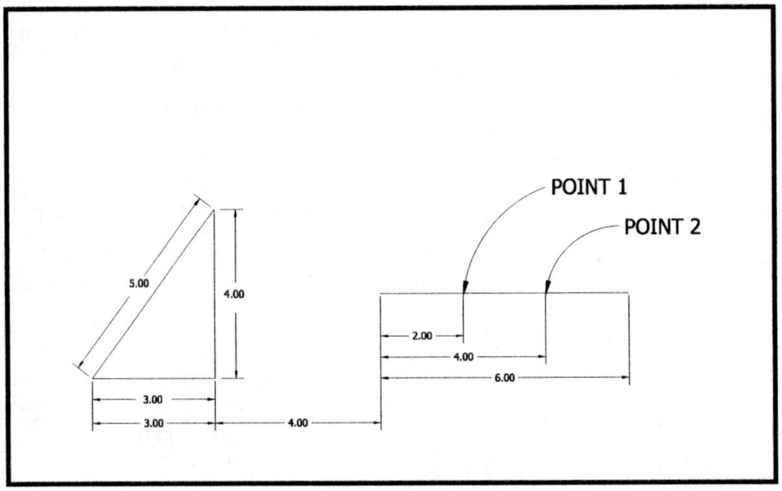

Figure 8.14

This point is two units from the left endpoint of the line. QDIM continues to prompt for points.

- **Pick Point 2, as shown in Figure 8.14.**

  This point is two units from the right endpoint of the line.

- **Press enter or the space bar to endpoint selection.**

  QDIM now divides the single 6.00 dimension into a series of three continuous 2.00 dimensions. But we are not done yet. We will choose to draw these three dimensions in Baseline format.

- **Type "b" for the Baseline option.**

  QDIM immediately switches the three dragged dimensions to a baseline form.

- **Pick a point so that the top, shortest, dimension of the three is positioned about 1.00 below the line.**

- **Press Enter or the space bar to exit QDIM.**

  Your screen will be redrawn with three baseline dimensions as shown in Figure 8.14. We will have more to say about this powerful command as we go along.

8.3.1 DIMBASELINE and DIMCONTINUE

Baseline and Continuous format dimensions can also be created one at a time using individual commands. The following general procedure is used with these commands.

1. Draw an initial linear dimension.
2. Select Baseline or Continue from the Dimension menu or the Baseline Dimension or Continue Dimension tool from the Dimension toolbar.
3. Pick a second extension line origin.
4. Pick another second extension line origin.
5. Press Enter to exit the command.

8.4 DRAWING ANGULAR DIMENSIONS

Angular dimensioning works much like linear dimensioning, except that you will be prompted to select objects that form an angle. AutoCAD will compute an angle based on the geometry that you select (two lines, an arc, part of a circle, or a vertex and two points) and construct extension lines, a dimension arc, and text specifying the angle. There is no angular option in the QDIM command.

For this exercise we will return to the triangle and add angular dimensions to two of the angles, as shown in Figure 8.16.

- **Select Angular from the Dimension menu or the Angular Dimension tool from the Dimension toolbar, as shown in Figure 8.15.**

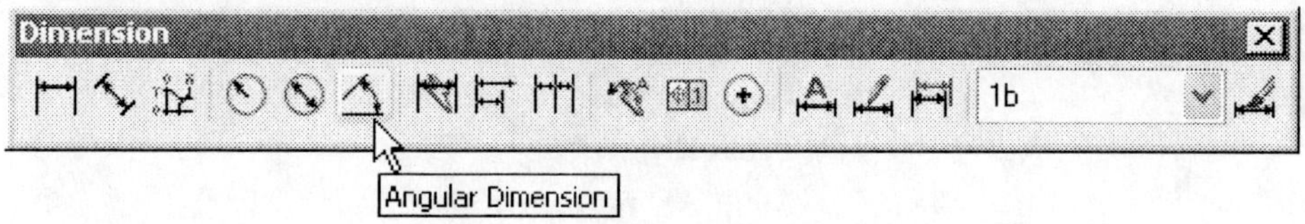

Figure 8.15

The first prompt will be

Select arc, circle, line, or <specify vertex>:

The prompt shows that you can use DIMANGULAR to dimension angles formed by arcs and portions of circles as well as angles formed by lines. If you press Enter, you can specify an angle manually by picking its vertex and a point on each side of the angle. We will begin by picking lines, the most common procedure in angular dimensioning.

⌗ **Select the base of the triangle.**

You will be prompted for another line:

Select second line:

⌗ **Select the hypotenuse.**

As in linear dimensioning, AutoCAD now shows you the dimension lines and lets you drag them into place. The prompt asks for a dimension arc location and also allows you the option of changing the text or the text angle.

Specify dimension arc line location or [Mtext/Text/Angle]:

⌗ **Move the cursor around to see how the dimension may be placed and then pick a point between the two selected lines, as shown in Figure 8.16.**

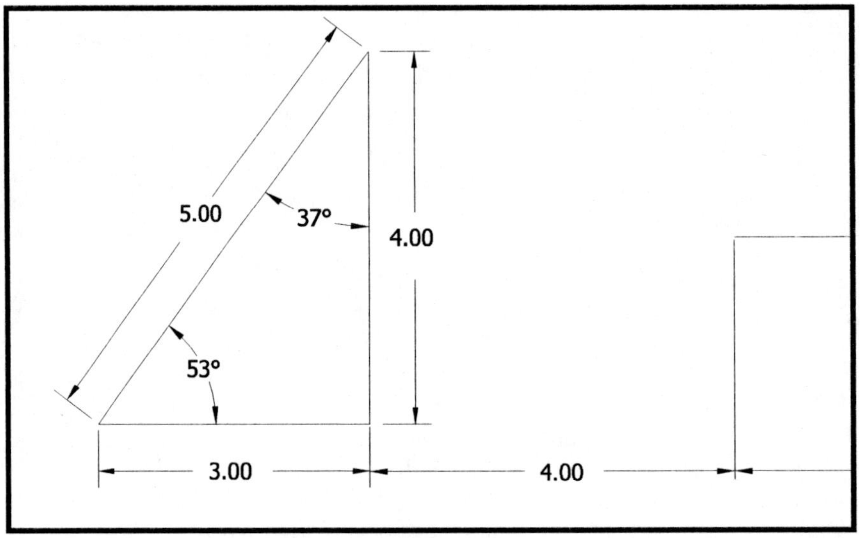

Figure 8.16

The lower left angle of your triangle should now be dimensioned, as in Figure 8.16. Notice that the degree symbol is added by default in angular dimension text.

We will dimension the upper angle by specifying its vertex.

⌗ **Repeat DIMANGULAR.**

⌗ **Press Enter.**

AutoCAD prompts for an angle vertex.

⌗ **Point to the vertex of the angle at the top of the triangle.**

AutoCAD prompts

Specify first angle endpoint:

⌖ **Pick a point along the hypotenuse.**

To be precise, this should be a snap point. The most dependable one will be the lower left corner of the triangle.

AutoCAD prompts

Specify second angle endpoint:

⌖ **Pick any point along the vertical side of the triangle.**

There should be many snap points on the vertical line, so you should have no problem.

⌖ **Move the cursor slowly up and down within the triangle.**

Notice how AutoCAD places the arrows outside the angle when you approach the vertex and things get crowded. Also notice that if you move outside the angle, AutoCAD switches to the outer angle.

⌖ **Pick a location for the dimension arc, as shown in Figure 8.16.**

8.5 DIMENSIONING ARCS AND CIRCLES

The basic process for dimensioning circles and arcs is as simple as those we have already covered. It can get tricky, however, when AutoCAD does not place the dimension where you want it. Text placement can be controlled by adjusting dimension variables. In this exercise we will create a center mark and some diameter and radius dimensions. Then we will return to the QDIM command to see how multiple circles can be dimensioned at once.

⌖ **To prepare for this exercise, draw two circles at the bottom of your screen, as shown in Figure 8.17.**

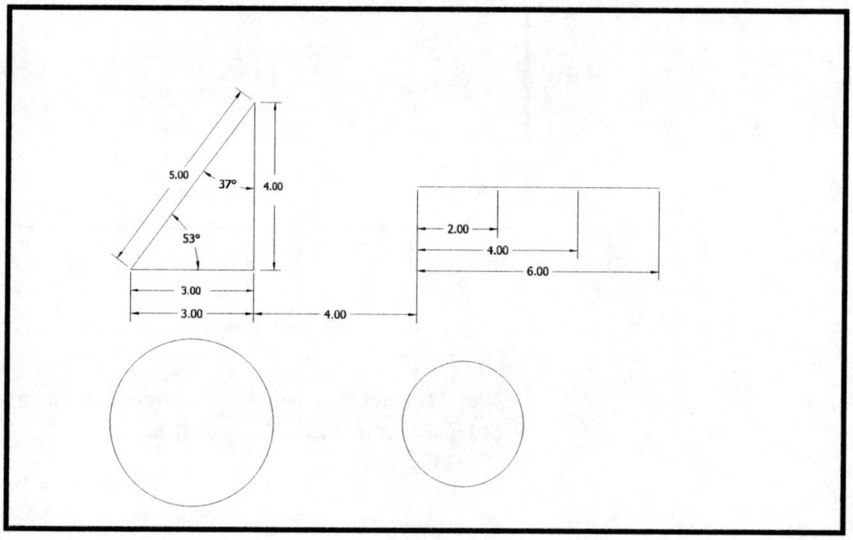

Figure 8.17

The circles we have used have radii of 2.00 and 1.50.

⌖ **Select Center Mark from the Dimension menu or the Center Mark tool from the Dimension toolbar, as shown in Figure 8.18.**

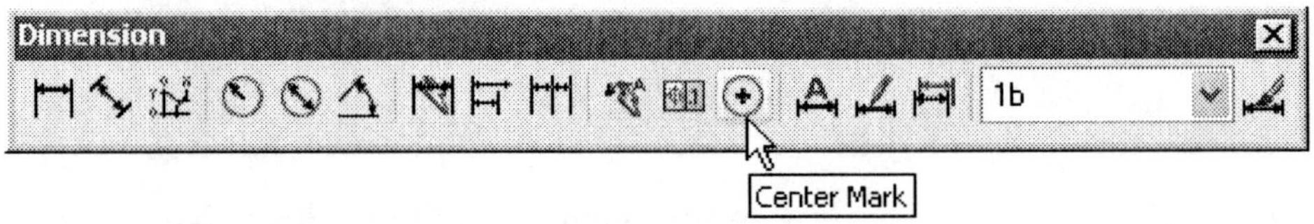

Figure 8.18

Center marks are the simplest of all dimension features to create and are created automatically as part of some radius and diameter dimensions.

AutoCAD prompts

Select arc or circle:

⌖ **Select the smaller circle.**

A center mark will be drawn in the 1.50 circle, as shown in Figure 8.19. The standard center mark is a small cross. The size of the cross can be changed in a small panel at the bottom right of the Lines and Arrows tab of the Modify Dimension Style dialog box. Here you also have a choice of standard continuous lines or broken center lines to form the mark.

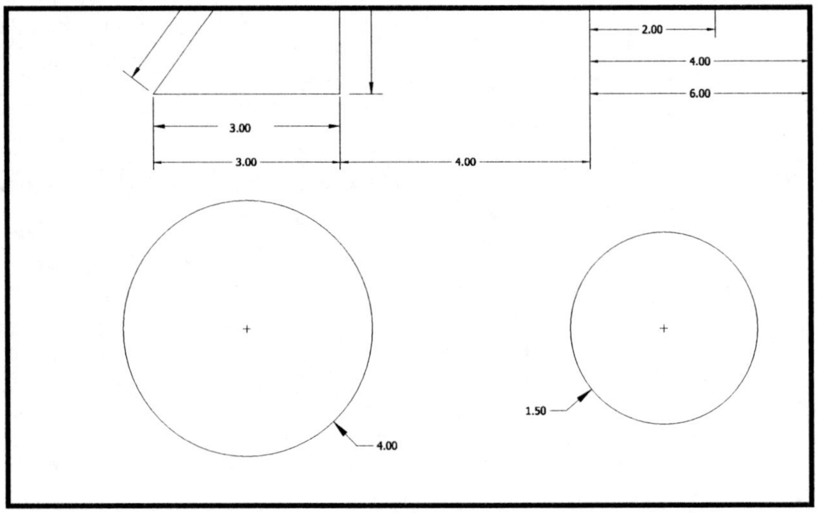

Figure 8.19

Now we will add the diameter dimension shown on the larger circle in Figure 8.19.

⌖ **Select Diameter from the Dimension menu or the Diameter Dimension tool from the Dimension toolbar.**

AutoCAD will prompt

Select arc or circle:

⌖ **Select the larger circle.**

AutoCAD will show a diameter dimension and ask for Dimension line location with the following prompt:

Specify dimension line location or [Mtext/Text/Angle]:

The Text and Angle options allow you to change the dimension text or put it at an angle. If you move your cursor around, you will see that you can position the dimension line anywhere around the circle.

⌖ **Pick a dimension position so that your screen resembles Figure 8.19.**

Notice that the diameter symbol prefix is added automatically by default.

8.5.1 Radius Dimensions

The procedures for radius dimensioning are exactly the same as those for diameter dimensions and the results look the same. The only differences will be the radius value of the text and the use of R for radius in place of the diameter symbol. Try adding a radius dimension to the smaller circle.

8.5.2 Dimensioning Circles and Arcs with QDIM

Multiple radius or diameter dimensions can be created with QDIM. When this technique is used, all leaders will be created at the same angle. Try this:

⌖ **Select QDIM from the Dimension menu, or the QDIM tool from the dimension toolbar.**

⌖ **Select both circles.**

⌖ **Right click to end object selection.**

⌖ **Type "r" for the radius option.**

QDIM prompts

Specify dimension line position, or
[Continuous/Staggered/Baseline/Ordinate/Radius/Diameter/datumPoint/Edit]
<Radius>:

⌖ **Specify a line position by picking a point, as shown in Figure 8.20.**

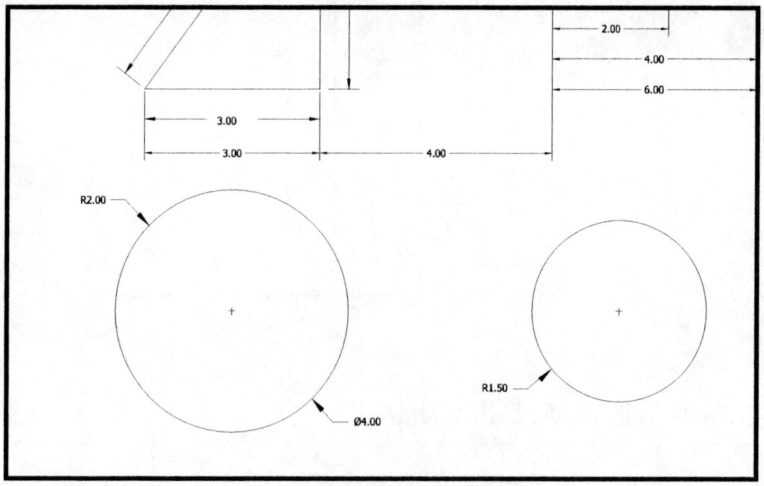

Figure 8.20

Radius dimensions will be added to both circles as shown in Figure 8.20. The diameter option works in exactly the same way.

8.5.3 Dimension Variables

The chart in Figure 8.21 shows some of the more common dimension variables that can be used to change the look and style of dimensions. Dimension variables can be changed through the Dimension Style dialog box, or by typing the name of the variable at the Command prompt and then entering a new value.

COMMONLY USED DIMENSION VARIABLES

Variable	Default Value	Appearance	DESCRIPTION	New Value	Appearance
dimaso	on	All parts of dim are one entity	Associative dimensioning	off	All parts of dim are separate entities
dimscale	1.00	2.00	Changes size of text & arrows, not value	2.00	2.00
dimasz	.18		Sets arrow size	.38	
dimcen	.09		Center mark size and appearance	-.09	
dimdli	.38		Spacing between continued dimension lines	.50	
dimexe	.18		Extension above dimension line	.25	
dimexo	0.06		Extension line origin offset	.12	
dimtp	0.00	1.50	Sets plus tolerance	.01	$1.50^{+0.01}_{-0.00}$
dimtm	0.00	1.50	Sets minus tolerance	.02	$1.50^{+0.00}_{-0.02}$
dimtol	off	1.50	Generate dimension tolerances (dimtp & dimtm must be set) (dimtol & dimlim cannot both be on)	on	$1.50^{+0.01}_{-0.02}$
dimlim	off	1.50	Generate dimension limits (dimtp & dimtm must be set) (dimtol & dimlim cannot both be on)	on	1.51 1.48
dimtad	off	1.50	Places text above the dimension line	on	1.50
dimtxt	.18	1.50	Sets height of text	.38	1.50
dimtsz	.18	1.50	Sets tick marks & tick height	.25	1.50
dimtih	on	1.50	Sets angle of text When off rotates text to the angle of the dimension	off	1.50
dimtix	off	ø0.71	Forces the text to inside of circles and arcs. Linear and angular dimensions are placed inside if there is sufficient room	on	ø0.71

Figure 8.21

8.6 USING THE BHATCH COMMAND

Automated hatching is another immense timesaver. AutoCAD includes two commands for use in crosshatching. Of the two, BHATCH and HATCH, BHATCH is more powerful and easier to use. BHATCH differs from HATCH in that it automatically defines the nearest boundary surrounding a point you have specified. The other big difference is that BHATCH creates associated hatch patterns. Associated hatching changes when the boundaries around it change. Nonassociated hatching is completely independent of the geometry that contains it.

⌖ **To prepare for this exercise, clear your screen of all previously drawn objects and then draw three rectangles, one inside the other, with the word "TEXT" at the center, as shown in Figure 8.22.**

Figure 8.22

⌖ **Select Hatch from the Draw menu, or the Hatch tool on the Draw toolbar, as shown in Figure 8.23.**

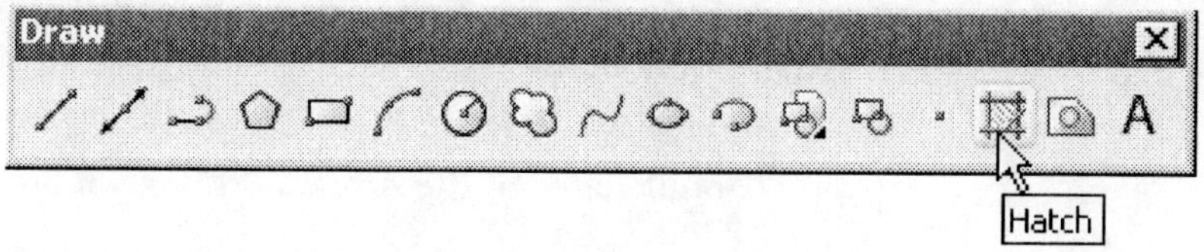

Figure 8.23

Both of these methods initiate the BHATCH command, which calls the Boundary Hatch dialog box shown in Figure 8.24. The Hatch tab gives you access to AutoCAD's library of over 50 standard hatch patterns. The Advanced tab provides more options for the way AutoCAD finds boundaries, creates boundaries, and handles objects within boundaries.

At the top of the Hatch tabbed card, you will see the Type box. Before we can hatch anything, we need to specify a hatch pattern. Later we will show AutoCAD what we wish to hatch using the Pick Points button on the right.

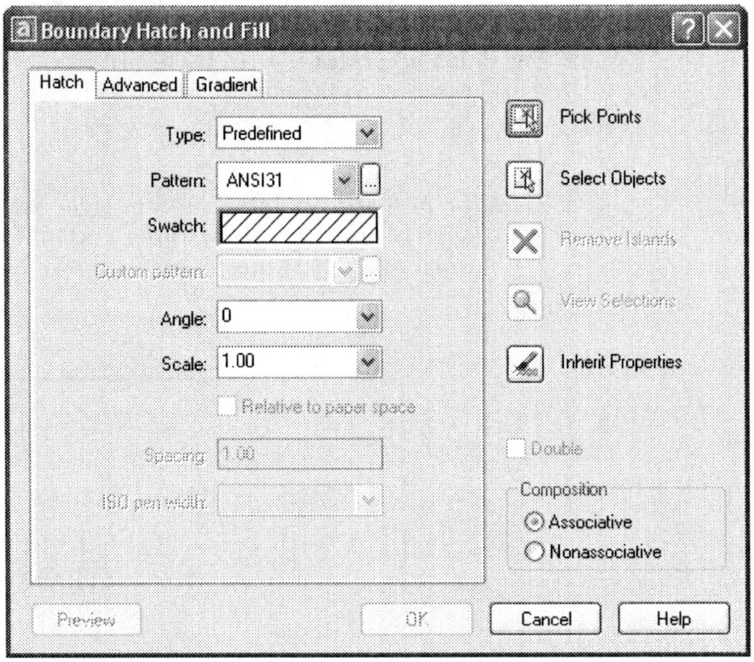

Figure 8.24

The Pattern type currently shown in the image box is a predefined pattern. Before we look at predefined patterns we will create a simple user-defined pattern of straight lines on a 45-degree angle.

⌗ **Click on the arrow to the right of "Predefined."**

This opens a list including Predefined, User-defined, and Custom patterns.

⌗ **Select User-defined.**

When you select a user-defined pattern, the swatch box, which shows an example of the pattern, will change to show a set of horizontal lines. To create our user-defined pattern, we will specify an angle and a spacing.

⌗ **Double click in the Angle edit box, and then type "45."**

⌗ **Double click in the Spacing edit box, and then type "0.5."**

Next we need to show AutoCAD where to place the hatching. To the right in the dialog box is a set of buttons with icons. The first two options are "Pick Points" and "Select Objects." Using the "Pick Points" option, you can have AutoCAD locate a boundary when you point to the area inside it. The "Select Objects" option can be used to create boundaries in the way that the older HATCH command works, by selecting entities that lie along the boundaries.

⌗ **Click on "Pick Points."**

The dialog box will disappear temporarily and you will be prompted as follows:

Select internal point:

Pick a point inside the largest, outer rectangle but outside the smaller rectangles.

AutoCAD displays these messages, though you may have to press F2 to see them:

Selecting everything...
Selecting everything visible...
Analyzing the selected data...
Analyzing internal islands...

In a large drawing this process can be time consuming because the program searches all visible entities to locate the appropriate boundary. When the process is complete, all of the rectangles and the text will be highlighted. It will happen very quickly in this case.

AutoCAD continues to prompt for internal points so that you can define multiple boundaries. Let's return to the dialog box and see what we've done so far.

Press Enter to end internal point selection.

The dialog box will reappear. You may not have noticed, but several of the options that were "grayed out" before are now accessible. We will make use of the "Preview" button at the bottom left of the dialog box. Preview allows us to see what has been specified without leaving the command, so that we can continue to adjust the hatching until we are satisfied.

Click on Preview.

Your screen should resemble Figure 8.25. Notice the way the command has recognized and treated internal boundaries. Boundaries are hatched or left clear in alternating fashion, beginning with the outermost boundary and working inward. This demonstrates the "normal" style of hatching. We will explore the effect of the other styles by looking at the Advanced tab. Before going on, also notice that BHATCH has recognized the text as well as the other interior boundaries.

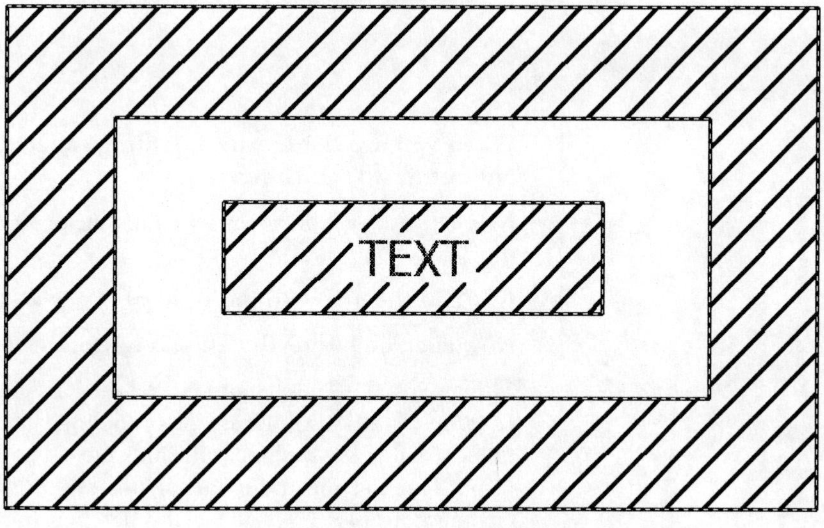

Figure 8.25

Hit Enter or right click to return to the Boundary Hatch dialog box.

Click on the Advanced tab.

This Advanced card is shown in Figure 8.26. In the Island Detection Style panel you will see that there are three basic options that determine how BHATCH will treat interior boundaries. "Normal" is the current style. "Normal" hatches alternate areas moving inward, "Outer" hatches only the outer area, and "Ignore" hatches through all interior boundaries. You can see the same effects in your own drawing, if you like, by clicking the Preview button after changing from the "Normal" style to either of the other styles. Of course, the three styles are indistinguishable if you do not have boundaries within boundaries to hatch.

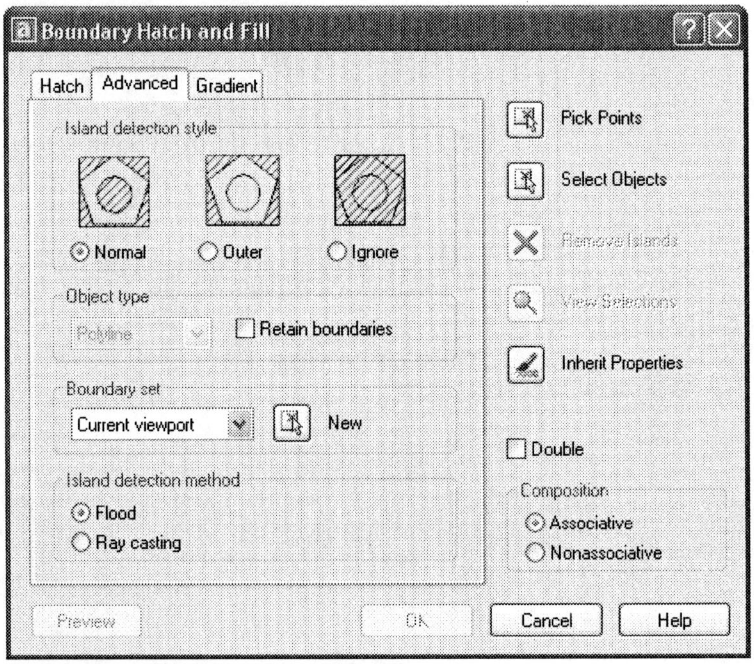

Figure 8.26

When you are done experimenting, select "Normal" style hatching again and return to the Hatch tab.

Now let's take a look at some of the fancier stored hatch patterns that AutoCAD provides.

Click on the arrow to the right of "User-Defined" and select "Predefined."

Now click on either the ellipsis button or the Swatch.

This opens the Hatch Pattern Palette, as shown in Figure 8.27. This Palette contains AutoCAD's library of predefined hatch patterns. They are shown in tabbed dialog box fashion with four tabs. The first three contain images of patterns. The Custom tab is empty unless you have created and saved your own custom patterns. To produce the hatched image in Figure 8.28, we chose the Escher pattern.

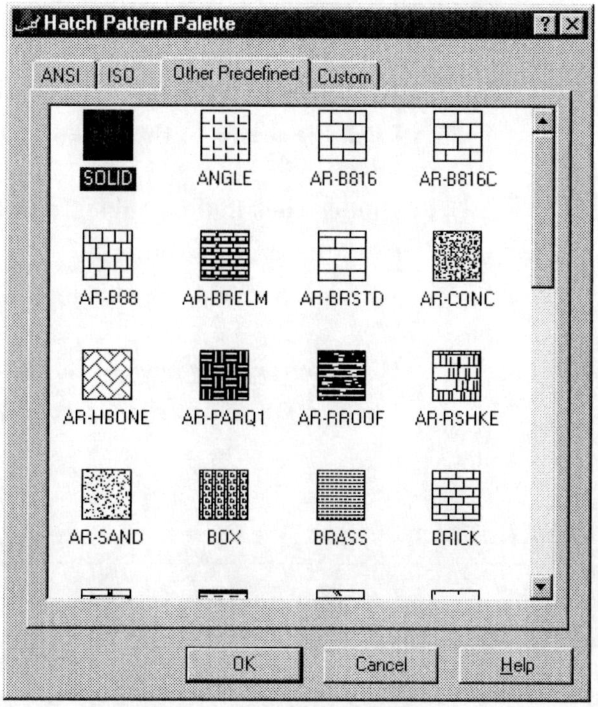

Figure 8.27

Figure 8.28

- **Select the Other Predefined tab.**
- **Scroll down the list until you come to "Escher."**

- **Select "Escher."**
- **Click on Okay to exit the Pattern Palette.**

To produce the figure we also used a larger scale in this hatching.

- **Click the arrow in the Scale list box to open the list of scale factors and select 1.50.**
- **Double click in the "Angle:" edit box and type "0."**
- **Click the Preview button.**

Your screen should resemble Figure 8.28, but remember this is still just the preview.

- **Hit Enter or right click to return to the dialog box.**
- **Click on OK to exit BHATCH and confirm the hatching.**

8.7 REVIEW MATERIAL

Questions

1. You are working in a drawing with units set to architectural, but when you begin dimensioning, AutoCAD provides four-place decimal units. What is the problem? What do you need to do so that your dimensioning units match your drawing units?
2. Describe at least one way to change the size of the arrowheads in the dimensions of a drawing.
3. What changes can be made with the Edit option of the QDIM command?
4. Describe the general selections you would make to draw dimensions for an angle.
5. Name three commonly used dimension variables.
6. What is the difference between HATCH and BHATCH?

Commands

BHATCH	DDIM	DIMALIGNED
DIMANGULAR	DIMBASELINE	DIMCONTINUE
DIMLINEAR	DIMSTYLE	QDIM
QLEADER		

8.8 DRAWING PROBLEMS

1. Create a new dimension style called "Dim-2." Dim-2 will use architectural units with 1/2" precision for all units except angles, which will use two-place decimals. Text in Dim-2 will be 0.5 units high.
2. Draw an isosceles triangle with vertexes at (4, 3), (14, 3), and (9, 11). Draw a 2" circle centered at the center of the triangle.
3. Dimension the base and one side of the triangle using the Dim-2 dimension style.
4. Add a diameter dimension to the circle and change a dimension variable so that the circle will be dimensioned with a diameter line drawn inside the circle.

5. Add an angle dimension to one of the base angles of the triangle. Make sure that the dimension is placed outside of the triangle.

6. Hatch the area inside the triangle and outside the circle using a predefined crosshatch pattern.

PROFESSIONAL SUCCESS

Using AutoCAD in Other Disciplines

Any recent release of AutoCAD is capable of producing the two- and three-dimensional engineering drawings described in this book. The basic release of AutoCAD is geared towards mechanical engineering, and includes symbols and primitives (e.g., dimensioning, linetype, crosshatch) which were designed to conform with accepted engineering standards. Other types of drawings, including architectural studies, electrical layouts, maps, and piping diagrams, may be produced by using the various extensions and companions to AutoCAD which are available. These extend the capabilities of the basic AutoCAD package, and allow industry-specific primitives and symbols to be specified directly.

One available extension to AutoCAD is AutoCAD Map, an add-on that allows maps and topological diagrams to be easily produced from within AutoCAD. Instead of constructing basic map symbols and geographic features using the geometric primitives (like line or circle) available in the standard AutoCAD package, AutoCAD map allows basic mapping primitives to be added directly to your drawing. This makes creating specialized drawings much easier, and helps to ensure that the symbols and layouts used are based on accepted industry standards.

There is most likely software available that will allow you to use AutoCAD to create the specialized drawings required by your specific field of study. Information about these is available through the AutoDesk website (http://www.autodesk.com), which contains complete descriptions on the available packages, as well as demonstrations that may be downloaded and tested.

DRAWING 1

Flanged Wheel

Most of the objects in this drawing are straightforward. The keyway is easily done using the TRIM command. If necessary, use DIMTEDIT or grips to move the diameter dimension, as shown in the reference.

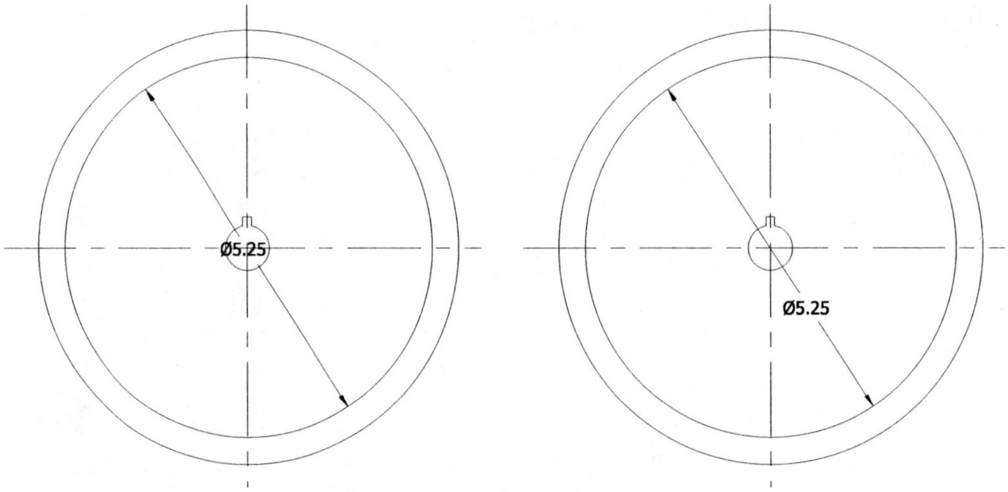

Drawing Suggestions

GRID = 0.25

SNAP = 0.0625

HATCH line spacing = 0.50

- You will need a 0.0625 snap to draw the keyway. Draw a 0.125 × 0.125 square at the top of the 0.63 diameter circle. Drop the vertical lines down into the circle so they may be used to TRIM the circle. TRIM the circle and the vertical lines, using a window to select both as cutting edges.
- Remember to set to layer "hatch" before hatching, layer "text" before adding text, and layer "dim" before dimensioning.

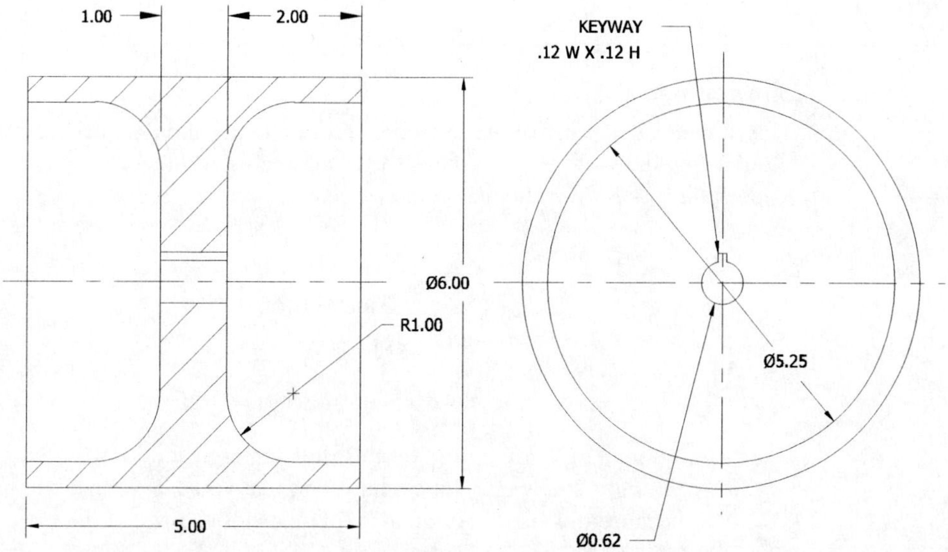

FLANGED WHEEL

DRAWING 2

Shower Head

This drawing makes use of the procedures for hatching and dimensioning you learned in the last two drawings. In addition, it uses an angular dimension, baseline dimensions, leaders, and "%%c" for the diameter symbol.

Drawing Suggestions

GRID = 0.50

SNAP = 0.125

HATCH line spacing = 0.25

- You can save some time on this drawing by using MIRROR to create half of the right-side view. Notice, however, that you cannot hatch before mirroring, because the mirror command will reverse the angle of the hatch lines.
- To achieve the angular dimension at the bottom of the right-side view, you will need to draw the vertical line coming down on the right. Select this line and the angular line at the right end of the shower head, and the angular extension will be drawn automatically. Add the text "2 PL" using the DIMEDIT command.
- Notice that the diameter symbols in the vertical dimensions at each end of the right-side view are not automatic. Use %%c to add the diameter symbol to the text.

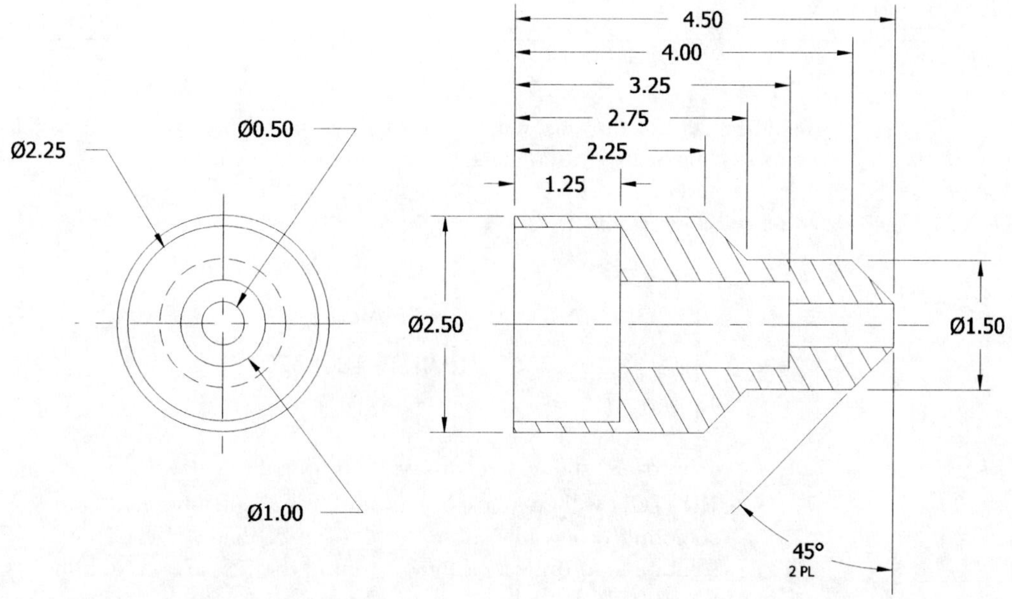

SHOWER HEAD

DRAWING 3

Plot Plan

This architectural drawing makes use of three hatch patterns and several dimension variable changes. Be sure to make these settings as shown.

Drawing Suggestions

GRID = 10'

SNAP = 1'

LIMITS = 180',120'

LTSCALE = 2'

- The "trees" shown here are symbols for oaks, willows, and evergreens.
- BHATCH will open a space around text inside a defined boundary; however, sometimes you will want more white space than BHATCH leaves. The simple solution is to draw a rectangle around the text area as an inner boundary. If the BHATCH style is set to "Normal," it will stop hatching at the inner boundary. Later you can erase the box, leaving an island of white space around the text.

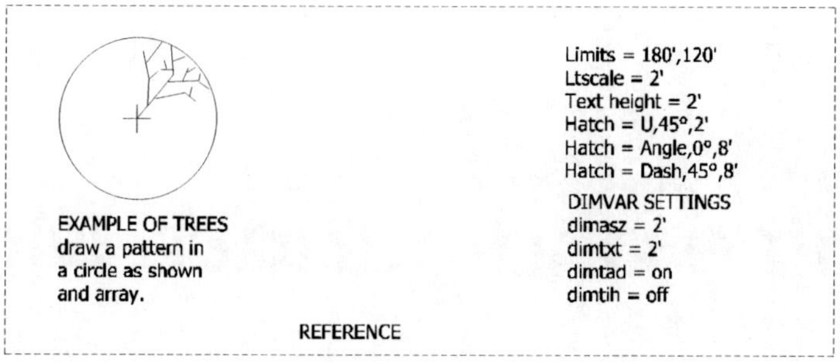

EXAMPLE OF TREES
draw a pattern in
a circle as shown
and array.
Limits = 180',120'
Ltscale = 2'
Text height = 2'
Hatch = U,45°,2'
Hatch = Angle,0°,8'
Hatch = Dash,45°,8'
DIMVAR SETTINGS
dimasz = 2'
dimtxt = 2'
dimtad = on
dimtih = off
REFERENCE

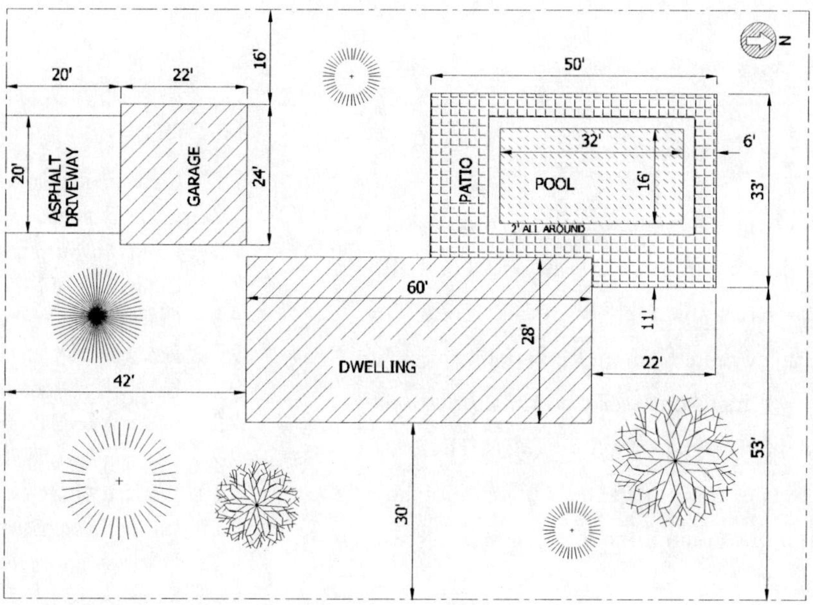

140'
16'
20'
22'
50'
N
20'
ASPHALT DRIVEWAY
GARAGE
24'
32'
6'
PATIO
POOL
16'
33'
2' ALL AROUND
60'
100'
11'
100'
28'
DWELLING
22'
42'
53'
30'
140'

PLOT PLAN

9

Wireframe and Surface Models

OVERVIEW

It is now time to begin thinking in three dimensions. Three-dimensional drawing in AutoCAD is logical and efficient. You can create wireframe models, surface models, or solid models and display them from multiple points of view. In this chapter we will focus on User Coordinate Systems, 3D viewpoints, and the three types of 3D models. These are the primary tools you will need to understand how AutoCAD allows you to work in three dimensions on a two-dimensional screen.

SECTIONS

OBJECTIVES

After reading this chapter, you should be able to:

- Create and view a 3D box and define and save three User Coordinate Systems.
- Use standard edit commands in a UCS and use multiple tiled viewports.
- Create flat surfaces with 3DFACE and remove hidden lines with HIDE.
- Use 3D polygon meshes.
- Create solid boxes and wedges and create the union of two solids.
- Work above the XY plane with ELEV.
- Create the subtraction of two solids and SHADE and RENDER solid objects.
- Draw a clamp, REVSURF designs, and a bushing mount.

9.1 CREATING AND VIEWING A 3D WIREFRAME BOX

In this section we will create a simple 3D box that we can edit in later tasks to form a more complex object. We have shown how to turn the coordinate system icon (see Figure 9.1) off and on. For drawing in 3D you will definitely want it on. If your icon is not visible, follow this procedure to turn it on:

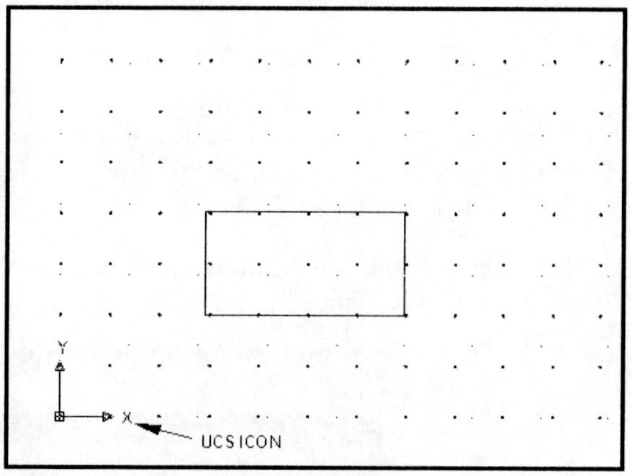

Figure 9.1

1. Open the View menu, highlight Display, and then UCS, as shown in Figure 9.2.
2. Select On from the submenu.

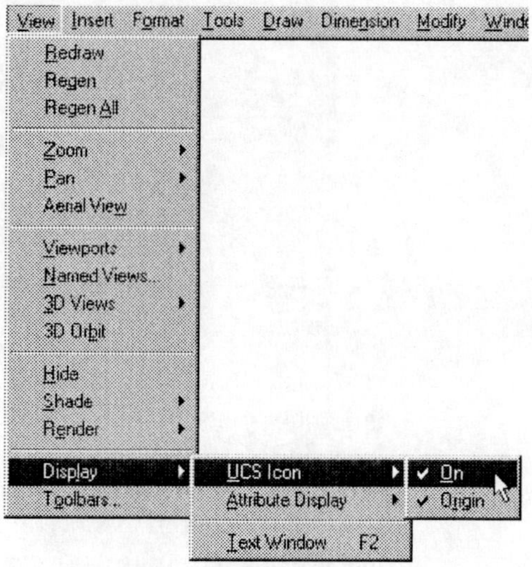

Figure 9.2

For now, simply observe the icon as you go through the process of creating the box, and be aware that you are currently working in the same coordinate system that you have always used in AutoCAD. It is called the World Coordinate System (WCS), to distinguish it from others you will create yourself beginning in Section 9.2.

Currently, the origin of the WCS is at the lower left of your grid. This is the point (0, 0, 0) when you are thinking 3D, or simply (0, 0) when you are in 2D. The x coordinates increase to the right horizontally across the screen, and y coordinates increase vertically up the screen as usual. The z axis, which we have ignored until now, currently extends out of the screen toward you and perpendicular to the x and y axes. This orientation of the three planes is called a plan view. Soon we will switch to a "front, right, top" or "southeast isometric" view.

Let's begin.

- **Draw a 2.00 by 4.00 rectangle near the middle of your screen, as shown in Figure 9.1. Do not use the RECTANG command to draw this figure because we will want to select individual line segments later on.**

9.1.1 Changing Viewpoints

To move immediately into a 3D mode of drawing and thinking, our first step will be to change our viewpoint on this object. The simplest and most efficient method is to use the Named Views dialog box introduced in the last chapter. For our purposes, this is the only method you will need.

- **Click the Named Views tool on the standard toolbar.**

This will open the View dialog box.

- **Select the Orthographic & Isometric Views tab, as shown in Figure 9.3.**

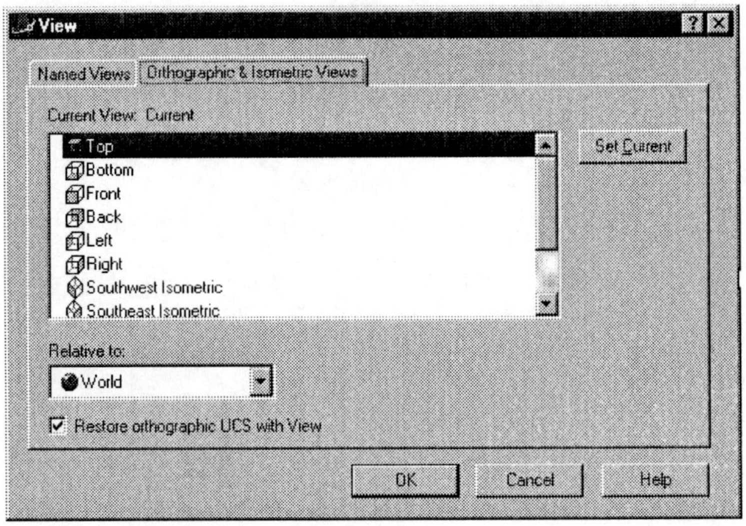

Figure 9.3

This dialog box uses simple cube images to show 10 standard preset views. Imagine your point of view to be perpendicular to the blue face of the cube in each case. In the six orthographic views, objects will be presented from points of view along each of the six axis directions. You will see objects in the drawing from directly above (Top, positive z) or directly below (Bottom, negative z), or by looking in along the positive or negative x axis (Left and Right) or the positive or negative y axis (Front and Back).

The four isometric views present objects at 45 degree angles from the XY axis and take you up 30 degrees out of the XY plane. We will use a southeast isometric view. It is simple if you imagine a compass. The lower right quadrant is the southeast. In a southeast isometric view you will be looking in from this quadrant and down at a 30-degree angle. Try it.

- **Select "SE Isometric" from the list of views.**
- **Click on Set Current.**

Click OK.

The dialog will disappear and the screen will be redrawn to the view shown in Figure 9.4. Notice how the grid and the coordinate system icon have altered to show our current orientation. These visual aids are extremely helpful in viewing 3D objects on the flat screen and imagining them as if they were positioned in space.

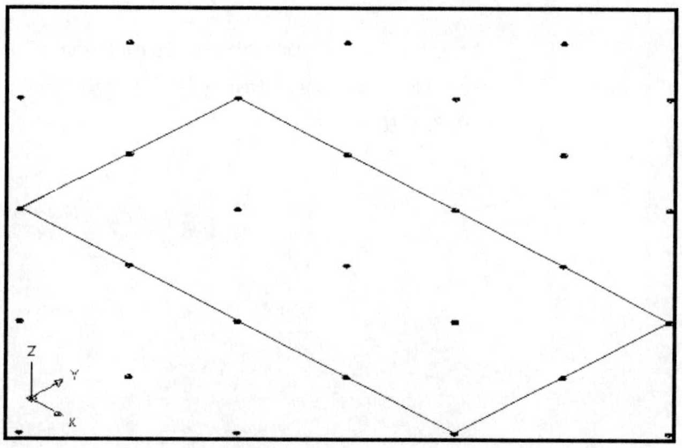

Figure 9.4

At this point you may wish to experiment with the other views in the View dialog box. You will probably find the isometric views most interesting at this point. Pay attention to the grid and the icon as you switch views. Variations of the icon you may encounter here and later on are shown in Figure 9.5. With some views you will have to think carefully and watch the icon to understand which way the object is being presented.

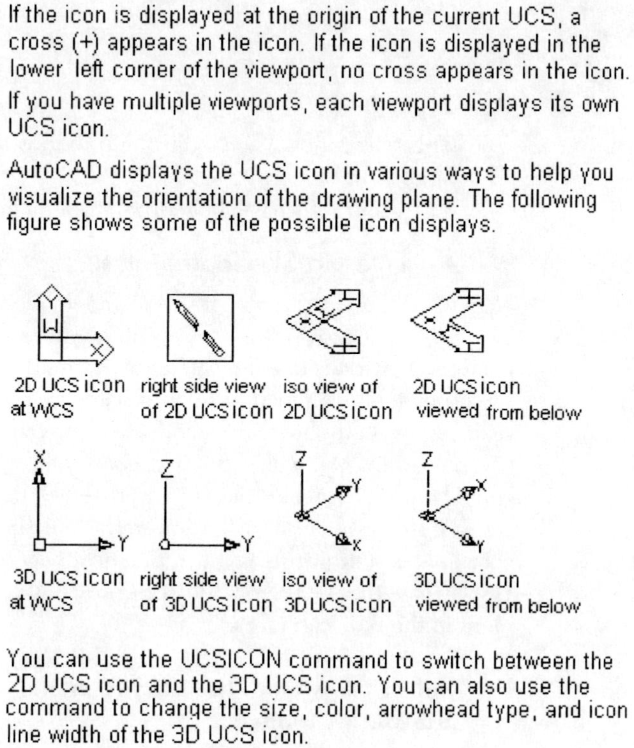

If the icon is displayed at the origin of the current UCS, a cross (+) appears in the icon. If the icon is displayed in the lower left corner of the viewport, no cross appears in the icon.

If you have multiple viewports, each viewport displays its own UCS icon.

AutoCAD displays the UCS icon in various ways to help you visualize the orientation of the drawing plane. The following figure shows some of the possible icon displays.

2D UCS icon at WCS
right side view of 2D UCS icon
iso view of 2D UCS icon
2D UCS icon viewed from below

3D UCS icon at WCS
right side view of 3D UCS icon
iso view of 3D UCS icon
3D UCS icon viewed from below

You can use the UCSICON command to switch between the 2D UCS icon and the 3D UCS icon. You can also use the command to change the size, color, arrowhead type, and icon line width of the 3D UCS icon.

Figure 9.5

When you are done experimenting, be sure to return to the southeast isometric view shown in Figure 9.4. We will use this view frequently throughout this chapter.

Whenever you change viewpoints, AutoCAD displays the drawing extents, so that the object fills the screen and is as large as possible. Often you will need to zoom out a bit to get some space to work in. This is easily done using the "Scale(X)" option of the ZOOM command.

⌖ **Open the View menu, highlight Zoom, and select Scale, or select the Zoom Scale tool from the Zoom flyout on the Standard toolbar, as shown in Figure 9.6.**

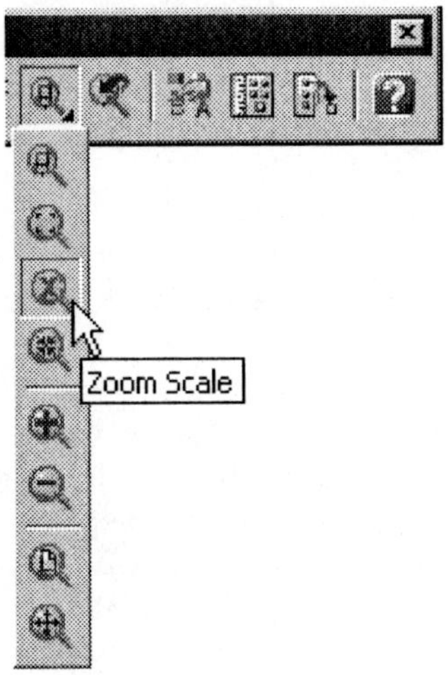

Figure 9.6

⌖ **Type "0.5."**

This tells AutoCAD to adjust and redraw the display so that objects appear half as large as before.

Your screen will be redrawn with the rectangle at half its previous magnification.

9.1.2 Entering 3D Coordinates

Next we will create a copy of the rectangle placed 1.25 above it. This brings up a basic 3D problem: AutoCAD interprets all pointer device point selections as being in the XY plane, so how does one indicate a point or a displacement in the Z direction? There are three possibilities: typed 3D coordinates, X/Y/Z point filters, and object snaps. Object snap requires an object already drawn above or below the XY plane, so it will be of no use right now. We will use typed coordinates first and then discuss how point filters could be used as an alternative. Later we will be using object snap as well.

3D coordinates can be entered from the keyboard in the same manner as 2D coordinates. Often this is an impractical way to enter individual points in a drawing. However, within COPY or MOVE it provides a simple method for specifying a displacement in the Z direction.

⌖ **Select Copy from the Modify menu, or select the Copy Object tool from the Modify toolbar.**

AutoCAD will prompt for object selection.

- **Select the complete rectangle.**
- **Press Enter, the space bar, or the enter equivalent button on your pointing device to end object selection.**

AutoCAD now prompts for the base point of a vector or a displacement value:

Specify base point or displacement, or [Multiple]:

Typically, you would respond to this prompt and the next by showing the two endpoints of a vector. However, we cannot show a displacement in the Z direction by pointing. This is important for understanding AutoCAD coordinate systems. Unless an object snap is used, all points picked on the screen with the pointing device will be interpreted as being in the XY plane of the current UCS. Without an entity outside the XY plane to use in an object snap, there is no way to point to a displacement in the Z direction.

- **Type "0, 0, 1.25."**

AutoCAD now prompts

Specify second point of displacement, or <use first point as displacement>:

You can type the coordinates of another point, or press Enter to tell AutoCAD to use the first entry as a displacement from (0, 0, 0). In this case, pressing Enter will indicate a displacement of 1.25 in the Z direction, and no change in X or Y.

- **Press Enter.**

AutoCAD will create a copy of the rectangle 1.25 units directly above the original. Your screen should resemble Figure 9.7.

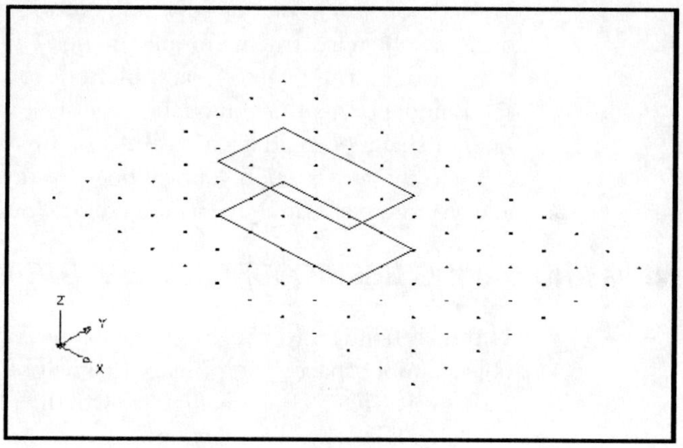

Figure 9.7

9.1.3 Using Object Snap

We now have two rectangles floating in space. Our next job is to connect the corners to form a wireframe box. This is done easily using Endpoint object snaps. This is a good example of how object snaps allow us to construct entities not in the XY plane of the current coordinate system.

- **Right click on the OSNAP button on the status bar.**
- **Select Settings... from the cursor menu.**
- **Click on Clear all to remove checks from all object snap boxes.**
- **Click the check box next to Endpoint.**
- **Click on OK.**

- **Click the OSNAP button so that it is in the down position.**

The running Endpoint object snap is now on and will affect all point selection. You will find that object snaps are very useful in 3D drawing and that Endpoint mode can be used frequently.

Now we will draw some lines.

- **Enter the LINE command and connect the upper and lower corners of the two rectangles, as shown in Figure 9.8.**

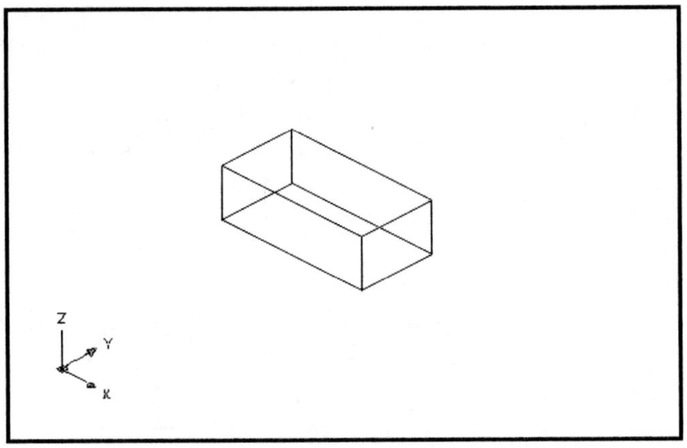

Figure 9.8

(We have removed the grid for clarity, but you will probably want to leave yours on.)

Before going on, pause a moment to be aware of what you have drawn. The box on your screen is a true wireframe model. Unlike an isometric drawing, it is a 3D model that can be turned, viewed, and plotted from any point in space. It is not, however, a solid model or a surface model. It is only a set of lines in 3D space. Removing hidden lines or shading would have no effect on this model.

In the next section you will begin to define your own coordinate systems that will allow you to perform drawing and editing functions in any plane you choose.

9.2 DEFINING AND SAVING USER COORDINATE SYSTEMS

In this section you will begin to develop new vocabulary and techniques for working with objects in 3D space. The primary tool will be the UCS command. You will also learn to use the UCSICON command to control the placement of the coordinate system icon.

Until now we have had only one coordinate system to work with. All coordinates and displacements have been defined relative to a single point of origin. Keep in mind that viewpoint and coordinate system are not the same, although they use similar vocabulary. In Section 9.1 we changed our point of view, but the UCS icon changed along with it, so that the orientations of the x, y, and z axes relative to the object were retained. With the UCS command you can free the coordinate system from the viewpoint and define new coordinate systems at any point and any angle in space. When you do, you can use the coordinate system icon and the grid to help you visualize the planes you are working in, and all commands and drawing aids will function relative to the new system.

The coordinate system we are currently using is unique. It is called the World Coordinate System and is the one we always begin with. The "W" at the base of the coordinate system icon indicates that we are working in the world system. A User Coordinate System is nothing more than a new point of origin and a new orientation for the x, y, and z axes.

We will begin by defining a User Coordinate System in the plane of the top of the box, as shown in Figure 9.9.

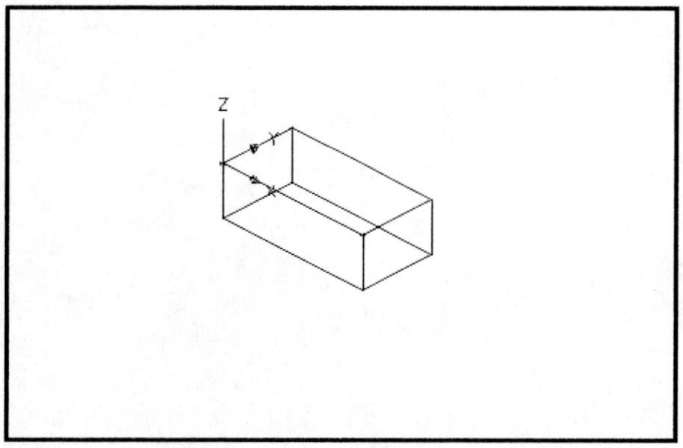

Figure 9.9

⌗ **Leave the Endpoint osnap mode on for this exercise.**

⌗ **Open the Tools menu and highlight New UCS.**

There is also a UCS tool on the UCS toolbar shown in Figure 9.10, but you will have to open the toolbar before you can access it. If you type "ucs" or select the tool from the toolbar, you will work with prompts at the command line. Here we will begin using the pull-down menu options and later use the command line as well.

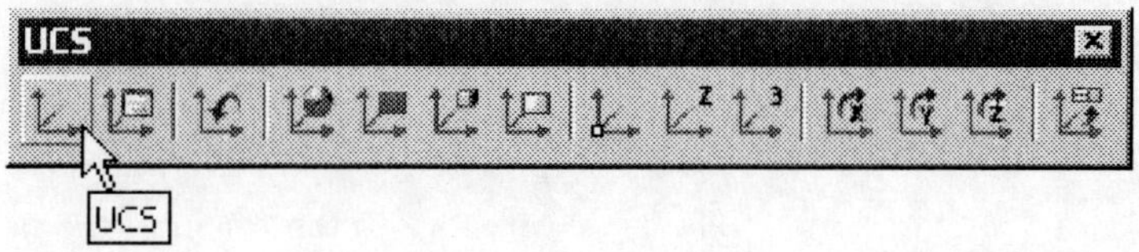

Figure 9.10

On the pull-down menu, you will see options on a submenu, as illustrated in Figure 9.11. We will begin by using "Origin" to create a UCS that is parallel to the WCS.

⌗ **Select Origin from the submenu.**

AutoCAD will prompt for a new origin:

Specify new origin point <0, 0, 0>:

This option does not change the orientation of the three axes. It simply shifts their intersection to a different point in space. We will use this procedure to define a UCS in the plane of the top of the box.

⌗ **Use the Endpoint object snap to select the top left front corner of the box, as shown by the location of the icon in Figure 9.9.**

You will notice that the "W" is gone from the icon. However, the icon has not moved. It is still at the lower left of the screen. It is visually helpful to place it at the origin of the new UCS, as in the figure. To do this we need the UCSICON command.

⌗ **Open the View menu, highlight "Display," and then "UCS Icon."**

⌗ **Select "Origin," so that there is a checkmark next to it.**

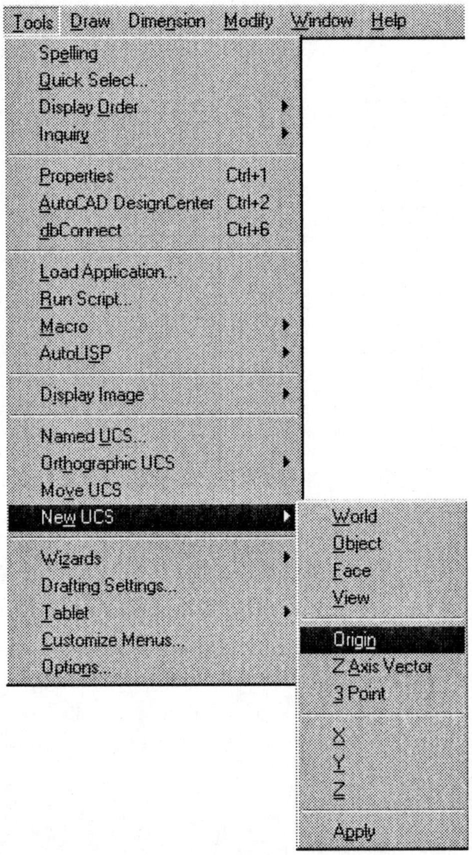

Figure 9.11

The icon will move to the origin of the new current UCS, as in Figure 9.9. With UCSICON set to origin, the icon will shift to the new origin whenever we define a new UCS. The only exception would be if the origin were not on the screen or too close to an edge for the icon to fit. In these cases the icon would be displayed in the lower left corner again.

The UCS we have just created will make it easy to draw and edit entities that are in the plane of the top of the box, and to perform editing in planes that are parallel to it, such as the bottom. In the next task we will begin drawing and editing using different coordinate systems, and you will see how this works. For now, we will spend a little more time on the UCS command itself. We will define two more user coordinate systems, but first let's save this one so that we can recall it quickly when we need it later.

⌖ **Open the Tools menu and highlight "Named UCS... ."**

The new UCS will be on the list as "Unnamed," along with World and Previous.

⌖ **Select "Unnamed."**

The word "Unnamed" should be selected for editing. We will name our coordinate system "top." It will be the UCS we use to draw and edit in the top plane. This UCS would also make it easy for us to create an orthographic top viewpoint later on.

⌖ **Type "top" and press Enter.**

The top UCS is now saved and can be recalled by opening this dialog, selecting it in the name list, and clicking the Set current button.

Next we will define a "left" UCS using the "3 point" option.

Open the Tools menu, highlight New UCS, and select "3 point" from the submenu.

AutoCAD prompts

Specify new origin point <0, 0, 0>:

In this option you will show AutoCAD a new origin point, as before, and then a new orientation for the axes as well. Notice that the default origin is the current one. If we retained this origin, we could define a UCS with the same origin and a different axis orientation.

Instead, we will define a new origin at the lower left corner of the left side of the box, as shown in Figure 9.12.

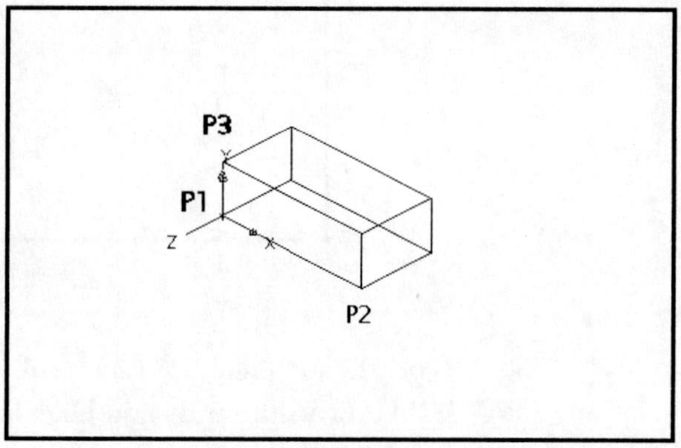

Figure 9.12

With the Endpoint osnap on, pick P1, as shown in Figure 9.12.

AutoCAD now prompts you to indicate the orientation of the x axis:

Specify point on positive portion of the X axis <1.00, 0.00, −1.25>:

Pick the right front corner of the box, P2, as shown.

The object snap ensures that the new x axis will now align with the left side of the object. AutoCAD prompts for the y axis orientation:

Specify point on positive-Y portion of the UCS XY plane <0.00, 1.00, −1.25>:

By definition, the y axis will be perpendicular to the x axis; therefore, AutoCAD needs only a point that shows the plane of the y axis and its positive direction. Because of this, any point on the positive side of the y plane will specify the y axis correctly. We have chosen a point that is on the y axis itself.

Pick P3, as shown.

When this sequence is complete, you will notice that the coordinate system icon has rotated along with the grid and moved to the new origin as well. This UCS will be convenient for drawing and editing in the left plane of the box, or editing in any plane parallel to the left plane, such as the back plane.

9.3 USING DRAW AND EDIT COMMANDS IN A UCS

Now the fun begins. Using our three new coordinate systems and one more we will define later, we will give the box a more interesting "slotted wedge" shape. In this task we will cut away a slanted surface on the right side of the box. Since the planes we will be working in are parallel to the left side of the box, we will begin by making the "left" UCS current. All our work in this task will be done in this UCS.

Look at Figure 9.13. We will draw a line down the middle of the left side (Line 1) and use it to trim another line coming in at an angle (Line 2).

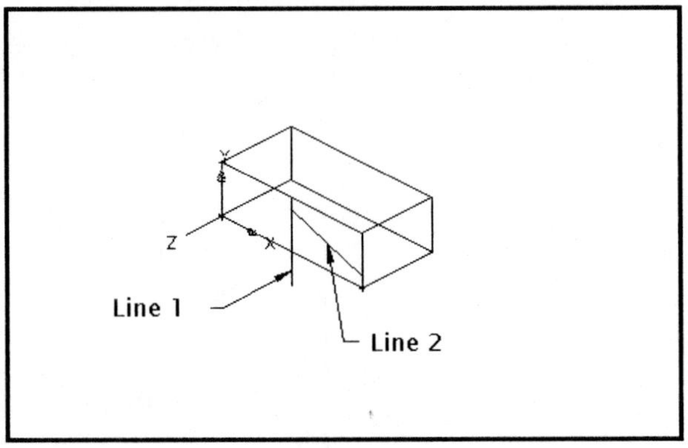

Figure 9.13

- **Type "L" or select the Line tool from the Draw toolbar.**
- **Hold down shift and right click to open the object snap cursor menu.**
- **Select Midpoint.**

  This will temporarily override the Endpoint object snap.
- **Point to the top edge of the left side of the box.**

  AutoCAD will snap to the midpoint of the line.
- **Make sure that Ortho is on (F8 or the ORTHO button).**

  Notice how Ortho works as usual, but relative to the current UCS.
- **Pick a second point anywhere below the box.**

  This line will be trimmed later, so the exact length does not matter.
- **Exit the LINE command.**

  Next we will draw Line 2 on an angle across the left side. This line will become one edge of a slanted surface. Your snap setting will need to be at 0.25 or smaller, and ortho will need to be off. The grid, snap, and coordinate display all work relative to the current UCS, so it is a simple matter to draw in this plane.
- **Turn Grid Snap on (F9 or the SNAP button) and check your snap setting by observing the coordinate display. Change it to 0.25 if necessary.**
- **Turn Ortho off.**
- **Turn Osnap off (F3 or the OSNAP button).**
- **Enter the LINE command.**
- **Use incremental snap to pick a point 0.25 down from the top edge of the box on Line 1, as shown in Figure 9.13.**

- **Pick a second point 0.25 up along the right front edge of the box, as shown.**
- **Exit the LINE command.**

Now trim Line 1.

- **Select the Trim tool from the Modify toolbar.**

AutoCAD will present the following message, though you may need to switch to the text screen to see it:

View is not plan to UCS. Command results may not be obvious.

In the language of AutoCAD 3D, a view is plan to the current UCS if the XY plane is in the plane of the monitor display and its axes are parallel to the sides of the screen. This is the usual 2D view, in which the y axis aligns with the left side of the display and the x axis aligns with the bottom of the display. In previous chapters we always worked in plan view. In this chapter we have not been in plan view since the beginning of Section 9.1.

With this message, AutoCAD is warning us that boundaries, edges, and intersections may not be obvious as we look at a 3D view of an object. For example, lines that appear to cross may be in different planes.

Having read the warning, we continue.

- **Select Line 2 as a cutting edge.**
- **Press Enter to end cutting edge selection.**
- **Point to the lower end of Line 1.**
- **Press Enter or the space bar to exit TRIM.**

Your screen should resemble Figure 9.14.

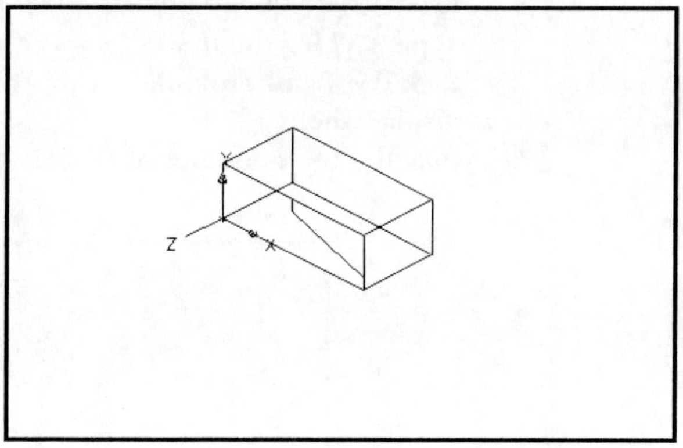

Figure 9.14

Now we will copy our two lines to the back of the box. Since we will be moving out of the left plane, which is also the XY plane in the current UCS, we will require the use of the Endpoint object snaps to specify the displacement vector.

- **Select the Copy Object tool from the Modify toolbar.**
- **Pick Lines 1 and 2. (You will probably need to zoom in on the box at this point to pick Line 1.)**
- **Press Enter to end object selection.**
- **Use the Endpoint Osnap to pick the lower front corner of the box, P1 as shown in Figure 9.15.**

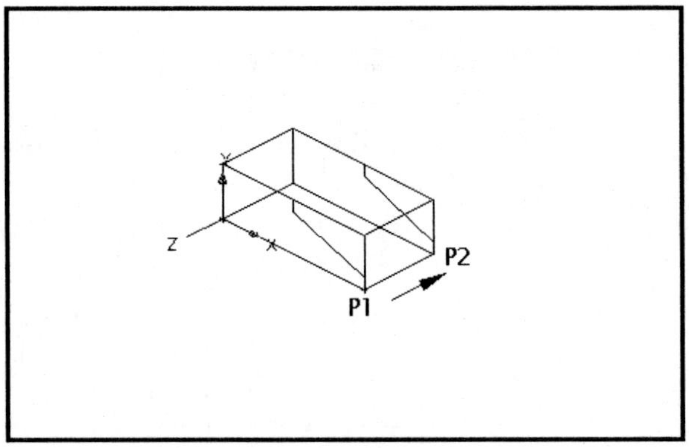

Figure 9.15

- **At the prompt for a second point of displacement, use the Endpoint osnap to pick the lower right back corner of the box, P2 as shown.**
  Your screen should now resemble Figure 9.15.

What remains is to connect the edges we have just outlined and then trim away the top of the box. We will continue to work in the left UCS and to use Endpoint Osnaps.

We will use a multiple COPY to copy one of the previously drawn edges in three new places.

- **Repeat COPY.**
- **Pick the bottom right edge for copying (the edge between p1 and p2 in Figure 9.15).**
- **Press Enter to end object selection.**
- **Type "m" for the multiple option.**
- **Pick the front endpoint of the selected edge to serve as a base point of displacement.**
- **Pick the top endpoint of Line 1 (P1 in Figure 9.16).**

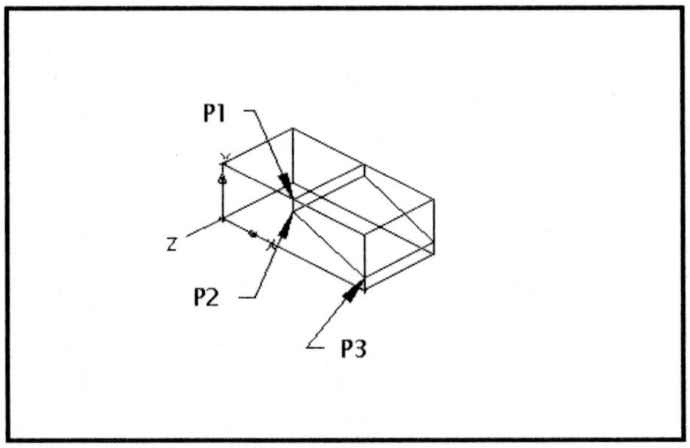

Figure 9.16

- **Pick the lower endpoint of Line 1 (P2) as another second point.**
- **Pick the right endpoint of Line 2 (P3) as another second point.**
- **Press Enter to exit the COPY command.**
  Finally, we need to do some trimming.

⌗ **Select the Trim tool from the Modify toolbar.**

For cutting edges, we want to select Lines 1 and 2 and their copies in the back plane (lines 3 and 4 in Figure 9.17). Since this can be difficult, a quick alternative to selecting these four separate lines is to use a crossing box to select the whole area. As long as your selection includes the four lines, it will be effective.

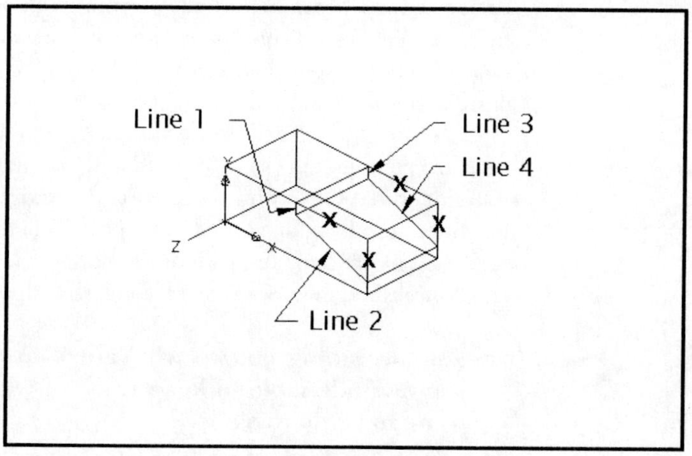

Figure 9.17

⌗ **Select the area around Lines 1 and 2 with a crossing box.**

NOTE: Trimming in 3D can be tricky. Remember where you are. Edges that do not run parallel to the current UCS may not be recognized at all.

⌗ **Press Enter to end cutting edge selection.**

⌗ **One by one, pick the top left and top back edges to the right of the cut, and the right front and right back edges above the cut, as shown by the x's in Figure 9.17.**

⌗ **Press Enter to exit the TRIM command.**

⌗ **Use the ERASE command to erase the top edge that is left hanging in space.**

We use ERASE here because this line does not intersect any edges.

Your screen should now resemble Figure 9.18.

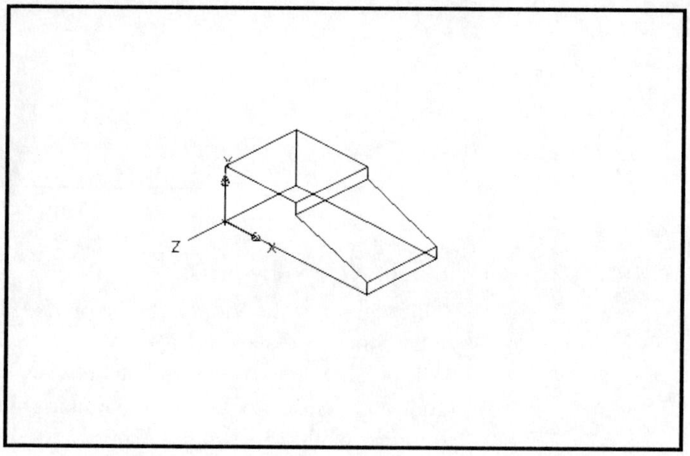

Figure 9.18

9.4 USING MULTIPLE TILED VIEWPORTS

A major feature needed to draw effectively in 3D is the ability to view an object from several different points of view simultaneously as you work on it. The VPORTS command is easy to use and can save you from having to jump back and forth between different views of an object. Viewports can be used in 2D to place several zoom magnifications on the screen at once. More important, viewports can be used to place several 3D viewpoints on the screen at once. This is a significant drawing aid. If you do not continually view an object from different points of view, it is easy to create entities that appear correct in the current view but that are clearly incorrect from other points of view.

In this task we will divide your screen in half and define two views so that you can visualize an object in plan view and a 3D isometric view at the same time. As you work, remember that this is only a display command. The viewports we use in this chapter will be simple model space "tiled" viewports. Tiled viewports cover the complete drawing area, do not overlap, and cannot be plotted simultaneously. Plotting multiple viewports is accomplished in paper space layouts with floating viewports.

- **Before going on, we will return to the World Coordinate System. It is always advisable to keep track of where you are in relation to the WCS and to begin there.**
- **Type "ucs" or select "Set UCS" from the View pull-down menu.**
- **Type "w" or select "World" from the submenu.**

Now we will move to two viewports.

- **Highlight Viewports on the View menu.**

This will open the submenu shown in Figure 9.19.

We will use the New Viewports option.

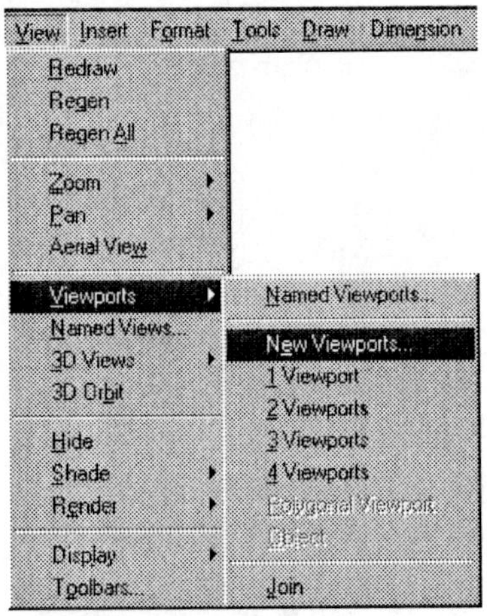

Figure 9.19

- **Select New Viewports....**

This will open the Viewports dialog box shown in Figure 9.20. The dialog has two tabs. Since you selected New Viewports from the menu, the New Viewports tab will be showing. If you had selected Named Viewports, the other tab would be showing. The two tabs are similar, but New Viewports contains predefined options, while the Named Viewports contains viewport configurations that have been previously created and saved in your drawing.

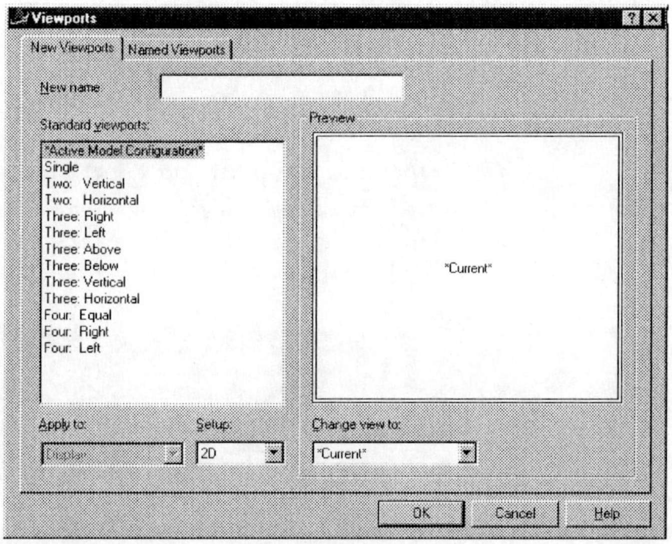

Figure 9.20

Looking at the New Viewport tab, at the top you see an edit box so that you can give a name to a viewport configuration when you define it. This is only useful if you create a configuration that is not already on the list. The white panel on the left lists predefined configurations. Active Model Configuration is basically the current configuration in the drawing. Single is the one viewport drawing area we have been working in since the beginning. The others are defined by number and location of viewports.

Select "Two Vertical:"

The Preview on the right will change to show two vertical viewports, as illustrated in Figure 9.21. Notice that both viewports currently contain the current model space display. Look at the three list boxes at the bottom of the dialog. The Apply to list gives you the choice of applying configuration changes to the whole display or just to a selected viewport. This means you can create viewports by dividing already defined viewports. For now, display should be selected in this list.

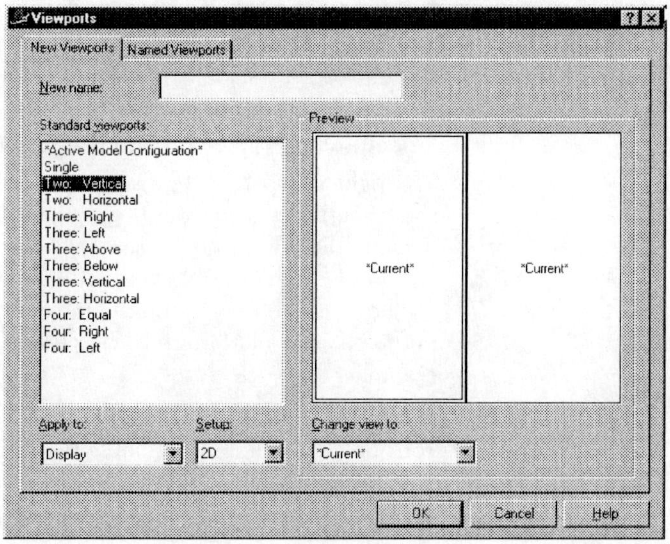

Figure 9.21

The Setup list has two options, 2D and 3D. Standard 2D configurations will always start with the current view in each viewport. 3D configurations add standard top, front, and southeast isometric views. If you look at the third list box, labeled "Change view to:", you will see that Current is the only choice. Now try this:

⌖ **Open the Setup list and select 3D.**

The preview will change to show a top view on the left and a southeast isometric view on the right, as shown in Figure 9.22. Notice that the top viewport is selected with a border in the preview and that "*Top*" is now showing in the Change view list.

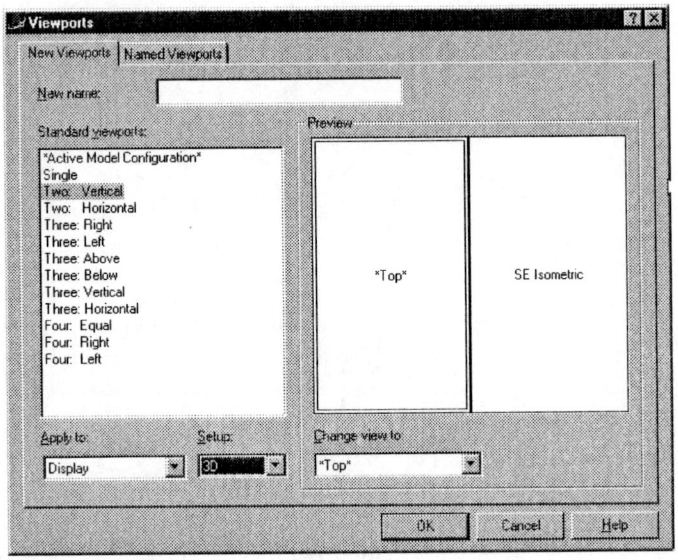

Figure 9.22

⌖ **Open the Change view to: list.**

In addition to Top, you will see Bottom, Front, Back, and Left viewpoint options. These are the standard options for the left viewport in a two-viewport vertical configuration. With this list you can change the view in any selected viewport to create your own configuration. Then if you add a name in the New name edit box at the top of the dialog, the named configuration will be added to a list on the Named Viewports tab.

⌖ **Select the right viewport in the preview by clicking anywhere inside it.**

The right viewport will be selected with a border and the Change view list will show Southeast isometric. If you open the list you will see that the other options here are the four standard isometric views: SW, SE, NW, and NE.

The standard Two: Vertical 3D viewport with a top view on the left and a southeast isometric view on the right is the configuration we will be working with in this chapter, but before leaving the dialog box, look at some other options. For example:

⌖ **Select "Three: Right."**

Your preview will now resemble the one in Figure 9.23. This is also a very common configuration.

⌖ **Select "Four: Equal," and any other configurations you wish to preview.**

⌖ **Select "Two: Vertical" before leaving the dialog.**

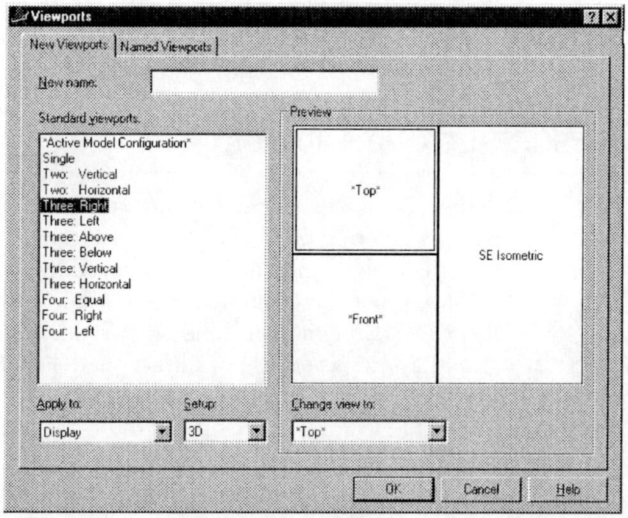

Figure 9.23

⌗ **Click OK to exit the dialog.**

Your screen will resemble Figure 9.24, except that the grid will be off in the right viewport.

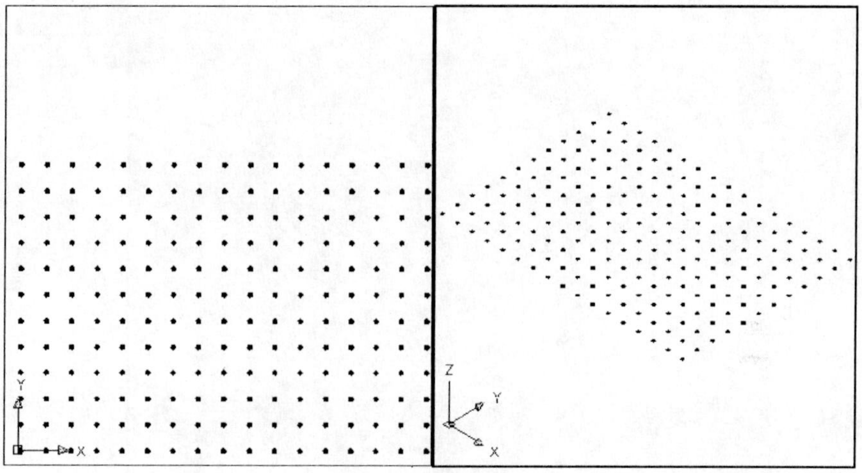

Figure 9.24

If you move your pointing device back and forth between the windows, you will see an arrow when you are on the left and the crosshairs when you are on the right. This indicates that the right window is currently active. Drawing and editing can be done only in the active window. To work in another window, you need to make it current by picking it with your pointing device. Often this can be done while a command is in progress.

⌗ **Move the cursor into the left window and press the pickbutton on your pointing device.**

Now the crosshairs will appear in the left viewport, and you will see the arrow when you move into the right viewport.

⌗ **Move the cursor back to the right and press the pickbutton again.**

This will make the right window active again.

⌗ **If the grid is off in your right viewport, turn it on (F7).**

We are now ready to begin drawing in this viewport configuration. Once you have defined viewports, any drawing or editing done in the active viewport will appear in all the viewports. As you draw, watch what happens in both viewports.

9.5 CREATING SURFACES WITH 3DFACE

3DFACE creates triangular and quadrilateral surfaces. Three-dimensional faces are built by entering points in groups of three or four to define the outlines of triangles or quadrilaterals, similar to objects formed by the 2D SOLID command. The surface of a 3D face is not shown on the screen, but it is recognized by the HIDE command and by the RENDER command, and other rendering programs such as 3D Studio.

Layering is critical in surface modeling. Surfaces quickly complicate a drawing so that object selection and object snap become difficult or impossible. Also, you may want to be able to turn layers off or freeze them to achieve the results you want from the HIDE command. You may eventually want a number of layers specifically defined for faces and surfaces, but this will not be necessary for the current exercise.

⌗ **Open the Draw menu and highlight Surfaces.**

This calls the submenu shown in Figure 9.25. There is also a Surface toolbar with a 3D Face tool, as shown in Figure 9.26.

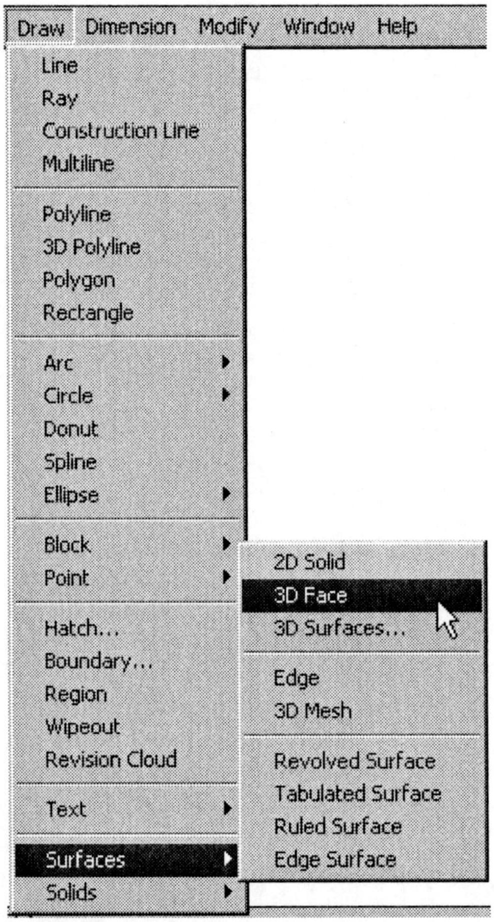

Figure 9.25

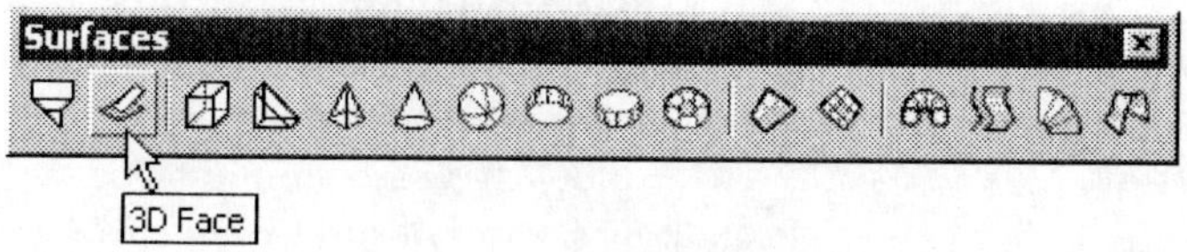

Figure 9.26

⌖ **Select "3D Face."**

AutoCAD will prompt

Specify first point or [Invisible]:

You can define points in either of the two viewports. In fact, you can even switch viewports in the middle of the command.

⌖ **Pick a point similar to P1, as shown in Figure 9.27.**

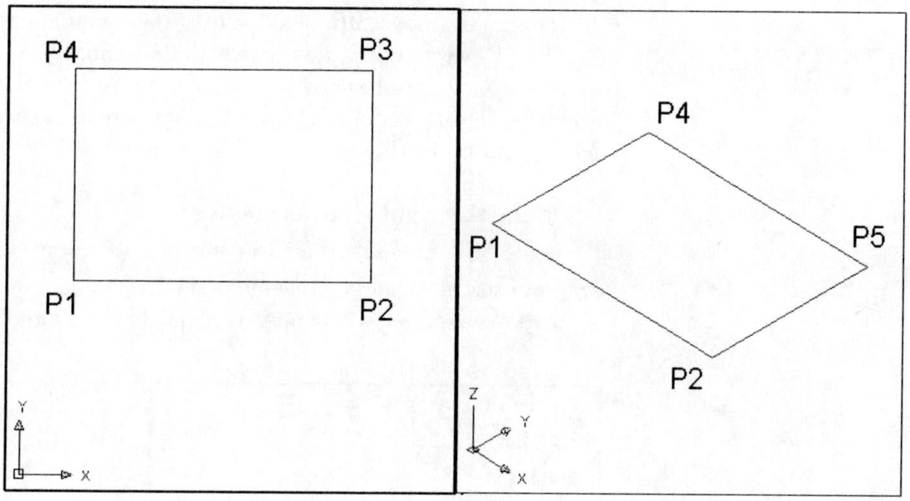

Figure 9.27

AutoCAD prompts

Specify second point or [Invisible]:

⌖ **Pick a second point, moving around the perimeter of the face, as shown.**

Be aware that the correct order for defining 3D faces is different from the 2D SOLID command. It is important to pick points in order around the face; otherwise you will get a bow tie or hourglass effect.

AutoCAD prompts

Specify third point or [Invisible]<exit>:

⌖ **Pick a third point, as shown.**

AutoCAD prompts

Specify fourth point or [Invisible]<create three-sided face>:

NOTE: If you pressed Enter now, AutoCAD would draw the outline of a triangular face, using the three points already given.

- **Pick the fourth point of the face.**

  AutoCAD draws the fourth edge of the face automatically when four points have been given, so it is not necessary to complete or close the rectangle.

  AutoCAD will continue to prompt for third and fourth points so that you can draw a series of surfaces to cover an area with more than four edges. Keep in mind, however, that drawing faces in series is only a convenience. The result is a collection of independent three- and four-sided faces.

- **Press Enter or the space bar to exit the 3DFACE command.**

In the next task we will demonstrate the HIDE command.

9.6 REMOVING HIDDEN LINES WITH HIDE

The HIDE command is easy to execute. However, execution may be slow in large drawings, and careful work may be required to create a drawing that hides the way you want it to. This is an important objective in surface modeling. When you've got everything right, HIDE will temporarily remove all lines and objects that would be obstructed in the current view, resulting in a more realistic representation of the object in space. A correctly surfaced model can also be used to create a shaded rendering. Hiding has no effect on wireframe drawings, since there are no surfaces to obstruct lines behind them.

- **Make the right viewport active.**
- **Type "hi" or open the View menu and select "Hide."**

  Your screen should be regenerated to resemble Figure 9.28. In this case the hiding and regeneration will happen very quickly. In a larger drawing you will have to wait.

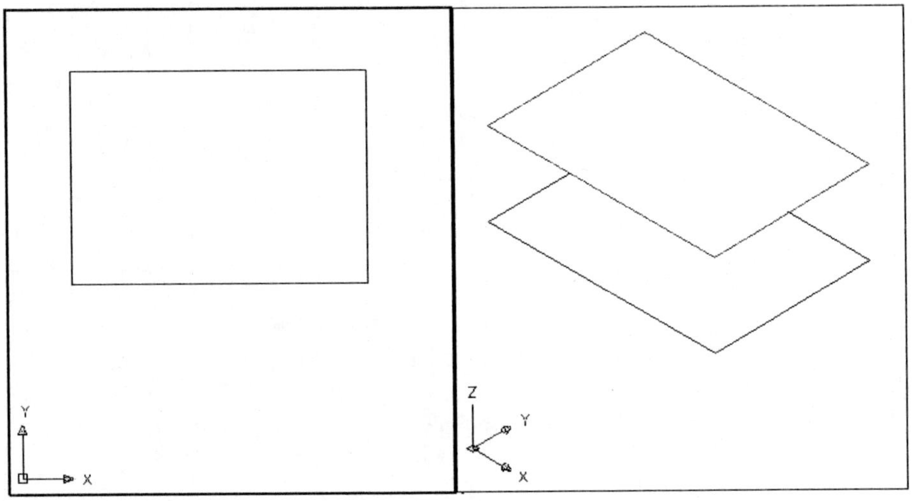

Figure 9.28

Following are some important points about hidden line removal that you should read before continuing:

1. Hidden line removal can be done from the plot configuration dialog box. However, due to the time involved and the difficulty of getting a hidden view

just right, it is usually better to experiment on the screen first and then plot with hidden lines removed when you know you will get the image you want.

2. Whenever the screen is regenerated, hidden lines are returned to the screen.
3. Layer control is important in hidden line removal. Layers that are frozen are ignored by the HIDE command, but layers that are off are treated like layers that are visible. This can, for example, create peculiar blank spaces in your display if you have left surfaces or solids on a layer that is off at the time of hidden line removal.

9.7 USING 3D POLYGON MESH COMMANDS

3DFACE can be used to create simple surfaces. However, most surface models require large numbers of faces to approximate the surfaces of real objects. Consider the number of faces in Figure 9.29. Obviously, you would not want to draw such an image one face at a time.

Figure 9.29

AutoCAD includes a number of commands that make the creation of some types of surfaces very easy. These powerful commands create 3D polygon meshes. Polygon meshes are made up of 3D faces and are defined by a matrix of vertices.

⌗ **To begin this task, ERASE the two faces from the last task and draw an arc and a line below it, as shown in Figure 9.30. Exact sizes and locations are not important.**

The entities may be drawn in either viewport.

Now we will define some 3D surfaces using the arc and line you have just drawn.

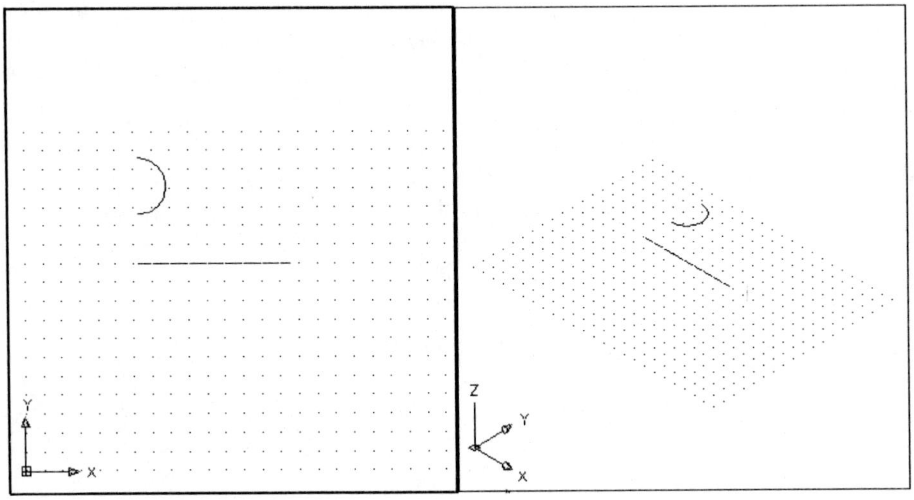

Figure 9.30

9.7.1 TABSURF

The first surface we will draw is called a "tabulated surface." To use the TABSURF command, you need a line or curve to define the shape of the surface and a vector to show its size and direction. The result is a surface generated by repeating the shape of the original curve at every point along the path specified by the vector.

- **Open the Draw menu, highlight Surfaces, and select Tabulated Surface.**

  There is also a Tabulated Surface tool on the Surface toolbar, shown previously in Figure 9.26. AutoCAD will prompt

- **Select object for path curve.**

  The path curve is the line or curve that will determine the shape of the surface. In our case it will be the arc.

- **Pick the arc.**

  AutoCAD will prompt for a vector:

  Select object for direction vector:

  We will use the line. Notice that the vector does not need to be connected to the path curve. Its location is not significant, only its direction and length.

  There is an oddity here to watch out for as you pick the vector. If you pick a point near the left end of the line, AutoCAD will interpret the vector as extending from left to right. Accordingly, the surface will be drawn to the right. By the same token, if your point is near the right end of the line, the surface will be drawn to the left. Most of the time you will avoid confusion by picking a point on the side of the vector nearest the curve itself.

- **Pick a point on the left side of the line.**

  Your screen will be redrawn to resemble Figure 9.31. Notice that this is a flat surface even though it may look 3D in the left viewport. Tabulated surfaces can be fully 3D, depending on the path and vector chosen to define them. In this case we have an arc and a vector that are both entirely in the XY plane, so the resulting surface is also in that plane.

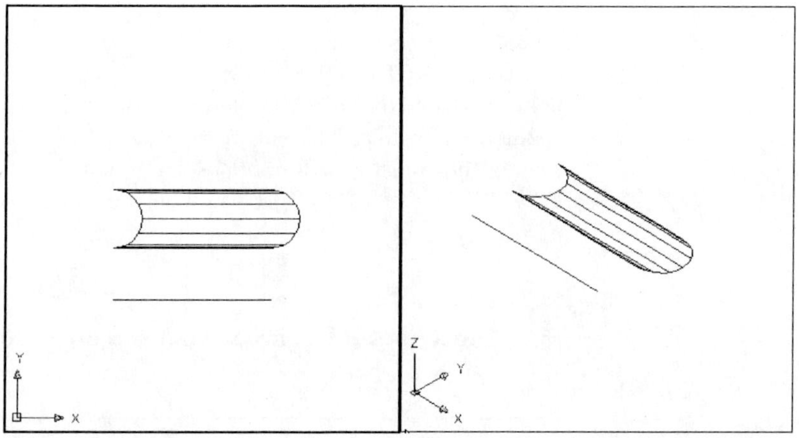

Figure 9.31

9.7.2 RULESURF

TABSURF is useful in defining surfaces that are the same on both ends, assuming you have one end and a vector. Often, however, you have no vector, or you need to draw a surface between two different paths. In these cases you will need the RULESURF command.

For example, what if we need to define a surface between the line and the arc? Let's try it.

⌖ **Type "u" to undo the last tabulated surface.**

⌖ **Open the Draw menu, highlight Surfaces, and select Ruled Surface.**

The first prompt is

Select first defining curve:

⌖ **Pick the arc, using a point near the bottom.**

Remember that you must pick points on corresponding sides of the two defining curves in order to avoid an hourglass effect.

AutoCAD prompts

Select second defining curve:

⌖ **Pick the line, using a point near the left end.**

Your screen should resemble Figure 9.32. Again, notice that this surface is within the XY plane even though it may look 3D. Ruled surfaces may be drawn just as easily between curves that are not coplanar.

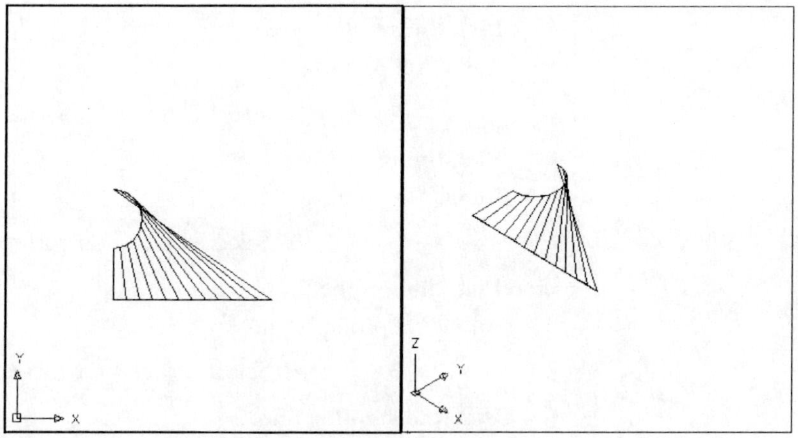

Figure 9.32

9.7.3 EDGESURF

TABSURF creates surfaces that are the same at both ends and move along a straight line vector. RULESURF draws surfaces between any two boundaries. EDGESURF draws surfaces that are bounded by four curves. Edge-defined surfaces have a lot of geometric flexibility. The only restriction is that they must be bounded on all four sides. That is, they must have four edges that touch.

To create an EDGESURF, we need to undo our last ruled surface and add two more edges.

⌖ **Type "u."**

⌖ **Add a line and an arc to your screen, as shown in Figure 9.33.**

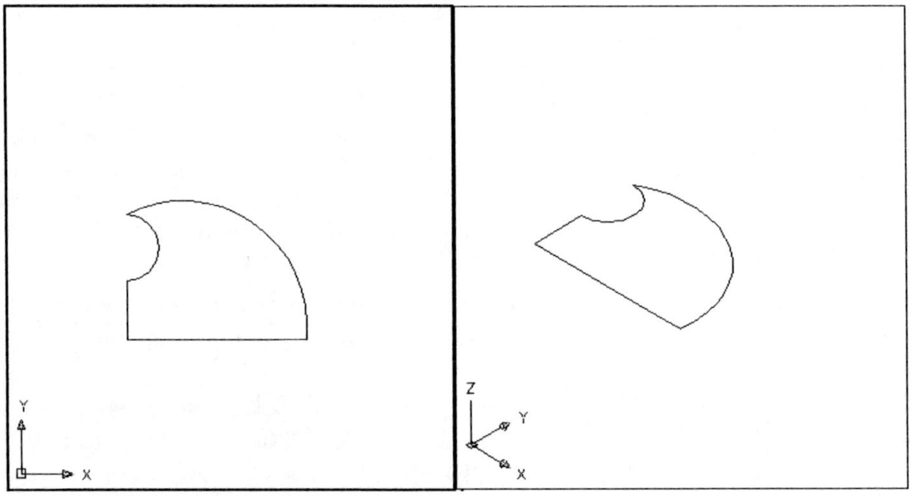

Figure 9.33

Remember, you can draw in either viewport.

⌖ **Open the Draw menu, highlight Surfaces, and select Edge Surface.**

AutoCAD will prompt for the four edges of the surface, one at a time:

Select object 1 for surface edge:

⌖ **Pick the smaller arc.**

AutoCAD prompts

Select object 2 for surface edge:

⌖ **Pick the larger arc.**

AutoCAD prompts

Select object 3 for surface edge:

⌖ **Pick the longer line.**

AutoCAD prompts

Select object 4 for surface edge:

⌖ **Pick the smaller line.**

Your screen should now resemble Figure 9.34.

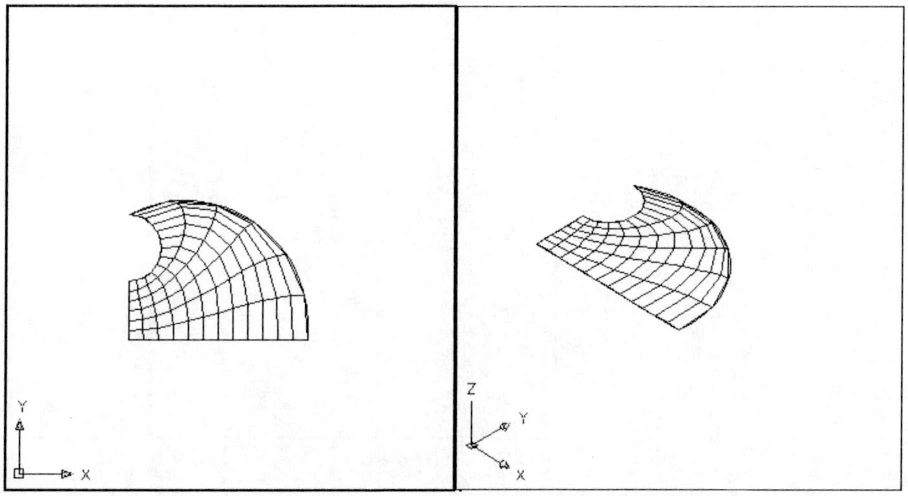

Figure 9.34

9.7.4 REVSURF

We have one more 3D polygon mesh command to explore, and this one is probably the most impressive of all. REVSURF creates surfaces by spinning a curve through a given angle around an axis of revolution. Just as tabulated surfaces are spread along a linear path, surfaces of revolution follow a circular or arc-shaped path. As a result, surfaces of revolution are always fully three dimensional, even if their defining geometry is in a single plane, as it will be here.

⌖ **In preparation for this exercise, undo the EDGESURF, so that your screen resembles Figure 9.33 again.**

We will use REVSURF to create a surface of revolution.

⌖ **Open the Draw menu, highlight Surfaces, and select Revolved Surface.**

AutoCAD needs an object to revolve and an axis of revolution to define the surface. The first prompt is

Select object to revolve:

⌖ **Pick the smaller arc.**

AutoCAD prompts

Select object that defines the axis of revolution:

⌖ **Pick the smaller line.**

AutoCAD now needs to know whether you want the surface to begin at the object itself or somewhere else around the circle of revolution:

Specify start angle <0>:

The default is to start at the object.

⌖ **Press Enter or the space bar.**

AutoCAD prompts

Specify included angle (+=ccw, −=cw) <360>:

Entering a positive or negative degree measure will cause the surface to be drawn around an arc rather than a full circle. The default will give us a complete circle.

⌖ **Press Enter or the space bar.**

Your screen should be drawn to resemble Figure 9.35

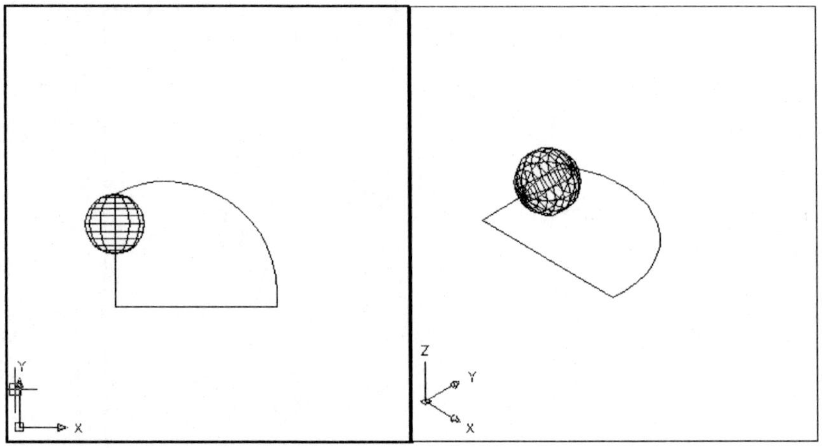

Figure 9.35

Next, we will move on to solid modeling, probably the most powerful type of 3D drawing.

9.8 CREATING SOLID BOXES AND WEDGES

Solid modeling requires a somewhat different type of thinking from any of the drawings you have done so far. Instead of focusing on lines and arcs, edges and surfaces, you will need to imagine how 3D objects might be pieced together by combining or subtracting basic solid shapes. This building block process is called constructive solid geometry and includes joining, subtracting, and intersecting operations. A simple washer, for example, could be made by cutting a small cylinder out of the middle of a larger cylinder. In AutoCAD solid modeling you can begin with a flat outer cylinder, then draw an inner cylinder with a smaller radius centered at the same point, and then subtract the inner cylinder from the outer, as illustrated in Figure 9.36.

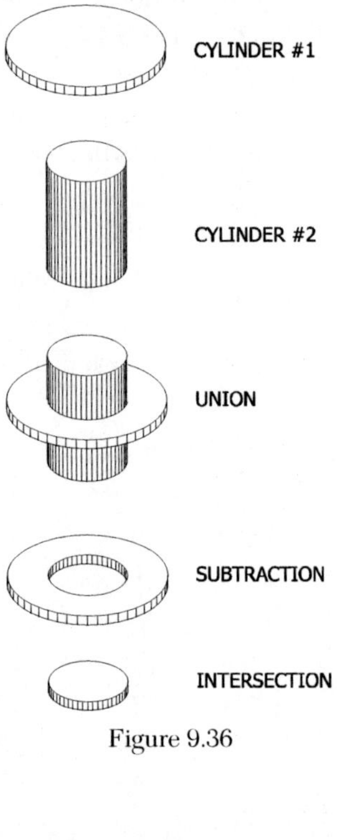

Figure 9.36

This operation, which uses the SUBTRACT command, is the equivalent of cutting a hole and is one of three Boolean operations (after the mathematician George Booles) used to create composite solids. UNION joins two solids to make a new solid, and INTERSECT creates a composite solid in the space where two solids overlap.

In this exercise, you will create a composite solid from the union and subtraction of several solid primitives. Primitives are 3D solid building blocks—boxes, cones, cylinders, spheres, wedges, and torus. They all are regularly shaped and can be defined by specifying a few points and distances.

For this exercise, we will return to a single 3D viewpoint.

⌗ **Erase objects left from the last task.**

⌗ **Make the right viewport active.**

⌗ **Select Tiled Viewports from the View pull-down menu.**

We are now ready to create new solid objects.

⌗ **Type "box" or open the Draw menu, highlight Solids, and select Box.**

There is also a Solids toolbar with a Box tool, as illustrated in Figure 9.37.

Figure 9.37

In the command area you will see the following prompt:

Specify corner of box or [CEnter] <0, 0, 0>:

"CEnter" allows you to begin defining a box by specifying its center point. Here we will use the "Corner of box" option to begin drawing a box in the base plane of the current UCS. We will draw a box with a length of 4, width of 3, and height of 1.5.

⌗ **Pick a corner point similar to Point 1 in Figure 9.38.**

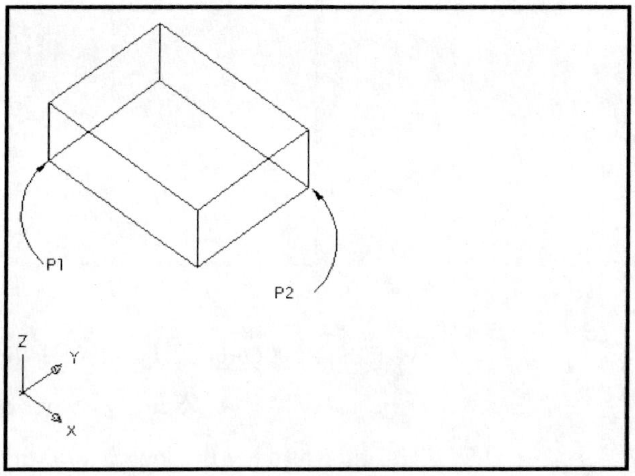

Figure 9.38

AutoCAD will prompt

Specify corner or [Cube/Length]:

With the "Cube" option you can draw a box with equal length, width, and height by specifying one distance. The "Length" option will allow you to specify length, width, and height separately. If you have simple measurements that fall on snap points, as we do, you can show the length and width at the same time by picking the other corner of the base of the box (the default method).

Move the crosshairs over 4 in the x direction and up 3 in the y direction to Point 2, as shown in the figure.

Notice that "length" is measured along the x axis, and "width" is measured along the y axis.

Pick Point 2 as shown.

Now AutoCAD prompts for a height. "Height" is measured along the z axis. As usual, you cannot pick points in the z direction unless you have objects to snap to. Instead, you can type a value or show a value by picking two points in the XY plane.

Type "1.5" or pick two points 1.5 units apart.

Your screen should resemble Figure 9.38.

Next we will create a solid wedge. The process will be exactly the same, but there will be no "Cube" option.

Type "we" or open the Draw menu, highlight Solids, and select Wedge.

AutoCAD prompts

Specify first corner of wedge or [CEnter] <0, 0, 0>:

Pick the front corner point of the box, as shown in Figure 9.39.

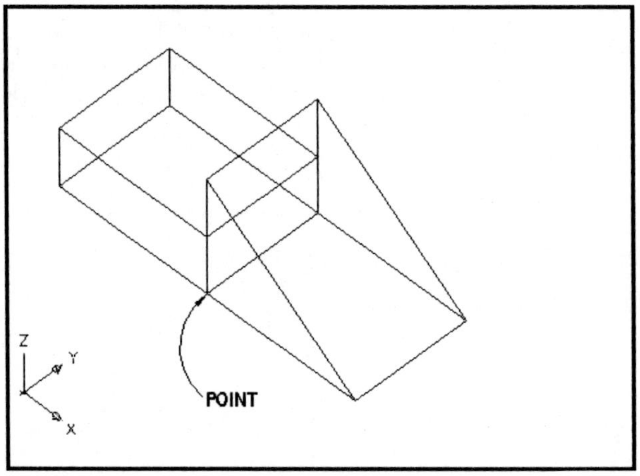

Figure 9.39

As in the BOX command, AutoCAD prompts for a cube, length, or the other corner:

Specify corner or [Cube/Length]:

This time let's use the length and width option.

Type "L."

The rubberband will disappear and AutoCAD will prompt for a length, which you can define by typing a number or showing two points.

Type "4" or show a length of 4.00 units.

AutoCAD now prompts for a width. Remember, length is measured in the x direction, and width is measured in the y direction.

⌗ **Type "3" or show a width of 3 units.**

AutoCAD prompts for a height.

⌗ **Type "3" or show a distance of 3 units.**

AutoCAD will draw the wedge you have specified. Notice that a wedge is simply half a box, cut along a diagonal plane.

Your screen should resemble Figure 9.39. Although the box and the wedge appear as wireframe objects, they are really quite different, as you will find. In the next section, we will join the box and the wedge to form a new composite solid.

9.9 CREATING THE UNION OF TWO SOLIDS

Unions are simple to create and usually easy to visualize. The union of two objects is an object that includes all points that are on either of the objects. Unions can be performed just as easily on more than two objects. The union of objects can be created even if the objects have no points in common (i.e., they do not touch or overlap).

Right now we have two distinct solids on the screen; with UNION we can join them.

⌗ **Open the Modify menu, highlight Solids Editing, and select Union.**

There is also a Union tool on the Solids Editing toolbar, as shown in Figure 9.40.

Figure 9.40

AutoCAD will prompt you to select objects.

⌗ **Point or use a crossing box to select both objects.**

⌗ **Press Enter to end object selection.**

Your screen should resemble Figure 9.41.

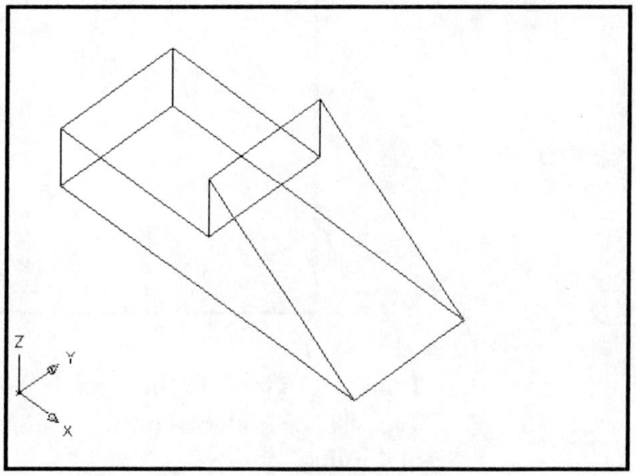

Figure 9.41

9.10 WORKING ABOVE THE XY PLANE USING ELEVATION

In this section we will draw two more solid boxes while demonstrating the use of elevation to position objects above the XY plane of the current UCS. Changing elevations simply adds a single Z value to all new objects as they are drawn and can be used as an alternative to creating a new UCS. With an elevation of 1.00, for example, new objects would be drawn 1.00 above the XY plane of the current UCS. You can also use a thickness setting to create 3D objects, but these will be created as surface models, not solids.

⌗ **To begin this task you should have the union of a wedge and a box on your screen, as shown in Figure 9.41.**

We will begin by drawing a second box positioned on top of the first box. Later we will move it, copy it, and subtract it to form a slot in the composite object.

⌗ **Type "Elev."**

AutoCAD prompts

Specify new default elevation <0.00>:

The elevation is always set at 0 unless you specify otherwise.

⌗ **Type "1.5."**

This will bring the elevation up 1.5 out of the XY plane, putting it even with the top of the first box you drew.

AutoCAD now prompts for a new thickness. Thickness does not apply to solid objects because they have their own thickness.

⌗ **Press Enter or the space bar to retain 0.00 thickness.**

This brings us back to the command prompt. If you watch closely you will see that the grid has also moved up into the new plane of elevation.

⌗ **Type "Box" or open the Draw menu, highlight Solids, and select Box.**

⌗ **Pick the far upper left corner of the box, Point 1 in Figure 9.42.**

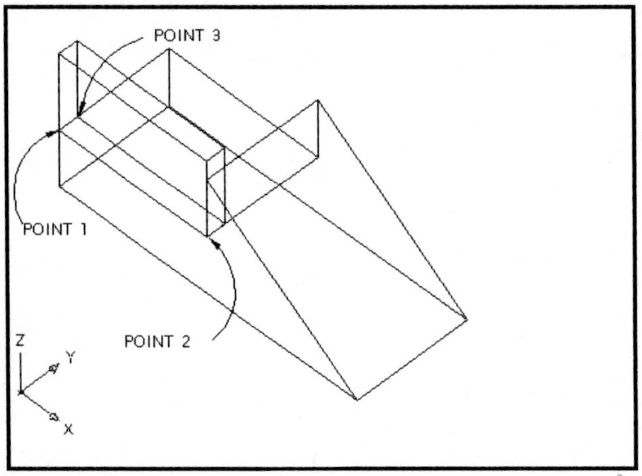

Figure 9.42

⌗ **Type "L" to initiate the "length" option.**

⌗ **Type "4" or pick two points (Points 1 and 2 in the figure) to show a length of 4 units.**

⌗ **Type "0.5" or pick two points (Points 1 and 3) to show a width of 0.5 units.**

⌗ **Type "2" or pick two points to show a height of 2 units.**

Your screen should resemble Figure 9.42. Notice how you were able to pick points on top of the box because of the change in elevation just as if we had changed coordinate systems. Before going on, return to 0.00 elevation.

⌗ **Type "elev."**

⌗ **Type "0."**

⌗ **Press Enter to retain 0.00 thickness.**

9.11 CREATING COMPOSITE SOLIDS WITH SUBTRACT

SUBTRACT is the logical opposite of UNION. In a union operation, all the points contained in one solid are added to the points contained in other solids to form a new composite solid. In a subtraction, all points in the solids to be subtracted are removed from the source solid. A new composite solid is defined by what is left.

In this exercise, we will use the objects already on your screen to create a slotted wedge. First we need to move the thin upper box into place, then we will copy it to create a longer slot, and finally we will subtract it from the union of the box and wedge.

⌗ **To begin this task, you should have the composite box and wedge solid and the thin box on your screen, as shown in Figure 9.42.**

Before subtracting, we will move the box to the position shown in Figure 9.43.

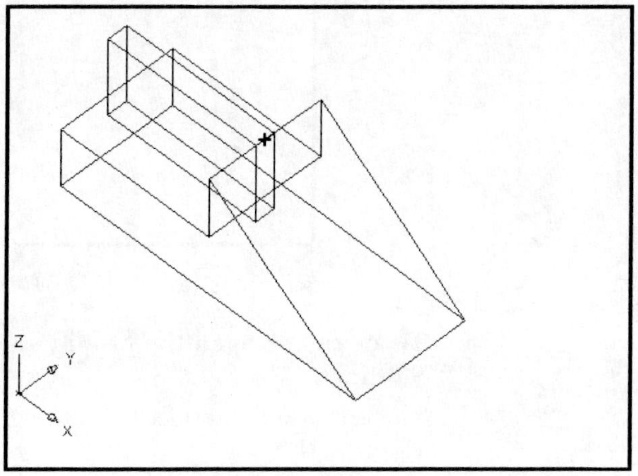

Figure 9.43

⌗ **Type "m" or select the Move tool from the Modify toolbar.**

⌗ **Select the narrow box drawn in the last task.**

⌗ **Right click to end object selection.**

⌗ **At the "Specify base point or displacement" prompt use a midpoint object snap to pick the midpoint of the top right edge of the narrow box.**

⌗ **At the "Specify second point of displacement" prompt use another midpoint object snap to pick the top edge of the wedge, as shown in Figure 9.43.**

This will move the narrow box over and down. If you were to perform the subtraction now, you would create a slot but it would only run through the box, not the wedge. We can create a longer slot by copying the narrow box over to the right using grips.

⌖ **Select the narrow box.**

⌖ **Pick any of the eight grips.**

⌖ **If ortho is off, turn it on.**

Now if you move the cursor in the x direction you will see a copy of the box moving with you. Solids cannot be stretched, so we must make a copy to lengthen the slot.

⌖ **Type "c."**

⌖ **Move the cursor between 2.00 and 4.00 units to the right and press the pick button.**

If you don't go far enough the slot will be too short. If you go past 4.00, the slot will be interrupted by the space between the box and the copy.

⌖ **Press Enter to leave the grip edit mode.**

Your screen will resemble Figure 9.44.

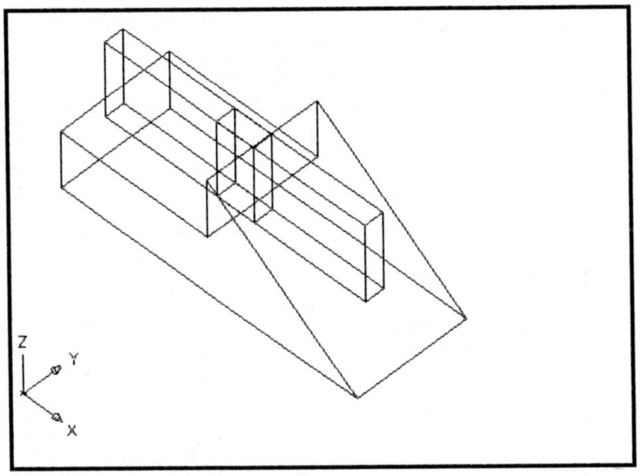

Figure 9.44

⌖ **Type "su" or open the Modify menu, highlight Solids Editing, and select Subtract.**

There is also a Subtract tool on the Solids Editing toolbar, shown previously in Figure 9.41.

AutoCAD asks you to select objects to subtract from first:

```
Select solids and regions to subtract from ...
Select objects:
```

⌖ **Pick the composite of the box and the wedge.**

⌖ **Right click to end selection of source objects.**

AutoCAD prompts for objects to be subtracted:

```
Select solids and regions to subtract...
Select objects:
```

⌖ **Pick the two narrow boxes.**

⌖ **Right click to end selection.**

Your screen will resemble Figure 9.45.

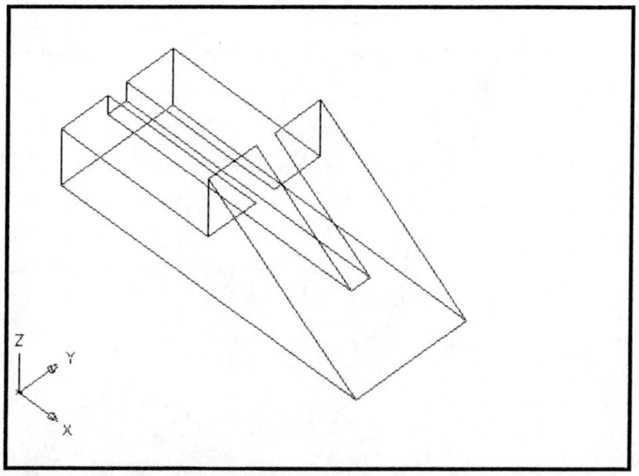

Figure 9.45

9.12 SHADING AND RENDERING

There are many ways to present a solid object. Once drawn, you can view it from any angle, create a perspective view using the DVIEW command, remove hidden lines, or create dramatic shaded or rendered images. Before leaving, try these three simple procedures. We hope that these will whet your appetite and that you will go on to learn much more about 3D imaging in AutoCAD.

⌖ **To remove hidden lines, type "hide."**

This will produce a simple hidden line image that clearly shows how AutoCAD is recognizing the surfaces of this solid object.

⌖ **To create a simple shaded image, type "shade."**

This will produce a shaded image similar to Figure 9.46.

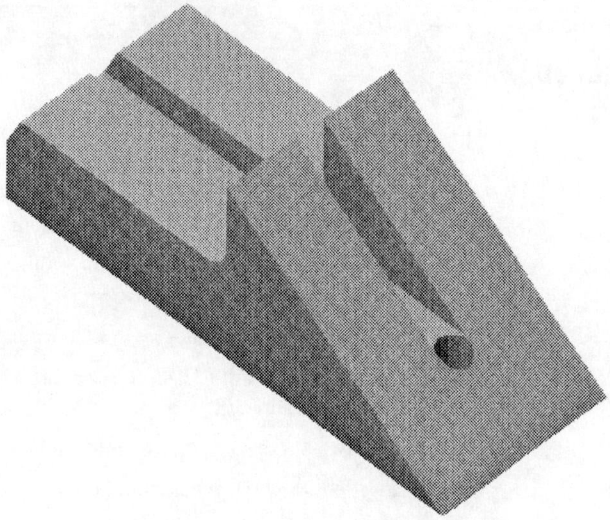

Figure 9.46

- **To create a simple rendering, type "render." This will call up the Render dialog box.**
- **In the Render dialog box, select "Render Scene" in the lower left corner.**

This will produce a simple rendered image similar to Figure 9.47. In a rendered image you can create and control effects to simulate light, shadow, and different materials. Although lighting is beyond the scope of this introduction to AutoCAD, we would encourage you to explore the LIGHT command, which allows you to add three different types of lighting to rendered images, and the RMAT and MATLIB commands, which allow you to create the effect of different materials. Good luck!

Figure 9.47

9.13 REVIEW MATERIAL

Questions

1. What is a wireframe model?
2. What is the significance of the W on the UCS icon?
3. What coordinates indicate a displacement of -5 in the z direction from the point (6, 6, 6)?
4. Why is it usually necessary to utilize Object Snap to select a point on an object outside of the XY plane of the current UCS?
5. What information defines a User Coordinate System?
6. Why is it important to keep two or more different views of an object on the screen as you are drawing and editing it?
7. What two basic geometric shapes can be drawn as a 3DFACE?
8. How does the HIDE command treat objects on layers that are turned off?
9. What geometry is needed to define a tabulated surface? A ruled surface? An edge surface? A revolved surface?

10. What 3D solid objects and commands would you use to create a square nut with a bolt hold in the middle?

11. What command allows you to draw outside of the xy plane of the current UCS without the use of typed coordinates, object snap, or point filters?

Commands

3DFACE	BOX	DDUCS
EDGESURF	REVSURF	RULESURF
TABSURF	UCS	UCSICON
UNON	WEDGE	

9.14 DRAWING PROBLEMS

1. Set up a southeast isometric 3D viewpoint in the World Coordinate System and draw a regular hexagon with a circumscribed radius of 4.0 units.

2. Create a half-sized scaled copy of the hexagon centered at the same center as the original hexagon; then move the smaller hexagon 5.0 units up in the z direction.

3. Connect corresponding corners of the two hexagons to create a tapered hexagonal prism in three dimensions.

4. Create a UCS aligned with any of the faces of the hexagonal prism.

PROFESSIONAL SUCCESS

Using Solid Models

Techniques have been developed that allow solid models to be used for purposes besides visualization. The solid model, which contains a complete mathematical representation of the object's surface and interior, is easily converted to specialized computer code. Such software is used in applications that include stress analysis and computer-aided manufacturing.

A finite element analysis (FEA) allows the deformation behavior of an object under mechanical or thermal loads to be studied in detail. The solid model is used by an FEA preprocessor program to subdivide the object under study into a three-dimensional mesh consisting of simple rectangular or triangular elements. The simple geometry of the finite elements allows a system of equations to be generated by the FEA software, which, when solved using the applied loads, provides stress, displacement (strain), and thermal maps of the solid. These maps are often displayed as color contour plots superimposed on the solid model, and allow areas of high stress and strain to be visualized.

Solid models may also be used to directly generate manufactured prototypes without any human intervention. Computer numerical control (CNC) machine tools are controlled with programs automatically generated from the solid model. Such programs control the trajectory of the tool as it travels over a part, causing the desired surfaces to be cut with high precision. CNC tools remove the surface variability associated with manual machine tools controlled by human operators, and allow many identical parts to be machined automatically.

DRAWING 1

Clamp

This drawing is similar to the one you did in the chapter. Two major differences are that it is drawn from a different viewpoint and that it includes dimensions in the 3D view. This will give you additional practice in defining and using User Coordinate Systems. Your drawing should include dimensions, border, and title.

Drawing Suggestions

- We drew the outline of the clamp in a horizontal position and then worked from a northeast isometric or back, left, top point of view.
- Begin in WCS plan view drawing the horseshoe-shaped outline of the clamp. This will include fillets on the inside and outside of the clamp. The more you can do in plan view before copying to the top plane, the less duplicate editing you will need to do later.
- When the outline is drawn, switch to a northeast isometric view.
- COPY the clamp outline up 1.50.
- Define User Coordinate Systems as needed, and save them whenever you are ready to switch to another UCS. You will need to use them in your dimensioning.
- The angled face, the slots, and the filleted surfaces can be drawn just as in the chapter.

Dimensioning in 3D The trick to dimensioning a 3D object is that you will need to restore the appropriate UCS for each set of dimensions. Think about how you want the text to appear. If text is to be aligned with the top of the clamp (for example, the 5.75 overall length), you will need to draw that dimension in a "top" UCS; if it is to align with the front of the object (the 17-degree angle and the 1.50 height), draw it in a "front" UCS, and so forth.

- Define a UCS with the "View" option to add the border and title. Type "UCS," and then "v." This creates a UCS aligned with your current viewing angle.

Setting Surftab1 Notice that there are eight lines defining the RULESURF fillets in this drawing, compared to six in the chapter. This number of lines is controlled by the setting of the variable Surftab1. You can change it by typing "Surftab1" and entering "8" for the new value.

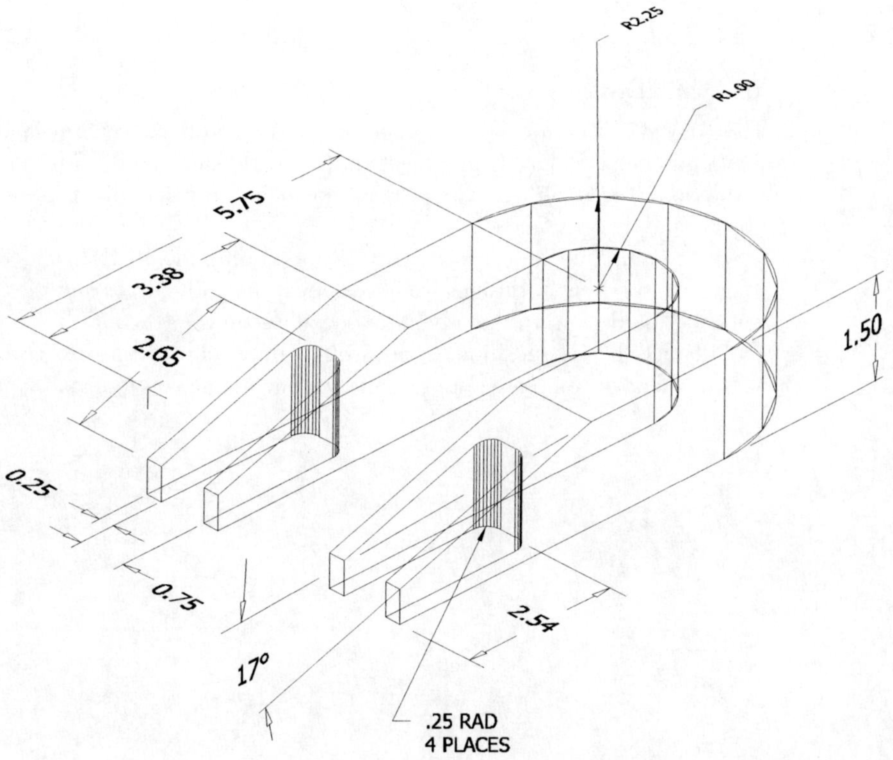

CLAMP

DRAWING 2

REVSURF Designs

The REVSURF command is fascinating and powerful. As you get familiar with it, you may find yourself identifying objects in the world that can be conceived as surfaces of revolution. To encourage this process, we have provided this page of 12 REVSURF objects and designs.

To complete the exercise, you will need only the PLINE and REVSURF commands. In the first six designs we have shown the path curves and axes of rotation used to create the design. In the other six you will be on your own.

Exact shapes and dimensions are not important in this exercise. Imagination is. When you have completed our designs, we encourage you to invent your own.

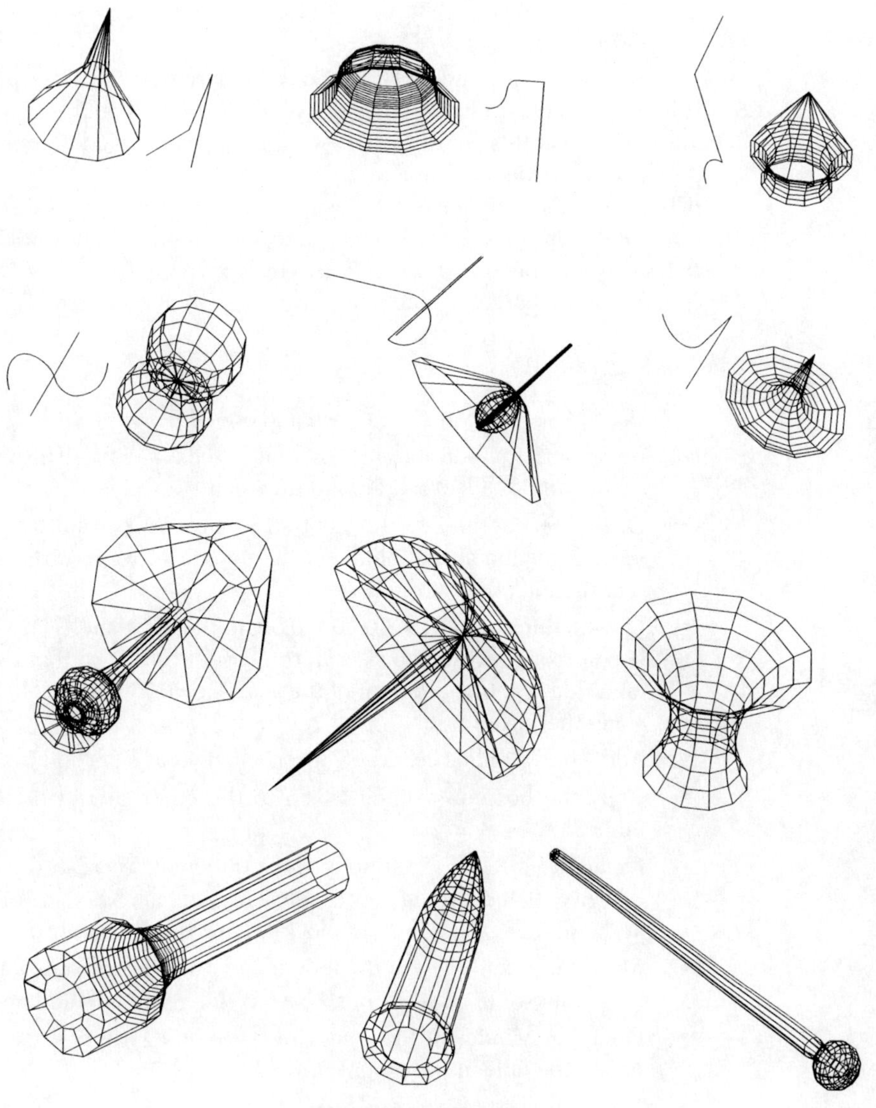

REVSURF DESIGNS

DRAWING 3

Bushing Mount

We offer the following drawing suggestions for Drawing 9.3. The principles demonstrated here will carry over into other drawings, and you should be capable of handling them on your own at this point. In all cases you are encouraged to experiment with renderings when the model is complete.

Use an efficient sequence in the construction of composite solids. In general, this will mean saving union, subtraction, and intersection operations until most of the solid objects have been drawn and positioned. This approach allows you to continue to use the geometry of the parts for snap points as you position other parts.

Drawing Suggestions

- Use at least two views, one plan and one 3D, as you work.
- Begin with the bottom of the mount in the XY plane. This will mean drawing a 6.00 × 4.00 × 0.50 solid box sitting on the XY plane.
- Draw a second box, 1.50 × 4.00 × 3.50, in the XY plane. This will become the upright section at the middle of the mount. Move it so that its own midpoint is at the midpoint of the base.
- Draw a third box, 1.75 × 0.75 × 0.50, in the XY plane. This will be copied and become one of the two slots in the base. Move it so that the midpoint of its long side is at the midpoint of the short side of the base. Then MOVE it 1.125 along the x axis.
- Add a 0.375 radius cylinder with 0.50 height at each end of the slot.
- Copy the box and cylinders 3.75 to the other side of the base to form the other slot.
- Create a new UCS 2.00 up in the z direction. You can use the origin option and give (0, 0, 2) as the new origin. This puts the XY plane of the UCS directly at the middle of the upright block, where you can easily draw the bushing.
- Move out to the right of the mount and draw the polyline outline of the bushing, as shown in the drawing. Use REVOLVE to create the solid bushing.
- Create a cylinder in the center of the mount, where it can be subtracted to create the hole in the mount upright.
- Union the first and second boxes.
- Subtract the boxes and cylinders to form the slots in the base and the bushing-sized cylinder to form the hole in the mount.

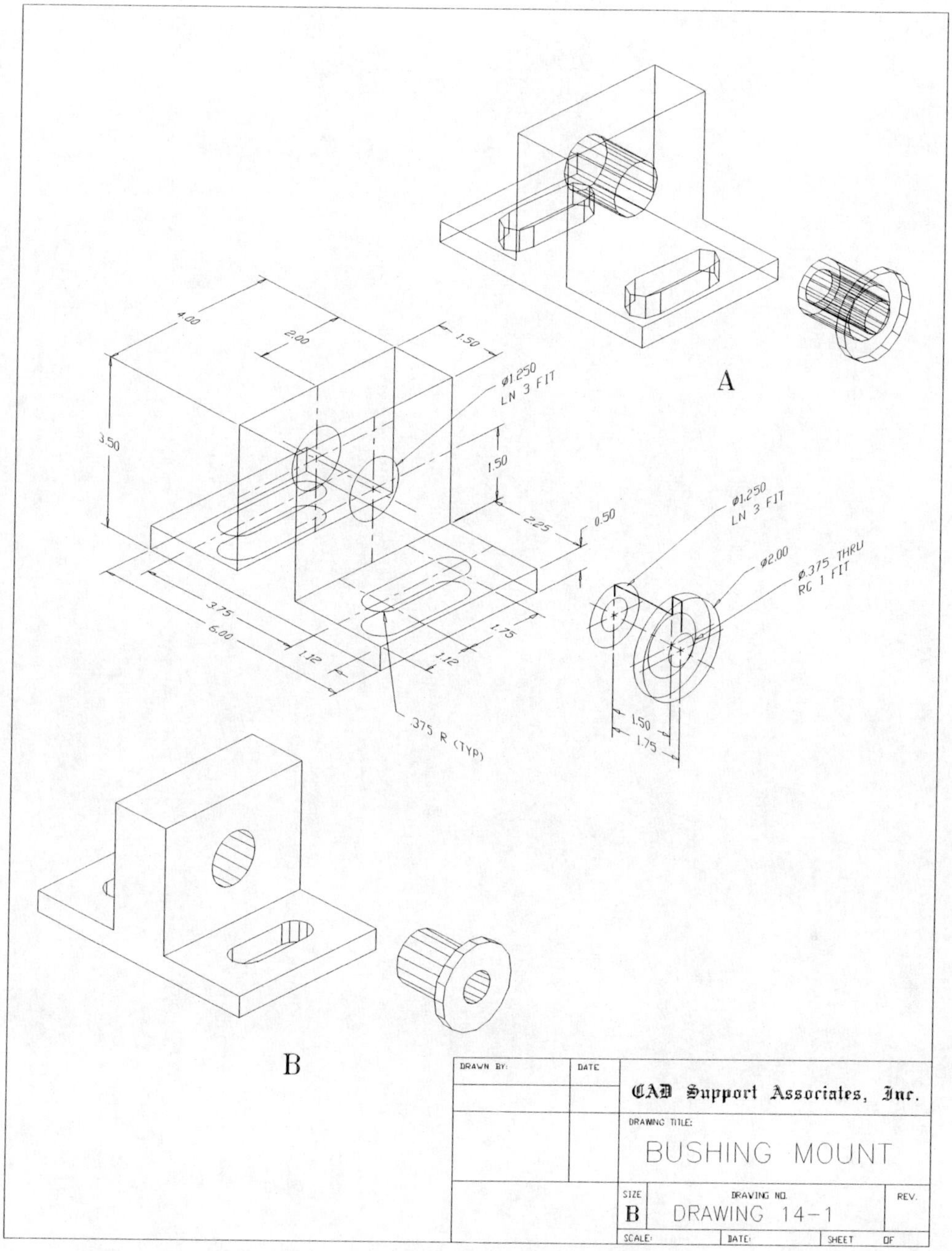
4.00
2.00
1.50
Ø1.250
LN 3 FIT
3.50
1.50
2.25
0.50
3.75
6.00
1.12
1.12
1.75
.375 R (TYP)
Ø1.250
LN 3 FIT
Ø2.00
Ø.375 THRU
RC 1 FIT
1.50
1.75
A
B
DRAWN BY:
DATE
CAD Support Associates, Inc.
DRAWING TITLE:
BUSHING MOUNT
SIZE
B
DRAWING NO.
DRAWING 14-1
REV.
SCALE:
DATE:
SHEET
OF

Index

Q

R

S

T